Springer Texts in Business and Economics

Springer Texts in Business and Economics (STBE) delivers high-quality instructional content for undergraduates and graduates in all areas of Business/Management Science and Economics. The series is comprised of self-contained books with a broad and comprehensive coverage that are suitable for class as well as for individual self-study. All texts are authored by established experts in their fields and offer a solid methodological background, often accompanied by problems and exercises.

Karolina Sobczak-Marcinkowska ·
Krzysztof Malaga

Workbook for Microeconomics

Exercises and Solutions

Springer

Karolina Sobczak-Marcinkowska
Institute of Informatics and Quantitative Economics
Poznań University of Economics and Business
Poznań, Poland

Krzysztof Malaga
Institute of Informatics and Quantitative Economics
Poznań University of Economics and Business
Poznań, Poland

ISSN 2192-4333 ISSN 2192-4341 (electronic)
Springer Texts in Business and Economics
ISBN 978-3-031-41946-1 ISBN 978-3-031-41947-8 (eBook)
https://doi.org/10.1007/978-3-031-41947-8

This Springer imprint is published by the registered company Springer Nature Switzerland AG
The registered company address is: Gewerbestrasse 11, 6330 Cham, Switzerland

Preface

This book presents solutions and answers to exercises included in *Microeconomics. Static and Dynamic Analysis* by Krzysztof Malaga and Karolina Sobczak-Marcinkowska (Cham, Switzerland: Springer Nature, 2022). Altogether, there are 62 exercises in five chapters.

Poznań, Poland

Krzysztof Malaga
Karolina Sobczak-Marcinkowska

Contents

About the Authors

Krzysztof Malaga, Dr. habil. is a distinguished economics professor at Poznań University of Economics and Business (Poland). With 4 monographs, 3 textbooks, 6 scripts and over 70 articles, he specializes in microeconomics, macroeconomics, economic growth and development. He has translated 11 French-language books with 29 editions in Poland. Formerly serving as the vice-dean and dean, he currently directs the Institute of Computer Science and Quantitative Economics and holds key positions as an editor-in-chief and scientific director in prominent international economic associations AIELF.

Karolina Sobczak-Marcinkowska, Ph.D. holds a dual doctorate in economic sciences from University Rennes 1 (France) and Poznań University of Economics and Business (Poland). As an assistant professor in the Department of Operations Research and Mathematical Economics, she delivers engaging lectures and classes on diverse subjects such as microeconomics, macroeconomics, mathematical economics and DSGE models. She has contributed as a co-author to a script and several textbooks focused on microeconomics.

Index of Mathematical Symbols

$\forall$	Universal quantifier: "for all"
$\exists$	Existential quantifier: "there exists"
$\exists_1$	Existential quantifier: "there exists exactly one"
$\exists_{>1}$	Existential quantifier: "there exists more than one"
$\neg$	Negation; $\neg p$ "not p"
$\wedge$	Conjunction: "and"
$\vee$	Disjunction: "or"
$\Rightarrow$	Implication; $p \Rightarrow q$ "if p then q"
$\Leftrightarrow$	Equivalence: "if and only if"
$a, \ \ x \in \mathbb{R}$	Numbers, scalars
$\mathbf{a} = (a_1, a_2, \ldots, a_n) \in \mathbb{R}^n$	Vector of parameters
$\mathbf{x} = (x_1, x_2, \ldots, x_n) \in \mathbb{R}^n$	Vector of variables
$A, \ X$	Sets
$\boldsymbol{A}, \ \boldsymbol{X}$	Matrices (with dimensions m by n) with m rows and n columns
$\sim$	Indifference relation
$\mathbf{x} \sim \mathbf{y}$	Bundle $\mathbf{x}$ is indifferent with respect to bundle $\mathbf{y}$
$\succ$	Strong preference relation
$\mathbf{x} \succ \mathbf{y}$	Bundle $\mathbf{x}$ is strongly preferred over bundle $\mathbf{y}$
$\succsim$	(Weak) preference relation
$\mathbf{x} \succsim \mathbf{y}$	Bundle $\mathbf{x}$ is (weakly) preferred over bundle $\mathbf{y}$
$\mathbb{R}$	Set of real numbers
$\mathbb{R}_+$	Set of nonnegative real numbers
$\text{int } \mathbb{R}_+ \subset \mathbb{R}_+$	Set of positive real numbers
$\mathbb{R}^n = \mathbb{R} \times \mathbb{R} \times \ldots \times \mathbb{R}$	n-dimensional space of real numbers, Cartesian product of set $\mathbb{R}$
$\mathbb{R}^n_+ = \{\, \mathbf{x} \in \mathbb{R}^n \mid \mathbf{x} \geq 0\} \subset \mathbb{R}^n$	Nonnegative orthant (subspace) of set $\mathbb{R}^n$

$\operatorname{int} \mathbb{R}_+^n \subset \mathbb{R}_+^n$	Interior of set $\mathbb{R}^n$
$f : X \to Y$	Function, X—Domain of a function (set of arguments of a function) Y—Codomain of a function (set of values of a function)
$y = f(x)$	Scalar function of one variable, x—Independent variable (argument/input of a function) y—Dependent variable (value of a function)
$y = f(x_1, x_2)$	Scalar function of two variables, x_1, x_2—Independent variables (arguments/inputs of a function) y—Dependent variable (value of a function)
$\frac{dy}{dx}, y', f'(x)$	First-order derivative order of function $y = f(x)$
$\frac{d^2y}{dx^2}, y'', f''(x)$	Second-order derivative of second order of function $y = f(x)$
$\frac{\partial y}{\partial x_i}, \frac{\partial f(x_1,x_2)}{\partial x_i}$	Partial first-order derivatives of function $y = f(x_1, x_2)$ with respect to variable x_i, $i = 1, 2$
$\frac{\partial^2 f(x_1,x_2)}{\partial x_i \partial x_j}, \frac{\partial^2 (x_1,x_2)}{\partial x_i^2}, i = 1, 2$	Partial second-order derivatives of function $y = f(x_1, x_2)$
$H(x_1, x_2) = \begin{bmatrix} \frac{\partial^2 f(x_1,x_2)}{\partial x_1^2} & \frac{\partial^2 f(x_1,x_2)}{\partial x_1 \partial x_2} \\ \frac{\partial^2 f(x_1,x_2)}{\partial x_2 \partial x_1} & \frac{\partial^2 f(x_1,x_2)}{\partial x_2^2} \end{bmatrix}$	Hessian, symmetric matrix of partial second-order derivatives of function $y = f(x_1, x_2)$
$\left.\frac{df(x)}{dx}\right\vert_{x=\bar{x}}$	Value of a derivative of an one-variable function at point $\bar{x}$
$\left.\frac{\partial f(x_1, x_2)}{\partial x_i}\right\vert_{\mathbf{x}=\bar{\mathbf{x}}}$	Value of a derivative of a two variable function with respect to variable x_i ($i = 1, 2$) at point $\bar{\mathbf{x}} = (\bar{x}_1, \bar{x}_2)$
$\langle \mathbf{p}, \mathbf{x} \rangle = \sum_{i=1}^{2} p_i x_i$	Scalar product of two vectors $\mathbf{p}, \mathbf{x} \in \mathbb{R}_+^2$
$\det(\mathbf{A})$ or $\vert\mathbf{A}\vert$	Determinant of matrix $\mathbf{A}$
$d_E(\mathbf{x^1}, \mathbf{x^2}) = \left(\sum_{i=1}^{2} (x_i^1 - x_i^2)^2\right)^{\frac{1}{2}}$	Euclidean metric (distance)
$d(\mathbf{x^1}, \mathbf{x^2}) = \max\limits_{i=1,2}\{\vert x_i^1 - x_i^2\vert\}$	Non-Euclidean metric (distance)
$\Vert\mathbf{x}\Vert_E = \left(\sum_{i=1}^{2} (x_i)^2\right)^{\frac{1}{2}}$	Euclidean norm

$\|\mathbf{x}\| = \max_{i=1,2}\{\|x_i\|\}$	Non-Euclidean norm
$t = 0,\ 1,\ 2, \ldots$	Time as discrete variable
$t \in [0; +\infty)$	Time as continuous variable

Chapter 1
Introduction

"It is not enough to have a fit mind, but to use it properly"
Réné Descartes.

We present to the Reader the Workbook which is a valuable and useful supplement to our textbook Malaga K., Sobczak K., *Microeconomics. Static and Dynamic Analysis*, Springer Nature Switzerland, Cham, 2022. The Workbook contains solutions to 62 exercises given in the textbook and assigned to five chapters:

- Chapter 2 Rationality of choices made by individual consumer
- Chapter 3 Rationality of choices made by a group of consumers
- Chapter 4 Rationality of choices made by individual producers
- Chapter 5 Rationality of choices made by a group of producers by exogenously determined function of demand for a product
- Chapter 6 Rationality of choices made by a group of producers and consumers.

These exercises are aimed at a more in-depth reflection on the microeconomic categories defined in the textbook, decision-making problems and microeconomic models. Unlike in the textbook, in the Workbook a symbol (*) marks these of solved exercises that we think are a bit more difficult.

We assume that this Workbook will be a supplement to our manual. In no case should it be treated as a substitute to the textbook or independent development. For this reason, in the solutions to the exercises, we draw the Reader's attention to methods of solving problems and on the results obtained. We leave their more comprehensive interpretation to students and professors, who should use the textbook itself, including the glossary and the mathematical appendix.

We consider additional materials enclosed in the form of twenty-seven MATLAB files and nine Excel files to be a very important supplement to the Workbook. We expect that they will be of particular interest to students and professors who are interested in dynamic analysis. The files allow to introduce own data if the form of

---

Supplementary Information The online version contains supplementary material available at https://doi.org/10.1007/978-3-031-41947-8_1.

K. Sobczak and K. Malaga, *Workbook for Microeconomics*, Springer Texts in Business and Economics, https://doi.org/10.1007/978-3-031-41947-8_1

functions and/or values of parameters and to control for these values to observe how they influence results. The Reader can use as well other type of software or create own files treating the enclosed files as exemplary.

We would like to thank Springer Nature Switzerland Publishing House for its publication, in particular to the following representatives of Springer: Dr. Johannes Glaeser, Senior Editor, Economics and Political Science, Springer of Heidelberg, and Mr. Vijay Kumar Selvaraj for their extraordinary professionalism and kindness during the editing of this book. We would also like to thank Dr. Giancarlo Ianulardo from the University of Exeter Business School in the UK for his encouragement in the development of this Workbook for Microeconomics.

The motto of the Workbook, taken from *Discourse on Method* by René Descartes, is intended to encourage students to use both the textbook and the Workbook in a way that will contribute to a full understanding of the issues and decision-making problems presented in these books, but above all in a way that will stimulate their imagination and creativity.

Krzysztof MALAGA

Karolina SOBCZAK

Poznań, 16.06.2023

Chapter 2
Rationality of Choices Made by Individual Consumer

This Chapter presents 15 exercises that help in understanding the problem of describing rational behaviour of an individual consumer. In particular they concern: relation of consumer preferences, a utility function as a numerical characteristic of the relation of consumer preferences, the Marshallian demand function understood as an optimal solution to utility maximization problem, the Hicksian demand function as an optimal solution to consumer spending minimization problem, relations between the Marshallian and Hicksian demand functions, as well as substitution and income effects of changes in prices of goods, presented in a form of the Slutsky equation.

E2.1. There is given an increasing and twice differentiable utility function $u\colon \mathbb{R}_+^2 \to \mathbb{R}$ of a form:

A. $u(\mathbf{x}) = a_1 e^{x_1} + a_2 e^{x_2} + a_3, a_i > 0, i = 1, 2, 3.$
B. $u(\mathbf{x}) = a_1 e^{\frac{1}{x_1}} + a_2 e^{\frac{1}{x_2}} + a_3, a_i > 0, i = 1, 2, 3.$
C. $u(\mathbf{x}) = \frac{x_1 x_2}{a_1 x_1 + a_2 x_2}, a_i > 0, i = 1, 2.$
D. $u(\mathbf{x}) = a_1 x_1 + a_2 x_2 + a x_1^{\alpha_1} x_2^{\alpha_2}, \quad a, a_i, \alpha_i > 0, \quad \alpha_1 + \alpha_2 < 1, \quad i = 1, 2.$
E. $u(\mathbf{x}) = a_1(x_1 + \ln x_1) + a_2(x_2 + \ln x_2), \quad a_i, x_i > 0, \quad i = 1, 2.$
F. $u(\mathbf{x}) = a_1 x_1 \left(1 + x_1^{\alpha-1}\right) + a_2 x_2 \left(1 + x_2^{\alpha-1}\right), \quad \alpha \in (0; 1), \quad a_i > 0, \quad i = 1, 2.$

1 Calculate a value and give economic interpretation of:

(a) a marginal utility of i-th good,
(b) a growth rate of consumption bundle utility with respect to quantity of i-th good,
(c) an elasticity of consumption bundle utility with respect to quantity of i-th good,
(d) a marginal rate of substitution of the first (second) good by the second (first) good,
(e) an elasticity of substitution of the first (second) good by the second (first) good,

for consumption bundles: $\mathbf{x}^1 = (1, 1), \mathbf{x}^2 = (1, 2).$

K. Sobczak and K. Malaga, *Workbook for Microeconomics*, Springer Texts in Business and Economics, https://doi.org/10.1007/978-3-031-41947-8_2

2. Check if the given function satisfies first Gossen's law.

Solutions

Ad A1a

$$T_1(\mathbf{x}) = \frac{\partial u(\mathbf{x})}{\partial x_1} = a_1 e^{x_1} \quad T_2(\mathbf{x}) = \frac{\partial u(\mathbf{x})}{\partial x_2} = a_2 e^{x_2}$$
$$T_1(\mathbf{x}^1) = a_1 e > 0 \quad T_2(\mathbf{x}^1) = a_2 e > 0$$
$$T_1(\mathbf{x}^2) = a_1 e > 0 \quad T_2(\mathbf{x}^2) = a_1 e^2 > 0$$

Ad A1b

$$s_1(\mathbf{x}) = \frac{T_1(\mathbf{x})}{u(\mathbf{x})} = \frac{a_1 e^{x_1}}{a_1 e^{x_1} + a_2 e^{x_2} + a_3} \quad s_2(\mathbf{x}) = \frac{T_2(\mathbf{x})}{u(x)} = \frac{a_2 e^{x_2}}{a_1 e^{x_1} + a_2 e^{x_2} + a_3}$$
$$s_1(\mathbf{x}^1) = \frac{a_1 e}{(a_1 + a_2)e + a_3} > 0[\%] \quad s_2(\mathbf{x}^1) = \frac{a_2 e}{(a_1 + a_2)e + a_3} > 0[\%]$$
$$s_1(\mathbf{x}^2) = \frac{a_1 e}{(a_1 + a_2 e)e + a_3} > 0[\%] \quad s_2(\mathbf{x}^2) = \frac{a_2 e^2}{(a_1 + a_2 e)e + a_3} > 0[\%]$$

Ad A1c

$$\varepsilon_1(\mathbf{x}) = s_1(\mathbf{x}) \cdot x_1 = \frac{a_1 e^{x_1} x_1}{a_1 e^{x_1} + a_2 e^{x_2} + a_3}$$
$$\varepsilon_2(\mathbf{x}) = s_2(\mathbf{x}) \cdot x_2 = \frac{a_1 e^{x_2} x_2}{a_1 e^{x_1} + a_2 e^{x_2} + a_3}$$
$$\varepsilon_1(\mathbf{x}^1) = \frac{a_1 e}{(a_1 + a_2)^{e+a_3}} > 0[\%]$$
$$\varepsilon_2(\mathbf{x}^1) = \frac{a_2 e}{(a_1 + a_2)e + a_3} > 0[\%]$$
$$\varepsilon_1(\mathbf{x}^2) = \frac{a_1 e}{(a_1 + a_2 e)e + a_3} > 0[\%]$$
$$\varepsilon_2(\mathbf{x}^2) = \frac{2a_2 e^2}{(a_1 + a_2 e)e + a_3} > 0[\%]$$

Ad A1d

$$\sigma_{12}(\mathbf{x}) = \frac{\frac{\partial u(\mathbf{x})}{\partial x_1}}{\frac{\partial u(x)}{\partial x_2}} = \frac{a_1 e^{x_1}}{a_2 e^{x_2}} \quad \sigma_{21}(\mathbf{x}) = \frac{1}{\sigma_{12}(\mathbf{x})} = \frac{a_2 e^{x_2}}{a_1 e^{x_1}}$$
$$\varepsilon_{12}(\mathbf{x}^1) = \frac{a_1}{a_2} > 0[\%] \quad \varepsilon_{21}(\mathbf{x}^1) = \frac{a_2}{a_1} > 0[\%]$$
$$\sigma_{12}(\mathbf{x}^2) = \frac{a_1}{a_2 e} \quad \sigma_{21}(\mathbf{x}^2) = \frac{a_2 e}{a_1}$$

Ad A1e

$$\varepsilon_{12}(\mathbf{x}) = \sigma_{12}(\mathbf{x})\frac{x_1}{x_2} = \frac{a_1 e^{x_1} x_1}{a_2 e^{x_2} x_2} \quad \varepsilon_{21}(\mathbf{x}) = \frac{1}{\varepsilon_{12}(\mathbf{x})} = \frac{a_2 e^{x_2} x_2}{a_1 e^{x_1 x_1}}$$

$$\varepsilon_{12}(\mathbf{x}^1) = \frac{a_1}{a_2} > 0[\%] \quad \varepsilon_{21}(\mathbf{x}^1) = \frac{a_2}{a_1} > 0[\%]$$

$$\varepsilon_{12}(\mathbf{x}^2) = \frac{a_1}{2a_2 e} > 0[\%] \quad \varepsilon_{21}(\mathbf{x}^2) = \frac{2a_2 e}{a_1} > 0[\%]$$

Ad A2

$$\frac{\partial^2 u(\mathbf{x})}{\partial x_1^2} = a_1 e^{x_1} \quad \frac{\partial^2 u(\mathbf{x})}{\partial x_1^2} = a_2 e^{x_2}$$

$$\left.\frac{\partial^2 u(\mathbf{x})}{\partial x_1^2}\right|_{\mathbf{x}=\mathbf{x}^1} = a_1 e > 0 \quad \left.\frac{\partial^2 u(\mathbf{x})}{\partial x_2^2}\right|_{\mathbf{x}=\mathbf{x}^1} = a_2 e > 0$$

$$\left.\frac{\partial^2 u(\mathbf{x})}{\partial x_1^2}\right|_{\mathbf{x}=\mathbf{x}^2} = a_1 e > 0 \quad \left.\frac{\partial^2 u(\mathbf{x})}{\partial x_2^2}\right|_{\mathbf{x}=\mathbf{x}^2} = a_2 e^2 > 0$$

Ad B1a

$$T_1(\mathbf{x}) = \frac{\partial u(\mathbf{x})}{\partial x_1} = -\frac{1}{x_1^2} a_1 e^{\frac{1}{x_1}} < 0$$

$$T_2(\mathbf{x}) = \frac{\partial u(\mathbf{x})}{\partial x_2} = -\frac{1}{x_2^2} a_2 e^{\frac{1}{x_2}} < 0$$

$$T_1(\mathbf{x}^1) = -a_1 e < 0 \quad T_2(\mathbf{x}^1) = -a_2 e < 0$$

$$T_1(\mathbf{x}^2) = -a_1 e < 0 \quad T_2(\mathbf{x}^2) = -\frac{1}{4} a_2 e^{\frac{1}{2}} < 0$$

Ad B1b

$$s_1(\mathbf{x}) = \frac{T_1(\mathbf{x})}{u(\mathbf{x})} = \frac{-\frac{1}{x_1^2} a_1 e^{\frac{1}{x_1}}}{a_1 e^{\frac{1}{x_1}} + a_2 e^{\frac{1}{x_2}} + a_3}$$

$$s_2(\mathbf{x}) = \frac{T_2(\mathbf{x})}{u(\mathbf{x})} = \frac{-\frac{1}{x_2^2} a_2 e^{\frac{1}{x_2}}}{a_1 e^{\frac{1}{x_1}} + a_2 e^{\frac{1}{x_2}} + a_3}$$

$$s_1(\mathbf{x}^1) = \frac{-a_1 e}{(a_1 + a_2)e + a_3} < 0[\%]$$

$$s_2(\mathbf{x}^1) = \frac{-a_2 e}{(a_1 + a_2)e + a_3} < 0[\%]$$

$$s_1(\mathbf{x}^2) = \frac{-a_1 e}{(a_1 + a_2)e + a_3} < 0[\%]$$

$$s_2\left(\mathbf{x}^2\right) = \frac{-\frac{1}{4}a_2 e^{\frac{1}{2}}}{a_1 e + a_2 e^{\frac{1}{2}} + a_3} < 0[\%]$$

Ad B1c

$$\varepsilon_1(\mathbf{x}) = s_1(\mathbf{x}) \cdot x_1 = \frac{-\frac{1}{x_1}a_1 e^{\frac{1}{x_1}}}{a_1 e^{\frac{1}{x_1}} + a_2 e^{\frac{1}{x_2}} + a_3} < 0$$

$$\varepsilon_2(\mathbf{x}) = s_2(\mathbf{x}) \cdot x_2 = \frac{-\frac{1}{x_2}a_2 e^{\frac{1}{x_2}}}{a_1 e^{\frac{1}{x_1}} + a_2 e^{\frac{1}{x_2}} + a_3} < 0$$

$$\varepsilon_1\left(\mathbf{x}^1\right) = \frac{-a_1 e}{(a_{1+}a_2)e + a_3} < 0[\%]$$

$$\varepsilon_2\left(\mathbf{x}^1\right) = \frac{-a_2 e}{(a_{1+}a_2)e + a_3} < 0[\%]$$

$$\varepsilon_1\left(\mathbf{x}^2\right) = \frac{-a_1 e}{(a_{1+}a_2)e + a_3} < 0[\%]$$

$$\varepsilon_2\left(\mathbf{x}^2\right) = \frac{-a_2 e}{a_1 e + a_2 e^{\frac{1}{2}} + a_3} < 0[\%]$$

Ad B1d

$$\sigma_{12}(\mathbf{x}) = \frac{\frac{\partial u(\mathbf{x})}{\partial x_1}}{\frac{\partial u(\mathbf{x})}{\partial x_2}} = \frac{-\frac{1}{x_1^2}a_1 e^{\frac{1}{x_1}}}{-\frac{1}{x_2^2}a_2 e^{\frac{1}{x_2}}} = \frac{x_2^2 a_1 e^{\frac{1}{x_1}}}{x_1^2 a_2 e^{\frac{1}{x_2}}} > 0$$

$$\sigma_{21}(\mathbf{x}) = \frac{1}{\sigma_{12}(\mathbf{x})} = \frac{x_1^2 a_2 e^{\frac{1}{x_2}}}{x_2^2 a_1 e^{\frac{1}{x_1}}} > 0$$

$$\sigma_{12}\left(\mathbf{x}^1\right) = \frac{a_1}{a_2} > 0 \quad \sigma_{21}\left(\mathbf{x}^1\right) = \frac{a_2}{a_1} > 0$$

$$\sigma_{12}\left(\mathbf{x}^2\right) = \frac{4a_1 e^{\frac{1}{2}}}{a_2} > 0 \quad \sigma_{21}\left(\mathbf{x}^2\right) = \frac{a_2}{4a_1 e^{\frac{1}{2}}} > 0$$

Ad B1e

$$\varepsilon_{12}(\mathbf{x}) = \sigma_{12}(\mathbf{x})\frac{x_1}{x_2} = \frac{x_2 a_1 e^{\frac{1}{x_1}}}{x_1 a_2 e^{\frac{1}{x_2}}} > 0[\%]$$

$$\varepsilon_{21}(\mathbf{x}) = \frac{1}{\varepsilon_{12}(\mathbf{x})} = \frac{x_1 a_2 e^{\frac{1}{x_2}}}{x_2 a_1 e^{\frac{1}{x_1}}} > 0[\%]$$

$$\varepsilon_{12}\left(\mathbf{x}^2\right) = \frac{2a_1 e^{\frac{1}{2}}}{a_2} > 0[\%] \quad \varepsilon_{21}\left(\mathbf{x}^2\right) = \frac{a_2}{2a_1 e^{\frac{1}{2}}} > 0[\%].$$

$$\varepsilon_{12}\left(\mathbf{x}^2\right) = \frac{2a_1 e^{\frac{1}{2}}}{a_2} > 0[\%] \quad \varepsilon_{21}\left(\mathbf{x}^2\right) = \frac{a_2}{2a_1 e^{\frac{1}{2}}} > 0[\%]$$

Ad B2

$$\frac{\partial^2 u(\mathbf{x})}{\partial x_1^2} = 2x_1^{-3} a_1 e^{\frac{1}{x_1}} + x_1^{-4} a_1 e^{\frac{1}{x_1}} > 0$$

$$\frac{\partial^2 u(\mathbf{x})}{\partial x_2^2} = 2x_2^{-3} a_2 e^{\frac{1}{x_2}} + x_2^{-4} a_2 e^{\frac{1}{x_2}} > 0$$

$$\left.\frac{\partial^2 u(\mathbf{x})}{\partial x_1^2}\right|_{\mathbf{x}=\mathbf{x}^1} = 3a_1 e > 0 \quad \left.\frac{\partial^2 u(\mathbf{x})}{\partial x_2^2}\right|_{\mathbf{x}=\mathbf{x}^1} = 3a_2 e > 0$$

$$\left.\frac{\partial^2 u(\mathbf{x})}{\partial x_1^2}\right|_{\mathbf{x}=\mathbf{x}^2} = 3a_1 e > 0 \quad \left.\frac{\partial^2 u(\mathbf{x})}{\partial x_2^2}\right|_{\mathbf{x}=\mathbf{x}^2} = \frac{5}{16} a_2 e^{\frac{1}{2}} > 0$$

Ad C1a

$$T_1(\mathbf{x}) = \frac{\partial u(\mathbf{x})}{\partial x_1} = \frac{a_2 x_2^2}{(a_1 x_1 + a_2 x_2)^2} \qquad T_2(\mathbf{x}) = \frac{\partial u(\mathbf{x})}{\partial x_2} = \frac{a_1 x_1^2}{(a_1 x_1 + a_2 x_2)^2}$$

$$T_1\left(\mathbf{x}^1\right) = \frac{a_2}{(a_1 + a_2)^2} > 0 \quad T_2\left(\mathbf{x}^1\right) = \frac{a_1}{(a_1 + a_2)^2} > 0$$

$$T_1\left(\mathbf{x}^2\right) = \frac{4a_2}{(a_1 + 2a_2)^2} > 0 \quad T_2\left(\mathbf{x}^2\right) = \frac{a_1}{(a_1 + 2a_2)^2} > 0$$

Ad C1b

$$s_1(\mathbf{x}) = \frac{T_1(x)}{u(x)} = \frac{a_2 x_2}{x_1(a_1 x_1 + a_2 x_2)} \qquad s_2(\mathbf{x}) = \frac{T_2(x)}{u(x)} = \frac{a_1 x_1}{x_2(a_1 x_1 + a_2 x_2)}$$

$$s_1\left(\mathbf{x}^1\right) = \frac{a_2}{a_1 + a_2} > 0[\%] \quad s_2\left(\mathbf{x}^1\right) = \frac{a_1}{a_1 + a_2} > 0[\%]$$

$$s_1\left(\mathbf{x}^2\right) = \frac{2a_2}{a_1 + 2a_2} > 0[\%] \quad s_2\left(\mathbf{x}^2\right) = \frac{2a_1}{2a_1 + 4a_2} > 0[\%]$$

Ad C1c

$$\varepsilon_1(\mathbf{x}) = s_1(\mathbf{x}) \cdot x_1 = \frac{a_2 x_2}{a_1 x_1 + a_2 x_2} \qquad \varepsilon_2(\mathbf{x}) = s_2(\mathbf{x}) \cdot x_2 = \frac{a_1 x_1}{a_1 x_1 + a_2 x_2}$$

$$\varepsilon_1\left(\mathbf{x}^1\right) = \frac{a_2}{a_1 + a_2} > 0[\%] \quad \varepsilon_2\left(\mathbf{x}^1\right) = \frac{a_1}{a_1 + a_2} > 0[\%]$$

$$\varepsilon_1\left(\mathbf{x}^2\right) = \frac{2a_2}{a_1 + 2a_2} > 0[\%] \quad \varepsilon_2\left(\mathbf{x}^2\right) = \frac{a_1}{a_1 + 2a_2} > 0[\%]$$

Ad C1d

$$\sigma_{12}(\mathbf{x}) = \frac{\frac{\partial u(\mathbf{x})}{\partial x_1}}{\frac{\partial u(\mathbf{x})}{\partial x_2}} = \frac{a_2 x_2^2}{a_1 x_1^2} \quad \sigma_{21}(\mathbf{x}) = \frac{1}{\sigma_{12}(\mathbf{x})} = \frac{a_1 x_1^2}{a_2 x_2^2}$$

$$\sigma_{12}(\mathbf{x}^1) = \frac{a_2}{a_1} > 0 \quad \sigma_{21}(\mathbf{x}^1) = \frac{a_1}{a_2} > 0$$

$$\sigma_{12}(\mathbf{x}^2) = \frac{4a_2}{a_1} > 0 \quad \sigma_{21}(\mathbf{x}^2) = \frac{a_1}{4a_2} > 0$$

Ad C1e

$$\varepsilon_{12}(\mathbf{x}) = \sigma_{12}(\mathbf{x})\frac{x_1}{x_2} = \frac{a_2 x_2}{a_1 x_1} \quad \varepsilon_{21}(\mathbf{x}) = \frac{1}{\varepsilon_{12}(\mathbf{x})} = \frac{a_1 x_1}{a_2 x_2}$$

$$\varepsilon_{12}(\mathbf{x}^1) = \frac{a_2}{a_1} > 0[\%] \quad \varepsilon_{21}(\mathbf{x}^1) = \frac{a_1}{a_2} > 0[\%]$$

$$\varepsilon_{12}(\mathbf{x}^2) = \frac{2a_2}{a_1} > 0[\%] \quad \varepsilon_{21}(\mathbf{x}^2) = \frac{a_1}{2a_2} > 0[\%]$$

Ad C2

$$\frac{\partial^2 u(\mathbf{x})}{\partial x_1^2} = \frac{-2a_1 a_2 x_2^2}{(a_1 x_1 + a_2 x_2)^3} < 0 \quad \frac{\partial^2 u(\mathbf{x})}{\partial x_1^2} = \frac{-2a_1 a_2 x_1^2}{(a_1 x_1 + a_2 x_2)^3} < 0$$

$$\left.\frac{\partial^2 u(\mathbf{x})}{\partial x_1^2}\right|_{\mathbf{x}=\mathbf{x}^1} = \frac{-2a_1 a_2}{(a_1 + a_2)^3} < 0 \quad \left.\frac{\partial^2 u(\mathbf{x})}{\partial x_2^2}\right|_{\mathbf{x}=\mathbf{x}^1} = \frac{-2a_1 a_2}{(a_1 + a_2)^3} < 0$$

$$\left.\frac{\partial^2 u(\mathbf{x})}{\partial x_1^2}\right|_{\mathbf{x}=\mathbf{x}^2} = \frac{-8a_1 a_2}{(a_1 + 2a_2)^3} < 0 \quad \left.\frac{\partial^2 u(\mathbf{x})}{\partial x_2^2}\right|_{\mathbf{x}=\mathbf{x}^2} = \frac{-2a_1 a_2}{(a_1 + 2a_2)^3} < 0$$

Ad D1a

$$T_1(\mathbf{x}) = \frac{\partial u(\mathbf{x})}{\partial x_1} = a_1 + a\alpha_1 x_1^{\alpha_1 - 1} x_2^{\alpha_2}$$

$$T_2(\mathbf{x}) = \frac{\partial u(\mathbf{x})}{\partial x_2} = a_2 + a\alpha_2 x_1^{\alpha_1} x^{\alpha_2 - 1}$$

$$T_1(\mathbf{x}^1) = a_1 + a\alpha_1 > 0 \qquad T_2(\mathbf{x}^1) = a_2 + a\alpha_2 > 0$$

$$T_1(\mathbf{x}^2) = a_1 + a\alpha_1 2^{\alpha_2} > 0 \qquad T_2(\mathbf{x}^2) = a_2 + a\alpha_2 2^{\alpha_2 - 1} > 0$$

Ad D1b

$$s_1(\mathbf{x}) = \frac{T_1(\mathbf{x})}{u(\mathbf{x})} = \frac{a_1 + a\alpha_1 x_1^{\alpha_1 - 1} x_2^{\alpha_2}}{a_1 x_1 + a_2 x_2 + a x_1^{\alpha_1} x_2^{\alpha_2}}$$

$$s_2(\mathbf{x}) = \frac{T_2(\mathbf{x})}{u(\mathbf{x})} = \frac{a_2 + a\alpha_2 x_1^{\alpha_1} x_2^{\alpha_2 - 1}}{a_1 x_1 + a_2 x_2 + a x_1^{\alpha_1} x_2^{\alpha_2}}$$

$$s_1(\mathbf{x}^1) = \frac{a_1 + a\alpha_1}{a_1 + a_2 + a} > 0[\%]$$

$$s_2(\mathbf{x}^1) = \frac{a_2 + a\alpha_2}{a_1 + 2a_2 + a} > 0[\%]$$

$$s_1(\mathbf{x}^2) = \frac{a_1 + a\alpha_1 2^{\alpha_2}}{a_1 + 2a_2 + a2^{\alpha_2}} > 0[\%]$$

$$s_2(\mathbf{x}^2) = \frac{a_2 + a\alpha_2 2^{\alpha_2 - 1}}{a_1 + 2a_2 + a2^{\alpha_2}} > 0[\%]$$

Ad D1c

$$\varepsilon_1(\mathbf{x}) = s_1(\mathbf{x}) \cdot x_1 = \frac{a_1 x_1 + a\alpha_1 x_1^{\alpha_1} x_2^{\alpha_2}}{a_1 x_1 + a_2 x_2 + a x_1^{\alpha_1} x_2^{\alpha_2}}$$

$$\varepsilon_2(\mathbf{x}) = s_2(\mathbf{x}) \cdot x_2 = \frac{a_2 x_2 + a\alpha_2 x_1^{\alpha_1} x_2^{\alpha_2}}{a_1 x_1 + a_2 x_2 + a x_1^{\alpha_1} x_2^{\alpha_2}}$$

$$\varepsilon_1(\mathbf{x}^1) = \frac{a_1 + +a\alpha_1}{a_1 + a_2 + a} > 0[\%]$$

$$\varepsilon_2(\mathbf{x}^1) = \frac{a_2 + a\alpha_2}{a_1 + a_2 + a} > 0[\%]$$

$$\varepsilon_1(\mathbf{x}^2) = \frac{a_1 + a\alpha_1 2^{\alpha_2}}{a_1 + 2a_2 + a2^{\alpha_2}} > 0[\%]$$

$$\varepsilon_2(\mathbf{x}^2) = \frac{a_2 + a\alpha_2 2^{\alpha_2}}{a_1 + 2a_2 + a2^{\alpha_2}} > 0[\%]$$

Ad D1d

$$\sigma_{12}(\mathbf{x}) = \frac{\frac{\partial u(\mathbf{x})}{\partial x_1}}{\frac{\partial u(\mathbf{x})}{\partial x_2}} = \frac{a_1 + a\alpha_1 x_1^{\alpha_1 - 1} x_2^{\alpha_2}}{a_2 + a\alpha_2 x_1^{\alpha_1} x^{\alpha_2 - 1}} \qquad \sigma_{21}(\mathbf{x}) = \frac{1}{\sigma_{12}(\mathbf{x})} = \frac{a_2 + a\alpha_2 x_1^{\alpha_1} x_2^{\alpha_2 - 1}}{a_1 + a\alpha_1 x_1^{\alpha_1 - 1} x^{\alpha_2}}$$

$$\sigma_{12}(\mathbf{x}^1) = \frac{a_1 + a\alpha_1}{a_2 + a\alpha_2} > 0 \qquad \sigma_{21}(\mathbf{x}^1) = \frac{a_2 + a\alpha_2}{a_1 + a\alpha_1} > 0$$

$$\sigma_{12}(\mathbf{x}^2) = \frac{a_1 + a\alpha_1 2^{\alpha_2}}{a_2 + a\alpha_2 2^{\alpha_2 - 1}} > 0 \qquad \sigma_{21}(\mathbf{x}^2) = \frac{a_2 + a\alpha_2 2^{\alpha_2 - 1}}{a_1 + a\alpha_1 2^{\alpha_2}} > 0$$

Ad D1e

$$\varepsilon_{12}(\mathbf{x}) = \sigma_{12}(\mathbf{x})\frac{x_1}{x_2} = \frac{a_1 + a\alpha_1 x_1^{\alpha_1} x_2^{\alpha_2}}{a_2 + a\alpha_2 x_1^{\alpha_1} x^{\alpha_2 - 1}}$$

$$\varepsilon_{21}(\mathbf{x}) = \frac{1}{\varepsilon_{12}(\mathbf{x})} = \frac{a_2 + a\alpha_2 x_1^{\alpha_1} x^{\alpha_2 - 1}}{a_1 + a\alpha_1 x_1^{\alpha_1} x_2^{\alpha_2}}$$

$$\varepsilon_{12}\left(\mathbf{x}^1\right) = \frac{a_1 + a\alpha_1}{a_2 + a\alpha_2} > 0[\%]$$

$$\varepsilon_{21}\left(\mathbf{x}^1\right) = \frac{a_2 + a\alpha_2}{a_1 + a\alpha_1} > 0[\%]$$

$$\varepsilon_{12}\left(\mathbf{x}^2\right) = \frac{a_1 + a\alpha_1 2^{\alpha_2}}{a_2 + a\alpha_2 2^{\alpha_2 - 1}} > 0[\%]$$

$$\varepsilon_{21}\left(\mathbf{x}^2\right) = \frac{a_2 + a\alpha_2 2^{\alpha_2 - 1}}{a_1 + a\alpha_1 2^{\alpha_2}} > 0[\%]$$

Ad D2

$$\frac{\partial^2 u(\mathbf{x})}{\partial x_1^2} = (\alpha_1 - 1)a\alpha_1 x_1^{\alpha_1 - 1} x_2^{\alpha_2} < 0$$

$$\frac{\partial^2 u(\mathbf{x})}{\partial x_1^2} = (\alpha_2 - 1)a\alpha_2 x_1^{\alpha_1} x_2^{\alpha_2 - 1} < 0$$

$$\left.\frac{\partial^2 u(\mathbf{x})}{\partial x_1^2}\right|_{\mathbf{x}=\mathbf{x}^1} = (\alpha_1 - 1)a\alpha_1 < 0$$

$$\left.\frac{\partial^2 u(\mathbf{x})}{\partial x_2^2}\right|_{\mathbf{x}=\mathbf{x}^1} = (\alpha_2 - 1)a\alpha_2 < 0$$

$$\left.\frac{\partial^2 u(\mathbf{x})}{\partial x_1^2}\right|_{\mathbf{x}=\mathbf{x}^2} = (\alpha_1 - 1)a\alpha_1 2^{\alpha_2} < 0$$

$$\left.\frac{\partial^2 u(\mathbf{x})}{\partial x_2^2}\right|_{x=\mathbf{x}^2} = (\alpha_2 - 1)a\alpha_2 2^{\alpha_2 - 1} < 0$$

Ad E1a

$$T_1(\mathbf{x}) = \frac{\partial u(\mathbf{x})}{\partial x_1} = a_1\left(1 + \frac{1}{x_1}\right)$$

$$T_2(\mathbf{x}) = \frac{\partial u(\mathbf{x})}{\partial x_2} = a_2\left(1 + \frac{1}{x_2}\right)$$

$$T_1\left(\mathbf{x}^1\right) = 2a_1 > 0 \qquad T_2\left(\mathbf{x}^1\right) = 2a_2 > 0$$

$$T_1\left(\mathbf{x}^2\right) = 2a_1 > 0 \qquad T_2\left(\mathbf{x}^2\right) = \frac{3}{2}a_2 > 0$$

Ad E1b

$$s_1(\mathbf{x}) = \frac{T_1(\boldsymbol{x})}{u(\mathbf{x})} = \frac{a_1\left(1+\frac{1}{x_1}\right)}{a_1(x_1+\ln x_1)+a_2(x_2+\ln x_2)+a_3}$$

$$s_2(\mathbf{x}) = \frac{T_2(\mathbf{x})}{u(\mathbf{x})} = \frac{a_2\left(1+\frac{1}{x_2}\right)}{a_1(x_1+\ln x_1)+a_2(x_2+\ln x_2)+a_3}$$

$$s_1\left(\mathbf{x}^1\right) = \frac{2a_1}{a_1+a_2+a_3} > 0[\%]$$

$$s_2\left(\mathbf{x}^1\right) = \frac{2a_2}{a_1+a_2+a_3} > 0[\%]$$

$$s_1\left(\mathbf{x}^2\right) = \frac{2a_1}{a_1+a_2(2+\ln 2)+a_3} > 0[\%]$$

$$s_2\left(\mathbf{x}^2\right) = \frac{\frac{3}{2}a_2}{a_1+a_2(2+\ln 2)+a_3} > 0[\%]$$

Ad E1c

$$\varepsilon_1(\mathbf{x}) = s_1(\mathbf{x})x_1 = \frac{a_1(x_1+1)}{a_1(x_1+\ln x_1)+a_2(x_2+\ln x_2)+a_3}$$

$$\varepsilon_2(\mathbf{x}) = s_2(\mathbf{x})x_2 \frac{a_2(x_2+1)}{a_1(x_1+\ln x_1)+a_2(x_2+\ln x_2)+a_3}$$

$$\varepsilon_1\left(\mathbf{x}^1\right) = \frac{2a_1}{a_1+a_2+a_3} > 0[\%] \quad \varepsilon_2\left(\mathbf{x}^1\right) = \frac{2a_2}{a_1+a_2+a_3} > 0[\%]$$

$$\varepsilon_1\left(\mathbf{x}^2\right) = \frac{2a_1}{a_1+a_2(2+\ln 2)+a_3} > 0[\%]$$

$$\varepsilon_2\left(\mathbf{x}^2\right) = \frac{2a_2}{a_1+a_2(2+\ln 2)+a_3} > 0[\%]$$

Ad E1d

$$\sigma_{12}(\mathbf{x}) = \frac{\frac{\partial u(\mathbf{x})}{\partial x_1}}{\frac{\partial u(\mathbf{x})}{\partial x_2}} = \frac{a_1\left(1+\frac{1}{x_1}\right)}{a_2\left(1+\frac{1}{x_2}\right)} > 0$$

$$\sigma_{21}(\mathbf{x}) = \frac{1}{\sigma_{12}(\mathbf{x})} = \frac{a_2\left(1+\frac{1}{x_2}\right)}{a_1\left(1+\frac{1}{x_1}\right)}$$

$$\sigma_{12}\left(\mathbf{x}^1\right) = \frac{a_2}{a_1} > 0 \quad \sigma_{21}\left(\mathbf{x}^1\right) = \frac{a_1}{a_2} > 0$$

$$\sigma_{12}\left(\mathbf{x}^2\right) = \frac{3a_2}{4a_1} > 0 \quad \sigma_{21}\left(\mathbf{x}^2\right) = \frac{4a_1}{3a_2} > 0$$

Ad E1e

$$\varepsilon_{12}(\mathbf{x}) = \sigma_{12}(\mathbf{x})\frac{x_1}{x_2} = \frac{a_1(x_1+1)}{a_2(x_2+1)}$$
$$\varepsilon_{21}(\mathbf{x}) = \frac{1}{\varepsilon_{12}(\mathbf{x})} = \frac{a_2(x_2+1)}{a_1(x_1+1)}$$
$$\varepsilon_{12}\left(\mathbf{x}^1\right) = \frac{a_2}{a_1} > 0[\%] \quad \varepsilon_{21}\left(\mathbf{x}^1\right) = \frac{a_1}{a_2} > 0[\%]$$
$$\varepsilon_{12}\left(\mathbf{x}^2\right) = \frac{3a_2}{2a_1} > 0[\%] \quad \varepsilon_{21}\left(\mathbf{x}^2\right) = \frac{2a_1}{3a_2} > 0[\%]$$

Ad E2

$$\frac{\partial^2 u(\mathbf{x})}{\partial x_1^2} = \frac{-a_1}{x_1^2} < 0 \quad \frac{\partial^2 u(\mathbf{x})}{\partial x_1^2} = \frac{-a_2}{x_2^2} < 0$$
$$\left.\frac{\partial^2 u(\mathbf{x})}{\partial x_1^2}\right|_{\mathbf{x}=\mathbf{x}^1} = -a_1 < 0 \quad \left.\frac{\partial^2 u(\mathbf{x})}{\partial x_2^2}\right|_{\mathbf{x}=\mathbf{x}^1} = -a_2 < 0$$
$$\left.\frac{\partial^2 u(\mathbf{x})}{\partial x_1^2}\right|_{\mathbf{x}=\mathbf{x}^2} = -a_1 < 0 \quad \left.\frac{\partial^2 u(\mathbf{x})}{\partial x_2^2}\right|_{\mathbf{x}=\mathbf{x}^2} = \frac{-a_2}{4} < 0$$

Ad F1a

$$T_1(\mathbf{x}) = \frac{\partial u(\mathbf{x})}{\partial x_1} = a_1 + \alpha a_1 x_1^{\alpha-1}$$
$$T_2(\mathbf{x}) = \frac{\partial u(\mathbf{x})}{\partial x_2} = a_2 + \alpha a_2 x_2^{\alpha-1}$$
$$T_1\left(\mathbf{x}^1\right) = a_1(1+\alpha) > 0 \quad T_2\left(\mathbf{x}^1\right) = a_2(1+\alpha) > 0$$
$$T_1\left(\mathbf{x}^2\right) = a_1(1+\alpha) > 0 \quad T_2\left(\mathbf{x}^2\right) = a_2(1+\alpha)2^{\alpha_2-1} > 0$$

Ad F1b

$$s_1(\mathbf{x}) = \frac{T_1(\mathbf{x})}{u(\mathbf{x})} = \frac{a_1 + \alpha a_1 x_1^{\alpha-1}}{a_1 x_1 + a_1 x_1^{\alpha} + a_2 + a_2 x_2^{\alpha}}$$
$$s_2(\mathbf{x}) = \frac{T_2(\mathbf{x})}{u(\mathbf{x})} = \frac{a_2 + \alpha a_2 x_2^{\alpha-1}}{a_1 x_1 + a_1 x_1^{\alpha} + a_2 + a_2 x_2^{\alpha}}$$
$$s_1\left(\mathbf{x}^1\right) = \frac{a_1(1+\alpha)}{2a_1 + 2a_2} > 0[\%] \quad s_2\left(\mathbf{x}^1\right) = \frac{a_2(1+\alpha)}{2a_1 + 2a_2} > 0[\%]$$
$$s_1\left(\mathbf{x}^2\right) = \frac{a_1(1+\alpha)}{2a_1 + a_2(1+2^{\alpha})} > 0[\%]$$

$$s_2(\mathbf{x}^2) = \frac{a_2(1+\alpha)2^{\alpha-1}}{2a_1 + a_2(1+2^\alpha)} > 0[\%]$$

Ad F1c

$$\varepsilon_1(\mathbf{x}) = s(\mathbf{x}) \cdot x_1 = \frac{a_1x_1 + \alpha a_1 x_1^\alpha}{a_1x_1 + a_1x_1^\alpha + a_2 + a_2x_2^\alpha}$$

$$\varepsilon_2(\mathbf{x}) = s(\mathbf{x}) \cdot x_2 = \frac{a_2x_2 + \alpha a_2 x_2^\alpha}{a_1x_1 + a_1x_1^\alpha + a_2 + a_2x_2^\alpha}$$

$$\varepsilon_1(\mathbf{x}^1) = \frac{a_1(1+\alpha)}{2a_1 + a_2(1+2^\alpha)} > 0[\%]$$

$$\varepsilon_2(\mathbf{x}^1) = \frac{a_2(1+\alpha)}{2a_1 + a_2(1+2^\alpha)} > 0[\%]$$

$$\varepsilon_1(\mathbf{x}^2) = \frac{a_1(1+\alpha)}{2a_1 + a_2(1+2^\alpha)} > 0[\%]$$

$$\varepsilon_2(\mathbf{x}^2) = \frac{a_2(2+\alpha 2^\alpha)}{2a_1 + a_2(1+2^\alpha)} > 0[\%]$$

Ad F1d

$$\sigma_{12}(\mathbf{x}) = \frac{\frac{\partial u(\mathbf{x})}{\partial x_1}}{\frac{\partial u(\mathbf{x})}{\partial x_2}} = \frac{a_1 + \alpha a_1 x_1^{\alpha-1}}{a_2 + \alpha a_2 x_2^{\alpha-1}}$$

$$\sigma_{21}(\mathbf{x}) = \frac{1}{\sigma_{12}(\mathbf{x})} = \frac{a_2 + \alpha a_2 x_2^{\alpha-1}}{a_1 + \alpha a_1 x_1^{\alpha-1}}$$

$$\sigma_{12}(\mathbf{x}^1) = \frac{a_1(1+\alpha)}{a_2(1+\alpha 2^{\alpha-1})} > 0$$

$$\sigma_{21}(\mathbf{x}^1) = \frac{a_2(1+\alpha 2^{\alpha-1})}{a_1(1+\alpha)} > 0$$

$$\sigma_{12}(\mathbf{x}^2) = \frac{a_1(1+\alpha)}{a_2(1+\alpha 2^{\alpha-1})} > 0$$

$$\sigma_{21}(\mathbf{x}^2) = \frac{a_2(1+\alpha 2^{\alpha-1})}{a_1(1+\alpha)} > 0$$

Ad F1e

$$\varepsilon_{12}(\mathbf{x}) = \sigma_{12}(\mathbf{x})\frac{x_1}{x_2} = \frac{a_1x_1 + \alpha a_1 x_1^\alpha}{a_2x_2 + \alpha a_2 x_2^\alpha}$$

$$\varepsilon_{21}(\mathbf{x}) = \frac{1}{\varepsilon_{12}(\mathbf{x})} = \frac{a_2x_2 + \alpha a_2 x_2^\alpha}{a_1x_1 + \alpha a_1 x_1^\alpha}$$

$$\varepsilon_{12}\left(\mathbf{x}^1\right) = \frac{a_1(1+\alpha)}{a_2(2+\alpha 2^{\alpha})} > 0[\%]$$
$$\varepsilon_{21}\left(\mathbf{x}^1\right) = \frac{a_2(2+\alpha 2^{\alpha})}{a_1(1+\alpha)} > 0[\%]$$
$$\varepsilon_{12}\left(\mathbf{x}^2\right) = \frac{a_1(1+\alpha)}{a_2(2+\alpha 2^{\alpha})} > 0[\%]$$
$$\varepsilon_{21}\left(\mathbf{x}^2\right) = \frac{a_2(2+\alpha 2^{\alpha})}{a_1(1+\alpha)} > 0[\%]$$

Ad F2

$$\frac{\partial^2 u(\mathbf{x})}{\partial x_1^2} = (\alpha-1)\alpha a_1 x_1^{\alpha-2} < 0 \quad \frac{\partial^2 u(\mathbf{x})}{\partial x_1^2} = (\alpha-1)\alpha a_2 x_2^{\alpha-2} < 0$$
$$\left.\frac{\partial^2 u(\mathbf{x})}{\partial x_1^2}\right|_{\mathbf{x}=\mathbf{x}^1} = (\alpha-1)\alpha a_1 < 0 \quad \left.\frac{\partial^2 u(\mathbf{x})}{\partial x_2^2}\right|_{\mathbf{x}=\mathbf{x}^1} = (\alpha-1)\alpha a_2 < 0$$
$$\left.\frac{\partial^2 u(\mathbf{x})}{\partial x_1^2}\right|_{\mathbf{x}=\mathbf{x}^2} = (\alpha-1)\alpha a_1 < 0 \quad \left.\frac{\partial^2 u(\mathbf{x})}{\partial x_2^2}\right|_{\mathbf{x}=\mathbf{x}^2} = (\alpha-1)\alpha a_2 2^{\alpha-2} < 0$$

E2.2. There are given utility functions $u\colon \mathbb{R}_+^2 \to \mathbb{R}$:

(a) $u_1(\mathbf{x}) = a_1x_1 + a_2x_2, \quad a_i > 0, i = 1, 2,$
(b) $u_2(\mathbf{x}) = A^{a_1x_1+a_2x_2}, \quad A \in (0; 1), a_i > 0, i = 1, 2,$
(c) $u_3(\mathbf{x}) = A^{a_1x_1+a_2x_2}, \quad A > 1, a_i > 0, i = 1, 2,$
(d) $u_4(\mathbf{x}) = \frac{1}{\ln(a_1x_1+a_2x_2)}, \quad a_i > 0, i = 1, 2,$
(e) $u_5(\mathbf{x}) = \ln(a_1x_1 + a_2x_2), \quad a_i > 0, i = 1, 2,$
(f) $u_6(\mathbf{x}) = ax_1^{\alpha}x_2^{\beta}, \quad a > 0, \alpha, \beta \in (0; 1),$
(g) $u_7(\mathbf{x}) = \alpha \ln x_1 + \beta \ln x_2, \alpha, \beta \in (0; 1),$
(h) $u_8(\mathbf{x}) = A^{ax_1^{\alpha}x_2^{\beta}}, \quad a > 0, A, \alpha, \beta \in (0; 1),$
(i) $u_9(\mathbf{x}) = A^{ax_1^{\alpha}x_2^{\beta}}, \quad a > 0, A > 1, \alpha, \beta \in (0; 1),$
(j) $u_{10}(\mathbf{x}) = \min\{a_1x_1, a_2x_2\}, \quad a_i > 0, \ i = 1, 2,$
(k) $u_{11}(\mathbf{x}) = a_1x_1^{\gamma} + a_2x_2^{\gamma}, \quad a_i > 0, i = 1, 2, \gamma \in (0; 1),$
(l) $u_{12}(\mathbf{x}) = \left(a_1x_1^{\gamma} + a_2x_2^{\gamma}\right)^{\frac{\theta}{\gamma}}, \quad \theta, a_i > 0, i = 1, 2, \gamma \in (0; 1).$

1. Which of these functions describe the same relation of consumer preference?
2. Which of them are positively homogeneous of degree $\theta > 0$?
3. Which of them have the same degree of the homogeneity?
4. Which of them are (weakly) increasing, which (weakly) decreasing?

Solutions

Ad 1

Pairs of utility functions that describe the same consumer preference relationships are following:

- functions $u_1(\mathbf{x})$ and $u_3(\mathbf{x})$, because $u_3(\mathbf{x})$ is a composition of an increasing exponential function with the function $u_1(\mathbf{x})$,
- functions $u_1(\mathbf{x})$ and $u_5(\mathbf{x})$, because $u_5(\mathbf{x})$ is a composition of an increasing logarithmic function with the function $u_1(\mathbf{x})$,
- functions $u_6(\mathbf{x})$ and $u_7(\mathbf{x})$, because $u_7(\mathbf{x})$ is a composition of an increasing logarithmic function with the function $u_6(\mathbf{x})$,
- functions $u_6(\mathbf{x})$ and $u_9(\mathbf{x})$, because $u_9(\mathbf{x})$ is a composition of an increasing exponential function with the function $u_6(x)$,
- functions $u_{11}(\mathbf{x})$ and $u_{12}(\mathbf{x})$, if $\gamma \to 1$.

Ad 2

Let us note that:

(a) $\forall\lambda > 0 u_1(\lambda\mathbf{x}) = a_1\lambda x_1 + a_2\lambda x_2 = \lambda u_1(\mathbf{x})$, which means that the degree of homogeneity of the linear utility function is equal to $\theta = 1$,

(b) $\forall\lambda > 0 u_2(\lambda\mathbf{x}) = A^{a_1\lambda x_1 + a_2\lambda x_2} \neq \lambda^\theta u_2(\mathbf{x})$, which means that the decreasing exponential utility function $u_2(\mathbf{x})$ is not a positively homogeneous function,

(c) $\forall\lambda > 0 u_3(\lambda x) = A^{a_1\lambda x_1 + a_2\lambda x_2} \neq \lambda^\theta u_3(\mathbf{x})$, which means that the increasing exponential utility function $u_3(\mathbf{x})$ is not a positively homogeneous function,

(d) $\forall\lambda > 0 u_4(\lambda\mathbf{x}) = \frac{1}{\ln(a_1\lambda x_1 + a_2\lambda x_2)} \neq \lambda^\theta u_4(\mathbf{x})$, which means that the inverse of a logarithmic function is not a positively homogeneous function,

(e) $\forall\lambda > 0 u_5(\lambda\mathbf{x}) = \ln(a_1\lambda x_1 + a_2\lambda x_2) \neq \lambda^\theta u_5(\mathbf{x})$, which means that the logarithmic function $u_5(\mathbf{x})$ is not a positively homogeneous function,

(f) $\forall\lambda > 0 u_6(\lambda\mathbf{x}) = a(\lambda x_1)^\alpha(\lambda x_2)^\beta = \lambda^{\alpha+\beta} u_6(\mathbf{x})$, which means that the power function $u_6(\mathbf{x})$ is a positively homogeneous function of the degree $\theta = \alpha + \beta > 0$,

(g) $\forall\lambda > 0 u_7(\lambda\mathbf{x}) = \alpha\ln\lambda x_1 + a_2\ln\lambda x_2 \neq \lambda^\theta u_7(\mathbf{x})$, which means that the logarithmic function $u_7(\mathbf{x})$ is not a positively homogeneous function,

(h) $\forall\lambda > 0 u_8(\lambda\mathbf{x}) = A^{a(\lambda x_1)^\alpha(\lambda x_2)^\beta} \neq \lambda^\theta u_8(\mathbf{x})$, which means that the decreasing exponential utility function $u_8(\mathbf{x})$ is not a positively homogeneous function,

(i) $\forall\lambda > 0 u_9(\lambda\mathbf{x}) = A^{a(\lambda x_1)^\alpha(\lambda x_2)^\beta} \neq \lambda^\theta u_9(\mathbf{x})$, which means that the increasing exponential utility function $u_9(\mathbf{x})$ is not a positively homogeneous function,

(j) $\forall\lambda > 0 u_{10}(\lambda\mathbf{x}) = \min\{\lambda a_1 x_1, \lambda a_2 x_2\} = \lambda \min\{a_1 x_1, a_2 x_2\} = \lambda u_{10}(\mathbf{x})$, which means that the Koopmans-Leontief utility function $u_{10}(\mathbf{x})$ is a positively homogeneous function of the degree $\theta = 1$,

(k) $\forall\lambda > 0 u_{11}(\lambda\mathbf{x}) = a_1(\lambda x_1)^\gamma + a_2(\lambda x_2)^\gamma = \lambda^\gamma u_{10}(\mathbf{x})$, which means that a subadditive utility function $u_{11}(\mathbf{x})$ is a positively homogeneous function of the degree $\theta = \gamma$,

(l) $\forall\lambda > 0 u_{12}(\lambda\mathbf{x}) = (a_1(\lambda x_1)^\gamma + a_2(\lambda x_2)^\gamma)^{\frac{\theta}{\gamma}} = \lambda^\theta u_{12}(\mathbf{x})$, which means that the CES utility function $u_{12}(\mathbf{x})$ is a positively homogeneous function of the degree $\theta > 0$.

Ad 3

Functions $u_1(\mathbf{x})$ and $u_{10}(\mathbf{x})$ are positively homogeneous of the degree $\theta = 1$. Functions $u_6(\mathbf{x})$, $u_{11}(\mathbf{x})$and $u_{12}(\mathbf{x})$ are positively homogeneous of the degree $\theta > 0$.

Ad 4

(a) $\frac{\partial u(\mathbf{x})}{\partial x_1} = a_1 > 0 \quad \frac{\partial u(\mathbf{x})}{\partial x_2} = a_2 > 0,$
(b) $\frac{\partial u(\mathbf{x})}{\partial x_1} = a_1 A^{a_1x_1+a_2x_2} \ln A < 0 \quad \frac{\partial u(\mathbf{x})}{\partial x_2} = a_2 A^{a_1x_1+a_2x_2} \ln A < 0,$
(c) $\frac{\partial u(\mathbf{x})}{\partial x_1} = a_1 A^{a_1x_1+a_2x_2} \ln A > 0 \quad \frac{\partial u(\mathbf{x})}{\partial x_2} = a_2 A^{a_1x_1+a_2x_2} \ln A > 0,$
(d) $\frac{\partial u(\mathbf{x})}{\partial x_1} = -\ln(a_1x_1 + a_2x_2)^{-2}\frac{a_1}{x_1} < 0 \quad \frac{\partial u(\mathbf{x})}{\partial x_2} = -\ln(a_1x_1 + a_2x_2)^{-2}\frac{a_2}{x_2} < 0,$
(e) $\frac{\partial u(\mathbf{x})}{\partial x_1} = \frac{a_1}{a_1x_1+a_2x_2} > 0 \quad \frac{\partial u(\mathbf{x})}{\partial x_2} = \frac{a_2}{a_1x_1+a_2x_2} > 0,$
(f) $\frac{\partial u(\mathbf{x})}{\partial x_1} = \alpha a x_1^{\alpha-1} x_2^\beta > 0 \quad \frac{\partial u(\mathbf{x})}{\partial x_2} = \beta a x_1^\alpha x_2^{\beta-1} > 0$
(g) $\frac{\partial u(\mathbf{x})}{\partial x_1} = \frac{a_1}{x_1} > 0 \quad \frac{\partial u(\mathbf{x})}{\partial x_2} = \frac{a_2}{x_2} > 0,$
(h) $\frac{\partial u(\mathbf{x})}{\partial x_1} = a_1 A^{ax_1^\alpha x_2^\beta} \alpha a x_1^{\alpha-1} x_2^\beta \ln A < 0 \quad \frac{\partial u(\mathbf{x})}{\partial x_2} = a_2 A^{ax_1^\alpha x_2^\beta} \beta a x_1^\alpha x_2^{\beta-1} \ln A < 0,$
(i) $\frac{\partial u(\mathbf{x})}{\partial x_1} = a_1 A^{ax_1^\alpha x_2^\beta} \alpha a x_1^{\alpha-1} x_2^\beta \ln A > 0 \quad \frac{\partial u(\mathbf{x})}{\partial x_2} = a_2 A^{ax_1^\alpha x_2^\beta} \beta a x_1^\alpha x_2^{\beta-1} \ln A > 0,$
(j) The Koopmans-Leontief utility function is not differentiable.
(k) $\frac{\partial u(\mathbf{x})}{\partial x_1} = \gamma a_1 x_1^{\gamma-1} > 0 \quad \frac{\partial u(\mathbf{x})}{\partial x_2} = \gamma a_2 x_2^{\gamma-1} > 0,$
(l) $\frac{\partial u(\mathbf{x})}{\partial x_1} = \frac{\theta}{\gamma}\left(a_1x_1^\gamma + a_2x_2^\gamma\right)^{\frac{\theta}{\gamma}-1} \gamma a_1 x_1^{\gamma-1} > 0$
$\frac{\partial u(\mathbf{x})}{\partial x_2} = \frac{\theta}{\gamma}\left(a_1x_1^\gamma + a_2x_2^\gamma\right)^{\frac{\theta}{\gamma}-1} \gamma a_2 x_2^{\gamma-1} > 0.$

E2.3. Determine if a given utility function $u: \mathbb{R}^2_+ \to \mathbb{R}$ of a form:

(a) $u(\mathbf{x}) = a_1x_1 - a_2x_2 + a_3, \quad a_i > 0, i = 1, 2,$
(b) $u(\mathbf{x}) = a_1 \ln x_1 - a_2 \ln x_2 + a_3, \quad a_i > 0, i = 1, 2,$
(c) $u(\mathbf{x}) = -a_1x_1^{\frac{1}{2}} + a_2x_2^{\frac{1}{2}} + a_3, \quad a_i > 0, i = 1, 2,$

is (weakly) increasing or (weakly) decreasing.

Solutions

Ad a

$$\frac{\partial u(\mathbf{x})}{\partial x_1} = a_1 > 0 \quad \frac{\partial u(\mathbf{x})}{\partial x_2} = -a_2 < 0$$

Ad b

$$\frac{\partial u(\mathbf{x})}{\partial x_1} = \frac{a_1}{x_1} > 0 \quad \frac{\partial u(\mathbf{x})}{\partial x_2} = -\frac{a_2}{x_2} < 0$$

Ad c

$$\frac{\partial u(\mathbf{x})}{\partial x_1} = -\frac{1}{2}a_1 x_1^{-\frac{1}{2}} < 0 \qquad \frac{\partial u(\mathbf{x})}{\partial x_2} = \frac{\partial u(\mathbf{x})}{\partial x_1} = \frac{1}{2}a_2 x_2^{-\frac{1}{2}} > 0$$

It follows that none of these utility functions is either (weakly) increasing or (weakly) decreasing.

E2.4. There are given:

- a budget set $D(\mathbf{p}, I) = \{\mathbf{x} \in \mathbb{R}_+^2 | p_1x_1 + p_2x_2 \leq I\} \subset X = \mathbb{R}_+^2$,
- a supply set $B = \{(x_1, x_2) \in \mathbb{R}_+^2 | x_1 \leq b_1, x_2 \leq b_2\} \subset X = \mathbb{R}_+^2$,

such that:

a. $\forall \alpha, \beta \geq 0, \alpha + \beta = 1 \quad 0 < b_1 < \frac{\alpha I}{p_1}$ and $0 < b_2 < \frac{\beta I}{P_2}$,
b. $0 < \frac{I}{p_1} \leq b_1$ and $0 < b_2 < \frac{I}{P_2}$,
c. $0 < b_1 < \frac{I}{p_1}$ and $0 \leq \frac{I}{P_2} < b_2$.
d. $0 < \frac{I - p_2 b_2}{p_1} < b_1 < \frac{I}{p_1}$ and $0 < \frac{I - p_1 b_1}{P_2} < b_2 < \frac{I}{p_2}$.

1. Using a geometric method, find a solution to a consumption utility maximization problem with a given utility function:

   A. linear: $u(\mathbf{x}) = a_1x_1 + a_2x_2, \quad a_i > 0, i = 1, 2,$
   B. a power function: $u(\mathbf{x}) = ax_1^{\alpha_1}x_2^{\alpha_2}, \quad a, \alpha_i > 0, \alpha_1 + \alpha_2 < 1, i = 1, 2,$
   C. logarithmic: $u(\mathbf{x}) = a_1 \ln x_1 + a_2 \ln x_2, \quad a_i > 0, x_i > 0, i = 1, 2,$
   D. subadditive: $u(\mathbf{x}) = a_1x_1^{\alpha} + a_2x_2^{\alpha}, \quad a_i > 0, i = 1, 2, \alpha \in (0; 1),$
   E. a Koopmans-Leontief function: $u(\mathbf{x}) = \min\{a_1x_1, a_2x_2\}, \quad a_i > 0, i = 1, 2,$
   F. a CES function: $u(\mathbf{x}) = (a_1x_1^{\gamma} + a_2x_2^{\gamma})^{\frac{\theta}{\gamma}}, \quad \theta, a_i > 0, i = 1, 2, \gamma \in (-1; 0) \cap (0; +\infty),$

knowing that a consumer chooses an optimal consumption bundle in a set $B \cap D(\mathbf{p}, I)$.

2. For each of considered sets $B \cap D(\mathbf{p}, I)$ of feasible solutions by each of utility functions, determine relationships between properties of the set (convex, bounded, closed, compact) and properties of the utility function (monotonicity, convexity or strict convexity). Write conclusions about number of optimal consumption bundles.

Solutions

Case 1

The budget set is a subset of the supply set: $D(\mathbf{p}, I) \subseteq B$, which means that the supply of each good is sufficiently big in comparison to the consumer's income. It is the case when:

$$0 < \frac{I}{p_1} \leq b_1 \quad \wedge \quad 0 < \frac{I}{P_2} \leq b_2.$$

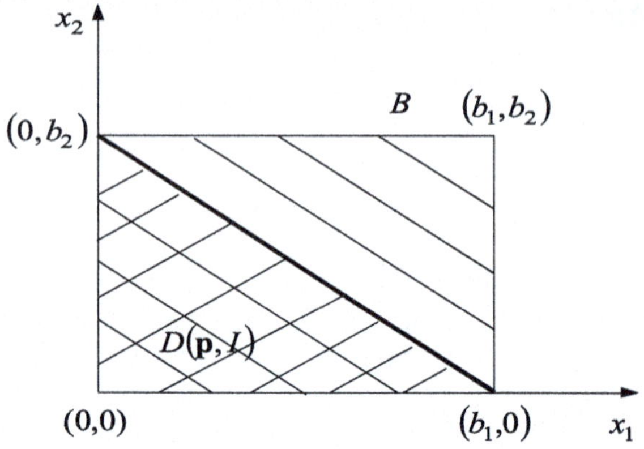

Fig. 2.1 Budget set as subset of supply set when $\frac{I}{p_i} = b_i, i = 1, 2$ (E2.4)

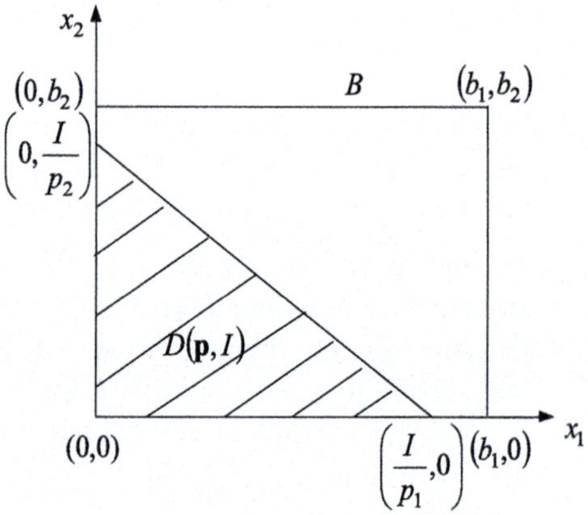

Fig. 2.2 Budget set as subset of supply set when $\frac{I}{p_i} < b_i, i = 1, 2$ (E2.4)

Then, the budget constraint is binding and a consumer chooses the optimal consumption bundle in the budget set $D(\mathbf{p}, I)$ (Figs. 2.1 and 2.2)

A.

$$\text{If } \exists \lambda > 0, \mathbf{p} = \lambda \mathbf{a} \text{ then } \bar{\mathbf{x}} = \left(\frac{\alpha I}{p_1}, \frac{\beta I}{p_2}\right)$$
$$= (\alpha b_1, \beta b_2), \forall \alpha, \beta \geq 0, \alpha + \beta = 1$$
$$\text{If } \neg \exists \lambda > 0, \mathbf{p} = \lambda \mathbf{a} \text{ then } \bar{\mathbf{x}}^1 = \left(\frac{I}{p_1}, 0\right)$$
$$= (b_1, 0) \text{ or } \bar{\mathbf{x}}^2 = \left(0, \frac{I}{p_2}\right) = (0, b_2)$$

B–F. $\exists_1 \alpha, \beta > 0, \alpha + \beta = 1 \quad \bar{\mathbf{x}} = \left(\frac{\alpha I}{p_1}, \frac{\beta I}{p_2}\right) = (\alpha b_1, \beta b_2)$

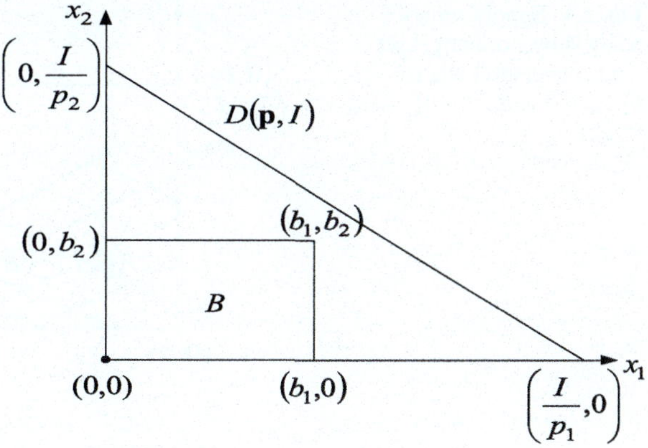

Fig. 2.3 Supply set as subset of budget set when $b_1 \in \left(0; \frac{\alpha I}{p_1}\right)$ and $b_2 \in \left(0; \frac{\beta I}{p_2}\right)$ (E2.4)

Case 2

The supply set is a proper subset of the budget set: $B \subset D(\mathbf{p}, I)$, which means that the supply of each good is sufficiently small in comparison to the consumer's income. It is the case when:

$$\forall \alpha, \beta \geq 0, \alpha + \beta = 1 \quad 0 < b_1 < \frac{\alpha I}{p_1} \quad \wedge \quad 0 < b_2 < \frac{\beta I}{P_2}.$$

Then, the supply constraint is binding and a consumer chooses the optimal consumption bundle in the supply set B (Fig. 2.3).

B–F. correct to points A-F (not B-F) $\overline{\mathbf{x}} = (b_1, b_2)$

Case 3

The budget set and the supply set are not disjoint but in the same time none of them is the proper subset of the other and the supply constraints are following:

$$\text{Case 3.1} \quad 0 < b_1 < \frac{I}{p_1} \quad \wedge \quad 0 < \frac{I}{p_2} < b_2 \quad \text{or}$$

$$\text{Case 3.2} \quad 0 < \frac{I}{p_1} < b_1 \quad \wedge \quad 0 < b_2 < \frac{I}{p_2}.$$

Then both budget and supply constraints are binding and a consumer chooses the optimal consumption bundle in a set $B \cap D(\mathbf{p}, I)$ which is not equal to B nor to $D(\mathbf{p}, I)$ (Figs. 2.4 and 2.5).

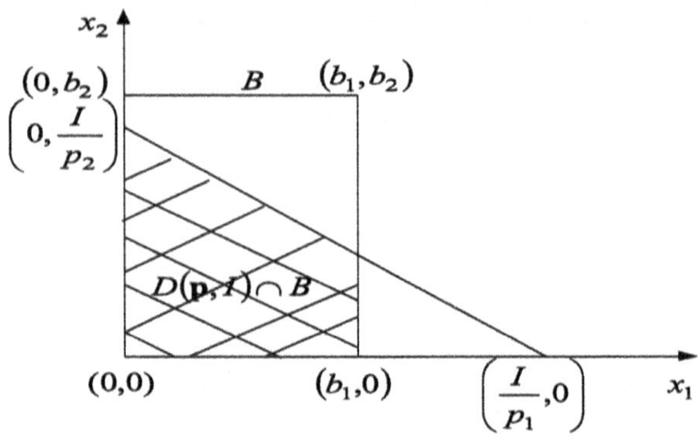

Fig. 2.4 Supply set not being subset of budget set (and conversely) when $0 < b_1 < \frac{I}{p_1}$ and $0 < \frac{I}{p_2} < b_2$ (E2.4)

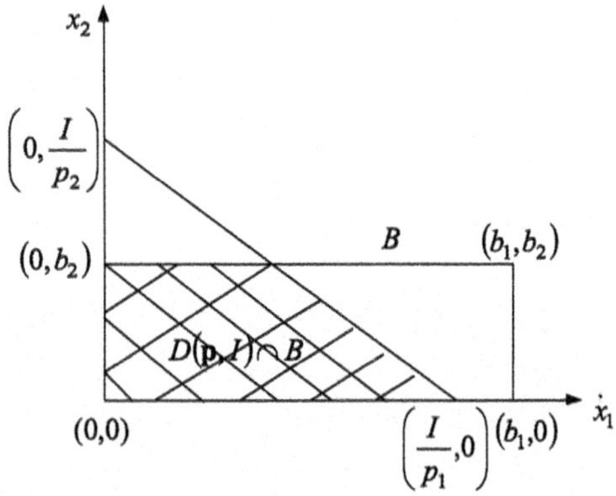

Fig. 2.5 Supply set not being subset of budget set (and conversely) when $0 < \frac{I}{p_1} < b_1$ and $0 < b_2 < \frac{I}{p_2}$ (E2.4)

A.

$$\text{If} \quad \exists\lambda > 0, \mathbf{p} = \lambda\mathbf{a} \quad \text{then} \quad \forall\alpha, \beta \geq 0, \alpha + \beta = 1$$

$$\text{Case 3.1} \quad \bar{\mathbf{x}} = \left(\alpha b_1, \frac{I - \alpha p_1 b_1}{p_2}\right), \quad \text{Case 3.2} \quad \bar{\mathbf{x}} = \left(\frac{I - \beta p_2 b_2}{p_1}, \beta b_2\right)$$

$$\text{If} \quad \neg\exists\lambda > 0, \mathbf{p} = \lambda\mathbf{a} \quad \text{then}$$

$$\text{Case 3.1} \quad \bar{\mathbf{x}}^1 = \left(b_1, \frac{I - p_1 b_1}{p_2}\right) \quad \text{or} \quad \bar{\mathbf{x}}^2 = \left(0, \frac{I}{p_2}\right)$$

$$\text{Case 3.2} \quad \bar{\mathbf{x}}^1 = \left(\frac{I}{p_1}, 0\right) \quad \text{or} \quad \bar{\mathbf{x}}^2 = \left(\frac{I - p_2 b_2}{p_1}, b_2\right)$$

B–F.

$$\exists_1 \alpha, \beta > 0, \alpha + \beta = 1 \quad \text{such that}$$

$$\text{Case 3.1} \quad \bar{\mathbf{x}} = \left(\alpha b_1, \frac{I - \alpha p_1 b_1}{p_2}\right), \quad \text{Case 3.2} \quad \bar{\mathbf{x}} = \left(\frac{I - \beta p_2 b_2}{p_1}, \beta b_2\right).$$

Case 4

The budget set and the supply set are not disjoint but in the same time none of them is the proper subset of the other. It is the case when:

Fig. 2.6 Supply set not being subset of budget set (and conversely) when $0 < \frac{I-p_2b_2}{p_1} < b_1 < \frac{I}{p_1}$ and $0 < \frac{I-p_1b_1}{P_2} < b_2 < \frac{I}{p_2}$. (E2.4)

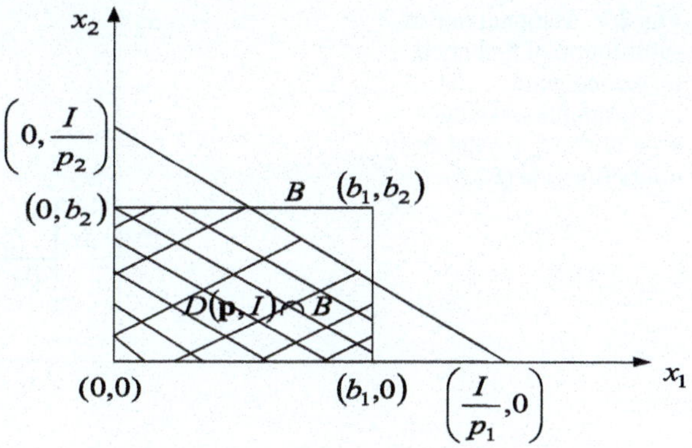

$$0 < \frac{I - p_2 b_2}{p_1} < b_1 < \frac{I}{p_1} \quad \text{and} \quad 0 < \frac{I - p_1 b_1}{P_2} < b_2 < \frac{I}{p_2}.$$

Then both budget and supply constraints are binding and a consumer chooses the optimal consumption bundle in a set $B \cap D(\mathbf{p}, I)$ which is not equal to B nor to $D(\mathbf{p}, I)$ (Fig. 2.6).

If $\exists\lambda > 0, \mathbf{p} = \lambda\mathbf{a}$ then

A. $\bar{\mathbf{x}} = \left(\alpha\left(b_1 + \frac{I - p_2b_2}{p_1}\right), \beta\left(b_2 + \frac{I - p_1b_1}{p_2}\right)\right) \quad \forall\alpha, \beta \geq 0, \alpha + \beta = 1$

If $\neg\exists\lambda > 0, \mathbf{p} = \lambda\mathbf{a}$ then $\bar{\mathbf{x}}^1 = \left(b_1, \frac{I - p_1b_1}{p_2}\right)$ or $\bar{\mathbf{x}}^2 = \left(\frac{I - p_2b_2,}{p_1}, b_2\right)$

B. B-F $\exists_1\alpha, \beta > 0, \alpha + \beta = 1$ $\bar{\mathbf{x}} = \left(\alpha\left(b_1 + \frac{I-p_2b_2}{p_1}\right), \beta\left(b_2 + \frac{I-p_1b_1}{p_2}\right)\right)$.

E2.5. Justify by geometric means that a linear utility function:

A. $u(\mathbf{x}) = a_1x_1 + a_2x_2 + a_3, a_i > 0, i = 1, 2, 3$

describes consumer goods which are perfect substitutes and not complementary for each other,

and that a Koopmans-Leontief utility function:

B. $u(\mathbf{x}) = \min\{a_1x_1, a_2x_2\} + a_3, a_i > 0, i = 1, 2, 3$

describes consumer goods which are perfect complements and not substitute for each other.

Solutions

Ad a

Notice that the indifference curve $u(\mathbf{x}) = a_1x_1 + a_2x_2 + a_3 = u > 0$ intersects the horizontal axis at the point $\mathbf{x}^1 = \left(\frac{u-a_1}{a_2}, 0\right)$, and the vertical axis at the point $\mathbf{x}^2 = \left(0, \frac{u-a_3}{a_2}\right)$ (Fig. 2.7).

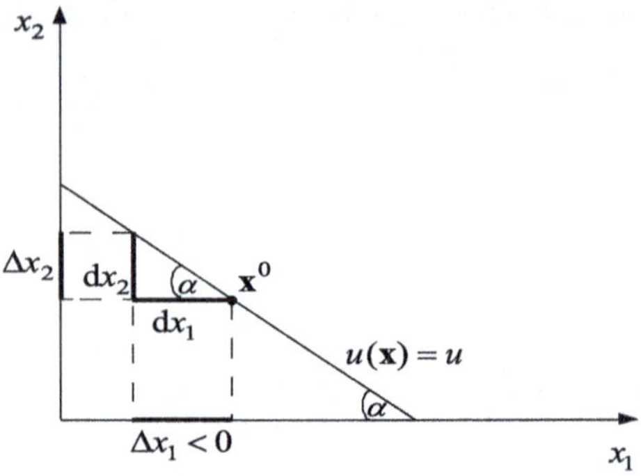

Fig. 2.7 Marginal rate of substitution of first good by second good in consumption bundle $\mathbf{x}^0 \in G \subset \mathbb{R}^2_+$ for linear utility function (E2.5)

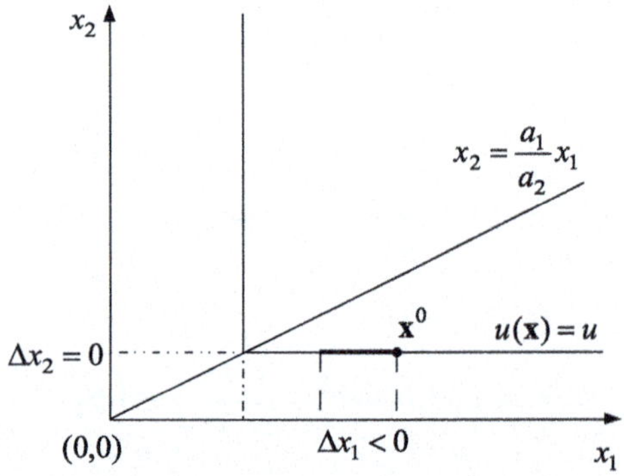

Fig. 2.8 Marginal rate of substitution of first good by second good in consumption bundle $\mathbf{x}^0 \in G \subset \mathbb{R}^2_+$ for Koopmans-Leontief utility function (E2.5)

Let us notice that $dx_1 = \Delta x_1$ and $dx_2 = \Delta x_2$. Since $s_{12}(\mathbf{x}) = -\frac{dx_2}{dx_1} = \text{tg}\alpha =$ const., we see that the marginal rate of substitution of the first (second) good by the second (first) in a consumption bundle $\mathbf{x}^0 \in \mathbb{R}^2_+$, which utility is described by the linear utility function, is constant. Thus, it does not depend on quantities of goods in the bundle. In this case, the goods are called **perfect substitutes**. In the same time, we can notice that in order to rise (reduce) the utility level of any consumption bundle $\mathbf{x} = (x_1, x_2) \in \mathbb{R}^2_+$, it is enough to increase (decrease) quantity of just one of the goods, not necessarily of both goods. This shows that the linear utility function describes goods which are not complementary for each other. Finally, the substitutability of consumer goods takes place when the utility of a consumption bundle $\mathbf{x} = (x_1, x_2) \in \mathbb{R}^2_+$ is described by an increasing or by a decreasing utility function (Fig. 2.8).

Ad b

Let us notice that for an indifference curve $\min\{a_1x_1, a_2x_2\} + a_3 = u$, we get that $\mathbf{x}^1 = \left(\frac{u-a_1}{a_2}, 0\right)$ and $\mathbf{x}^2 = \left(0, \frac{u-a_3}{a_2}\right)$.

Let us also notice that $dx_1 = \Delta x_1$ and $dx_2 = \Delta x_2 = 0$. Since $s_{12}(\mathbf{x}) \cong -\frac{dx_2}{dx_1}$, we see that the marginal rate of substitution of the first good by the second in a consumption bundle $\mathbf{x}^0 \in \mathbb{R}^2_+$ is equal to $s_{12}(\mathbf{x}^0) = 0$, while that the marginal rate of substitution of the second good by the first good is undefined (its value is infinite). This shows that the Koopmans-Leontief utility function describes goods which are not substitute for each other. In the same time, we can notice that in order to rise (reduce) the utility level of any consumption bundle $\mathbf{x} = (x_1, x_2) \in \mathbb{R}^2_+$, it is necessary to increase (decrease) quantities of both goods in some fixed proportion, not just one of the goods. In this case, the goods are called **perfect complements**. Finally, the complementarity of consumer goods takes place when the utility of a consumption bundle $\mathbf{x} = (x_1, x_2) \in \mathbb{R}^2_+$ is described by a weakly increasing or by a weakly decreasing utility function.

E2.6. There are given a power utility function $u(\mathbf{x}) = ax_1^{\alpha_1}x_2^{\alpha_2}, a, \alpha_i > 0, \alpha_1 + \alpha_2 < 1, i = 1, 2$ and a utility function $u_2(\mathbf{x}) = \alpha_1 \ln x_1 + \alpha_2 \ln x_2 + \ln a, x_i > 0, i = 1, 2,$ which is a composition of the function u with an increasing logarithmic function. We know that u and u_2 describe the same relation of consumer preference. Solving consumption utility maximization problems with each of these functions check if they correspond to the same Marshallian demand function.

Solution

Let us notice that if $u(\mathbf{x}) = ax_1^{\alpha_1}x_2^{\alpha_2}$, then $u_2(\mathbf{x}) = \ln[u(\mathbf{x})] = \alpha_1 \ln x_1 + \alpha_2 \ln x_2 + \ln a$.

Thus, two problems of maximizing the utility of consumption are given:

(P2) $u(\mathbf{x}) = ax_1^{\alpha_1}x_2^{\alpha_2} \to \max$

(1) $p_1x_1 + p_2x_2 \leq I$
(2) $x_1, x_2 \geq 0$

(P2) $u_2(\mathbf{x}) = \alpha_1 \ln x_1 + \alpha_2 \ln x_2 + \ln a_3 \to \max$

(1) $p_1x_1 + p_2x_2 \leq I$
(2) $x_1, x_2 \geq 0.$

The optimal solution to the problem (T1) is to solve the system of equations:

(1) $s_{12}(\mathbf{x}) = \frac{\frac{\partial u(\mathbf{x})}{\partial x_1}}{\frac{\partial u(\mathbf{x})}{\partial x_2}} = \frac{p_1}{p_2},$
(2) $p_1x_1 + p_2x_2 = I.$

From Eq. (1), it follows that:

(3) $\frac{\alpha_1 ax_1^{\alpha-1}x_2^{\beta}}{\alpha_2 ax_1^{\alpha}x_2^{\beta-1}} = \frac{\alpha_1 x_2}{\alpha_2 x_1} = \frac{p_1}{p_2}.$

From where:

(4) $x_2 = \frac{\alpha_2}{\alpha_1}\frac{p_1}{p_2}x_1$.

Substituting (4) into (2) we get:

(5) $p_1x_1 + p_2\frac{\alpha_2}{\alpha_1}\frac{p_1}{p_2}x_1 = I$

(6) $p_1x_1\left(\frac{\alpha_1+\alpha_2}{\alpha_1}\right) = I$

(7) $x_1 = \frac{\alpha_1}{(\alpha_1+\alpha_2)}\frac{I}{p_1}$

Substituting (7) into (4), we get:

(8) $x_2 = \frac{\alpha_2}{\alpha_1}\frac{p_1}{p_2}\frac{\alpha_1}{(\alpha_1+\alpha_2)}\frac{I}{p_1} = \frac{\alpha_2}{(\alpha_1+\alpha_2)}\frac{I}{p_2}$

Finally, the optimal bundle of goods in the problem (T1) has the form: $\overline{\mathbf{x}}^1 = \left(\frac{\alpha_1}{(\alpha_1+\alpha_2)}\frac{I}{p_1}, \frac{\alpha_2}{(\alpha_1+\alpha_2)}\frac{I}{p_2}\right)$, and the maximum utility is $u(\overline{\mathbf{x}}^1) = a\left(\frac{\alpha_1}{p_1}\right)^{\alpha_1}\left(\frac{\alpha_2}{p_2}\right)^{\alpha_2}\left(\frac{I}{\alpha_1+\alpha_2}\right)^{\alpha_1+\alpha_2}$

The optimal solution to the problem (T2) is to solve the system of equations:

(1) $s_{12}(\mathbf{x}) = \frac{\frac{\partial u(\mathbf{x})}{\partial x_1}}{\frac{\partial u(\mathbf{x})}{\partial x_2}} = \frac{p_1}{p_2}$,

(2) $p_1x_1 + p_2x_2 = I$

From Eq. (1), it follows that:

(3) $\frac{\frac{\alpha_1}{x_1}}{\frac{\alpha_2}{x_2}} = \frac{\alpha_1x_2}{\alpha_2x_1} = \frac{p_1}{p_2}$

From where:

(4) $x_2 = \frac{\alpha_2}{\alpha_1}\frac{p_1}{p_2}x_1$

Substituting (4) into (2), we get:

(5) $p_1x_1 + p_2\frac{\alpha_2}{\alpha_1}\frac{p_1}{p_2}x_1 = I$

(6) $p_1x_1\left(\frac{\alpha_1+\alpha_2}{\alpha_1}\right) = I$

(7) $x_1 = \frac{\alpha_1}{(\alpha_1+\alpha_2)}\frac{I}{p_1}$

Substituting (4) into (2), we get:

(8) $x_2 = \frac{\alpha_2}{\alpha_1}\frac{p_1}{p_2}\frac{\alpha_1}{(\alpha_1+\alpha_2)}\frac{I}{p_1} = \frac{\alpha_2}{(\alpha_1+\alpha_2)}\frac{I}{p_2}$

Finally, the optimal bundle of goods in the problem (T2) has the form: $\overline{\mathbf{x}}^2 = \left(\frac{\alpha_1}{(\alpha_1+\alpha_2)}\frac{I}{p_1}, \frac{\alpha_2}{(\alpha_1+\alpha_2)}\frac{I}{p_2}\right)$, and the maximum utility is $u_2(\overline{\mathbf{x}}^2) = \ln a\left(\frac{\alpha_1}{p_1}\right)^{\alpha_1}\left(\frac{\alpha_2}{p_2}\right)^{\alpha_2}\left(\frac{I}{\alpha_1+\alpha_2}\right)^{\alpha_1+\alpha_2}$

It follows that: $\overline{\mathbf{x}}^1 = \overline{\mathbf{x}}^2$ and $u_2(\overline{\mathbf{x}}^2) = \ln[u(\overline{\mathbf{x}}^1)]$, but $u(\overline{\mathbf{x}}^1) \neq u_2(\overline{\mathbf{x}}^2)$

E2.7. Using the Kuhn-Tucker theorem,[1] find an optimal solution to a consumption utility maximization problem with an additional constraint on the supply of both goods: $0 \le x_i \le b_i, i = 1, 2$, when a utility function is:

[1] The theorem (Theorem A.6) is presented in a Mathematical appendix of the textbook Malaga K., Sobczak K, *Microeconomics. Static and Dynamic Analysis*, Springer Nature Switzerland, 2022.

A. a power function: $u(\mathbf{x}) = ax_1^{\alpha_1}x_2^{\alpha_2}, a, \alpha_i > 0, \alpha_1 + \alpha_2 < 1,\ i = 1, 2,$
B. logarithmic: $u(\mathbf{x}) = a_1 \ln x_1 + a_2 \ln x_2, a_i > 0, x_i > 0,\ i = 1, 2,$
C. subadditive: $u(\mathbf{x}) = a_1x_1^{\alpha} + a_2x_2^{\alpha}, a_i > 0,\ i = 1, 2, \alpha \in (0; 1).$

Solutions

There are given:

- a budget set $D(\mathbf{p}, I) = \left\{\mathbf{x} \in \mathbb{R}_+^2 | p_1x_1 + p_2x_2 \leq I\right\} \subset X = \mathbb{R}_+^2,$
- a supply set $B = \{(x_1, x_2) \in \mathbb{R}_+^2 | x_1 \leq b_1, x_2 \leq b_2\} \subset X = \mathbb{R}_+^2,$

such that:

(a) If $0 < b_1 < \frac{I-p_2b_2}{p_1}$ and $0 < b_2 < \frac{I-p_1b_1}{P_2}$ then $D(\mathbf{p}, I) \cap B = B$.
(b) If $0 < \frac{I}{p_1} < b_1$ and $0 < \frac{I}{P_2} < b_2$ then $D(\mathbf{p}, I) \cap B = D(\mathbf{p}, I)$.
(c) If $0 < b_1 < \frac{I}{p_1}$ and $0 < b_2 < \frac{I}{P_2}$ then $D(\mathbf{p}, I) \cap B = C$.

A Lagrange function has the following form:

$$L(x_1, x_2, \lambda_1, \lambda_2, \lambda_3) = u(\mathbf{x}) + \lambda_1(b_1 - x_1) + \lambda_2(b_2 - x_2) + \lambda_3(I - p_1x_1 - p_2x_2).$$

Ad a

$$\text{If} \left.\frac{\partial L(\overline{\mathbf{x}}, \lambda)}{\partial \lambda_1}\right|_{\lambda_1 = \overline{\lambda}_1} = b_1 - \overline{x}_1 = 0 \text{ then } \overline{x}_1 = b_1.$$

$$\text{If} \left.\frac{\partial L(\overline{\mathbf{x}}, \lambda)}{\partial \lambda_2}\right|_{\lambda_2 = \overline{\lambda}_2} = b_2 - \overline{x}_2 = 0 \text{ then } \overline{x}_2 = b_2$$

Ad A

$$\overline{\mathbf{x}} = (\overline{x}_1, \overline{x}_2) = (b_1, b_2) > (0, 0) \text{ and } u(\overline{\mathbf{x}}) = ab_1^{\alpha_1}b_2^{\alpha_2} > 0$$

Ad B

$$\overline{\mathbf{x}} = (\overline{x}_1, \overline{x}_2) = (b_1, b_2) > (0, 0) \text{ and } u(\overline{\mathbf{x}}) = a_1 \ln b_1 + a_2 \ln b_2.$$

Ad C

$$\overline{\mathbf{x}} = (\overline{x}_1, \overline{x}_2) = (b_1, b_2) > (0, 0) \text{ and } u(\overline{\mathbf{x}}) = a_1b_1^{\alpha} + a_2b_2^{\alpha} > 0.$$

Ad b

(1) $\left.\frac{\partial L(\mathbf{x},\lambda)}{\partial x_1}\right|_{\mathbf{x}=\overline{\mathbf{x}}} = \left.\frac{\partial u(\mathbf{x})}{\partial x_1}\right|_{\mathbf{x}=\overline{\mathbf{x}}} - \overline{\lambda}_3 p_1 = 0$

(2) $\left.\frac{\partial L(\mathbf{x},\lambda)}{\partial x_2}\right|_{\mathbf{x}=\overline{\mathbf{x}}} = \left.\frac{\partial u(\mathbf{x})}{\partial x_2}\right|_{\mathbf{x}=\overline{\mathbf{x}}} - \overline{\lambda}_3 p_2 = 0$

(3) $\left.\frac{\partial L(\overline{\mathbf{x}},\lambda)}{\partial \lambda_3}\right|_{\lambda_3=\overline{\lambda}_3} = I - p_1\overline{x}_1 - p_2\overline{x}_2 = 0$

(4) $\frac{\left.\frac{\partial u(\mathbf{x})}{\partial x_1}\right|_{\mathbf{x}=\overline{\mathbf{x}}}}{\left.\frac{\partial u(\mathbf{x})}{\partial x_2}\right|_{\mathbf{x}=\overline{\mathbf{x}}}} = \frac{p_1}{p_2}$

(5) $p_1\overline{x}_1 + p_2\overline{x}_2 = I.$

Ad A

(6) $\frac{\alpha_1 a\overline{x}_1^{\alpha_1-1}\overline{x}_2^{\alpha_2}}{\alpha_2 a\overline{x}_1^{\alpha_1}\overline{x}_2^{\alpha_2-1}} = \frac{\alpha_1\overline{x}_2}{\alpha_2\overline{x}_1} = \frac{p_1}{p_2}$

(7) $\overline{x}_2 = \frac{\alpha_2 p_1}{\alpha_1 p_2}\overline{x}_1$

(8) $p_1\overline{x}_1 + p_2\frac{\alpha_2 p_1}{\alpha_1 p_2}\overline{x}_1 = I$

(9) $\overline{x}_1 = \frac{\alpha_1 I}{(\alpha_1+\alpha_2)p_1}$

(10) $\overline{x}_2 = \frac{\alpha_2 I}{(\alpha_1+\alpha_2)p_2}$

(11) $\overline{\mathbf{x}} = \left(\frac{\alpha_1 I}{(\alpha_1+\alpha_2)p_1}, \frac{\alpha_2 I}{(\alpha_1+\alpha_2)p_2}\right)$

(12) $\exists_1 \alpha, \beta > 0, \alpha + \beta = 1; \overline{\mathbf{x}} = \left(\frac{\alpha I}{p_1}, \frac{\beta I}{p_2}\right)$ where $\alpha = \frac{\alpha_1}{\alpha_1+\alpha_2} > 0$ and $\beta = \frac{\alpha_2}{\alpha_1+\alpha_2} > 0$

(13) $u(\overline{\mathbf{x}}) = a\left(\frac{\alpha_1}{p_1}\right)^{\alpha_1}\left(\frac{\alpha_2}{p_2}\right)^{\alpha_2}\left(\frac{I}{\alpha_1+\alpha_2}\right)^{\alpha_1+\alpha_2} > 0.$

Ad B

(6) $\frac{\frac{a_1}{\overline{x}_1}}{\frac{a_2}{\overline{x}_2}} = \frac{a_1\overline{x}_2}{a_2\overline{x}_1} = \frac{p_1}{p_2}$

(7) $\overline{x}_2 = \frac{a_2 p_1}{a_1 p_2}\overline{x}_1$

(8) $p_1\overline{x}_1 + p_2\frac{a_2 p_1}{a_1 p_2}\overline{x}_1 = I$

(9) $\overline{x}_1 = \frac{a_1 I}{(a_1+a_2)p_1}$

(10) $\overline{x}_2 = \frac{a_2 I}{(a_1+a_2)p_2}$

(11) $\overline{\mathbf{x}} = \left(\frac{a_1 I}{(a_1+a_2)p_1}, \frac{a_2 I}{(a_1+a_2)p_2}\right)$

(12) $\exists_1 \alpha, \beta > 0, \alpha + \beta = 1; \overline{\mathbf{x}} = \left(\frac{\alpha I}{p_1}, \frac{\beta I}{p_2}\right)$ where $\alpha = \frac{a_1}{a_1+a_2} > 0$ and $\beta = \frac{a_2}{a_1+a_2} > 0$

(13) $u(\overline{\mathbf{x}}) = \ln\left[\left(\frac{a_1}{p_1}\right)^{a_1}\left(\frac{a_2}{p_2}\right)^{a_2}\left(\frac{I}{a_1+a_2}\right)^{a_1+a_2}\right].$

Ad C

(6) $\frac{\alpha a_1\overline{x}_1^{\alpha-1}}{\alpha a_2\overline{x}_2^{\alpha-1}} = \frac{a_1\overline{x}_2^{1-\alpha}}{a_2\overline{x}_1^{1-\alpha}} = \frac{p_1}{p_2}$

(7) $\overline{x}_2 = \left(\frac{a_2 p_1}{a_1 p_2}\right)^{\frac{1}{1-\alpha}}\overline{x}_1$

(8) $p_1\overline{x}_1 + p_2\left(\frac{a_2 p_1}{a_1 p_2}\right)^{\frac{1}{1-\alpha}}\overline{x}_1 = I$

(9) $\overline{x}_1 = \frac{(p_2 a_1)^{\frac{1}{1-\alpha}} I}{\left(p_1 p_2^{\frac{1}{1-\alpha}} a_1^{\frac{1}{1-\alpha}} + p_2 p_1^{\frac{1}{1-\alpha}} a_2^{\frac{1}{1-\alpha}}\right)}$

(10) $\overline{x}_2 = \frac{(p_1 a_2)^{\frac{1}{1-\alpha}} I}{\left(p_1 p_2^{\frac{1}{1-\alpha}} a_1^{\frac{1}{1-\alpha}} + p_2 p_1^{\frac{1}{1-\alpha}} a_2^{\frac{1}{1-\alpha}}\right)}$

(11)
$$\overline{\mathbf{x}} = \left(\frac{(p_2 a_1)^{\frac{1}{1-\alpha}} I}{\left(p_1 p_2^{\frac{1}{1-\alpha}} a_1^{\frac{1}{1-\alpha}} + p_2 p_1^{\frac{1}{1-\alpha}} a_2^{\frac{1}{1-\alpha}}\right)}, \frac{(p_1 a_2)^{\frac{1}{1-\alpha}} I}{\left(p_1 p_2^{\frac{1}{1-\alpha}} a_1^{\frac{1}{1-\alpha}} + p_2 p_1^{\frac{1}{1-\alpha}} a_2^{\frac{1}{1-\alpha}}\right)} \right)$$
$$= \left(\frac{(p_2 a_1)^{\frac{1}{1-\alpha}} I}{\left(p_2^{\frac{1}{1-\alpha}} a_1^{\frac{1}{1-\alpha}} + p_2 p_1^{\frac{\alpha}{1-\alpha}} a_2^{\frac{1}{1-\alpha}}\right) p_1}, \frac{(p_1 a_2)^{\frac{1}{1-\alpha}} I}{\left(p_1 p_2^{\frac{\alpha}{1-\alpha}} a_1^{\frac{1}{1-\alpha}} + p_1^{\frac{1}{1-\alpha}} a_2^{\frac{1}{1-\alpha}}\right) p_2} \right)$$

(12) $\exists_1 \alpha, \beta > 0, \alpha + \beta = 1; \overline{\mathbf{x}} = \left(\frac{\alpha I}{p_1}, \frac{\beta I}{p_2}\right)$ where $\alpha = \frac{a_1^{\frac{1}{1-\alpha}}}{a_1^{\frac{1}{1-\alpha}} + a_2^{\frac{1}{1-\alpha}}} > 0, \beta = \frac{a_2^{\frac{1}{1-\alpha}}}{a_1^{\frac{1}{1-\alpha}} + a_2^{\frac{1}{1-\alpha}}} > 0$

(13)
$$u(\overline{\mathbf{x}}) = a_1 \left(\frac{a_1^{\frac{1}{1-\alpha}} I}{\left((a_1^{\frac{1}{1-\alpha}} + a_2^{\frac{1}{1-\alpha}} \right) p_1} \right)^{\alpha} + a_2 \left(\frac{a_2^{\frac{1}{1-\alpha}} I}{\left((a_1^{\frac{1}{1-\alpha}} + a_2^{\frac{1}{1-\alpha}} \right) p_2} \right)^{\alpha}$$
$$= \left(\frac{I}{p_1 p_2} \right)^{\alpha} \left(a_1^{\frac{1}{1-\alpha}} p_1^{\alpha} + a_2^{\frac{1}{1-\alpha}} p_2^{\alpha} \right).$$

Ad c

(1) $\left.\frac{\partial L(\mathbf{x}, \overline{\lambda})}{\partial x_1}\right|_{\mathbf{x}=\overline{\mathbf{x}}} = \left.\frac{\partial u(\mathbf{x})}{\partial x_1}\right|_{\mathbf{x}=\overline{\mathbf{x}}} - \overline{\lambda}_3 p_1 = 0$

(2) $\left.\frac{\partial L(\mathbf{x}, \overline{\lambda})}{\partial x_2}\right|_{\mathbf{x}=\overline{\mathbf{x}}} = \left.\frac{\partial u(\mathbf{x})}{\partial x_2}\right|_{\mathbf{x}=\overline{\mathbf{x}}} - \overline{\lambda}_3 p_2 = 0$

(3) $\left.\frac{\partial L(\overline{\mathbf{x}}, \lambda)}{\partial \lambda_3}\right|_{\lambda_3=\overline{\lambda}_3} = I - p_1 \overline{x}_1 - p_2 \overline{x}_2 = 0$

(4) $\frac{\left.\frac{\partial u(\mathbf{x})}{\partial x_1}\right|_{\mathbf{x}=\overline{\mathbf{x}}}}{\left.\frac{\partial u(\mathbf{x})}{\partial x_2}\right|_{\mathbf{x}=\overline{\mathbf{x}}}} = \frac{p_1}{p_2}$

(5) $p_1 \overline{x}_1 + p_2 \overline{x}_2 = I.$

Ad A

(6) $\frac{\alpha_1 a \overline{x}_1^{\alpha_1 - 1} \overline{x}_2^{\alpha_2}}{\alpha_2 a \overline{x}_1^{\alpha_1} \overline{x}_2^{\alpha_2 - 1}} = \frac{\alpha_1 \overline{x}_2}{\alpha_2 \overline{x}_1} = \frac{p_1}{p_2}$

(7) $\overline{x}_2 = \frac{\alpha_2 p_1}{\alpha_1 p_2} \overline{x}_1$

(8) $p_1 \overline{x}_1 + p_2 \frac{\alpha_2 p_1}{\alpha_1 p_2} \overline{x}_1 = I$

(9) $\overline{x}_1 = \frac{\alpha_1 I}{(\alpha_1 + \alpha_2) p_1}$

(10) $\overline{x}_2 = \frac{\alpha_2 I}{(\alpha_1 + \alpha_2) p_2}$

(11) $\overline{\mathbf{x}} = \left(\frac{\alpha_1 I}{(\alpha_1 + \alpha_2) p_1}, \frac{\alpha_2 I}{(\alpha_1 + \alpha_2) p_2} \right)$

(12) $\exists_1 \alpha, \beta > 0, \alpha + \beta = 1 \;\; \bar{\mathbf{x}} = \left(\frac{\alpha I}{p_1}, \frac{\beta I}{p_2}\right)$ where $\alpha = \frac{\alpha_1}{\alpha_1+\alpha_2} > 0$ and $\beta = \frac{\alpha_2}{\alpha_1+\alpha_2} > 0$

(13) $\bar{x}_1 \in \left[\frac{I-p_2 b_2}{p_2}; b_1\right], \;\; \bar{x}_2 \in \left[\frac{I-p_1 b_1}{p_1}; b_2\right]$

(14) $u(\bar{\mathbf{x}}) = a\left(\frac{\alpha_1}{p_1}\right)^{\alpha_1}\left(\frac{\alpha_2}{p_2}\right)^{\alpha_2}\left(\frac{I}{\alpha_1+\alpha_2}\right)^{\alpha_1+\alpha_2} > 0.$

Ad B

(6) $\frac{\frac{a_1}{\bar{x}_1}}{\frac{a_2}{\bar{x}_2}} = \frac{a_1 \bar{x}_2}{a_2 \bar{x}_1} = \frac{p_1}{p_2}$

(7) $\bar{x}_2 = \frac{a_2 p_1}{a_1 p_2}\bar{x}_1$

(8) $p_1\bar{x}_1 + p_2\frac{a_2 p_1}{a_1 p_2}\bar{x}_1 = I$

(9) $\bar{x}_1 = \frac{a_1 I}{(a_1+a_2)p_1}$

(10) $\bar{x}_2 = \frac{a_2 I}{(a_1+a_2)p_2}$

(11) $\bar{\mathbf{x}} = \left(\frac{a_1 I}{(a_1+a_2)p_1}, \frac{a_2 I}{(a_1+a_2)p_2}\right)$

(12)
$$\exists_1 \alpha, \beta > 0, \alpha + \beta = 1 \;\; \bar{\mathbf{x}} = \left(\frac{\alpha I}{p_1}, \frac{\beta I}{p_2}\right) \text{ where}$$
$$\alpha = \frac{a_1}{a_1 + a_2} > 0 \text{ and } \beta = \frac{a_2}{a_1 + a_2} > 0$$

(13) $\bar{x}_1 \in \left[\frac{I-p_2 b_2}{p_2}; b_1\right], \bar{x}_2 \in \left[\frac{I-p_1 b_1}{p_1}; b_2\right]$

(14) $u(\bar{\mathbf{x}}) = \ln\left[\left(\frac{a_1}{p_1}\right)^{a_1}\left(\frac{a_2}{p_2}\right)^{a_2}\left(\frac{I}{a_1+a_2}\right)^{a_1+a_2}\right].$

Ad C

(6) $\frac{\alpha a_1 \bar{x}_1^{\alpha-1}}{\alpha a_2 \bar{x}_2^{\alpha-1}} = \frac{a_1 \bar{x}_2^{1-\alpha}}{a_2 \bar{x}_1^{1-\alpha}} = \frac{p_1}{p_2}$

(7) $\bar{x}_2 = \left(\frac{a_2 p_1}{a_1 p_2}\right)^{\frac{1}{1-\alpha}}\bar{x}_1$

(8) $p_1\bar{x}_1 + p_2\left(\frac{a_2 p_1}{a_1 p_2}\right)^{\frac{1}{1-\alpha}}\bar{x}_1 = I$

(9) $\bar{x}_1 = \frac{(p_2 a_1)^{\frac{1}{1-\alpha}} I}{\left(p_1 p_2^{\frac{1}{1-\alpha}} a_1^{\frac{1}{1-\alpha}} + p_2 p_1^{\frac{1}{1-\alpha}} a_2^{\frac{1}{1-\alpha}}\right)}$

(10) $\bar{x}_2 = \frac{(p_1 a_2)^{\frac{1}{1-\alpha}} I}{\left(p_1 p_2^{\frac{1}{1-\alpha}} a_1^{\frac{1}{1-\alpha}} + p_2 p_1^{\frac{1}{1-\alpha}} a_2^{\frac{1}{1-\alpha}}\right)}$

(11)
$$\mathbf{N} = \left(\frac{(p_2 a_1)^{\frac{1}{1-\alpha}} I}{\left(p_1 p_2^{\frac{1}{1-\alpha}} a_1^{\frac{1}{1-\alpha}} + p_2 p_1^{\frac{1}{1-\alpha}} a_2^{\frac{1}{1-\alpha}}\right)}, \frac{(p_1 a_2)^{\frac{1}{1-\alpha}} I}{\left(p_1 p_2^{\frac{1}{1-\alpha}} a_1^{\frac{1}{1-\alpha}} + p_2 p_1^{\frac{1}{1-\alpha}} a_2^{\frac{1}{1-\alpha}}\right)}\right)$$
$$= \left(\frac{(p_2 a_1)^{\frac{1}{1-\alpha}} I}{\left(p_2^{\frac{1}{1-\alpha}} a_1^{\frac{1}{1-\alpha}} + p_2 p_1^{\frac{\alpha}{1-\alpha}} a_2^{\frac{1}{1-\alpha}}\right) p_1}, \frac{(p_1 a_2)^{\frac{1}{1-\alpha}} I}{\left(p_1 p_2^{\frac{\alpha}{1-\alpha}} a_1^{\frac{1}{1-\alpha}} + p_1^{\frac{1}{1-\alpha}} a_2^{\frac{1}{1-\alpha}}\right) p_2}\right)$$

$$\exists_1 \alpha, \beta > 0, \alpha + \beta = 1 \quad \overline{\mathbf{x}} = \left(\frac{\alpha I}{p_1}, \frac{\beta I}{p_2}\right) \text{ where}$$

(12)
$$\alpha = \frac{\frac{1}{a_1^{1-\alpha}}}{a_1^{\frac{1}{1-\alpha}} + a_2^{\frac{1}{1-\alpha}}} > 0, \beta = \frac{\frac{1}{a_2^{1-\alpha}}}{a_1^{\frac{1}{1-\alpha}} + a_2^{\frac{1}{1-\alpha}}} > 0$$

(13) $\overline{x}_1 \in \left[\frac{I - p_2 b_2}{p_2}; b_1\right], \overline{x}_2 \in \left[\frac{I - p_1 b_1}{p_1}; b_2\right]$

(14)
$$u(\overline{\mathbf{x}}) = a_1 \left(\frac{a_1^{\frac{1}{1-\alpha}} I}{\left(a_1^{\frac{1}{1-\alpha}} + a_2^{\frac{1}{1-\alpha}}\right) p_1}\right)^{\alpha} + a_2 \left(\frac{a_2^{\frac{1}{1-\alpha}} I}{\left(a_1^{\frac{1}{1-\alpha}} + a_2^{\frac{1}{1-\alpha}}\right) p_2}\right)^{\alpha}$$
$$= \left(\frac{I}{p_1 p_2}\right)^{\alpha} \left(a_1^{\frac{1}{1-\alpha}} p_1^{\alpha} + a_2^{\frac{1}{1-\alpha}} p_2^{\alpha}\right).$$

E2.8. There is given a market of two consumer goods, where:

$\mathbf{x} = (x_1, x_2) \in \mathbb{R}_+^2$—a consumption bundle, $\mathbf{p} = (p_1, p_2) \in \operatorname{int} \mathbb{R}_+^2$—a vector of prices of goods, $I > 0$—a consumer's income and a utility function describing a relation of consumer preference of a form:

A. $u(\mathbf{x}) = \min\{a_1 x_1, a_2 x_2\}, \quad a_i > 0, \ i = 1, 2,$
B. $u(\mathbf{x}) = a_1 \ln x_1 + a_2 \ln x_2, \quad a_i > 0, \quad x_i > 0, \ i = 1, 2,$
C. $u(\mathbf{x}) = a x_1^{\alpha} x_2^{\beta}, \quad a > 0, \ \alpha, \beta \in (0; 1).$

1. Write a form of a consumption utility maximization problem.
2. Determine a Marshallian demand function and an indirect utility function.
3. Write a form of a consumer expenditure minimization problem.
4. Determine a Hicksian demand function and a consumer expenditure function.
5. Knowing that $I = e(\mathbf{p}, u)$ and that $u = v(p, I)$, check if following Slutsky equations are true:

a. $\frac{\partial \varphi_1(\mathbf{p}, I)}{\partial p_1} = \frac{\partial f_1(\mathbf{p}, u)}{\partial p_1} - \frac{\partial \varphi_1(\mathbf{p}, I)}{\partial I} \varphi_1(\mathbf{p}, I),$
b. $\frac{\partial \varphi_1(\mathbf{p}, I)}{\partial p_2} = \frac{\partial f_1(\mathbf{p}, u)}{\partial p_2} - \frac{\partial \varphi_1(\mathbf{p}, I)}{\partial I} \varphi_2(\mathbf{p}, I),$
c. $\frac{\partial \varphi_2(\mathbf{p}, I)}{\partial p_2} = \frac{\partial f_2(\mathbf{p}, u)}{\partial p_2} - \frac{\partial \varphi_2(\mathbf{p}, I)}{\partial I} \varphi_2(\mathbf{p}, I),$
d. $\frac{\partial \varphi_2(\mathbf{p}, I)}{\partial p_1} = \frac{\partial f_2(\mathbf{p}, u)}{\partial p_1} - \frac{\partial \varphi_2(\mathbf{p}, I)}{\partial I} \varphi_1(\mathbf{p}, I),$

6. Present graphic illustrations of the Slutsky equations of point 5.

Solutions

Ad A1

(P2) $\min\{a_1 x_1, a_2 x_2\} \to \max$

(1) $p_1 x_1 + p_2 x_2 \leq I$
(2) $x_1, x_2 \geq 0.$

Ad B1

(P2) $a_1 \ln x_1 + a_2 \ln x_2 \to \max$

(1) $p_1x_1 + p_2x_2 \le I$
(2) $x_1, x_2 \ge 0.$

Ad C1

(P2) $ax_1^{\alpha}x_2^{\beta} \to \max$

(1) $p_1x_1 + p_2x_2 \le I$
(2) $x_1, x_2 \ge 0.$

Ad A2

An optimal solution satisfies conditions:

(3) $\min\{a_1\overline{x}_1, a_2\overline{x}_2\} = u.$
(4) $a_1\overline{x}_1 = a_2\overline{x}_2.$

To find the optimal solution, one needs to solve the equation system (3)–(4). The solution has a form:

$$\overline{\mathbf{x}} = \left(\frac{a_2I}{a_2p_1 + a_1p_2}, \frac{a_1I}{a_2p_1 + a_1p_2}\right) = \left(\frac{p_1a_2}{p_1a_2 + p_2a_1}\frac{I}{p_1}, \frac{p_2a_1}{p_1a_2 + p_2a_1}\frac{I}{p_2}\right)$$

(5) $$= \left(\alpha\frac{I}{p_1}, \beta\frac{I}{p_2}\right) = \varphi(\mathbf{p}, I), \quad \text{where}$$

$$\alpha = \frac{p_1a_2}{p_1a_2 + p_2a_1} > 0, \beta = \frac{p_2a_1}{p_1a_2 + p_2a_1} > 0$$
such that $\alpha + \beta = 1$.

(6) $u(\overline{\mathbf{x}}) = \min\left\{\frac{a_1a_2I}{a_2p_1+a_1p_2}, \frac{a_1a_2I}{a_2p_1+a_1p_2}\right\} = \frac{a_1a_2I}{a_2p_1+a_1p_2} = v(\mathbf{p}, I).$

Ad B2

An optimal solution satisfies conditions:

(3) $$s_{12}(\overline{x}_1, \overline{x}_2) = \frac{\left.\frac{\partial u(x_1,x_2)}{\partial x_1}\right|_{\mathbf{x} = \overline{\mathbf{x}}}}{\left.\frac{\partial u(x_1,x_2)}{\partial x_2}\right|_{\mathbf{x} = \overline{\mathbf{x}}}} = \frac{\frac{a_1}{\overline{x}_1}}{\frac{a_2}{\overline{x}_2}} = \frac{a_1\overline{x}_2}{a_1\overline{x}_1} = \frac{p_1}{p_2},$$

(4) $p_1\overline{x}_1 + p_2\overline{x}_2 = I.$

To find the optimal solution one needs to solve the equation system (3)–(4). The solution has a form:

(5) $\overline{\mathbf{x}} = \left(\frac{a_1I}{(a_1+a_2)p_1}, \frac{a_2I}{(a_1+a_2)p_2}\right) = \left(\alpha\frac{I}{p_1}, \beta\frac{I}{p_2}\right) = \varphi(\mathbf{p}, I),$

where $\alpha = \frac{a_1}{a_1+a_2} > 0, \beta = \frac{a_2}{a_1+a_2} > 0$, such that $\alpha + \beta = 1$.

(6) $u(\overline{\mathbf{x}}) = \ln \frac{a_1 a_2 I^2}{(a_1+a_2)^2 p_1 p_2} = v(\mathbf{p}, I)$.

Ad C2

An optimal solution satisfies conditions:

(3) $$s_{12}(\overline{x}_1, \overline{x}_2) = \frac{\left.\frac{\partial u(x_1,x_2)}{\partial x_1}\right|_{\mathbf{x}=\overline{\mathbf{x}}}}{\left.\frac{\partial u(x_1,x_2)}{\partial x_2}\right|_{\mathbf{x}=\overline{\mathbf{x}}}} = \frac{\alpha a \overline{x}_1^{\alpha-1} \overline{x}_2^{\beta}}{\beta a \overline{x}_1^{\alpha} \overline{x}_2^{\beta-1}} = \frac{\alpha \overline{x}_2}{\beta \overline{x}_1} = \frac{p_1}{p_2}$$

(4) $p_1 \overline{x}_1 + p_2 \overline{x}_2 = I$

To find the optimal solution. One needs to solve the equation system (3)–(4). The solution has a form:

(5) $$\overline{\mathbf{x}} = \left(\frac{\alpha I}{(\alpha+\beta)p_1}, \frac{\beta I}{(\alpha+\beta)p_2}\right) = \left(\alpha' \frac{I}{p_1}, \beta' \frac{I}{p_2}\right) = \varphi(\mathbf{p}, I),$$

where $\alpha' = \frac{\alpha}{\alpha+\beta} > 0, \beta' = \frac{\beta}{\alpha+\beta} > 0$, such that $\alpha' + \beta' = 1$.

(6) $$u(\overline{\mathbf{x}}) = a\left(\frac{\alpha}{p_1}\right)^{\alpha}\left(\frac{\beta}{p_2}\right)^{\beta}\left(\frac{I}{\alpha+\beta}\right)^{\alpha+\beta} = v(\mathbf{p}, I).$$

Ad A3

(P4) $w(x) = p_1 x_1 + p_2 x_2 \to \min$

(7) $\min\{a_1 x_1, a_2 x_2\} = u$.
(8) $x_1, x_2 \geq 0$.

Ad B3

(P4) $w(x) = p_1 x_1 + p_2 x_2 \to \min$

(9) $a_1 \ln x_1 + a_2 \ln x_2 = u$.
(10) $x_1, x_2 \geq 0$.

Ad C3

(P4) $w(x) = p_1 x_1 + p_2 x_2 \to \min$

(11) $a x_1^{\alpha} x_2^{\beta} = u$.
(12) $x_1, x_2 \geq 0$.

Ad A4

An optimal solution satisfies conditions:

(12) $\min\{a_1\tilde{x}_1, a_2\tilde{x}_2\} = u,$
(13) $a_1\tilde{x}_1 = a_2\tilde{x}_2.$

To find the optimal solution. One needs to solve the equation system (12)–(13). The solution has a form:

(14) $\tilde{\mathbf{x}} = \left(\frac{u}{a_1}, \frac{u}{a_2}\right) = f(\mathbf{p}, u)$
(15) $w(\tilde{\mathbf{x}}) = p_1\frac{u}{a_1} + p_2\frac{u}{a_2} = \frac{u(p_1a_2+p_2a_1)}{a_1a_2} = e(\mathbf{p}, I).$

Ad B4

An optimal solution satisfies conditions:

(16) $$\frac{\left.\frac{\partial u(x_1,x_2)}{\partial x_1}\right|_{\mathbf{x}=\tilde{\mathbf{x}}}}{\left.\frac{\partial u(x_1,x_2)}{\partial x_2}\right|_{\mathbf{x}=\tilde{\mathbf{x}}}} = \frac{p_1}{p_2}$$
(17) $u(\tilde{x}_1, \tilde{x}_2) = u.$

To find the optimal solution, one needs to solve the equation system (12)–(13). The solution has a form:

(18) $\frac{\frac{a_1}{\tilde{x}_1}}{\frac{a_2}{\tilde{x}_2}} = \frac{a_1\tilde{x}_2}{a_2\tilde{x}_1} = \frac{p_1}{p_2},$
(19) $a_1\ln\tilde{x}_1 + a_2\ln\tilde{x}_2 = u.$
(20) $$\tilde{\mathbf{x}} = \left(e^{\frac{u}{a_1+a_2}}\left(\frac{a_1p_2}{a_2p_1}\right)^{\frac{a_2}{a_1+a_2}}, e^{\frac{u}{a_1+a_2}}\left(\frac{a_2p_1}{a_1p_2}\right)^{\frac{a_1}{a_1+a_2}}\right) = f(\mathbf{p}, u)$$
(21) $$w(\tilde{\mathbf{x}}) = \frac{a_1+a_2}{a_1^{\frac{a_1}{a_1+a_2}}a_2^{\frac{a_2}{a_1+a_2}}}e^{\frac{u}{a_1+a_2}}p_1^{\frac{a_1}{a_1+a_2}}p_2^{\frac{a_2}{a_1+a_2}} = e(\mathbf{p}, u)$$

Ad C4

An optimal solution satisfies conditions:

(22) $$\frac{\left.\frac{\partial u(x_1,x_2)}{\partial x_1}\right|_{\mathbf{x}=\tilde{\mathbf{x}}}}{\left.\frac{\partial u(x_1,x_2)}{\partial x_2}\right|_{\mathbf{x}=\tilde{\mathbf{x}}}} = \frac{p_1}{p_2}$$
(23) $u(\tilde{x}_1, \tilde{x}_2) = u.$

To find the optimal solution, one needs to solve the equation system (22)–(23). The solution has a form:

(24) $\frac{\alpha a\tilde{x}_1^{\alpha-1}\tilde{x}_2^{\beta}}{\beta a\tilde{x}_1^{\alpha}\tilde{x}_2^{\beta-1}} = \frac{\alpha\tilde{x}_2}{\beta\tilde{x}_1} = \frac{p_1}{p_2}$
(25) $a_1\ln\tilde{x}_1 + a_2\ln\tilde{x}_2 = u.$
(26) $$\tilde{\mathbf{x}} = \left(\left(\frac{u}{a}\right)^{\frac{1}{\alpha+\beta}}\left(\frac{\alpha p_2}{\beta p_1}\right)^{\frac{\beta}{\alpha+\beta}}; \left(\frac{u}{a}\right)^{\frac{1}{\alpha+\beta}}\left(\frac{\beta p_1}{\alpha p_2}\right)^{\frac{\alpha}{\alpha+\beta}}\right) = f(\mathbf{p}, u)$$
(27) $$w(\tilde{\mathbf{x}}) = \frac{\alpha+\beta}{\alpha^{\frac{\alpha}{\alpha+\beta}}\beta^{\frac{\beta}{\alpha+\beta}}}\left(\frac{u}{a}\right)^{\frac{1}{\alpha+\beta}}p_1^{\frac{\alpha}{\alpha+\beta}}p_2^{\frac{\beta}{\alpha+\beta}} = e(\mathbf{p}, u).$$

Ad 5A

$$\varphi(\mathbf{p}, I) = \left(\frac{a_2 I}{a_2 p_1 + a_1 p_2}, \frac{a_1 I}{a_2 p_1 + a_1 p_2}\right),$$
$$f(\mathbf{p}, u) = \left(\frac{u}{a_1}, \frac{u}{a_2}\right),$$
$$e(\mathbf{p}, u) = \frac{u \cdot (p_1 a_2 + p_2 a_1)}{a_1 a_2} = I \Rightarrow u \cdot (p_1 a_2 + p_2 a_1) = I a_1 a_2$$

$$\frac{\partial \varphi_1(\mathbf{p}, I)}{\partial p_1} = \frac{\partial f_1(\mathbf{p}, u)}{\partial p_1} - \frac{\partial \varphi_1(\mathbf{p}, I)}{\partial I} \varphi_1(\mathbf{p}, I),$$

a.
$$L = \frac{\partial \varphi_1(\mathbf{p}, I)}{\partial p_1} = \frac{-a_2^2 I}{(a_2 p_1 + a_1 p_2)^2} < 0$$
$$R = 0 - \frac{-a_2^2 I}{(a_2 p_1 + a_1 p_2)^2} = \frac{-a_2^2 I}{(a_2 p_1 + a_1 p_2)^2} < 0$$
$$L = R$$

$$\frac{\partial \varphi_1(\mathbf{p}, I)}{\partial p_2} = \frac{\partial f_1(\mathbf{p}, u)}{\partial p_2} - \frac{\partial \varphi_1(\mathbf{p}, I)}{\partial I} \varphi_2(\mathbf{p}, I),$$

b.
$$L = \frac{\partial \varphi_1(\mathbf{p}, I)}{\partial p_2} = \frac{-a_1 a_2 I}{(a_2 p_1 + a_1 p_2)^2} < 0$$
$$R = 0 - \frac{-a_1 a_2 I}{(a_2 p_1 + a_1 p_2)^2} = \frac{-a_1 a_2 I}{(a_2 p_1 + a_1 p_2)^2} < 0$$
$$L = R$$

$$\frac{\partial \varphi_2(\mathbf{p}, I)}{\partial p_2} = \frac{\partial f_2(\mathbf{p}, u)}{\partial p_2} - \frac{\partial \varphi_2(\mathbf{p}, I)}{\partial I} \varphi_2(\mathbf{p}, I),$$

c.
$$L = \frac{\partial \varphi_2(\mathbf{p}, I)}{\partial p_2} = \frac{-a_1^2 I}{(a_2 p_1 + a_1 p_2)^2} < 0$$
$$R = 0 - \frac{-a_1^2 I}{(a_2 p_1 + a_1 p_2)^2} = \frac{-a_1^2 I}{(a_2 p_1 + a_1 p_2)^2} < 0$$
$$L = R$$

$$\frac{\partial \varphi_2(\mathbf{p}, I)}{\partial p_1} = \frac{\partial f_2(\mathbf{p}, u)}{\partial p_1} - \frac{\partial \varphi_2(\mathbf{p}, I)}{\partial I} \varphi_1(\mathbf{p}, I),$$

d.
$$L = \frac{\partial \varphi_2(\mathbf{p}, I)}{\partial p_1} = \frac{-a_1 a_2 I}{(a_2 p_1 + a_1 p_2)^2} < 0$$
$$R = 0 - \frac{-a_1 a_2 I}{(a_2 p_1 + a_1 p_2)^2} = \frac{-a_1 a_2 I}{(a_2 p_1 + a_1 p_2)^2} < 0$$
$$L = R.$$

Ad 5B

$$\varphi(\mathbf{p}, I) = \left(\frac{\alpha_1 I}{(a_1 + a_2)p_1}, \frac{\alpha_2 I}{(a_1 + a_2)p_2}\right),$$

$$f(\mathbf{p}, u) = \left(e^{\frac{u}{a_1+a_2}} \left(\frac{a_1 p_2}{a_2 p_1}\right)^{\frac{a_2}{a_1+a_2}}, e^{\frac{u}{a_1+a_2}} \left(\frac{a_2 p_1}{a_1 p_2}\right)^{\frac{a_1}{a_1+a_2}}\right),$$

$$e(\mathbf{p}, u) = \frac{a_1 + a_2}{a_1^{\frac{a_1}{a_1+a_2}} a_2^{\frac{a_2}{a_1+a_2}}} e^{\frac{u}{a_1+a_2}} p_1^{\frac{a_1}{a_1+a_2}} p_2^{\frac{a_2}{a_1+a_2}} = I \Rightarrow e^{\frac{u}{a_1+a_2}} = \frac{a_1^{\frac{a_1}{a_1+a_2}} a_2^{\frac{a_2}{a_1+a_2}} I}{(a_1 + a_2) p_1^{\frac{a_1}{a_1+a_2}} p_2^{\frac{a_2}{a_1+a_2}}}$$

a.

$$\frac{\partial \varphi_1(\mathbf{p}, I)}{\partial p_1} = \frac{\partial f_1(\mathbf{p}, u)}{\partial p_1} - \frac{\partial \varphi_1(\mathbf{p}, I)}{\partial I} \varphi_1(\mathbf{p}, I),$$

$$L = \frac{\partial \varphi_1(\mathbf{p}, I)}{\partial p_1} = \frac{-a_1 I}{(a_1 + a_2) p_1^2} < 0$$

$$R = -\frac{a_2}{a_1 + a_2} e^{\frac{u}{a_1+a_2}} a_1^{\frac{a_2}{a_1+a_2}} p_2^{\frac{a_2}{a_1+a_2}} a_2^{-\frac{a_2}{a_1+a_2}} p_2^{\frac{-2a_2-a_1}{a_1+a_2}}$$

$$= -\frac{a_2}{a_1 + a_2} \frac{a_1^{\frac{a_1}{a_1+a_2}} a_2^{\frac{a_2}{a_1+a_2}} I}{(a_1 + a_2) p_1^{\frac{a_1}{a_1+a_2}} p_2^{\frac{a_2}{a_1+a_2}}} a_1^{\frac{a_2}{a_1+a_2}} p_2^{\frac{a_2}{a_1+a_2}} a_2^{-\frac{a_2}{a_1+a_2}} p_2^{\frac{-2a_2-a_1}{a_1+a_2}}$$

$$= -\frac{a_1 a_2 I}{(a_1 + a_2)^2 p_1^2} - \frac{a_1^2 I}{(a_1 + a_2)^2 p_1^2} = \frac{-a_1 I}{(a_1 + a_2) p_1^2}$$

$L = R$.

b.

$$\frac{\partial \varphi_1(\mathbf{p}, I)}{\partial p_2} = \frac{\partial f_1(\mathbf{p}, u)}{\partial p_2} - \frac{\partial \varphi_1(\mathbf{p}, I)}{\partial I} \varphi_2(\mathbf{p}, I),$$

$$L = \frac{\partial \varphi_1(\mathbf{p}, I)}{\partial p_2} = 0$$

$$R = \frac{a_2}{a_1 + a_2} e^{\frac{u}{a_1+a_2}} a_1^{\frac{a_2}{a_1+a_2}} p_2^{\frac{a_2}{a_1+a_2}} a_2^{-\frac{a_2}{a_1+a_2}} p_1^{\frac{-a_2}{a_1+a_2}} - \frac{a_1 a_2 l}{(a_1 + a_2)^2 p_1 p_2}$$

$$= \frac{a_2}{a_1 + a_2} \frac{a_1^{\frac{a_1}{a_1+a_2}} a_2^{\frac{a_2}{a_1+a_2}} I}{(a_1 + a_2) p_1^{\frac{a_1}{a_1+a_2}} p_2^{\frac{a_2}{a_1+a_2}}} a_1^{\frac{a_2}{a_1+a_2}} p_2^{\frac{-a_1}{a_1+a_2}} a_2^{-\frac{a_2}{a_1+a_2}} p_1^{\frac{-a_2}{a_1+a_2}}$$

$$- \frac{a_1 a_2 I}{(a_1 + a_2)^2 p_1 p_2} = \frac{a_1 a_2 I}{(a_1 + a_2)^2 p_1 p_2} - \frac{a_1 a_2 I}{(a_1 + a_2)^2 p_1 p_2} = 0$$

$L = R$.

c.

$$\frac{\partial \varphi_2(\mathbf{p}, I)}{\partial p_2} = \frac{\partial f_2(\mathbf{p}, u)}{\partial p_2} - \frac{\partial \varphi_2(\mathbf{p}, I)}{\partial I}\varphi_2(\mathbf{p}, I),$$

$$L = \frac{\partial \varphi_2(\mathbf{p}, I)}{\partial p_2} = \frac{-a_2 I}{(a_1 + a_2)p_2^2} < 0$$

$$R = -\frac{a_1}{a_1 + a_2} e^{\frac{u}{a_1+a_2}} a_2^{\frac{a_1}{a_1+a_2}} p_1^{\frac{a_1}{a_1+a_2}} a_1^{-\frac{-a_1}{a_1+a_2}} p_2^{\frac{-2a_1-a_2}{a_1+a_2}}$$

$$= -\frac{a_1}{a_1 + a_2} \frac{a_1^{\frac{a_1}{a_1+a_2}} a_2^{\frac{a_2}{a_1+a_2}} I}{(a_1 + a_2)p_1^{\frac{a_1}{a_1+a_2}} p_2^{\frac{a_2}{a_1+a_2}}} a_2^{\frac{a_1}{a_1+a_2}} p_1^{\frac{a_1}{a_1+a_2}} a_1^{-\frac{a_1}{a_1+a_2}} p_2^{\frac{-2a_1-a_2}{a_1+a_2}}$$

$$= -\frac{a_1 a_2 I}{(a_1 + a_2)^2 p_2^2} - \frac{a_2^2 I}{(a_1 + a_2)^2 p_2^2} = \frac{-a_2 I}{(a_1 + a_2)p_2^2}$$

$$L = R$$

d.

$$\frac{\partial \varphi_2(\mathbf{p}, I)}{\partial p_1} = \frac{\partial f_2(\mathbf{p}, u)}{\partial p_1} - \frac{\partial \varphi_2(\mathbf{p}, I)}{\partial I}\varphi_1(\mathbf{p}, I),$$

$$L = \frac{\partial \varphi_2(\mathbf{p}, I)}{\partial p_1} = 0$$

$$R = \frac{a_1}{a_1 + a_2} e^{\frac{u}{a_1+a_2}} a_2^{\frac{a_1}{a_1+a_2}} p_1^{\frac{a_1}{a_1+a_2}} a_1^{-\frac{a_1}{a_1+a_2}} p_2^{\frac{-a_1}{a_1+a_2}} - \frac{a_1 a_2 I}{(a_1 + a_2)^2 p_1 p_2}$$

$$= \frac{a_1}{a_1 + a_2} \frac{a_1^{\frac{a_1}{a_1+a_2}} a_2^{\frac{a_2}{a_1+a_2}} I}{(a_1 + a_2)p_1^{\frac{a_1}{a_1+a_2}} p_2^{\frac{a_2}{a_1+a_2}}} a_2^{\frac{a_1}{a_1+a_2}} p_1^{\frac{-a_2}{a_1+a_2}} a_1^{\frac{-a_1}{a_1+a_2}} p_2^{\frac{-a_1}{a_1+a_2}}$$

$$- \frac{a_1 a_2 I}{(a_1 + a_2)^2 p_1 p_2} = \frac{a_1 a_2 I}{(a_1 + a_2)^2 p_1 p_2} - \frac{a_1 a_2 I}{(a_1 + a_2)^2 p_1 p_2} = 0$$

$$L = R.$$

Ad 5C

$$\varphi(\mathbf{p}, I) = \left(\frac{\alpha I}{(\alpha + \beta)p_1}, \frac{\beta I}{(\alpha + \beta)p_2}\right)$$

$$f(\mathbf{p}, u) = \left(\left(\frac{u}{a}\right)^{\frac{1}{\alpha+\beta}} \left(\frac{\alpha p_2}{\beta p_1}\right)^{\frac{\beta}{\alpha+\beta}}, \left(\frac{u}{a}\right)^{\frac{1}{\alpha+\beta}} \left(\frac{\beta p_1}{\alpha p_2}\right)^{\frac{\alpha}{\alpha+\beta}}\right)$$

$$e(\mathbf{p}, u) = \frac{\alpha + \beta}{\alpha^{\frac{\alpha}{\alpha+\beta}} \beta^{\frac{\beta}{\alpha+\beta}}} \left(\frac{u}{a}\right)^{\frac{1}{\alpha+\beta}} p_1^{\frac{\alpha}{\alpha+\beta}} p_2^{\frac{\beta}{\alpha+\beta}} = I \Rightarrow \left(\frac{u}{a}\right)^{\frac{1}{\alpha+\beta}} = \frac{\alpha^{\frac{\alpha}{\alpha+\beta}} \beta^{\frac{\beta}{\alpha+\beta}} I}{(\alpha + \beta)p_1^{\frac{\alpha}{\alpha+\beta}} p_2^{\frac{\beta}{\alpha+\beta}}}$$

a.

$$\frac{\partial \varphi_1(\mathbf{p}, I)}{\partial p_1} = \frac{\partial f_1(\mathbf{p}, u)}{\partial p_1} - \frac{\partial \varphi_1(\mathbf{p}, I)}{\partial I} \varphi_1(\mathbf{p}, I),$$

$$L = \frac{\partial \varphi_1(\mathbf{p}, I)}{\partial p_1} = \frac{-\alpha I}{(\alpha+\beta) p_1^2} < 0$$

$$R = -\frac{\beta}{\alpha+\beta}\left(\frac{u}{a}\right)^{\frac{1}{\alpha+\beta}} \alpha^{\frac{\alpha}{\alpha+\beta}} p_2^{\frac{\beta}{\alpha+\beta}} \beta^{-\frac{\beta}{\alpha+\beta}} p_1^{\frac{-2\beta-\alpha}{\alpha+\beta}} - \frac{\alpha I}{(\alpha+\beta) p_1} \frac{\alpha}{(\alpha+\beta) p_1}$$

$$= -\frac{\beta}{\alpha+\beta} \frac{\alpha^{\frac{\alpha}{\alpha+\beta}} \beta^{\frac{\beta}{\alpha+\beta}} I}{(\alpha+\beta) p_1^{\frac{\alpha}{\alpha+\beta}} p_2^{\frac{\beta}{\alpha+\beta}}} \alpha^{\frac{\alpha}{\alpha+\beta}} p_2^{\frac{\beta}{\alpha+\beta}} \beta^{-\frac{\beta}{\alpha+\beta}}$$

$$- \frac{\alpha^2 I}{(\alpha+\beta)^2 p_1^2} = -\frac{\alpha\beta I}{(\alpha+\beta)^2 p_1^2} - \frac{\alpha^2 I}{(\alpha+\beta)^2 p_1^2} = \frac{-\alpha I}{(\alpha+\beta) p_1^2}$$

$$L = R.$$

b.

$$\frac{\partial \varphi_1(\mathbf{p}, I)}{\partial p_2} = \frac{\partial f_1(\mathbf{p}, u)}{\partial p_2} - \frac{\partial \varphi_1(\mathbf{p}, I)}{\partial I} \varphi_2(\mathbf{p}, I),$$

$$L = \frac{\partial \varphi_1(\mathbf{p}, I)}{\partial p_2} = 0$$

$$R = \frac{\alpha\beta}{(\alpha+\beta)^2 p_2} - \frac{\alpha\beta}{(\alpha+\beta)^2 p_2} = 0$$

$$L = R$$

c.

$$\frac{\partial \varphi_2(\mathbf{p}, I)}{\partial p_2} = \frac{\partial f_2(\mathbf{p}, u)}{\partial p_2} - \frac{\partial \varphi_2(\mathbf{p}, I)}{\partial I} \varphi_2(\mathbf{p}, I),$$

$$L = \frac{\partial \varphi_2(\mathbf{p}, I)}{\partial p_2} = \frac{-\beta I}{(\alpha+\beta) p_2^2} < 0$$

$$R = -\frac{\alpha}{\alpha+\beta}\left(\frac{u}{a}\right)^{\frac{1}{\alpha+\beta}} \beta^{\frac{\alpha}{\alpha+\beta}} p_1^{\frac{\alpha}{\alpha+\beta}} \alpha^{-\frac{\alpha}{\alpha+\beta}} p_2^{\frac{-2\alpha-\beta}{\alpha+\beta}}$$

$$- \frac{\beta I}{(\alpha+\beta) p_2} \frac{\beta}{(\alpha+\beta) p_2} = -\frac{\alpha\beta I}{(\alpha+\beta)^2 p_2^2} - \frac{\beta^2 I}{(\alpha+\beta)^2 p_1^2}$$

$$= \frac{-\beta I}{(\alpha+\beta) p_2^2}$$

$$L = R.$$

d.

$$\frac{\partial \varphi_2(\mathbf{p}, I)}{\partial p_1} = \frac{\partial f_2(\mathbf{p}, u)}{\partial p_1} - \frac{\partial \varphi_2(\mathbf{p}, I)}{\partial I} \varphi_1(\mathbf{p}, I),$$

$$L = \frac{\partial \varphi_2(\mathbf{p}, I)}{\partial p_1} = 0$$

$$R = \frac{\alpha\beta I}{(\alpha+\beta)^2 p_1 p_2} - \frac{\alpha\beta I}{(\alpha+\beta)^2 p_1 p_2} = 0$$

$$L = R$$

Ad A6

See Fig. 2.9

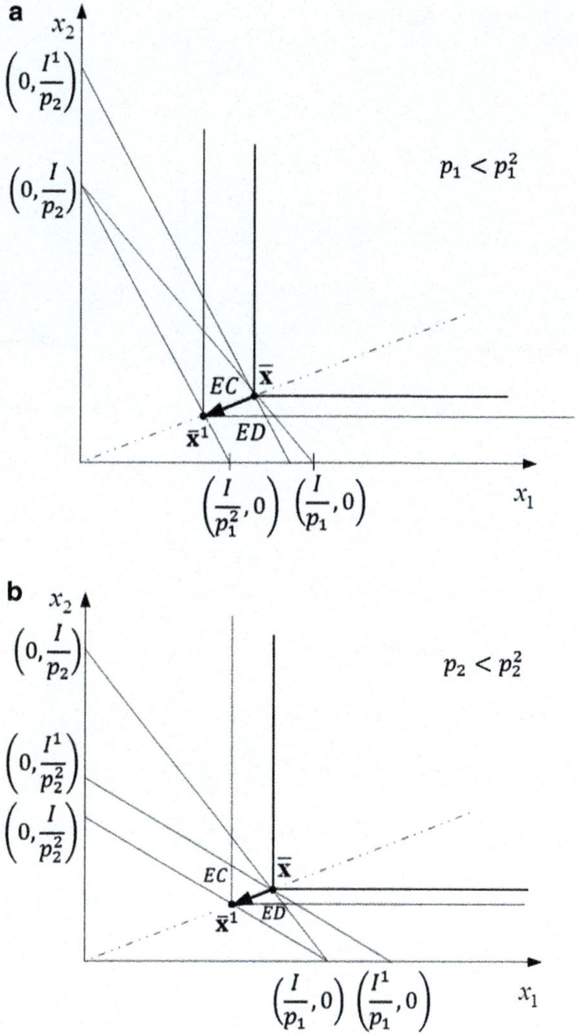

Fig. 2.9 Slutsky equation **a** and **b** (E2.8) Ad A6

Ad B6

See Fig. 2.10

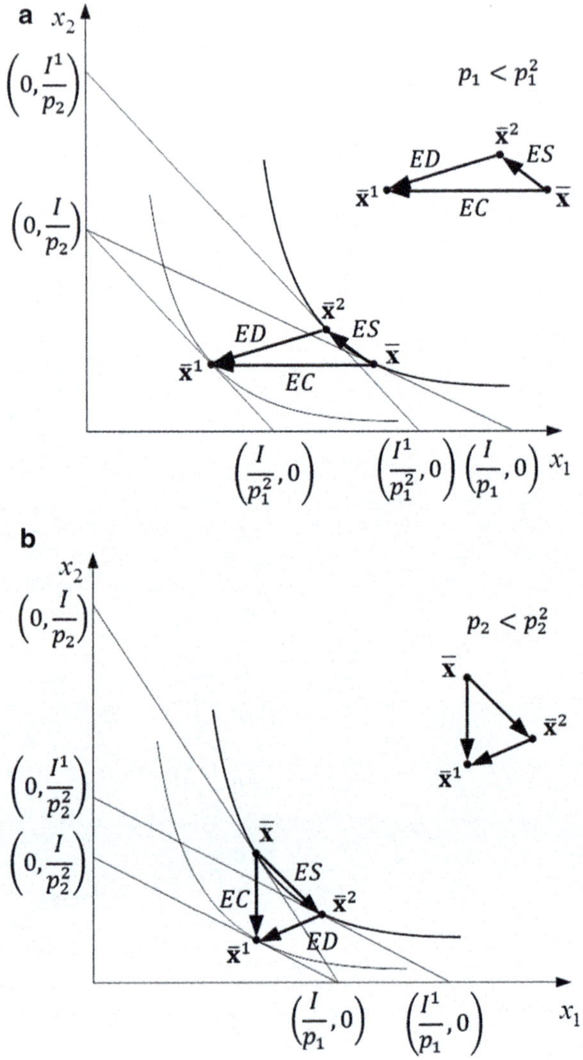

Fig. 2.10 Slutsky equation **a** and **b** (E2.8) Ad B6 and Ad C6

E2.9. Check properties of Marshallian demand functions which are optimal solutions to consumption utility maximization problems of Exercise 2.6. Check properties of the corresponding indirect utility functions.

Solutions

When a utility function is a power function: $u(\mathbf{x}) = ax_1^{\alpha_1}x_2^{\alpha_2}, a, \alpha_i > 0, \alpha_1 + \alpha_2 < 1, i = 1, 2$ or a logarithmic function $u_2(\mathbf{x}) = \alpha_1 \ln x_1 + \alpha_2 \ln x_2 + \ln a, x_i > 0, i = 1, 2$ then, according to the solution to Exercise 2.6, the Marshallian demand function is the same and given as:

$$\varphi(\mathbf{p}, I) = \left(\frac{\alpha_1 I}{(a_1 + a_2)p_1}, \frac{\alpha_2 I}{(a_1 + a_2)p_2}\right).$$

The corresponding indirect utility functions are:

$v(\mathbf{p}, I) = u(\overline{\mathbf{x}}) = a\left(\frac{\alpha_1}{p_1}\right)^{\alpha_1}\left(\frac{\alpha_2}{p_2}\right)^{\alpha_2}\left(\frac{I}{\alpha_1+\alpha_2}\right)^{\alpha_1+\alpha_2}$ in case of the power utility function.

$v_2(\mathbf{p}, I) = u_2(\overline{\mathbf{x}}) = \ln\left[a\left(\frac{\alpha_1}{p_1}\right)^{\alpha_1}\left(\frac{\alpha_2}{p_2}\right)^{\alpha_2}\left(\frac{I}{\alpha_1+\alpha_2}\right)^{\alpha_1+\alpha_2}\right]$ in case of the logarithmic utility function.

Let us check properties of the Marshallian demand function and of the corresponding demand functions:

1. Homogeneity of degree 0 of the Marshallian demand function:

$$\forall\lambda > 0 \quad \varphi(\lambda\mathbf{p}, \lambda I) = \left(\frac{\alpha_1 \lambda I}{(a_1 + a_2)\lambda p_1}, \frac{\alpha_2 \lambda I}{(a_1 + a_2)\lambda p_2}\right)$$
$$= \left(\frac{\alpha_1 I}{(a_1 + a_2)p_1}, \frac{\alpha_2 I}{(a_1 + a_2)p_2}\right) = \varphi(\mathbf{p}, I)$$

This shows us that when all prices and the consumer's income increase ($\lambda > 1$)/ decrease ($\lambda < 1$) λ-times then a consumer chooses the same consumption bundle as before the changes of prices and of the income.

Homogeneity of degree 0 of the indirect utility functions:

$$\forall\,\lambda > 0 \quad v(\lambda\mathbf{p}, \lambda I) = a\left(\frac{\alpha_1}{\lambda p_1}\right)^{\alpha_1}\left(\frac{\alpha_2}{\lambda p_2}\right)^{\alpha_2}\left(\frac{\lambda I}{\alpha_1 + \alpha_2}\right)^{\alpha_1+\alpha_2}$$
$$= a\left(\frac{\alpha_1}{p_1}\right)^{\alpha_1}\left(\frac{\alpha_2}{p_2}\right)^{\alpha_2}\left(\frac{I}{\alpha_1 + \alpha_2}\right)^{\alpha_1+\alpha_2} \cdot \frac{\lambda^{\alpha_1+\alpha_2}}{\lambda^{\alpha_1}\lambda^{\alpha_2}} = v(\mathbf{p}, I)$$

$$\forall\,\lambda > 0 \quad v_2(\lambda\mathbf{p}, \lambda I) = \ln\left[a\left(\frac{\alpha_1}{\lambda p_1}\right)^{\alpha_1}\left(\frac{\alpha_2}{\lambda p_2}\right)^{\alpha_2}\left(\frac{\lambda I}{\alpha_1 + \alpha_2}\right)^{\alpha_1+\alpha_2}\right]$$

$$= \ln\left[a\left(\frac{\alpha_1}{p_1}\right)^{\alpha_1}\left(\frac{\alpha_2}{p_2}\right)^{\alpha_2}\left(\frac{I}{\alpha_1+\alpha_2}\right)^{\alpha_1+\alpha_2}\cdot\frac{\lambda^{\alpha_1+\alpha_2}}{\lambda^{\alpha_1}\lambda^{\alpha_2}}\right] = v_2(\mathbf{p}, I).$$

This shows us that when all prices and the consumer's income increase ($\lambda > 1$)/ decrease ($\lambda < 1$) λ-times then a bundle chosen by a consumer as optimal has the same utility as before the changes of prices and of the income.

2. The Roy's identity

In case of the solution derived for the power utility function:

$$-\frac{\frac{\partial v(\mathbf{p},I)}{\partial p_1}}{\frac{\partial v(\mathbf{p},I)}{\partial I}} = -\frac{a\alpha_1^{\alpha_1}\left(\frac{\alpha_2}{p_2}\right)^{\alpha_2}\left(\frac{I}{\alpha_1+\alpha_2}\right)^{\alpha_1+\alpha_2}(-\alpha_1)p_1^{-\alpha_1-1}}{a\left(\frac{\alpha_1}{p_1}\right)^{\alpha_1}\left(\frac{\alpha_2}{p_2}\right)^{\alpha_2}\left(\frac{1}{\alpha_1+\alpha_2}\right)^{\alpha_1+\alpha_2}(\alpha_1+\alpha_2)I^{\alpha_1+\alpha_2-1}}$$

$$= \frac{\alpha_1 I}{(a_1+a_2)p_1} = \varphi_1(\mathbf{p}, I)$$

$$-\frac{\frac{\partial v(\mathbf{p},I)}{\partial p_2}}{\frac{\partial v(\mathbf{p},I)}{\partial I}} = -\frac{a\left(\frac{\alpha_1}{p_1}\right)^{\alpha_1}\alpha_2^{\alpha_2}\left(\frac{I}{\alpha_1+\alpha_2}\right)^{\alpha_1+\alpha_2}(-\alpha_2)p_2^{-\alpha_2-1}}{a\left(\frac{\alpha_1}{p_1}\right)^{\alpha_1}\left(\frac{\alpha_2}{p_2}\right)^{\alpha_2}\left(\frac{1}{\alpha_1+\alpha_2}\right)^{\alpha_1+\alpha_2}(\alpha_1+\alpha_2)I^{\alpha_1+\alpha_2-1}}$$

$$= \frac{\alpha_2 I}{(a_1+a_2)p_2} = \varphi_2(\mathbf{p}, I).$$

In case of the solution derived for the logarithmic utility function:

$$-\frac{\frac{\partial v_2(\mathbf{p},I)}{\partial p_1}}{\frac{\partial v_2(\mathbf{p},I)}{\partial I}} = \frac{a\alpha_1^{\alpha_1}\left(\frac{\alpha_2}{p_2}\right)^{\alpha_2}\left(\frac{I}{\alpha_1+\alpha_2}\right)^{\alpha_1+\alpha_2}(-\alpha_1)p_1 - \alpha_1 - 1}{a\left(\frac{\alpha_1}{p_1}\right)^{\alpha_1}\left(\frac{\alpha_2}{p_2}\right)^{\alpha_2}\left(\frac{I}{\alpha_1+\alpha_2}\right)^{\alpha_1+\alpha_2}}.$$

$$\frac{a\left(\frac{\alpha_1}{p_1}\right)^{\alpha_1}\left(\frac{\alpha_2}{p_2}\right)^{\alpha_2}\left(\frac{I}{\alpha_1+\alpha_2}\right)^{\alpha_1+\alpha_2}}{a\left(\frac{\alpha_1}{p_1}\right)^{\alpha_1}\left(\frac{\alpha_2}{p_2}\right)^{\alpha_2}\left(\frac{1}{\alpha_1+\alpha_2}\right)^{\alpha_1+\alpha_2}(\alpha_1+\alpha_2)I^{\alpha_1+\alpha_2-1}} = \frac{\alpha_1 I}{(a_1+a_2)p_1} = \varphi_1(\mathbf{p}, I)$$

$$-\frac{\frac{\partial v_2(\mathbf{p},I)}{\partial p_2}}{\frac{\partial v_2(\mathbf{p},I)}{\partial I}} = \frac{a\left(\frac{\alpha_1}{p_1}\right)^{\alpha_1}\alpha_2^{\alpha_2}\left(\frac{I}{\alpha_1+\alpha_2}\right)^{\alpha_1+\alpha_2}(-\alpha_2)p_2^{-\alpha_2-1}}{a\left(\frac{\alpha_1}{p_1}\right)^{\alpha_1}\left(\frac{\alpha_2}{p_2}\right)^{\alpha_2}\left(\frac{I}{\alpha_1+\alpha_2}\right)^{\alpha_1+\alpha_2}}.$$

$$\frac{a\left(\frac{\alpha_1}{p_1}\right)^{\alpha_1}\left(\frac{\alpha_2}{p_2}\right)^{\alpha_2}\left(\frac{I}{\alpha_1+\alpha_2}\right)^{\alpha_1+\alpha_2}}{a\left(\frac{\alpha_1}{p_1}\right)^{\alpha_1}\left(\frac{\alpha_2}{p_2}\right)^{\alpha_2}\left(\frac{1}{\alpha_1+\alpha_2}\right)^{\alpha_1+\alpha_2}(\alpha_1+\alpha_2)I^{\alpha_1+\alpha_2-1}} = \frac{\alpha_2 I}{(a_1+a_2)p_2} = \varphi_2(\mathbf{p}, I).$$

3. When the consumer's income increases. Then the demand for at least one good in a consumption bundle increases:

$$\frac{\partial\varphi_1(\mathbf{p},I)}{\partial I}=\frac{\alpha_1}{(a_1+a_2)p_1}>0$$
$$\frac{\partial\varphi_2(\mathbf{p},I)}{\partial I}=\frac{\alpha_2}{(a_1+a_2)p_2}>0.$$

Here, the demand for both goods increases, which shows that both are normal goods.

4. When a price of a good increases, then the demand for at least one good in a consumption bundle increases:

$$\frac{\partial\varphi_1(\mathbf{p},I)}{\partial p_1}=-\frac{\alpha_1 I}{(a_1+a_2)p_1^2}<0 \qquad \frac{\partial\varphi_1(\mathbf{p},I)}{\partial p_2}=0$$
$$\frac{\partial\varphi_2(\mathbf{p},I)}{\partial p_2}=-\frac{\alpha_2 I}{(a_1+a_2)p_2^2}<0 \qquad \frac{\partial\varphi_2(\mathbf{p},I)}{\partial p_1}=0.$$

Here, the demand for each good decreases when a price of this good increases. These negative reactions of the demand show that both goods are ordinary goods. We can also see that the demand for each good does not change when a price of the other good increases. This shows that two goods in the consumption bundle are independent goods.

5. A marginal utility of a consumer's income is equal to a marginal utility of a money unit for the purchase of each good:

$$\frac{\partial v(p_1,p_2,I)}{\partial I}=\frac{1}{p_i}\frac{\partial u(x_1,x_2)}{\partial x_i}\bigg|_{\mathbf{x}=\overline{\mathbf{x}}}=\overline{\lambda}>0,\quad i=1,2.$$

In case of the solution derived for the power utility function:

$$L=\frac{\partial v(\mathbf{p},I)}{\partial I}=a\left(\frac{\alpha_1}{p_1}\right)^{\alpha_1}\left(\frac{\alpha_2}{p_2}\right)^{\alpha_2}\left(\frac{1}{\alpha_1+\alpha_2}\right)^{\alpha_1+\alpha_2}(\alpha_1+\alpha_2)I^{\alpha_1+\alpha_2-1}$$
$$=a\left(\frac{\alpha_1}{p_1}\right)^{\alpha_1}\left(\frac{\alpha_2}{p_2}\right)^{\alpha_2}\left(\frac{I}{\alpha_1+\alpha_2}\right)^{\alpha_1+\alpha_2-1}$$

$$R(p_1)=\frac{1}{p_1}\frac{\partial u(\mathbf{x})}{\partial x_1}\bigg|_{\mathbf{x}=\overline{\mathbf{x}}}=\frac{1}{p_1}a\alpha_1\overline{x}_1^{\alpha_1-1}\overline{x}_2^{\alpha_2}$$
$$=\frac{1}{p_1}a\alpha_1\left(\frac{\alpha_1 I}{(a_1+a_2)p_1}\right)^{\alpha_1-1}\left(\frac{\alpha_2 I}{(a_1+a_2)p_2}\right)^{\alpha_2}$$
$$=a\left(\frac{\alpha_1}{p_1}\right)^{\alpha_1}\left(\frac{\alpha_2}{p_2}\right)^{\alpha_2}\left(\frac{I}{\alpha_1+\alpha_2}\right)^{\alpha_1+\alpha_2-1}=L$$

$$R(p_2)=\frac{1}{p_2}\frac{\partial u(\mathbf{x})}{\partial x_2}\bigg|_{\mathbf{x}=\overline{\mathbf{x}}}=\frac{1}{p_2}a\alpha_2\overline{x}_1^{\alpha_1}\overline{x}_2^{\alpha_2-1}$$
$$=\frac{1}{p_2}a\alpha_2\left(\frac{\alpha_1 I}{(a_1+a_2)p_2}\right)^{\alpha_1}\left(\frac{\alpha_2 I}{(a_1+a_2)p_2}\right)^{\alpha_2-1}$$

$$= a\left(\frac{\alpha_1}{p_1}\right)^{\alpha_1}\left(\frac{\alpha_2}{p_2}\right)^{\alpha_2}\left(\frac{I}{\alpha_1+\alpha_2}\right)^{\alpha_1+\alpha_2-1} = L.$$

In case of the solution derived for the logarithmic utility function:

$$L = \frac{\partial v_2(\mathbf{p}, I)}{\partial I} = \frac{a\left(\frac{\alpha_1}{p_1}\right)^{\alpha_1}\left(\frac{\alpha_2}{p_2}\right)^{\alpha_2}\left(\frac{1}{\alpha_1+\alpha_2}\right)^{\alpha_1+\alpha_2}(\alpha_1+\alpha_2)I^{\alpha_1+\alpha_2-1}}{a\left(\frac{\alpha_1}{p_1}\right)^{\alpha_1}\left(\frac{\alpha_2}{p_2}\right)^{\alpha_2}\left(\frac{I}{\alpha_1+\alpha_2}\right)^{\alpha_1+\alpha_2}} = \frac{a_1+a_2}{I}$$

$$R(p_1) = \frac{1}{p_1}\frac{\partial u_2(\mathbf{x})}{\partial x_1}\bigg|_{\mathbf{x}=\overline{\mathbf{x}}} = \frac{1}{p_1}\cdot\frac{\alpha_1}{\overline{x}_1} = \frac{\alpha_1}{p_1}\cdot\frac{(a_1+a_2)p_1}{\alpha_1 I} = \frac{a_1+a_2}{I}$$

$$R(p_2) = \frac{1}{p_2}\frac{\partial u_2(\mathbf{x})}{\partial x_2}\bigg|_{\mathbf{x}=\overline{\mathbf{x}}} = \frac{1}{p_2}\cdot\frac{\alpha_2}{\overline{x}_2} = \frac{\alpha_2}{p_2}\cdot\frac{(a_1+a_2)p_2}{\alpha_2 I} = \frac{a_1+a_2}{I}.$$

E2.10. Using the Kuhn-Tucker theorem,[2] find an optimal solution to a consumer expenditure minimization problem with an additional constraint on the supply of both goods: $0 \le x_i \le b_i, i = 1, 2$, when a utility function is:

(a) a power function: $u(\mathbf{x}) = ax_1^{\alpha_1}x_2^{\alpha_2}, a, \alpha_i > 0, \alpha_1 + \alpha_2 < 1,\ i = 1, 2,$
(b) logarithmic: $u(\mathbf{x}) = a_1 \ln x_1 + a_2 \ln x_2, a_i > 0, x_i > 0,\ i = 1, 2,$
(c) subadditive: $u(\mathbf{x}) = a_1x_1^{\alpha} + a_2x_2^{\alpha}, a_i > 0,\ i = 1, 2, \alpha \in (0; 1).$

Solutions

The consumer's expenditure minimization problem has a general form:

$$w(x_1, x_2) = \{p_1x_1 + p_2x_2\} \to \min$$

(P4) $u(x_1, x_2) = u = \text{const.}$

$$x_1, x_2 \ge 0$$

In this exercise, one imposes the additional constraints on quantities of consumption goods:

$$x_i \le b_i \quad i = 1, 2.$$

For the conditional optimization problem with three constraints, one uses the following Lagrange function:

$$L(\mathbf{x}, \lambda) = w(\mathbf{x}) + \lambda_1(b_1 - x_1) + \lambda_2(b_2 - x_2) + \lambda_3(u - u(\mathbf{x})),\ \lambda_i \ge 0,$$

which in case of (a)–(c) utility functions takes different forms:

$$\text{(a)}\quad L(\mathbf{x}, \lambda) = p_1x_1 + p_2x_2 + \lambda_1(b_1 - x_1)$$

---

[2] The theorem (Theorem A.6) is presented in a Mathematical appendix of the textbook Malaga K., Sobczak K, *Microeconomics. Static and Dynamic Analysis*, Springer Nature Switzerland, 2022.

$$+\lambda_2(b_2-x_2)+\lambda_3\left(u-ax_1^{\alpha_1}x_2^{\alpha_2}\right)$$

$$\text{(b)}\quad L(\mathbf{x},\lambda)=p_1x_1+p_2x_2+\lambda_1(b_1-x_1)+\lambda_2(b_2-x_2)+\lambda_3(u-a_1\ln x_1-a_2\ln x_2)$$

$$\text{(c)}\quad L(\mathbf{x},\lambda)=p_1x_1+p_2x_2+\lambda_1(b_1-x_1)+\lambda_2(b_2-x_2)+\lambda_3\left(u-a_1x_1^{\alpha}-a_2x_2^{\alpha}\right).$$

A necessary condition[3] for existence of a minimum is the following system of equations:

$$\text{(a)}\quad\begin{cases}\frac{\partial L(\mathbf{x},\lambda)}{\partial x_1}=p_1-\lambda_1-\lambda_3a\alpha_1x_1^{\alpha_1-1}x_2^{\alpha_2}=0\\ \frac{\partial L(\mathbf{x},\lambda)}{\partial x_2}=p_2-\lambda_2-\lambda_3a\alpha_2x_1^{\alpha_1}x_2^{\alpha_2-1}=0\\ \frac{\partial L(\mathbf{x},\lambda)}{\partial \lambda_1}=b_1-x_1=0\\ \frac{\partial L(\mathbf{x},\lambda)}{\partial \lambda_2}=b_2-x_2=0\\ \frac{\partial L(\mathbf{x},\lambda)}{\partial \lambda_3}=u-ax_1^{\alpha_1}x_2^{\alpha_2}=0\end{cases}$$

$$\text{(b)}\quad\begin{cases}\frac{\partial L(\mathbf{x},\lambda)}{\partial x_1}=p_1-\lambda_1-\lambda_3\frac{a_1}{x_1}=0\\ \frac{\partial L(\mathbf{x},\lambda)}{\partial x_2}=p_2-\lambda_2-\lambda_3\frac{a_2}{x_2}=0\\ \frac{\partial L(\mathbf{x},\lambda)}{\partial \lambda_1}=b_1-x_1=0\\ \frac{\partial L(\mathbf{x},\lambda)}{\partial \lambda_2}=b_2-x_2=0\\ \frac{\partial L(\mathbf{x},\lambda)}{\partial \lambda_3}=u-a_1\ln x_1-a_2\ln x_2=0\end{cases}$$

$$\text{(c)}\quad\begin{cases}\frac{\partial L(\mathbf{x},\lambda)}{\partial x_1}=p_1-\lambda_1-\lambda_3a_1\alpha x_1^{\alpha-1}=0\\ \frac{\partial L(\mathbf{x},\lambda)}{\partial x_2}=p_2-\lambda_2-\lambda_3a_2\alpha x_2^{\alpha-1}=0\\ \frac{\partial L(\mathbf{x},\lambda)}{\partial \lambda_1}=b_1-x_1=0\\ \frac{\partial L(\mathbf{x},\lambda)}{\partial \lambda_2}=b_2-x_2=0\\ \frac{\partial L(\mathbf{x},\lambda)}{\partial \lambda_3}=u-a_1x_1^{\alpha}-a_2x_2^{\alpha}=0\end{cases}$$

From the Kuhn-Tucker theorem, we know that the constraints can be considered in case they are binding and in case they are not binding. Let us first consider the case when constraints on quantities of goods are not binding, that is when $\lambda_1=\lambda_2=0$. Then the necessary condition consists of only three equations:

$$\text{(a)}\quad\begin{cases}p_1-\lambda_3a\alpha_1x_1^{\alpha_1-1}x_2^{\alpha_2}=0\\ p_2-\lambda_2a\alpha_2x_1^{\alpha_1}x_2^{\alpha_2-1}=0\\ u-ax_1^{\alpha_1}x_2^{\alpha_2}=0\end{cases}\Leftrightarrow\begin{cases}p_1x_1=\lambda_3\alpha_1u\\ p_2x_2=\lambda_3\alpha_2u\\ u=ax_1^{\alpha_1}x_2^{\alpha_2}\end{cases},$$

$$\text{(b)}\quad\begin{cases}p_1-\lambda_3\frac{a_1}{x_1}=0\\ p_2-\lambda_3\frac{a_2}{x_2}=0\\ u-a_1\ln x_1-a_2\ln x_2=0\end{cases}\Leftrightarrow\begin{cases}p_1x_1=\lambda_3a_1\\ p_2x_2=\lambda_3a_2\\ u=a_1\ln x_1+a_2\ln x_2\end{cases},$$

[3] A sufficient condition takes a more complex form and involves checking properties of a Hessian of the Lagrange function. But we can notice that the expenditure function $w(\mathbf{x})$ is convex and the utility function $u(\mathbf{x})$ is strictly concave in each (a)-(c) case; hence, the Lagrange function is strictly convex and the sufficient condition for existence of a minimum is satisfied.

$$\text{(c)} \quad \begin{cases} p_1 - \lambda_3 a_1 \alpha x_1^{\alpha-1} = 0 \\ p_2 - \lambda_3 a_2 \alpha x_2^{\alpha-1} = 0 \\ u - a_1 x_1^{\alpha} - a_2 x_2^{\alpha} = 0 \end{cases} \Leftrightarrow \begin{cases} p_1 x_1 = \lambda_3 a_1 \alpha x_1^{\alpha} \\ p_2 x_2 = \lambda_3 a_2 \alpha x_2^{\alpha} \\ u = a_1 x_1^{\alpha} + a_2 x_2^{\alpha} \end{cases},$$

which, after a division of first two equations one by the other, gives a relationship between quantities of both goods:

(a) $x_2 = \frac{p_1 \alpha_2}{p_2 \alpha_1} x_1$
(b) $x_2 = \frac{p_1 a_2}{p_2 a_1} x_1$
(c) $x_2 = \left(\frac{p_1 a}{p_2 a_1} \right)^{\frac{1}{\alpha - 1}} x_1.$

Substituting this relationship into the third equation gives the global solution, that is a solution obtained when the constraints are not binding:

$$\text{(a)} \quad \overline{\mathbf{x}}^G = \left(\overline{x}_1^G, \overline{x}_2^G\right) = \left(\left[\frac{u}{a} \left(\frac{p_2 \alpha_1}{p_1 \alpha_2} \right)^{\alpha_2} \right]^{\frac{1}{\alpha_1 + \alpha_2}}, \left[\frac{u}{a} \left(\frac{p_1 \alpha_2}{p_2 \alpha_1} \right)^{\alpha_1} \right]^{\frac{1}{\alpha_1 + \alpha_2}} \right)$$

$$\text{(b)} \quad \overline{\mathbf{x}}^G = \left(\overline{x}_1^G, \overline{x}_2^G\right) = \left(\left[e^u \left(\frac{p_2 a_1}{p_1 a_2} \right)^{a_2} \right]^{\frac{1}{a_1 + a_2}}, \left[e^u \left(\frac{p_1 a_2}{p_2 a_1} \right)^{a_1} \right]^{\frac{1}{a_1 + a_2}} \right)$$

$$\text{(c)} \quad \overline{\mathbf{x}}^G = \left(\overline{x}_1^G, \overline{x}_2^G\right) = \left(\left[a_1 + a_2 \left(\frac{p_2 a_1}{p_1 a_2} \right)^{\frac{\alpha}{\alpha-1}} \right]^{-\frac{1}{\alpha}} u^{\frac{1}{\alpha}}, \left[a_2 \left(\frac{p_1 a_2}{p_2 a_a} \right)^{\frac{\alpha}{\alpha-1}} + a_2 \right]^{-\frac{1}{\alpha}} u^{\frac{1}{\alpha}} \right)$$

Now, we can consider a few cases depending on whether the constraints are binding or not:

(1) None of the constraints is binding:

$$\text{if } \ \overline{x}_i^G \le b_i, i = 1, 2 \ \text{ then } \ \overline{x}_i = \overline{x}_i^G.$$

(2) The constraint on the quantity of the first good is binding
if $\overline{x}_1^G > b_1$ and $\overline{x}_2^G \le b_2$ then $\overline{x}_1 = b_1$ while
(a) $\overline{x}_2^L = \left(\frac{u}{a} b_1^{-\alpha_1}\right)^{\frac{1}{\alpha_2}}$ (b) $\overline{x}_2^L = \left(e^u b_1^{-a_1}\right)^{\frac{1}{a_2}}$ (c) $\overline{x}_2^L = \left(u - a_1 b_1^{\alpha}\right)^{\frac{1}{\alpha}} a_2^{\frac{1}{\alpha}}$
If now $\overline{x}_2^L \le b_2$ then the solution is:
(a) $\overline{\mathbf{x}} = \left(b_1, \left(\frac{u}{a} b_1^{-\alpha_1}\right)^{\frac{1}{\alpha_2}}\right)$ (b) $\overline{\mathbf{x}} = \left(b_1, \left(e^u b_1^{-a_1}\right)^{\frac{1}{a_2}}\right)$ (c) $\overline{\mathbf{x}} = \left(b_1, \left(u - a_1 b_1^{\alpha}\right)^{\frac{1}{\alpha}} a_2^{\frac{1}{\alpha}}\right)$
Because of the constraint on the quantity of the first good, a consumer chooses the bigger quantity of the second good than it results from the optimization problem with no constraints on quantities of goods.
If $\overline{x}_2^L > b_2$ then there is no solution satisfying $u(\overline{\mathbf{x}}) = u$.

(3) The constraint on the quantity of the second good is binding:
if $\overline{x}_2^G > b_2$ and $\overline{x}_1^G \le b_1$ then $\overline{x}_2 = b_2$ while
(a) $\overline{x}_1^L = \left(\frac{u}{a} b_2^{-\alpha_2}\right)^{\frac{1}{\alpha_1}}$ (b) $\overline{x}_1^L = \left(e^u b_2^{-a_2}\right)^{\frac{1}{a_1}}$ (c) $\overline{x}_1^L = \left(u - a_2 b_2^{\alpha}\right)^{\frac{1}{\alpha}} a_1^{\frac{1}{\alpha}}.$
If now $\overline{x}_1^L \le b_1$ then the solution is:

(a) $\overline{\mathbf{x}} = \left(\left(\frac{u}{a} b_2^{-\alpha_2}\right)^{\frac{1}{\alpha_1}}, b_2\right)$ (b) $\overline{\mathbf{x}} = \left(\left(e^u b_2^{-a_2}\right)^{\frac{1}{a_1}}, b_2\right)$ (c) $\overline{\mathbf{x}} = \left(\left(u - a_2 b_2^{\alpha}\right)^{\frac{1}{\alpha}} a_1^{\frac{1}{\alpha}}, b_2\right)$.

Because of the constraint on thequantity of the second good. A consumer chooses the bigger quantity of the first good than it results from the optimization problem with no constthe raints on quantities of goods.

If $\overline{x}_1^L > b_1$ then there is no solution satisfying $u(\overline{\mathbf{x}}) = u$.

(4) The constraints on quantities of both goods are binding:
if $\overline{x}_1^G > b_1$ and $\overline{x}_2^G > b_2$, then there is no solution satisfying $u(\overline{\mathbf{x}}) = u$.

E2.11. Check properties of Hicksian demand functions which are optimal solutions to consumer expenditure minimization problems of Exercise 2.8. Check properties of the corresponding consumer's expenditure functions.

Solutions

The Hicksian demand functions and the corresponding consumer's expenditure functions are obtained in Exercise 2.8 for the following utility functions:

(a) a Koopmans-Leontief function: $u(\mathbf{x}) = \min\{a_1 x_1, a_2 x_2\}, a_i > 0, i = 1, 2,$
(b) logarithmic: $u(\mathbf{x}) = a_1 \ln x_1 + a_2 \ln x_2, a_i > 0, x_i > 0, i = 1, 2,$
(c) a power function: $u(\mathbf{x}) = a x_1^{\alpha} x_2^{\beta}, a > 0, \alpha, \beta \in (0; 1)$.

The Hicksian (compensated) demand functions are:

(a) $f(\mathbf{p}, u) = \left(\frac{u}{a_1}, \frac{u}{a_2}\right)$

(b) $f(\mathbf{p}, u) = \left(\left(\frac{p_2 a_1}{p_1 a_2}\right)^{\frac{a_2}{a_1+a_2}} e^{\frac{u}{a_1+a_2}}, \left(\frac{p_1 a_2}{p_2 a_1}\right)^{\frac{a_1}{a_1+a_2}} e^{\frac{u}{a_1+a_2}}\right)$

(c) $f(\mathbf{p}, u) = \left(\left(\frac{\alpha p_2}{\beta p_1}\right)^{\frac{\beta}{\alpha+\beta}} \left(\frac{u}{a}\right)^{\frac{1}{\alpha+\beta}}, \left(\frac{\beta p_1}{\alpha p_2}\right)^{\frac{\alpha}{\alpha+\beta}} \left(\frac{u}{a}\right)^{\frac{1}{\alpha+\beta}}\right)$.

The corresponding consumer's expenditure functions are:

(a) $e(\mathbf{p}, u) = u\left(\frac{p_1}{a_1} + \frac{p_2}{a_2}\right)$

(b) $e(\mathbf{p}, u) = e^{\frac{u}{a_1+a_2}} (a_1 + a_2) \left(\frac{p_1}{a_1}\right)^{\frac{a_1}{a_1+a_2}} \left(\frac{p_2}{a_2}\right)^{\frac{a_2}{a_1+a_2}}$

(c) $e(\mathbf{p}, u) = \left(\frac{u}{a}\right)^{\frac{1}{\alpha+\beta}} (\alpha + \beta) \left(\frac{p_1}{\alpha}\right)^{\frac{\alpha}{\alpha+\beta}} \left(\frac{p_2}{\beta}\right)^{\frac{\beta}{\alpha+\beta}}$.

The properties are stated in Theorem 2.4. We are interested in properties[4] (3)–(7).

(3) Homogeneity of degree 1 of the consumer's expenditure function with respect to prices of goods:

(a) $\forall \lambda > 0 \quad e(\lambda \mathbf{p}, u) = u\left(\frac{\lambda p_1}{a_1} + \frac{\lambda p_2}{a_2}\right) = \lambda e(\mathbf{p}, u)$

[4] The theorem (Theorem 2.4) is presented in subchapter 2.5 of the textboook Malaga K., Sobczak K., *Microeconomics. Static and Dynamic Analysis*, Springer Nature Switzerland, 2022. In properties (1) and (2) one states that a Hicksian demand function and a consumer's expenditure function are differentiable in their domains.

(b) $$\forall\lambda > 0 \quad e(\lambda\mathbf{p}, u) = e^{\frac{u}{a_1+a_2}}(a_1 + a_2)\left(\frac{\lambda p_1}{a_1}\right)^{\frac{a_1}{a_1+a_2}}\left(\frac{\lambda p_2}{a_2}\right)^{\frac{a_2}{a_1+a_2}}$$
$$= \lambda^{\frac{a_1}{a_1+a_2}+\frac{a_2}{a_1+a_2}} e(\mathbf{p}, u) = \lambda^1 e(\mathbf{p}, u) = \lambda e(\mathbf{p}, u)$$

(c) $$\forall\lambda > 0 \quad e(\lambda\mathbf{p}, u) = \left(\frac{u}{a}\right)^{\frac{1}{\alpha+\beta}}(\alpha + \beta)\left(\frac{\lambda p_1}{\alpha}\right)^{\frac{\alpha}{\alpha+\beta}}\left(\frac{\lambda p_2}{\beta}\right)^{\frac{\beta}{\alpha+\beta}}$$
$$= \lambda^{\frac{\alpha}{\alpha+\beta}+\frac{\beta}{\alpha+\beta}} e(\mathbf{p}, u) = \lambda^1 e(\mathbf{p}, u) = \lambda e(\mathbf{p}, u).$$

This property shows us that when prices of both goods increase ($\lambda > 1$)/decrease ($\lambda < 1$) λ times, then the consumer's expenditure on an optimal consumption bundle also increases/decreases λ times.

(4) Homogeneity of degree 1 of the Hicksian (compensated) demand function with respect to prices of goods:

$$\text{(a)} \quad \forall\lambda > 0 \quad f(\lambda\mathbf{p}, u) = \left(\frac{u}{a_1}, \frac{u}{a_2}\right) = f(\mathbf{p}, u)$$

Values of this function do not depend on prices.

$$\text{(b)} \quad \forall\lambda > 0 \quad f(\lambda\mathbf{p}, u) = \left(\left(\frac{\lambda p_2 a_1}{\lambda p_1 a_2}\right)^{\frac{a_2}{a_1+a_2}} e^{\frac{u}{a_1+a_2}}, \left(\frac{\lambda p_1 a_2}{\lambda p_2 a_1}\right)^{\frac{a_1}{a_1+a_2}} e^{\frac{u}{a_1+a_2}}\right) = f(\mathbf{p}, u)$$

$$\text{(c)} \quad \forall\lambda > 0 \quad f(\lambda\mathbf{p}, u) = \left(\left(\frac{\alpha\lambda p_2}{\beta\lambda p_1}\right)^{\frac{\beta}{\alpha+\beta}}\left(\frac{u}{a}\right)^{\frac{1}{\alpha+\beta}}, \left(\frac{\beta\lambda p_1}{\alpha\lambda p_2}\right)^{\frac{\alpha}{\alpha+\beta}}\left(\frac{u}{a}\right)^{\frac{1}{\alpha+\beta}}\right) = f(\mathbf{p}, u).$$

This property shows us that when prices of both goods increase ($\lambda > 1$)/decrease ($\lambda < 1$) λ times. then the compensated demand of a consumer does not change.

(5) Relationship between a compensated demand for a good and a change in the consumer's expenditure when a price of this good increases:

$$\frac{\partial e(\mathbf{p}, u)}{\partial p_i} = f_i(\mathbf{p}, u), i = 1, 2,$$

(a) $\frac{\partial e(\mathbf{p},u)}{\partial p_1} = \frac{u}{a_1} = f_1(\mathbf{p}, u) \quad \frac{\partial e(\mathbf{p},u)}{\partial p_2} = \frac{u}{a_2} = f_2(\mathbf{p}, u)$

(b)

$$\frac{\partial e(\mathbf{p},u)}{\partial p_1} = e^{\frac{u}{a_1+a_2}}(a_1+a_2)a_1^{-\frac{a_1}{a_1+a_2}}\frac{a_1}{a_1+a_2}p_1^{-\frac{a_2}{a_1+a_2}}\left(\frac{p_2}{a_2}\right)^{\frac{a_2}{a_1+a_2}}$$

$$= \left(\frac{p_2a_1}{p_1a_2}\right)^{\frac{a_2}{a_1+a_2}} e^{\frac{u}{a_1+a_2}} = f_1(\mathbf{p},u)$$

$$\frac{\partial e(\mathbf{p},u)}{\partial p_2} = e^{\frac{u}{a_1+a_2}}(a_1+a_2)\left(\frac{p_1}{a_1}\right)^{\frac{1}{a_1+a_2}} a_2^{-\frac{a_2}{a_1+a_2}}\frac{a_2}{a_1+a_2}p_2^{-\frac{a_1}{a_1+a_2}}$$

$$= \left(\frac{p_1a_2}{p_2a_1}\right)^{\frac{a_1}{a_1+a_2}} e^{\frac{u}{a_1+a_2}} = f_2(\mathbf{p},u)$$

(c)

$$\frac{\partial e(\mathbf{p},u)}{\partial p_1} = \left(\frac{u}{a}\right)^{\frac{1}{\alpha+\beta}}(\alpha+\beta)\alpha^{-\frac{\alpha}{\alpha+\beta}}\frac{\alpha}{\alpha+\beta}p_1^{-\frac{\beta}{\alpha+\beta}}\left(\frac{p_2}{\beta}\right)^{\frac{\beta}{\alpha+\beta}}$$

$$= \left(\frac{\alpha p_2}{\beta p_1}\right)^{\frac{\beta}{\alpha+\beta}}\left(\frac{u}{a}\right)^{\frac{1}{\alpha+\beta}} = f_1(\mathbf{p},u)$$

$$\frac{\partial e(\mathbf{p},u)}{\partial p_2} = \left(\frac{u}{a}\right)^{\frac{1}{\alpha+\beta}}(\alpha+\beta)\left(\frac{p_1}{\alpha}\right)^{\frac{\alpha}{\alpha+\beta}}\beta^{-\frac{\beta}{\alpha+\beta}}\frac{\beta}{\alpha+\beta}p_2^{-\frac{\alpha}{\alpha+\beta}}$$

$$= \left(\frac{\beta p_1}{\alpha p_2}\right)^{\frac{\alpha}{\alpha+\beta}}\left(\frac{u}{a}\right)^{\frac{1}{\alpha+\beta}} = f_2(\mathbf{p},u)$$

The value of the compensated demand for a given good shows how the consumer's expenditure will change (increase) if a price of this good increases by one unit and the consumer is interested in keeping a given level of utility from a consumption bundle.

(6) An increase in a price of a good results in a decrease of the compensated demand for this good:

$$\frac{\partial f_i(\mathbf{p},u)}{\partial p_i} < 0, \quad i = 1,2$$

(a) $\frac{\partial f_1(\mathbf{p},u)}{\partial p_1} = 0 \quad \frac{\partial f_2(\mathbf{p},u)}{\partial p_2} = 0.$

In case of the Koopmans-Leontief function. this property is not satisfied, because a consumer perceives both goods as perfect complementary goods. As a result. he/she wants to have them only in a specific proportion (a_2 units of the first good per a_1 units of the second good) which does not depend on prices when it comes to the compensated demand.

(b)

$$\frac{\partial f_1(\mathbf{p},u)}{\partial p_1} = \left(\frac{p_2a_1}{a_2}\right)^{\frac{a_2}{a_1+a_2}}\left(-\frac{a_2}{a_1+a_2}\right)p_1^{-\frac{a_2}{a_1+a_2}-1}e^{\frac{u}{a_1+a_2}} < 0$$

$$\frac{\partial f_2(\mathbf{p},u)}{\partial p_2} = \left(\frac{p_1a_2}{a_1}\right)^{\frac{a_1}{a_1+a_2}}\left(-\frac{a_1}{a_1+a_2}\right)p_2^{-\frac{a_1}{a_1+a_2}-1}e^{\frac{u}{a_1+a_2}} < 0$$

(c)
$$\frac{\partial f_1(\mathbf{p},u)}{\partial p_1} = \left(\frac{\alpha p_2}{\beta}\right)^{\frac{\beta}{\alpha+\beta}} \left(-\frac{\beta}{\alpha+\beta}\right) p_1^{-\frac{\beta}{\alpha+\beta}-1} \left(\frac{u}{a}\right)^{\frac{1}{\alpha+\beta}} < 0$$
$$\frac{\partial f_2(\mathbf{p},u)}{\partial p_2} = \left(\frac{\beta p_1}{\alpha}\right)^{\frac{\alpha}{\alpha+\beta}} \left(-\frac{\alpha}{\alpha+\beta}\right) p_2^{-\frac{\alpha}{\alpha+\beta}-1} \left(\frac{u}{a}\right)^{\frac{1}{\alpha+\beta}} < 0.$$

(7) An effect of an increase in the second good's price on the compensated demand for the first good is the same as an effect of an increase in the first good's price on the compensated demand for the second good:

$$\frac{\partial f_1(\mathbf{p},u)}{\partial p_2} = \frac{\partial f_2(\mathbf{p},u)}{\partial p_1}$$

(a) $\frac{\partial f_1(\mathbf{p},u)}{\partial p_2} = 0 = \frac{\partial f_2(\mathbf{p},u)}{\partial p_1}$

(b)
$$\frac{\partial f_1(\mathbf{p},u)}{\partial p_2} = \left(\frac{a_1}{p_1 a_2}\right)^{\frac{a_2}{a_1+a_2}} \frac{a_2}{a_1+a_2} p_2^{-\frac{a_1}{a_1+a_2}} e^{\frac{u}{a_1+a_2}}$$
$$= \left(\frac{a_1}{p_1}\right)^{\frac{a_2}{a_1+a_2}} \left(\frac{a_2}{p_2}\right)^{\frac{a_1}{a_1+a_2}} \frac{1}{a_1+a_2} e^{\frac{u}{a_1+a_2}}$$
$$\frac{\partial f_2(\mathbf{p},u)}{\partial p_1} = \left(\frac{a_2}{p_2 a_1}\right)^{\frac{a_1}{a_1+a_2}} \frac{a_1}{a_1+a_2} p_1^{-\frac{a_2}{a_1+a_2}} e^{\frac{u}{a_1+a_2}}$$
$$= \left(\frac{a_1}{p_1}\right)^{\frac{a_2}{a_1+a_2}} \left(\frac{a_2}{p_2}\right)^{\frac{a_1}{a_1+a_2}} \frac{1}{a_1+a_2} e^{\frac{u}{a_1+a_2}}$$

(c)
$$\frac{\partial f_1(\mathbf{p},u)}{\partial p_2} = \left(\frac{\alpha}{\beta p_1}\right)^{\frac{\beta}{\alpha+\beta}} \frac{\beta}{\alpha+\beta} p_2^{-\frac{\alpha}{\alpha+\beta}} \left(\frac{u}{a}\right)^{\frac{1}{\alpha+\beta}}$$
$$= \left(\frac{\alpha}{p_1}\right)^{\frac{\beta}{\alpha+\beta}} \left(\frac{\beta}{p_2}\right)^{\frac{\alpha}{\alpha+\beta}} \frac{1}{\alpha+\beta} \left(\frac{u}{a}\right)^{\frac{1}{\alpha+\beta}}$$
$$\frac{\partial f_2(\mathbf{p},u)}{\partial p_1} = \left(\frac{\beta}{\alpha p_2}\right)^{\frac{\alpha}{\alpha+\beta}} \frac{\alpha}{\alpha+\beta} p_1^{-\frac{\beta}{\alpha+\beta}} \left(\frac{u}{a}\right)^{\frac{1}{\alpha+\beta}}$$
$$= \left(\frac{\alpha}{p_1}\right)^{\frac{\beta}{\alpha+\beta}} \left(\frac{\beta}{p_2}\right)^{\frac{\alpha}{\alpha+\beta}} \frac{1}{\alpha+\beta} \left(\frac{u}{a}\right)^{\frac{1}{\alpha+\beta}}.$$

E2.12. Knowing Hicksian and Marshallian demand functions which are optimal solutions to consumption utility maximization problems (E2.6) and to consumer expenditure minimization problems (E2.8), analyse income and substitutive effects of changes in prices of goods. For this purpose, use a Slutsky equation for i-th good, $i = 1, 2$.

Solutions

Let us recall the Slutsky equation considered for a single good:

$$\frac{\partial \varphi_i(\mathbf{p},I)}{\partial p_i} = \frac{\partial f_i(\mathbf{p},u)}{\partial p_i} - \frac{\partial \varphi_i(\mathbf{p},I)}{\partial I}\varphi_i(\mathbf{p},I) \quad i = 1, 2,$$

where $\frac{\partial \varphi_i(\mathbf{p},I)}{\partial p_i}$ is called a price effect, $\frac{\partial f_i(\mathbf{p},u)}{\partial p_i} < 0$ is called a substitution effect and $-\frac{\partial \varphi_i(\mathbf{p},I)}{\partial I}\varphi_i(\mathbf{p}, I)$ is called an income effect.

When a utility function is a power function: $u(\mathbf{x}) = ax_1^{\alpha_1}x_2^{\alpha_2}a, \alpha_i > 0, \alpha_1 + \alpha_2 < 1,\ i = 1, 2$ or a logarithmic function $u_2(\mathbf{x}) = \alpha_1 \ln x_1 + \alpha_2 \ln x_2 + \ln a, x_i > 0, i = 1, 2$ then, according to the solution to Exercise 2.6, the Marshallian demand function is the same and given as:

$$\varphi(\mathbf{p}, I) = \left(\frac{\alpha_1 I}{(\alpha_1 + \alpha_2)p_1}, \frac{\alpha_2 I}{(\alpha_1 + \alpha_2)p_2}\right).$$

The corresponding Hicksian (compensated) demand functions are:

$f(\mathbf{p}, u) = \left(\left(\frac{p_2\alpha_1}{p_1\alpha_2}\right)^{\frac{\alpha_2}{\alpha_1+\alpha_2}}\left(\frac{u}{a}\right)^{\frac{1}{\alpha_1+\alpha_2}}, \left(\frac{p_1\alpha_2}{p_2\alpha_1}\right)^{\frac{\alpha_1}{\alpha_1+\alpha_2}}\left(\frac{u}{a}\right)^{\frac{1}{\alpha_1+\alpha_2}}\right)$ in case of the power utility function.

$f(\mathbf{p}, u) = \left(\left(\frac{p_2\alpha_1}{p_1\alpha_2}\right)^{\frac{\alpha_2}{\alpha_1+\alpha_2}}\left(\frac{e^u}{a}\right)^{\frac{1}{\alpha_1+\alpha_2}}, \left(\frac{p_1\alpha_2}{p_2\alpha_1}\right)^{\frac{\alpha_1}{\alpha_1+\alpha_2}}\left(\frac{e^u}{a}\right)^{\frac{1}{\alpha_1+\alpha_2}}\right)$ in case of the logarithmic utility function.

Let us first analyse the price effect:

$$\mathrm{PE}_1 = \frac{\partial \varphi_1(\mathbf{p}, I)}{\partial p_1} = -\frac{\alpha_1 I}{(\alpha_1 + \alpha_2)p_1^2} < 0, \qquad \mathrm{PE}_2 = \frac{\partial \varphi_2(\mathbf{p}, I)}{\partial p_2} = \frac{\alpha_2 I}{(\alpha_1 + \alpha_2)p_2^2} < 0,$$

which shows us that both goods are ordinary goods.

Let us now analyse the substitution effect:

- in case of the solution obtained for the power utility function

$$\mathrm{SE}_1 = \frac{\partial f_1(\mathbf{p}, u)}{\partial p_1} = \left(\frac{p_2\alpha_1}{\alpha_2}\right)^{\frac{\alpha_2}{\alpha_1+\alpha_2}}\left(-\frac{\alpha_2}{\alpha_1 + \alpha_2}\right)p_1^{-\frac{\alpha_2}{\alpha_1+\alpha_2}-1}\left(\frac{u}{a}\right)^{\frac{1}{\alpha_1+\alpha_2}} < 0$$

$$\mathrm{SE}_2 = \frac{\partial f_2(\mathbf{p}, u)}{\partial p_2} = \left(\frac{p_1\alpha_2}{\alpha_1}\right)^{\frac{\alpha_1}{\alpha_1+\alpha_2}}\left(-\frac{\alpha_1}{\alpha_1 + \alpha_2}\right)p_2^{-\frac{\alpha_1}{\alpha_1+\alpha_2}-1}\left(\frac{u}{a}\right)^{\frac{1}{\alpha_1+\alpha_2}} < 0$$

- in case of the solution obtained for the logarithmic utility function

$$\mathrm{SE}_1 = \frac{\partial f_1(\mathbf{p}, u)}{\partial p_1} = \left(\frac{p_2\alpha_1}{\alpha_2}\right)^{\frac{\alpha_2}{\alpha_1+\alpha_2}}\left(-\frac{\alpha_2}{\alpha_1 + \alpha_2}\right)p_1^{-\frac{\alpha_2}{\alpha_1+\alpha_2}-1}\left(\frac{e^u}{a}\right)^{\frac{1}{\alpha_1+\alpha_2}} < 0$$

$$\mathrm{SE}_2 = \frac{\partial f_2(\mathbf{p}, u)}{\partial p_2} = \left(\frac{p_1\alpha_2}{\alpha_1}\right)^{\frac{\alpha_1}{\alpha_1+\alpha_2}}\left(-\frac{\alpha_1}{\alpha_1 + \alpha_2}\right)p_2^{-\frac{\alpha_1}{\alpha_1+\alpha_2}-1}\left(\frac{e^u}{a}\right)^{\frac{1}{\alpha_1+\alpha_2}} < 0,$$

which shows us that the substitution effect for both goods is, as it should be, negative.[5]

Let us now analyse the income effect:

$$\frac{\partial \varphi_1(\mathbf{p}, I)}{\partial I} = \frac{\alpha_1}{(\alpha_1 + \alpha_2)p_1} > 0 \qquad \frac{\partial \varphi_2(\mathbf{p}, I)}{\partial I} = \frac{\alpha_2}{(\alpha_1 + \alpha_2)p_2} > 0,$$

which shows us that both goods are normal goods. In the Slutsky equation, one considers the income effect in the following form:

$$\mathrm{IE}_1 = -\frac{\partial \varphi_1(\mathbf{p}, I)}{\partial I}\varphi_1(\mathbf{p}, I) = -\frac{\alpha_1 \varphi_1(\mathbf{p}, I)}{(\alpha_1 + \alpha_2)p_1} < 0$$

$$\mathrm{IE}_2 = -\frac{\partial \varphi_2(\mathbf{p}, I)}{\partial I}\varphi_2(\mathbf{p}, I) = -\frac{\alpha_2 \varphi_2(\mathbf{p}, I)}{(\alpha_1 + \alpha_2)p_2} < 0.$$

Let us now show that the substitution effect and the income effect compose together the price effect, that is the Slutsky equation is satisfied. Using the fact that $u = a\overline{x}_1^{\alpha_1}\overline{x}_2^{\alpha_2}$ in case of the power utility function or $u = \ln(a\overline{x}_1^{\alpha_1}\overline{x}_2^{\alpha_2})$ in case of the logarithmic utility function, thus:

$$u = a\left(\frac{\alpha_1 I}{(\alpha_1 + \alpha_2)p_1}\right)^{\alpha_1}\left(\frac{\alpha_2 I}{(\alpha_1 + \alpha_2)p_2}\right)^{\alpha_2}$$

$$= a\left(\frac{\alpha_1}{p_1}\right)^{\alpha_1}\left(\frac{\alpha_2}{p_2}\right)^{\alpha_2}\left(\frac{I}{\alpha_1 + \alpha_2}\right)^{\alpha_1+\alpha_2}\left(\frac{u}{a}\right)^{\frac{1}{\alpha_1+\alpha_2}}$$

$$= \left(\frac{\alpha_1}{p_1}\right)^{\frac{\alpha_1}{\alpha_1+\alpha_2}}\left(\frac{\alpha_2}{p_2}\right)^{\frac{\alpha_2}{\alpha_1+\alpha_2}}\frac{I}{\alpha_1 + \alpha_2}$$

or

$$u = \ln\left[a\left(\frac{\alpha_1}{p_1}\right)^{\alpha_1}\left(\frac{\alpha_2}{p_2}\right)^{\alpha_2}\left(\frac{I}{\alpha_1 + \alpha_2}\right)^{\alpha_1+\alpha_2}\right]$$

$$\left(\frac{e^u}{a}\right)^{\frac{1}{\alpha_1+\alpha_2}} = \left(\frac{\alpha_1}{p_1}\right)^{\frac{\alpha_1}{\alpha_1+\alpha_2}}\left(\frac{\alpha_2}{p_2}\right)^{\frac{\alpha_2}{\alpha_1+\alpha_2}}\frac{I}{\alpha_1 + \alpha_2}$$

we can calculate the right-hand side ($i = 1, 2$) of the Slutsky equation and show that it is equal to the left-hand side of this equation. In case of the first good and the power utility function, the right-hand side of the Slutsky equation takes a form:

$$\mathrm{SE}_1 + \mathrm{IE}_1 = \frac{\partial f_1(\mathbf{p}, u)}{\partial p_1} - \frac{\partial \varphi_1(\mathbf{p}, I)}{\partial I}\varphi_1(\mathbf{p}, I)$$

[5] The exception is the substitution effect for a Hicksian (compensated) demand function obtained when the utility is described by a Koopmans-Leontief function, thus regarding perfect complementary goods. In such a case, the substitution effect has the value zero showing that in this case, the compensated demand for goods does not depend on prices of goods.

$$= -\left(\frac{p_2\alpha_1}{p_1\alpha_2}\right)^{\frac{\alpha_2}{\alpha_1+\alpha_2}} \frac{\alpha_2}{(\alpha_1+\alpha_2)p_1}\left(\frac{u}{a}\right)^{\frac{1}{\alpha_1+\alpha_2}} - \frac{\alpha_1}{(\alpha_1+\alpha_2)p_1} \cdot \frac{\alpha_1 I}{(\alpha_1+\alpha_2)p_1}$$

$$= -\frac{\alpha_2}{(\alpha_1+\alpha_2)p_1} \cdot \frac{I}{\alpha_1+\alpha_2} \cdot \frac{\alpha_1}{p_1} - \frac{\alpha_1^2 I}{(\alpha_1+\alpha_2)^2 p_1^2}$$

$$= -\frac{\alpha_1 I}{(\alpha_1+\alpha_2)^2 p_1^2}(\alpha_2+\alpha_1) = -\frac{\alpha_1 I}{(\alpha_1+\alpha_2)p_1^2}$$

$$= \frac{\partial \varphi_1(\mathbf{p}, I)}{\partial p_1} = \mathrm{PE}_1$$

in case of the logarithmic utility function:

$$\mathrm{SE}_1 + \mathrm{IE}_1 = \frac{\partial f_1(\mathbf{p}, u)}{\partial p_1} - \frac{\partial \varphi_1(\mathbf{p}, I)}{\partial I}\varphi_1(\mathbf{p}, I)$$

$$= -\left(\frac{p_2\alpha_1}{p_1\alpha_2}\right)^{\frac{\alpha_2}{\alpha_1+\alpha_2}} \frac{\alpha_2}{(\alpha_1+\alpha_2)p_1}\left(\frac{e^u}{a}\right)^{\frac{1}{\alpha_1+\alpha_2}} - \frac{\alpha_1}{(\alpha_1+\alpha_2)p_1} \cdot \frac{\alpha_1 I}{(\alpha_1+\alpha_2)p_1}$$

$$= -\frac{\alpha_2}{(\alpha_1+\alpha_2)p_1} \cdot \frac{I}{\alpha_1+\alpha_2} \cdot \frac{\alpha_1}{p_1} - \frac{\alpha_1^2 I}{(\alpha_1+\alpha_2)^2 p_1^2}$$

$$= -\frac{\alpha_1 I}{(\alpha_1+\alpha_2)^2 p_1^2}(\alpha_2+\alpha_1) = -\frac{\alpha_1 I}{(\alpha_1+\alpha_2)p_1^2}$$

$$= \frac{\partial \varphi_1(\mathbf{p}, I)}{\partial p_1} = PE_1$$

In case of the second good and the power utility function, the right-hand side of the Slutsky equation takes a form:

$$\mathrm{SE}_2 + \mathrm{IE}_2 = \frac{\partial f_2(\mathbf{p}, u)}{\partial p_2} - \frac{\partial \varphi_2(\mathbf{p}, I)}{\partial I}\varphi_1(\mathbf{p}, I)$$

$$= -\left(\frac{p_1\alpha_2}{p_2\alpha_1}\right)^{\frac{\alpha_1}{\alpha_1+\alpha_2}} \frac{\alpha_1}{(\alpha_1+\alpha_2)p_2}\left(\frac{u}{a}\right)^{\frac{1}{\alpha_1+\alpha_2}} - \frac{\alpha_2}{(\alpha_1+\alpha_2)p_1} \cdot \frac{\alpha_2 I}{(\alpha_1+\alpha_2)p_1}$$

$$= -\frac{\alpha_1}{(\alpha_1+\alpha_2)p_2} \cdot \frac{I}{\alpha_1+\alpha_2} \cdot \frac{\alpha_2}{p_2} - \frac{\alpha_2^2 I}{(\alpha_1+\alpha_2)^2 p_2^2}$$

$$= -\frac{\alpha_2 I}{(\alpha_1+\alpha_2)^2 p_2^2}(\alpha_1+\alpha_2) = -\frac{\alpha_2 I}{(\alpha_1+\alpha_2)p_2^2}$$

$$= \frac{\partial \varphi_2(\mathbf{p}, I)}{\partial p_2} = \mathrm{PE}_2$$

in case of the logarithmic utility function:

$$\mathrm{SE}_2 + \mathrm{IE}_2 = \frac{\partial f_2(\mathbf{p}, u)}{\partial p_2} - \frac{\partial \varphi_2(\mathbf{p}, I)}{\partial I}\varphi_1(\mathbf{p}, I)$$

$$= -\left(\frac{p_1\alpha_2}{p_2\alpha_1}\right)^{\frac{\alpha_1}{\alpha_1+\alpha_2}} \frac{\alpha_1}{(\alpha_1+\alpha_2)p_2}\left(\frac{e^u}{a}\right)^{\frac{1}{\alpha_1+\alpha_2}} - \frac{\alpha_2}{(\alpha_1+\alpha_2)p_1} \cdot \frac{\alpha_2 I}{(\alpha_1+\alpha_2)p_1}$$
$$= -\frac{\alpha_1}{(\alpha_1+\alpha_2)p_2} \cdot \frac{I}{\alpha_1+\alpha_2} \cdot \frac{\alpha_2}{p_2} - \frac{\alpha_2^2 I}{(\alpha_1+\alpha_2)^2 p_2^2}$$
$$= -\frac{\alpha_2 I}{(\alpha_1+\alpha_2)^2 p_2^2}(\alpha_1+\alpha_2) = -\frac{\alpha_2 I}{(\alpha_1+\alpha_2)p_2^2}$$
$$= \frac{\partial\varphi_2(\mathbf{p}, I)}{\partial p_2} = \mathrm{PE}_2$$

E2.13. At each moment $t \in [0; 20]$ a consumer's income, the price of the first good and the price of the second good change according to equations:

$$I(t) = 10 \cdot 1.05^{-t}$$
$$p_1(t) = 4 \cdot 0.98^{-t}$$
$$p_2(t) = -0.006t^2 + 01t + 3$$

Consumers' preferences towards consumption bundles are described by a Koopmans-Leontief function of a form: $u(\mathbf{x}(t)) = \min\{2x_1(t), x_2(t)\}$. Solve a consumption utility maximization problem in the dynamic approach. Present trajectories of the demand for the first and the second goods and a trajectory of indirect utility.

Solution

From the static approach, we know that a solution to the consumption utility maximization problem can be found from a system:

$$\begin{cases} 2x_1(t) = x_2(t) \\ p_1(t)x_1(t) + p_2(t)x_2(t) = I(t) \end{cases}$$

hence is given as:

$$\begin{cases} \overline{x}_1(t) = \frac{I(t)}{p_1(t)+2p_2(t)} \\ \overline{x}_2(t) = \frac{2I(t)}{p_1(t)+2p_2(t)}. \end{cases}$$

Having optimal quantities of goods in a consumption bundle, we can also write a Marshallian demand function:

$$\varphi(\mathbf{p}(t), I(t)) = \overline{\mathbf{x}}(t) = \left(\frac{I(t)}{p_1(t)+2p_2(t)}, \frac{2I(t)}{p_1(t)+2p_2(t)}\right) \quad t \in [0; 20]$$

and an indirect utility function:

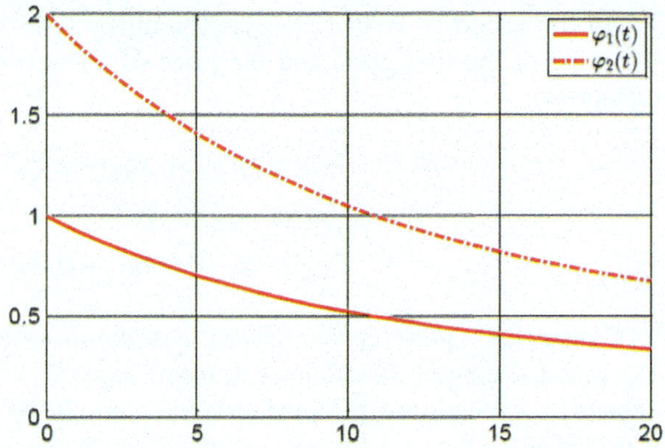

Fig. 2.11 Trajectories of demand for goods (E2.13)

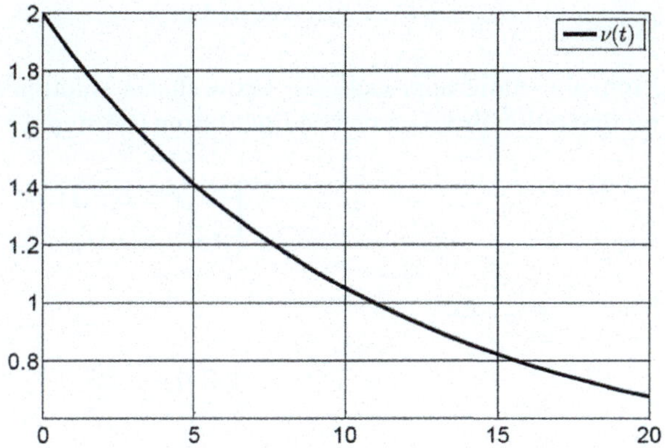

Fig. 2.12 Trajectory of indirect utility (E2.13)

$$
\begin{aligned}
v(\mathbf{p}(t), I(t)) &= u(\overline{\mathbf{x}}(t)) \\
&= \min\left\{\frac{2I(t)}{p_1(t)+2p_2(t)}, \frac{2I(t)}{p_1(t)+2p_2(t)}\right\} \\
&= \frac{2I(t)}{p_1(t)+2p_2(t)} \qquad t \in [0; 20]
\end{aligned}
$$

From the formula of the Marshallian demand function, we can notice that in the case of the Koopmans-Leontief utility function, a consumer wants to have the first and the second good always in the same proportion 1:2 (twice as much units of the second goods as units of the first good). This can be also seen in Fig. 2.11 in which trajectories[6] of the demand for goods are presented. Trajectory of the indirect utility is presented in Fig. 2.12.

[6] Trajectories of the demand for goods and of the indirect utility can be obtained using a MATLAB file called Exercise_2_13.m.

E2.14. In periods $t = 0, 1, 2, \ldots, 20$ a utility level a consumer wants to achieve, the price of the first good and the price of the second good change according to equations:

$$u(t) = 1 - 0.1\ln(t+1)$$
$$p_1(t) = 4 \cdot 0.98^{-t}$$
$$p_2(t) = -0.006t^2 + 0,1t + 3$$

Consumers' preferences toward consumption bundles are described by a Koopmans-Leontief function of a form: $u(\mathbf{x}(t)) = \min\{2x_1(t), x_2(t)\}$. Solve a consumer expenditure minimization problem in the dynamic approach. Present trajectories of the compensated demand for the first and the second goods and a trajectory of consumer's expenditure.

Solution

From the static approach, we know that a solution to the consumer expenditure minimization problem can be found from a system:

$$\begin{cases} 2x_1(t) = u(t) \\ x_2(t) = u(t) \end{cases}$$

hence is given as:

$$\begin{cases} \tilde{x}_1(t) = \frac{u(t)}{2} \\ \tilde{x}_2(t) = u(t). \end{cases}$$

Having optimal quantities of goods in a consumption bundle, we can also write a Hicksian (compensated) demand function:

$$f(\mathbf{p}(t), u(t)) = \tilde{\mathbf{x}}(t) = \left(\frac{1}{2}u(t), u(t)\right) \quad t = 0, 1, 2, \ldots, 20$$

and a consumer's expenditure function:

$$\begin{aligned} e(\mathbf{p}(t), u(t)) &= p_1(t)\tilde{x}_1(t) + p_2(t)\tilde{x}_2(t) \\ &= u(t)\left(\frac{1}{2}p_1(t) + p_2(t)\right) \quad t = 0, 1, 2, \ldots, 20 \end{aligned}$$

From the formula of the Hicksian (compensated) demand function, we can notice that in the case of the Koopmans-Leontief utility function, the compensated demand does not depend on prices of goods. Moreover, we can also notice that a consumer wants to have the first and the second good always in the same proportion 1 : 2 (twice as much units of the second goods as units of the first good). This can be also seen in

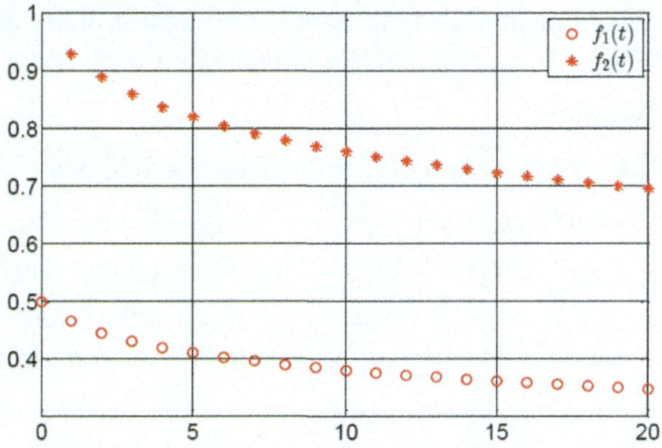

Fig. 2.13 Trajectories of compensated demand for goods (E2.14)

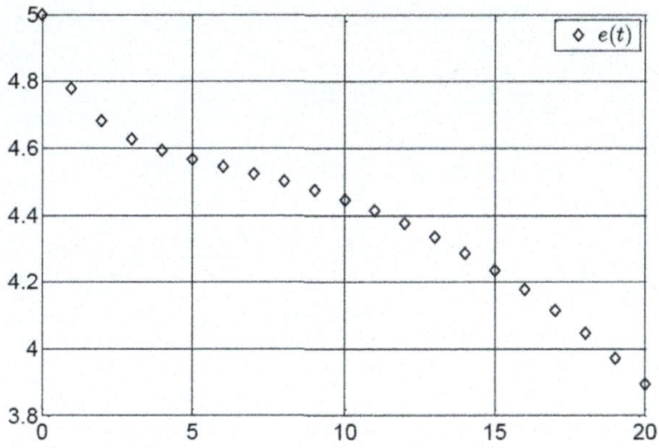

Fig. 2.14 Trajectory of consumer's expenditure (E2.14)

Fig. 2.13 in which trajectories[7] of the compensated demand for goods are presented. Trajectory of the consumer's expenditure is presented in Fig. 2.14.

E2.15. At each moment $t \in [0; 20]$ a consumer's income, the price of the first good and the price of the second good change according to equations:

$$I(t) = 10 \cdot 1.05^{-t}$$
$$p_1(t) = 4 \cdot 0.98^{-t}$$
$$p_2(t) = -0.006t^2 + 0.1t + 3$$

Consumers' preferences toward consumption bundles are described by a Koopmans-Leontief function of a form: $u(\mathbf{x}(t)) = \min\{2x_1(t), x_2(t)\}$. A utility level a consumer wants to achieve evolves at each moment according to an indirect

[7] Trajectories of the compensated demand for goods and of the consumer's expenditure can be obtained using a MATLAB file called Exercise_2_14.m.

utility function resulting from a consumption utility maximization problem. Present trajectories of price, income and substitutive effects for the first and the second goods.

Solution

Let us recall results obtained in Exercise 2.13 and 2.14:

$\varphi(\mathbf{p}(t), I(t)) = \left(\frac{I(t)}{p_1(t)+2p_2(t)}, \frac{2I(t)}{p_1(t)+2p_2(t)}\right)$ the Marshallian demand function.
$v(\mathbf{p}(t), I(t)) = \frac{2I(t)}{p_1(t)+2p_2(t)}$ the indirect utility function.
$f(\mathbf{p}(t), u(t)) = \left(\frac{1}{2}u(t), u(t)\right)$ the Hicksian (compensated) demand function.
$e(\mathbf{p}(t), u(t)) = u(t)\left(\frac{1}{2}p_1(t) + p_2(t)\right)$ the consumer's expenditure function.

The price, income and substitutive effects constitute the Slutsky equation. Let us consider this equation in a form in which the effects for one good are presented:

$$\frac{\partial \varphi_i(\mathbf{p}(t), I(t))}{\partial p_i(t)} = \frac{\partial f_i(\mathbf{p}(t), u(t))}{\partial p_i(t)} - \frac{\partial \varphi_i(\mathbf{p}(t), I(t))}{\partial I(t)}\varphi_i(\mathbf{p}(t), I(t))$$
$$i = 1, 2, \ t \in [0; 20].$$

The price effect has the following form:

$$\mathrm{PE}_1 = \frac{\partial \varphi_1(\mathbf{p}(t), I(t))}{\partial p_1(t)} = -\frac{I(t)}{(p_1(t) + 2p_2(t))^2} < 0$$
$$\mathrm{PE}_2 = \frac{\partial \varphi_2(\mathbf{p}(t), I(t))}{\partial p_2(t)} = -\frac{4I(t)}{(p_1(t) + 2p_2(t))^2} < 0,$$

which shows that both goods are ordinary goods,

while the income effect:

$$\mathrm{IE}_1 = -\frac{\partial \varphi_1(\mathbf{p}(t), I(t))}{\partial I(t)}\varphi_1(\mathbf{p}(t), I(t)) = -\frac{I(t)}{(p_1(t) + 2p_2(t))^2} < 0$$
$$\mathrm{IE}_2 = -\frac{\partial \varphi_2(\mathbf{p}(t), I(t))}{\partial I(t)}\varphi_2(\mathbf{p}(t), I(t)) = -\frac{4I(t)}{(p_1(t) + 2p_2(t))^2} < 0,$$

which shows that both goods are normal goods,

and the substitutive effect:

$$\mathrm{SE}_1 = \frac{\partial f_1(\mathbf{p}(t), u(t))}{\partial p_1(t)} = 0, \qquad \mathrm{SE}_2 = \frac{\partial f_2(\mathbf{p}(t), u(t))}{\partial p_2(t)} = 0.$$

We can see now that for both goods, the Slutsky equation is satisfied:

$$\mathrm{PE}_1 = \mathrm{SE}_1 + \mathrm{IE}_1, \qquad \mathrm{PE}_2 = \mathrm{SE}_2 + \mathrm{IE}_2.$$

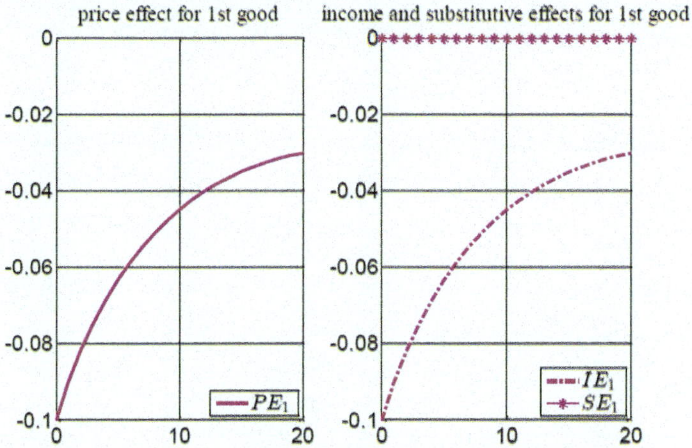

Fig. 2.15 Trajectories of price, income and substitutive effect for first good (E2.15)

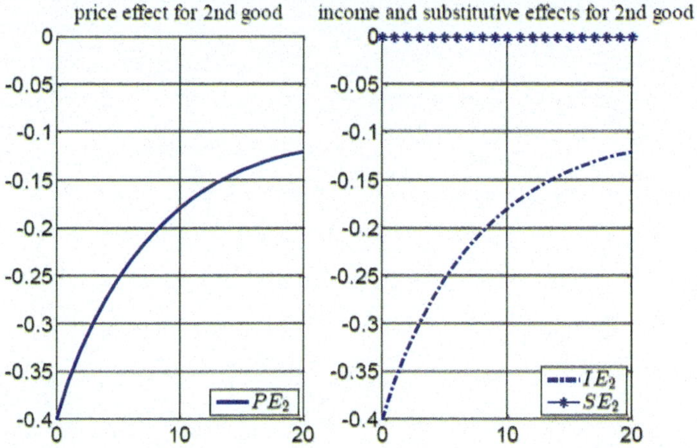

Fig. 2.16 Trajectories of price, income and substitutive effect for second good (E2.15)

The substitutive effect for both goods has value 0 because in the case of the Koopmans-Leontief utility function, the compensated demand for goods does not depend on prices of goods. Trajectories[8] of all effects are presented in Figs. 2.15 and 2.16.

[8] Trajectories of the effects can be obtained using a MATLAB file called Exercise_2_15.m.

Chapter 3
Rationality of Choices Made by a Group of Consumers

This Chapter presents 8 exercises that help in understanding the problem of describing rational decisions made by a group of consumers. They concern a simple exchange model, the static Arrow-Hurwicz model and the dynamic Arrow-Hurwicz model, in a discrete-time and continuous-time versions. In particular the focus of the exercises is to deal with a concept of the Walras general equilibrium and its global asymptotic stability.

E3.1. There is given a market of two traders and two goods described by the simple model of exchange, in which:

$i = 1, 2$—consumer goods,

$k = 1, 2$—traders (consumers),

$X^k = \mathbb{R}_+^2$—a goods' space of k-th trader,

$u^k \colon \mathbb{R}_+^2 \to \mathbb{R}$—a utility function of k-th trader describing her/his preferences (relation of k-th consumer's preference),

$\mathbf{a}^k = (a_{k1}, a_{k2}) \in \mathbb{R}_+^2$—an initial bundle the k-th consumer comes to the market with,

$\mathbf{x}^k = (x_{k1}, x_{k2}) \in \mathbb{R}_+^2$—a consumption bundle the k-th consumer wants to purchase.

The k-th ($k = 1, 2$) consumer aims to purchase such a bundle of goods $\overline{\mathbf{x}}^k = (\overline{x}_{k1}, \overline{x}_{k2})$, whose utility would be maximum and at the same time not less than of the initial bundle of goods $\mathbf{a}^k = (a_{k1}, a_{k2})$.

Let us consider cases when:

A. $u^k\left(\mathbf{x}^k\right) = a_{k1} \ln x_{k1} + a_{k2} \ln x_{k2} \to \max,$
B. $u^k\left(\mathbf{x}^\mathbf{k}\right) = a_{k1} x_{k1}^\alpha + a_{k2} x_{k2}^\alpha \to \max.$

Using the Edgeworth box:

1. Present geometric illustration of sets of allocations: feasible with regard to an initial allocation, accepted by traders, Pareto optimal,
2. Determine which allocations are blocked by traders,
3. Justify that $C(\mathbf{a}) \subseteq S(\mathbf{a}) \subseteq F(\mathbf{a}) \subset \mathbb{R}_+^4$.

K. Sobczak and K. Malaga, *Workbook for Microeconomics*, Springer Texts in Business and Economics, https://doi.org/10.1007/978-3-031-41947-8_3

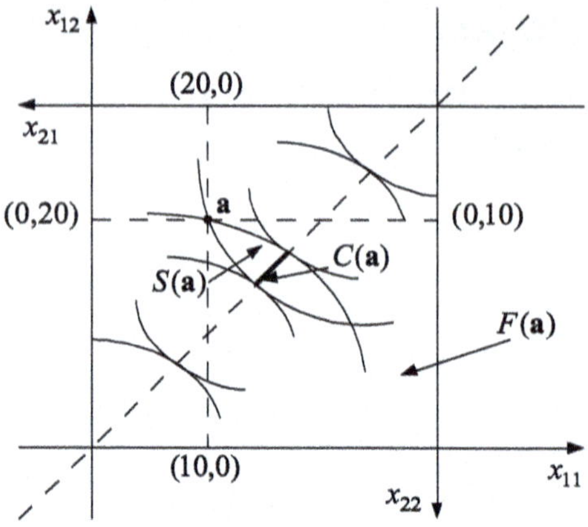

Fig. 3.1 Edgeworth box in case of logarithmic utility functions (E3.1)

Let us assume that there are given:

- Initial bundles both consumers come to the market with: $\mathbf{a}^1 = (10,\ 20)$, $\mathbf{a}^2 = (20,\ 10)$, which means that the initial allocation has a form: $\mathbf{a} = (10, 20, 20, 10)$,
- Values of parameters in the logarithmic and in the subadditive utility functions: $a_{k1} = a_{k2} = 1$,
- Values of parameters in the subadditive utility function: $\alpha = \frac{1}{4}$.

Solutions

Ad A

Figure 3.1 shows the initial allocation $\mathbf{a} = (10, 20, 20, 10)$, consisting of bundles of goods owned by both traders. Since the total amount of the first and second goods brought to the market by both traders is the same and amounts to 30 units, the Edgeworth box in the considered example is a square. It is created by putting together two coordinate systems: of each of two traders (from her/his point of view). It is not hard to notice that any vector $\mathbf{x} = (x_{11}, x_{12}, x_{21}, x_{22}) \in \mathbb{R}_+^4$, belonging to the Edgeworth box, is an allocation feasible with regard to the initial allocation because $\forall \mathbf{x} \in F(\mathbf{a}) \quad x_{11} + x_{21} = 30, x_{12} + x_{22} = 30.$

Since both traders use power utility functions when choosing the optimal bundles of goods, the corresponding indifference curves are strictly convex in the respective coordinate system of a given trader.

Let us notice that if $u^1(\mathbf{x}^1) = \ln x_{11} + \ln x_{12} = \ln x_{11}x_{12} = u$ then $x_{12} = \frac{e^u}{x_{11}}$. Similarly, if $u^2(\mathbf{x}^2) = \ln x_{21} + \ln x_{22} = \ln x_{21}x_{22} = u$ then $x_{22} = \frac{e^u}{x_{21}}$.

The lens-shaped area $S(\mathbf{a})$, within the indifference curves of both traders containing the initial allocation, consists of all the allocations accepted by both traders, because utility of the consumption bundles belonging to this area is not less than of the bundles of goods the traders entered the market with.

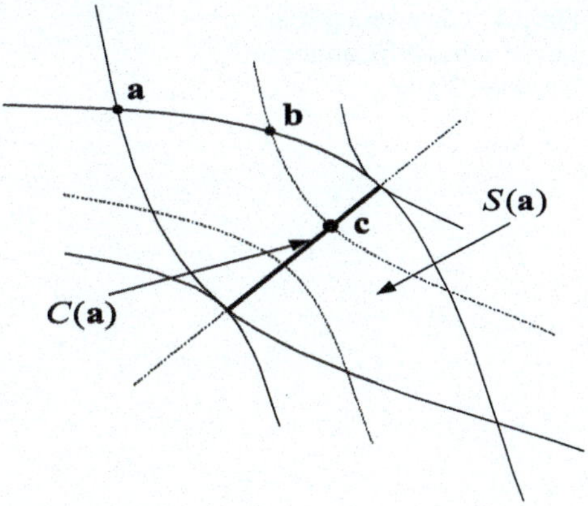

Fig. 3.2 Set of allocations accepted by both traders—case of logarithmic utility functions (E3.1)

According to definition 3.7[1], the allocations that are at the tangency points of the indifference curves of both traders are Pareto optimal allocations. There are infinitely many of them and they create a so-called **contract curve**, depicted in Fig. 3.1 as a dashed line connecting the origins of the coordinate systems of both traders. This part of the Pareto optimal allocations which belongs also to the set of allocations accepted by traders forms the exchange core denoted by a symbol $C(\mathbf{a})$.

From Fig. 3.1, it follows that $C(\mathbf{a}) \subset S(\mathbf{a}) \subset F(\mathbf{a}) \subset \mathbb{R}^4_+$, which means that any Pareto optimal allocation accepted by traders is the feasible allocation with regard to the initial allocation. At the same time, not every Pareto optimal allocation is accepted by traders. Not every allocation accepted by traders is Pareto optimal and not every feasible allocation is an allocation accepted by traders or Pareto optimal.

Figure 3.2 shows the set of allocations accepted by both traders $S(\mathbf{a})$ and the exchange core $C(\mathbf{a})$. Using Fig. 3.2, one can explain the mechanism according to which both traders choose one of the accepted allocations, which is at the same time the Pareto optimal allocation.

Let us suppose the first trader proposes an allocation **b** that is better for him/her than the initial allocation **a** because it belongs to an indifference curve that is higher up than the indifference curve of the first trader containing the initial allocation.

For the second trader, the allocation **b** is just as good as the initial allocation **a** because both of these allocations belong to the same indifference curve. The second trader however should block this allocation and propose a different allocation to the first trader, not worse for the first trader than the allocation **b** and at the same time better than the initial allocation **a** for the second trader. An example of such an allocation is an allocation **c** which is a Pareto optimal allocation too. The allocation **c** lies at the point where the indifference curves of both traders are tangent to each other. Neither of traders can block it and propose a different allocation which, being better than the allocation **c** for one of them, would also not be worse than the allocation **c** for the other trader.

---

[1] The definition is presented in a textbook Malaga K., Sobczak K, *Microeconomics. Static and Dynamic Analysis*, Springer Nature Switzerland, 2022.

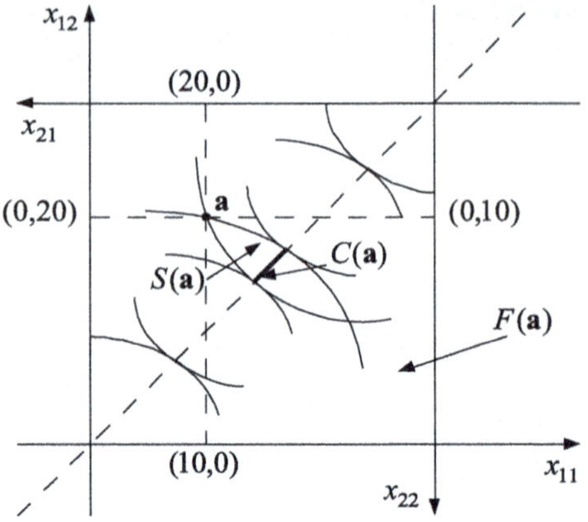

Fig. 3.3 Edgeworth box in case of subadditive utility functions (E3.1)

A reasonable question arises: since every allocation belonging to the exchange core is Pareto optimal, accepted by both traders and as such cannot be blocked by any trader, which one of them should be eventually chosen by traders?

In order to answer this question, it is necessary to define an additional criterion for choice of the optimal allocation in the set of Pareto optimal allocations. This would be the optimum of optima. There seems to be a need to define such an additional criterion since not all allocations Pareto optimal and accepted by traders are equally beneficial to them. For example, such an allocation optimal in the Pareto sense, that belongs to the indifference curve of the first (second) trader bounding the set of allocations accepted by both traders from the bottom (top), is the most advantageous allocation among the Pareto optimal allocations for the second (first) trader and the least favourable for the first (second) trader.

The fairest choice would be a Pareto optimal allocation lying in the middle of a segment identified with the exchange core. A Pareto optimal allocation defined in such a way would guarantee an identical increase in the utility of the bundle of goods purchased by each trader with regard to the bundle each of them entered the market with in order to exchange for another bundle whose utility would be maximum and at the same time not less than the utility of the initial bundle.

Ad B

Figure 3.3 shows the initial allocation $\mathbf{a} = (10, 20, 20, 10)$, consisting of bundles of goods owned by both traders. Since the total amount of the first and second goods brought to the market by both traders is the same and amounts to 30 units, the Edgeworth box in the considered example is a square. It is created by putting together two coordinate systems: of each of two traders (from her/his point of view). It is not hard to notice that any vector $\mathbf{x} = (x_{11}, x_{12}, x_{21}, x_{22}) \in \mathbb{R}^4_+$, belonging to the Edgeworth box, is an allocation feasible with regard to the initial allocation because $\forall \mathbf{x} \in F(\mathbf{a}) \quad x_{11} + x_{21} = 30, x_{12} + x_{22} = 30.$

Since both traders use power utility functions when choosing the optimal bundles of goods, the corresponding indifference curves are strictly convex in the respective coordinate system of a given trader.

Let us notice that if $u^1(\mathbf{x}^1) = x_{11}^{\frac{1}{4}} + x_{12}^{\frac{1}{4}} = u$ then $x_{12} = \left(u - x_{11}^{\frac{1}{4}}\right)$. Similarly, if $u^2(\mathbf{x}^2) = x_{21}^{\frac{1}{4}} + x_{22}^{\frac{1}{4}} = u$ then $x_{22} = \left(u - x_{21}^{\frac{1}{4}}\right)$.

The lens-shaped area $S(\mathbf{a})$, within the indifference curves of both traders containing the initial allocation, consists of all the allocations accepted by both traders, because utility of the consumption bundles belonging to this area is not less than of the bundles of goods the traders entered the market with.

According to definition 3.7[2], the allocations that are at the tangency points of the indifference curves of both traders are Pareto optimal allocations. There are infinitely many of them and they create a so-called **contract curve**, depicted in Fig. 3.3 as a dashed line connecting the origins of the coordinate systems of both traders. This part of the Pareto optimal allocations which belongs also to the set of allocations accepted by traders forms the exchange core denoted by a symbol $C(\mathbf{a})$.

From Fig. 3.3, it follows that $C(\mathbf{a}) \subset S(\mathbf{a}) \subset F(\mathbf{a}) \subset \mathbb{R}_+^4$, which means that any Pareto optimal allocation accepted by traders is the feasible allocation with regard to the initial allocation. At the same time, not every Pareto optimal allocation is accepted by traders. Not every allocation accepted by traders is Pareto optimal and not every feasible allocation is an allocation accepted by traders or Pareto optimal.

A reasonable question arises: since every allocation belonging to the exchange core is Pareto optimal, accepted by both traders and as such cannot be blocked by any trader, which one of them should be eventually chosen by traders?

In order to answer this question, it is necessary to define an additional criterion for choice of the optimal allocation in the set of Pareto optimal allocations. This would be the optimum of optima. There seems to be a need to define such an additional criterion since not all allocations Pareto optimal and accepted by traders are equally beneficial to them. For example, such an allocation optimal in the Pareto sense, that belongs to the indifference curve of the first (second) trader bounding the set of allocations accepted by both traders from the bottom (top), is the most advantageous allocation among the Pareto optimal allocations for the second (first) trader and the least favourable for the first (second) trader.

The fairest choice would be a Pareto optimal allocation lying in the middle of a segment identified with the exchange core. A Pareto optimal allocation defined in such a way would guarantee an identical increase in the utility of the bundle of goods purchased by each trader with regard to the bundle each of them entered the market with in order to exchange for another bundle whose utility would be maximum and at the same time not less than the utility of the initial bundle.

E3.2. There is given a market of two traders and two goods described by the static Arrow-Hurwicz model, in which:

---

[2] The definition is presented in a textbook Malaga K., Sobczak K, Microeconomics. Static and Dynamic Analysis, Springer Nature Switzerland, 2022.

$i = 1, 2$—consumer goods,
$k = 1, 2$—traders (consumers),
$X = \mathbb{R}^2_+$—a goods' space,
$\mathbf{a}^1 = (10, 20)$, $\mathbf{a}^2 = (20, 10)$—initial bundles the consumers come to the market with,
$\mathbf{p} = (p_1, p_2) \in \text{int}\mathbb{R}^2_+$—a vector of goods' prices,
$\mathbf{x}^k = (x_{k1}, x_{k2}) \in \mathbb{R}^2_+$—a consumption bundle the k-th consumer wants to purchase,
$I^1(p_1, p_2) = 10p_1 + 20p_2$, $I^2(p_1, p_2) = 20p_1 + 10p_2$—incomes of traders.
Utility functions of traders have forms:

(a) $u^1(x_{11}, x_{12}) = \ln x_{11} + \ln x_{12}, \quad u^2(x_{21}, x_{22}) = \ln x_{21} + \ln x_{22}$—logarithmic,
(b) $u^1(x_{11}, x_{12}) = x_{11}^{\frac{1}{4}} + x_{11}^{\frac{1}{4}}, \quad u^2(x_{21}, x_{22}) = x_{21}^{\frac{1}{4}} + x_{21}^{\frac{1}{4}}$—subadditive.

1. Find solution of the utility maximization problem of each trader—a demand function of each trader.
2. Determine functions of global supply and global demand.
3. Determine an excess demand function and justify that it is homogenous of degree 0 and that it satisfies Walras's law.
4. Determine a Walrasian equilibrium price vector.
5. Explain what it means that the Walrasian equilibrium price vector is determined to an accuracy of a structure (multiplication by a positive number).
6. Determine a Walrasian equilibrium allocation.
7. Present geometric illustrations of:
   - A set of allocations feasible with regard to the initial allocation,
   - A set of Pareto optimal allocations,
   - A set of Walrasian equilibrium allocations.
8. Justify by geometric means that: $W(\mathbf{a}) \subseteq C(\mathbf{a}) \subseteq S(\mathbf{a}) \subseteq F(\mathbf{a}) \subset \mathbb{R}^4_+$.

Solutions

Ad A

We know that the optimal solution to the consumption utility maximization problem in the case of the power utility function $u^k(x_{k1}, x_{k2}) = \ln x_{k1} + \ln x_{k1}$ has a form:

(1) $\overline{\mathbf{x}}^k(\mathbf{p}) = \left(\frac{1}{2}\frac{I^k(\mathbf{p})}{p_1}, \frac{1}{2}\frac{I^k(\mathbf{p})}{p_2}\right)$.

Substituting the parameters of the utility function of both traders into (1), we get the demand function of the first trader:

(2) $\overline{\mathbf{x}}^1(\mathbf{p}) = \left(\frac{10p_1+20p_2}{2p_1}, \frac{10p_1+20p_2}{2p_2}\right)$,

and of the second trader:

(3) $\overline{\mathbf{x}}^2(\mathbf{p}) = \left(\frac{20p_1+10p_2}{2p_1}, \frac{20p_1+10p_2}{2p_2}\right)$.

Adding the demand functions of both traders, we get the global demand function for both consumer goods:

(4) $\overline{\mathbf{x}}(\overline{\mathbf{p}}) = \overline{\mathbf{x}}^1(\mathbf{p}) + \overline{\mathbf{x}}^2(\mathbf{p}) = \left(\frac{30p_1+30p_2}{2p_1}, \frac{30p_1+30p_2}{2p_2}\right)$.

The global supply function (vector) has a form:

(5) $\overline{\mathbf{a}} = \mathbf{a}^1 + \mathbf{a}^2 = (30, 30)$.

The excess demand function then has a form:

(6) $\mathbf{z}(\mathbf{p}) = \overline{\mathbf{x}}(\mathbf{p}) - \overline{\mathbf{a}} = \left(\frac{30p_1+30p_2}{2p_1}, \frac{30p_1+30p_2}{2p_2}\right) - (30, 30) = \left(\frac{-30p_1+30p_2}{2p_1}, \frac{30p_1-30p_2}{2p_2}\right)$.

Let us notice that the excess demand function is homogeneous of degree 0 because:

(7) $\forall\lambda > 0 \;\; \mathbf{z}(\lambda\mathbf{p}) = \left(\frac{-30\lambda p_1+30\lambda p_2}{2\lambda p_1}, \frac{30\lambda p_1-30\lambda p_2}{2\lambda p_2}\right) = \mathbf{z}(\mathbf{p})$,

which means that the excess demand for any commodity does not depend on the absolute price level of both goods, but on the relationship between the prices of goods.

Moreover the function of excess demand satisfies Walras's law, because:

(8) $\forall\mathbf{p} > 0 \;\; \langle\mathbf{p}, \mathbf{z}(\mathbf{p})\rangle = p_1\frac{-30p_1+30p_2}{2p_1} + p_2\frac{30p_1-30p_2}{2p_2} = 0$,

which means that for any positive vector of consumer goods' prices, the value of global demand is equal to the value of global supply of both goods.

Let us determine the Walrasian equilibrium price vector $\overline{\mathbf{p}} > 0$ as a solution of a following system of equations:

(9) $\mathbf{z}(\mathbf{p}) = \left(\frac{-30\overline{p}_1+30\overline{p}_2}{2\overline{p}_1}, \frac{-30\overline{p}_1+30\overline{p}_2}{2\overline{p}_2}\right) = (0, 0)$

which can be written in an equivalent form:

(10) $$\begin{aligned} -30\overline{p}_1 + 30\overline{p}_2 &= 0 \\ 30\overline{p}_1 - 30\overline{p}_2 &= 0 \end{aligned}$$

resulting in:

(11) $\overline{p}_1 = \overline{p}_2 = \lambda > 0$,

therefore, the Walrasian equilibrium price vector, determined to an accuracy of a structure, has the following form:

(12) $\overline{\mathbf{p}} = \lambda(1, 1)$.

Having this, after substituting (12) to (2) and (3), we can determine the values of the demand functions of both traders when prices are given by the Walrasian equilibrium price vector:

(13) $\overline{\mathbf{x}}^1(\overline{\mathbf{p}}) = (15, 15)$
(14) $\overline{\mathbf{x}}^2(\overline{\mathbf{p}}) = (15, 15)$

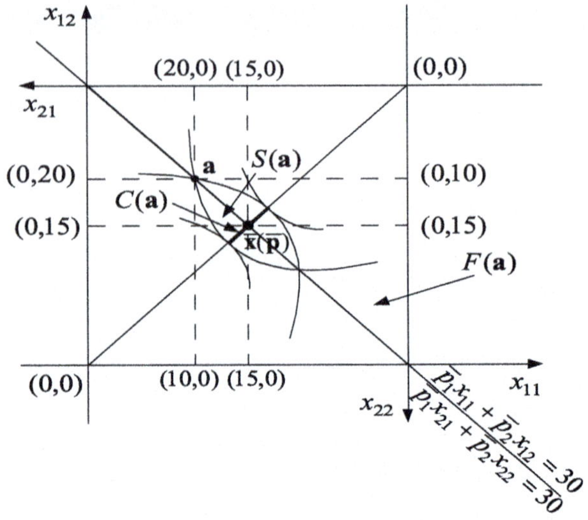

Fig. 3.4 Edgeworth box in case of logarithmic utility functions (E3.2)

and the Walrasian equilibrium allocation:

(15) $\overline{\mathbf{x}}(\overline{\mathbf{p}}) = \left(\overline{\mathbf{x}}^1(\overline{\mathbf{p}}), \overline{\mathbf{x}}^2(\overline{\mathbf{p}})\right) = (15, 15, 15, 15)$,

while the initial allocation is:

(16) $\mathbf{a} = \left(\mathbf{a}^1, \mathbf{a}^2\right) = (10, 20, 20, 10)$.

Let us notice that in the Walrasian equilibrium state, the relation between equilibrium prices is 1 : 1. This means that traders exchange goods in the relation 1 unit of the first good for 1 unit of the second good.

Since the utility functions of both traders are the same, their preferences to own each of the goods are also the same. Thus, in the Walrasian equilibrium state, as a result of the exchange made by the Walrasian equilibrium prices, both traders will have identical bundles of goods. It is also worth noticing that in the only state of the Walrasian equilibrium, an increase in utility of bundles of goods purchased by traders with respect to utility of the initial consumption bundles will be the same for both traders.

Figure 3.4 presents geometrical illustrations of sets of allocations: of the Walrasian equilibrium $W(\mathbf{a})$ (indicated by a single point $\overline{\mathbf{x}}(\overline{\mathbf{p}})$), optimal in the Pareto sense and accepted in the same time $C(\mathbf{a})$, as well as a set $F(\mathbf{a})$ of the allocations feasible with regard to the initial allocation: $\mathbf{a} = (10, 20, 20, 10)$.

Since the optimal solutions to both consumption utility maximization problems must lie on the budget lines respective to each of the traders, having the Walrasian equilibrium price vector, we get:

$$\overline{p}_1\overline{x}_{11} + \overline{p}_2\overline{x}_{12} = 10\overline{p}_1 + 20\overline{p}_2 \iff \overline{x}_{11} + \overline{x}_{12} = 30, \tag{3.1}$$

and

$$\overline{p}_1\overline{x}_{21} + \overline{p}_2\overline{x}_{22} = 10\overline{p}_1 + 20\overline{p}_2 \iff \overline{x}_{21} + \overline{x}_2 = 30. \tag{3.2}$$

This means that the budget lines of traders are not only parallel but also coincide, because each of them includes the initial bundle of goods each of the traders came to the market with. It is not difficult to notice that an angle of incline of both budget lines with respect to the horizontal axes is 45° in the coordinate system of each of the traders.

It is also easy to notice that: $W(\mathbf{a}) \subset C(\mathbf{a}) \subset S(\mathbf{a}) \subset F(\mathbf{a}) \subset \mathbb{R}^4_+$. This means that the only Walrasian equilibrium allocation corresponding to the only Walrasian equilibrium price vector, determined to an accuracy of a structure, is a Pareto optimal allocation, accepted and feasible with regard to an initial allocation.

Ad B

The consumption utility maximization problems for two traders are given:

(1) $u^1(x_{11}, x_{12}) = x_{11}^{\frac{1}{4}} + x_{12}^{\frac{1}{4}} \to \max$
(2) $p_1x_{11} + p_2x_{12} \leq 10p_1 + 20p_2,$
(3) $x_{11}, x_{12} \geq 0,$

and

(4) $u^2(x_{21}, x_{22}) = x_{21}^{\frac{1}{4}} + x_{22}^{\frac{1}{4}} \to \max$
(5) $p_1x_{21} + p_2x_{22} \leq 20p_1 + 10p_2,$
(6) $x_{21}, x_{22} \geq 0.$

We know that the optimal solution to the consumption utility maximization problem in case of the subadditive utility function $u(x_1, x_2) = a_1x_1^\alpha + a_2x_2^\alpha$ has a form:

(7) $$\overline{\mathbf{x}}(\mathbf{p}) = \left(\frac{(a_1p_2)^{\frac{1}{1-\alpha}} I}{a_1^{\frac{1}{1-\alpha}} p_2^{\frac{2-\alpha}{1-\alpha}} + a_2^{\frac{1}{1-\alpha}} p_1^{\frac{2-\alpha}{1-\alpha}}}, \frac{(a_2p_1)^{\frac{1}{1-\alpha}} I}{a_1^{\frac{1}{1-\alpha}} p_2^{\frac{2-\alpha}{1-\alpha}} + a_2^{\frac{1}{1-\alpha}} p_1^{\frac{2-\alpha}{1-\alpha}}} \right).$$

Substituting the parameters of the utility function of both traders into (7), we get the demand function of the first trader:

(8) $$\overline{\mathbf{x}}^1(\mathbf{p}) = \left(\frac{p_2^{\frac{4}{3}}(10p_1+20p_2)}{p_1^{\frac{7}{3}}+p_2^{\frac{7}{3}}}, \frac{p_1^{\frac{4}{3}}(10p_1+20p_2)}{p_1^{\frac{7}{3}}+p_2^{\frac{7}{3}}} \right),$$

and of the second trader:

(9) $$\overline{\mathbf{x}}^2(\mathbf{p}) = \left(\frac{p_2^{\frac{4}{3}}(20p_1+10p_2)}{p_1^{\frac{7}{3}}+p_2^{\frac{7}{3}}}, \frac{p_1^{\frac{4}{3}}(20p_1+10p_2)}{p_1^{\frac{7}{3}}+p_2^{\frac{7}{3}}} \right).$$

Adding the demand functions of both traders, we get the global demand function for both consumer goods:

(10) $$\overline{\mathbf{x}}(\overline{\mathbf{p}}) = \overline{\mathbf{x}}^1(\mathbf{p}) + \overline{\mathbf{x}}^2(\mathbf{p}) = \left(\frac{p_2^{\frac{4}{3}}(30p_1+30p_2)}{p_1^{\frac{7}{3}}+p_2^{\frac{7}{3}}}, \frac{p_1^{\frac{4}{3}}(30p_1+30p_2)}{p_1^{\frac{7}{3}}+p_2^{\frac{7}{3}}} \right).$$

The global supply function (vector) has a form:

(11) $\bar{\mathbf{a}} = \mathbf{a}^1 + \mathbf{a}^2 = (30, 30).$

The excess demand function then has a form:

$$\mathbf{z}(\mathbf{p}) = \bar{\mathbf{x}}(\mathbf{p}) - \bar{\mathbf{a}} = \left(\frac{p_2^{\frac{4}{3}}(30p_1 + 30p_2)}{p_1^{\frac{7}{3}} + p_2^{\frac{7}{3}}}, \frac{p_1^{\frac{4}{3}}(30p_1 + 30p_2)}{p_1^{\frac{7}{3}} + p_2^{\frac{7}{3}}} \right) - (30, 30)$$

(12)

$$= \left(\frac{30p_1\left(p_2^{\frac{4}{3}} - p_1^{\frac{4}{3}}\right)p_2^{\frac{4}{3}}}{p_1^{\frac{7}{3}} + p_2^{\frac{7}{3}}}, \frac{30p_2\left(p_1^{\frac{4}{3}} - p_2^{\frac{4}{3}}\right)p_1^{\frac{4}{3}}}{p_1^{\frac{7}{3}} + p_2^{\frac{7}{3}}} \right) = \mathbf{z}(\mathbf{p})$$

Let us notice that the excess demand function is homogeneous of degree 0 because:

$$\forall \lambda > 0 \quad \mathbf{z}(\lambda \mathbf{p}) = \left(\frac{\lambda^{\frac{7}{3}}\left(p_2^{\frac{4}{3}}(30p_1 + 30p_2) - 30p_1^{\frac{7}{3}} - 30p_2^{\frac{7}{3}}\right)}{\lambda^{\frac{7}{3}}\left(p_1^{\frac{7}{3}} + p_2^{\frac{7}{3}}\right)}, \right.$$

(13)

$$\left. \frac{\lambda^{\frac{7}{3}}\left(p_2^{\frac{4}{3}}(30p_1 + 30p_2) - 30p_1^{\frac{7}{3}} - 30p_2^{\frac{7}{3}}\right)}{\lambda^{\frac{7}{3}}\left(p_1^{\frac{7}{3}} + p_2^{\frac{7}{3}}\right)} \right)$$

$$= \left(\frac{30p_1\left(p_2^{\frac{4}{3}} - p_1^{\frac{4}{3}}\right)p_2^{\frac{4}{3}}}{p_1^{\frac{7}{3}} + p_2^{\frac{7}{3}}}, \frac{30p_2\left(p_1^{\frac{4}{3}} - p_2^{\frac{4}{3}}\right)p_1^{\frac{4}{3}}}{p_1^{\frac{7}{3}} + p_2^{\frac{7}{3}}} \right) = \mathbf{z}(\mathbf{p})$$

Which means that the excess demand for any commodity does not depend on the absolute price level of both goods, but on the relationship between the prices of goods.

Moreover, the function of excess demand satisfies Walras's law, because:

(14) $$\forall \mathbf{p} > 0 \quad \langle \mathbf{p}, \mathbf{z}(\mathbf{p}) \rangle = p_1 \frac{30p_1\left(p_2^{\frac{4}{3}} - p_1^{\frac{4}{3}}\right)p_2^{\frac{4}{3}}}{p_1^{\frac{7}{3}} + p_2^{\frac{7}{3}}} + p_2 \frac{30p_2\left(p_1^{\frac{4}{3}} - p_2^{\frac{4}{3}}\right)p_1^{\frac{4}{3}}}{p_1^{\frac{7}{3}} + p_2^{\frac{7}{3}}} = 0,$$

which means that for any positive vector of consumer goods' prices, the value of global demand is equal to the value of global supply of both goods.

Let us determine the Walrasian equilibrium price vector $\bar{\mathbf{p}} > 0$ as a solution of a following system of equations:

(15) $$\mathbf{z}(\mathbf{p}) = \left(\frac{30p_1\left(p_2^{\frac{4}{3}} - p_1^{\frac{4}{3}}\right)p_2^{\frac{4}{3}}}{p_1^{\frac{7}{3}} + p_2^{\frac{7}{3}}}, \frac{30p_2\left(p_1^{\frac{4}{3}} - p_2^{\frac{4}{3}}\right)p_2^{\frac{4}{3}}}{p_1^{\frac{7}{3}} + p_2^{\frac{7}{3}}} \right) = (0, 0),$$

which can be written in an equivalent form:

(17) $$\begin{aligned} -\bar{p}_1^{\frac{4}{3}} + \bar{p}_2^{\frac{4}{3}} &= 0 \\ \bar{p}_2^{\frac{4}{3}} - \bar{p}_1^{\frac{4}{3}} &= 0 \end{aligned}$$

resulting in:

(18) $\overline{p}_1 = \overline{p}_2 = \lambda > 0$,

therefore, the Walrasian equilibrium price vector, determined to an accuracy of a structure, has the following form:

(19) $\overline{\mathbf{p}} = \lambda(1, 1)$.

Having this, after substituting (19) to (8) and (9), we can determine the values of the demand functions of both traders when prices are given by the Walrasian equilibrium price vector:

(20) $\overline{\mathbf{x}}^1(\overline{\mathbf{p}}) = (15, 15)$
(21) $\overline{\mathbf{x}}^2(\overline{\mathbf{p}}) = (15, 15)$

and the Walrasian equilibrium allocation:

(22) $\overline{\mathbf{x}}(\overline{\mathbf{p}}) = \left(\overline{\mathbf{x}}^1(\overline{\mathbf{p}}), \overline{\mathbf{x}}^2(\overline{\mathbf{p}})\right) = (15, 15, 15, 15)$,

while the initial allocation is:

(23) $\mathbf{a} = \left(\mathbf{a}^1, \mathbf{a}^2\right) = (10, 20, 20, 10)$.

Let us notice that in the Walrasian equilibrium state, the relation between equilibrium prices is 1 : 1. This means that traders exchange goods in the relation 1 unit of the first good for 1 unit of the second good.

Since the utility functions of both traders are the same, their preferences to own each of the goods are also the same. Thus, in the Walrasian equilibrium state, as a result of the exchange made by the Walrasian equilibrium prices, both traders will have identical bundles of goods. It is also worth noticing that in the only state of the Walrasian equilibrium, an increase in utility of bundles of goods purchased by traders with respect to utility of the initial consumption bundles will be the same for both traders.

Figure 3.5 presents geometrical illustrations of sets of allocations: of the Walrasian equilibrium $W(\mathbf{a})$ (indicated by a single point $\overline{\mathbf{x}}(\overline{\mathbf{p}})$), optimal in the Pareto sense and accepted in the same time $C(\mathbf{a})$, as well as a set $F(\mathbf{a})$ of the allocations feasible with regard to the initial allocation:$\mathbf{a} = (10, 20, 20, 10)$.

Since the optimal solutions to both consumption utility maximization problems must lie on the budget lines respective to each of the traders, having the Walrasian equilibrium price vector we get:

(24) $\overline{p}_1\overline{x}_{11} + \overline{p}_2\overline{x}_{12} = 10\overline{p}_1 + 20\overline{p}_2 \iff \overline{x}_{11} + \overline{x}_{12} = 30$,

and

(25) $\overline{p}_1\overline{x}_{21} + \overline{p}_2\overline{x}_{22} = 10\overline{p}_1 + 20\overline{p}_2 \iff \overline{x}_{21} + \overline{x}_2 = 30$.

This means that the budget lines of traders are not only parallel but also coincide, because each of them includes the initial bundle of goods each of the traders came to the market with. It is not difficult to notice that an angle of incline of both budget

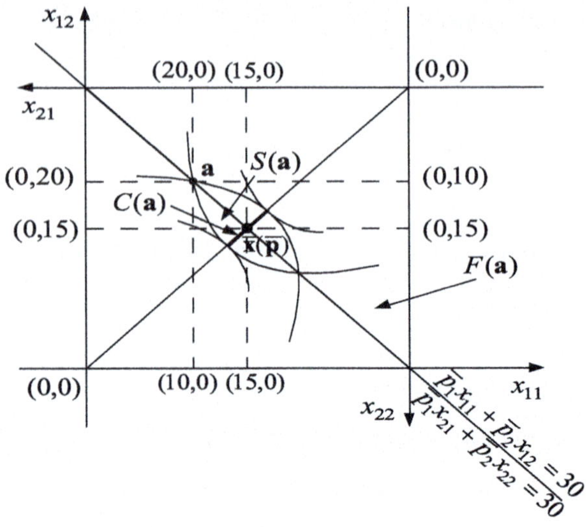

Fig. 3.5 Edgeworth box in case of subadditive utility functions (E3.2)

lines with respect to the horizontal axes is 45° in the coordinate system of each of the traders.

It is also easy to notice that: $W(\mathbf{a}) \subset C(\mathbf{a}) \subset S(\mathbf{a}) \subset F(\mathbf{a}) \subset \mathbb{R}^4_+$. This means that the only Walrasian equilibrium allocation corresponding to the only Walrasian equilibrium price vector, determined to an accuracy of a structure, is a Pareto optimal allocation, accepted and feasible with regard to an initial allocation.

E3.3. Using the Edgeworth box for the static Arrow-Hurwicz model of a market with two traders and two goods present a geometric illustration of a case when there exists no Walrasian equilibrium price vector in this model.

Solution

There is given a market of two traders and two goods described by the static Arrow-Hurwicz model, in which:

$i = 1, 2$—consumer goods,

$k = 1, 2$—traders (consumers),

$X = \mathbb{R}^2_+$—a goods' space,

$\mathbf{a}^1 = (a_{11}, a_{12})$, $\mathbf{a}^2 = (a_{21}, a_{22})$,—initial bundles the consumers come to the market with,

$\mathbf{p} = (p_1, p_2) \in \text{int}\mathbb{R}^2_+$—a vector of goods' prices,

$\mathbf{x}^k = (x_{k1}, x_{k2}) \in \mathbb{R}^2_+$—a consumption bundle the k-th consumer wants to purchase,

$I^1(p_1, p_2) = 10p_1 + 20p_2$, $I^2(p_1, p_2) = 20p_1 + 10p_2$—incomes of traders.

Utility functions of traders have forms: $u^1(x_{11}, x_{12})$, $u^1(x_{11}, x_{12})$.

The consumption utility maximization problems for two traders are given:

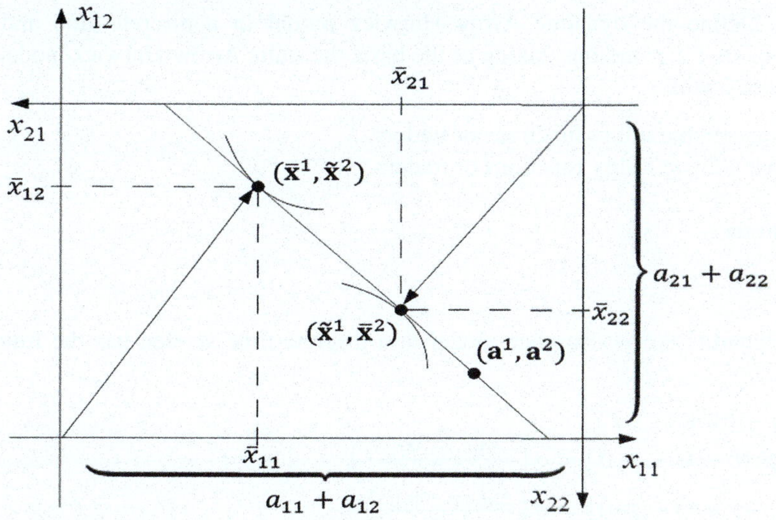

Fig. 3.6 Optimal baskets of goods of both traders in case of disequilibrium (E3.3)

$$\begin{aligned} &u^1(x_{11}, x_{12}) \to \max, && u^2(x_{21}, x_{22}) \to \max, \\ &p_1x_{11} + p_2x_{12} \leq 10a_{11} + 20a_{12}, && p_1x_{21} + p_2x_{22} \leq 10a_{21} + 20a_{22}, \\ &x_{11}, x_{12} \geq 0. && x_{21}, x_{22} \geq 0. \end{aligned}$$

Let us denote by $\left(\overline{\mathbf{x}}^1, \overset{\sim 2}{\mathbf{x}}\right)$ an allocation feasible with regard to the initial allocation $(\mathbf{a}^1, \mathbf{a}^2)$, in which the first trader receives an optimal bundle of goods $\overline{\mathbf{x}}^1$ and by $\left(\overset{\sim 1}{\mathbf{x}}, \overline{\mathbf{x}}^2\right)$ an allocation feasible with regard to the initial allocation $(\mathbf{a}^1, \mathbf{a}^2)$, in which the second trader receives an optimal bundle of goods $\overline{\mathbf{x}}^2$. If the price vector $\mathbf{p} = (p_1, p_2)$ is not a Walrasian equilibrium price vector, then allocations $\left(\overline{\mathbf{x}}^1, \overset{\sim 2}{\mathbf{x}}\right)$ and $\left(\overset{\sim 1}{\mathbf{x}}, \overline{\mathbf{x}}^2\right)$ are not Walrasian equilibrium allocations. In Fig. 3.6, it has been shown that although both allocations are feasibly located on the overlapping budget lines of both traders, the bundles $\overset{\sim 1}{\mathbf{x}}$ and $\overset{\sim 2}{\mathbf{x}}$ are not the optimal bundles of both traders, as they are located on lower indifference curves than the optimal bundles $\overline{\mathbf{x}}^1$ and $\overline{\mathbf{x}}^2$.

Let us notice that: $p_1\overline{x}_{11} + p_2\overline{x}_{12} < p_1a_{11} + p_2a_{12}$ and that $p_1\overline{x}_{21} + p_2\overline{x}_{22} > p_1a_{21} + +p_2a_{22}$.

This means that in the case of the first good, there is a surplus of the global supply over the global demand, and in the case of the second good there is an excess of the global demand over the global supply.

E3.4. Define the dynamic Arrow-Hurwicz model in a discrete-time and in a continuous-time versions, taking as the basis the static Arrow-Hurwicz model from Exercise 2 with:

A. logarithmic utility functions of traders,
B. subadditive utility functions of traders.

Solutions

Ad A

The dynamic Arrow-Hurwicz model in a discrete-time version has the following form:

(1) $t \in [0, 1, \ldots, T)$
(2) $p_1(t+1) - p_1(t) = \sigma\left(\frac{-30p_1(t)+30p_2(t)}{2p_1(t)}\right)$
(3) $p_2(t+1) - p_2(t) = \sigma\left(\frac{30p_1(t)-30p_2(t)}{2p_2(t)}\right)$
(4) $p_1(0) = p_1^0 > 0$
(5) $p_2(0) = p_2^0 > 0.$

The dynamic Arrow-Hurwicz model in a continuous-time version takes a form:

(6) $t \in [0, T)$
(7) $\frac{dp_1(t)}{dt} = \sigma\left(\frac{-30p_1(t)+30p_2(t)}{2p_1(t)}\right)$
(8) $\frac{dp_2(t)}{dt} = \sigma\left(\frac{30p_1(t)-30p_2(t)}{2p_2(t)}\right)$
(9) $p_1(0) = p_1^0 > 0$
(10) $p_2(0) = p_2^0 > 0.$

Ad B

The dynamic Arrow-Hurwicz model in a discrete-time version takes a form:

(11) $t \in [0, 1, \ldots, T)$

(12) $p_1(t+1) - p_1(t) = \sigma\left(\frac{30p_1(t)\left(p_2^{\frac{4}{3}}(t)-p_1^{\frac{4}{3}}(t)\right)p_2^{\frac{4}{3}}(t)}{p_1^{\frac{7}{3}}(t)+p_2^{\frac{7}{3}}(t)}\right)$

(13) $p_2(t+1) - p_2(t) = \sigma\left(\frac{30p_2(t)\left(p_1^{\frac{4}{3}}(t)-p_2^{\frac{4}{3}}(t)\right)p_1^{\frac{4}{3}}(t)}{p_1^{\frac{7}{3}}(t)+p_2^{\frac{7}{3}}(t)}\right)$

(14) $p_1(0) = p_1^0 > 0$
(15) $p_2(0) = p_2^0 > 0.$

The dynamic Arrow-Hurwicz model in a continuous-time version has the following form:

(16) $t \in [0, T)$

(17) $\frac{dp_1(t)}{dt} = \sigma\left(\frac{30p_1(t)\left(p_2^{\frac{4}{3}}(t) - p_1^{\frac{4}{3}}(t)\right)p_2^{\frac{4}{3}}(t)}{p_1^{\frac{7}{3}}(t) + p_2^{\frac{7}{3}}(t)}\right)$

(18) $\frac{dp_2(t)}{dt} = \sigma\left(\frac{30p_2(t)\left(p_1^{\frac{4}{3}}(t) - p_2^{\frac{4}{3}}(t)\right)p_1^{\frac{4}{3}}(t)}{p_1^{\frac{7}{3}}(t) + p_2^{\frac{7}{3}}(t)}\right)$

(19) $p_1(0) = p_1^0 > 0$

(20) $p_2(0) = p_2^0 > 0.$

E3.5. For the dynamic Arrow-Hurwicz model in a discrete-time version from Exercise 3.4 with logarithmic utility functions of traders and the Walrasian equilibrium price vector known from Exercise 3.2 determine a feasible price trajectory for a few subsequent periods taking some value of parameter $\sigma_i = \sigma > 0$. Present a geometric illustration of this trajectory in the state space and in the phase space.

Solution

Utility functions of traders are given in the following form:

$$u^1(x_{11}, x_{12}) = \ln x_{11} + \ln x_{12}, \quad u^2(x_{21}, x_{22}) = \ln x_{21} + \ln x_{22}.$$

Their initial bundles and incomes are of the following form:

$$\mathbf{a}^1 = (10, 20), \mathbf{a}^2 = (20, 10), \quad I^1(\mathbf{p}) = 10p_1 + 20p_2, I^2(\mathbf{p}) = 20p_1 + 10p_2$$

From the solutions to the utility maximization problems in Exercise 3.2, we know that demand functions of traders are given as:

$$\varphi^1(\mathbf{p}, I^1(\mathbf{p})) = \left(\frac{I^1(\mathbf{p})}{2p_1}, \frac{I^1(\mathbf{p})}{2p_2}\right) = \left(5 + 10\frac{p_2}{p_1}, 5\frac{p_1}{p_2} + 10\right) = \varphi^1(\mathbf{p}) = \overline{\mathbf{x}}_1(\mathbf{p})$$

$$\varphi^2(\mathbf{p}, I^2(\mathbf{p})) = \left(\frac{I^2(\mathbf{p})}{2p_1}, \frac{I^2(\mathbf{p})}{2p_2}\right) = \left(10 + 5\frac{p_2}{p_1}, 10\frac{p_1}{p_2} + 5\right) = \varphi^2(\mathbf{p}) = \overline{\mathbf{x}}_2(\mathbf{p}).$$

From Exercise 3.2, we also know that a function of global demand has a form:

$$\overline{\mathbf{x}}(\mathbf{p}) = \overline{\mathbf{x}}^1(\mathbf{p}) + \overline{\mathbf{x}}^2(\mathbf{p}) = \left(15 + 15\frac{p_2}{p_1}, 15\frac{p_1}{p_2} + 15\right).$$

Hence, a function of excess demand has a form:

$$\mathbf{z}(\mathbf{p}) = \overline{\mathbf{x}}(\mathbf{p}) - \overline{\mathbf{a}} = \left(15 + 15\frac{p_2}{p_1}, 15\frac{p_1}{p_2} + 15\right)$$
$$- (30, 30) = \left(15\frac{p_2}{p_1} - 15, 15\frac{p_1}{p_2} - 15\right)$$

Thus, the resulting Walrasian equilibrium price vector is given as:

$$\overline{\mathbf{p}} = \lambda(1, 1), \quad \lambda > 0.$$

Table 3.1 Price trajectories by different values of σ (E3.5)

	1st good	2nd good
equilibrium prices:	1	1
equilibrium prices ratio p2/p1:	1	

sigma	0,05			
prices	p_1	p_2	p_2/p_1	comparison with equilibrium
0	6	3	0,5	0,5
1	5,625	3,75	0,666667	0,333333333
2	5,375	4,125	0,767442	0,23255814
3	5,20058	4,35227	0,836882	0,163118045
4	5,07824	4,49846	0,885829	0,114170871
5	4,99261	4,59512	0,920384	0,07961643
6	4,9329	4,66	0,944677	0,05532325
7	4,89141	4,70392	0,96167	0,038330337
8	4,86266	4,73381	0,973503	0,026497431
9	4,84279	4,75423	0,981713	0,018287187
10	4,82907	4,7682	0,987394	0,01260588
11	4,81962	4,77777	0,991318	0,008682263
12	4,81311	4,78434	0,994024	0,005976342
13	4,80863	4,78885	0,995888	0,004112052
14	4,80554	4,79195	0,997171	0,002828506
15	4,80342	4,79408	0,998055	0,001945224
16	4,80198	4,79554	0,998662	0,001337589
17	4,80096	4,79654	0,99908	0,000919675
18	4,80027	4,79723	0,999368	0,000632293
19	4,79979	4,79771	0,999565	0,000434693
20	4,79947	4,79803	0,999701	0,000298838
21	4,79924	4,79826	0,999795	0,000205435
22	4,79909	4,79841	0,999859	0,000141224
23	4,79898	4,79852	0,999903	9,70825E-05

sigma	0,35			
prices	p_1	p_2	p_2/p_1	comparison with equilibrium
0	6	3	0,5	0,5
1	3,375	8,25	2,44444	1,444444444
2	10,9583	5,14773	0,46975	0,53024542
3	8,17454	11,0738	1,35467	0,354665734
4	10,0365	9,69927	0,9664	0,033604146
5	9,86012	9,88183	1,0022	0,002201681
6	9,87168	9,87029	0,99986	0,000140141
7	9,87094	9,87103	1,00001	8,93093E-06
8	9,87099	9,87098	1	5,69108E-07
9	9,87099	9,87099	1	3,62656E-08
10	9,87099	9,87099	1	2,31098E-09
11	9,87099	9,87099	1	1,47264E-10
12	9,87099	9,87099	1	9,38427E-12
13	9,87099	9,87099	1	5,97966E-13
14	9,87099	9,87099	1	3,79696E-14
15	9,87099	9,87099	1	2,44249E-15
16	9,87099	9,87099	1	2,22045E-16
17	9,87099	9,87099	1	2,22045E-16
18	9,87099	9,87099	1	2,22045E-16
19	9,87099	9,87099	1	2,22045E-16
20	9,87099	9,87099	1	2,22045E-16
21	9,87099	9,87099	1	2,22045E-16
22	9,87099	9,87099	1	2,22045E-16
23	9,87099	9,87099	1	2,22045E-16

sigma	1,25			
prices	p_1	p_2	p_2/p_1	comparison with equilibrium
0	6	3	0,5	0,5
1	-3,375	21,75	-6,44444	7,444444444
2	-142,958	0,09052	-0,00063	1,000633172
3	-161,72	-29631,5	183,2267	182,2266849
4	3255,03	-29650,1	-9,10901	10,10901083
5	3065,49	-29670,9	-9,67902	10,67902362
6	2865,25	-29691,6	-10,3626	11,36263984
7	2652,2	-29712,2	-11,2028	12,20281419
8	2423,4	-29732,6	-12,2689	13,26894284
9	2174,61	-29752,9	-13,6819	14,68193278
10	1899,32	-29773	-15,6756	16,67557347
11	1586,66	-29792,9	-18,7772	19,7771782
12	1215,83	-29812,7	-24,5203	25,52034692
13	737,328	-29832,2	-40,4599	41,45988098
14	-40,0451	-29851,4	745,4454	744,4454289
15	13918,3	-29870,1	-2,1461	3,146103709
16	13859,3	-29897,6	-2,15722	3,157221445
17	13800,1	-29925,1	-2,16846	3,168463719
18	13740,7	-29952,5	-2,17983	3,17983302
19	13681,1	-29979,8	-2,19133	3,191331907
20	13621,3	-30007,1	-2,20296	3,202963012
21	13561,2	-30034,4	-2,21473	3,214729042
22	13500,9	-30061,6	-2,22683	3,226832781
23	13440,4	-30088,8	-2,23868	3,238677098

A dynamic discrete-time Arrow-Hurwicz model for the data given in the exercise takes a form:

$$\begin{cases} p_1(t+1) = p_1(t) + \sigma\left(15\frac{p_2}{p_1} - 15\right) \\ p_2(t+1) = p_2(t) + \sigma\left(15\frac{p_1}{p_2} - 15\right) \end{cases}$$

where initial prices are given:

$$\begin{cases} p_1(0) = p_1^0 > 0 \\ p_2(0) = p_2^0 > 0 \end{cases}$$

and prices change over time given as a discrete variable $t = 0, 1, 2, \dots T$.

Let us take the initial prices, for example $p_1(0) = 6$, $p_2(0) = 3$ and consider a few values for σ, for example 0.05, 0.35, 1.25. The price trajectories are obtained in an Excel file named Exercise 3.5.xlsx and presented in Table 3.1.

When $\sigma = 0.05$, the price trajectories are feasible and a structure of prices stabilizes around the equilibrium price structure in 23-rd period with prices' levels $\overline{p}_1 = \overline{p}_2 \approx 4.8$. When $\sigma = 0.35$, the price trajectories are feasible and a structure of prices stabilizes around the equilibrium price structure in seventh period with levels $\overline{p}_1 = \overline{p}_2 \approx 9.87$. When $\sigma = 1.25$, the price trajectories are infeasible.

The price trajectories in the state space and in the phase space are presented in Figs. 3.7 and 3.8.[3]

E3.6. For the dynamic Arrow-Hurwicz model in a discrete-time version from Exercise 3.4 with subadditive utility functions of traders and the Walrasian equilibrium price vector known from Exercise 3.2 determine a feasible price trajectory for a few

[3] The price trajectories in the state space are obtained using an Excel file named Exercise 3.5.xlsx and a MATLAB file named Exercise_3_5_1.m. In the phase space, they are obtained using a MATLAB file named Exercise_3_5_2.m.

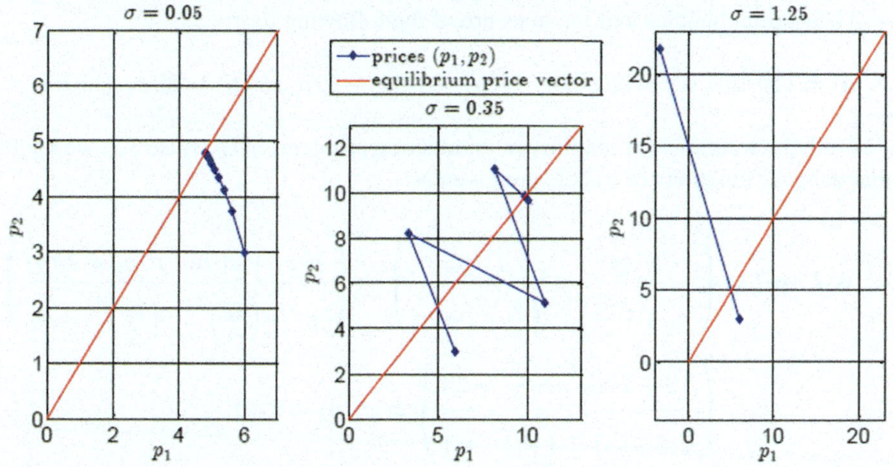

Fig. 3.7 Price trajectories in state space (E3.5)

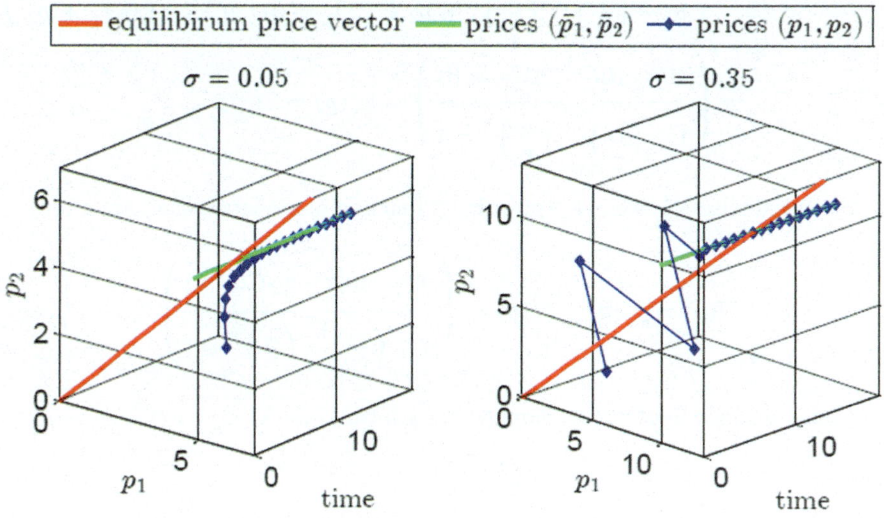

Fig. 3.8 Price trajectories in phase space (E3.5)

subsequent periods taking some value of parameter $\sigma_i = \sigma > 0$. Present a geometric illustration of this trajectory in the state space and in the phase space.

Solution

Utility functions of traders are given in the following form:

$$u^1(x_{11}, x_{12}) = x_{11}^{\frac{1}{4}} + x_{11}^{\frac{1}{4}}, \quad u^2(x_{21}, x_{22}) = x_{21}^{\frac{1}{4}} + x_{21}^{\frac{1}{4}}.$$

Their initial bundles and incomes are of the following form:

$$\mathbf{a}^1 = (10, 20), \mathbf{a}^2 = (20, 10) \quad I^1(\mathbf{p}) = 10p_1 + 20p_2, I^2(\mathbf{p}) = 20p_1 + 10p_2$$

From the solutions to the utility maximization problems in Exercise 3.2, we know that demand functions of traders are given as:

$$\varphi^1(\mathbf{p}, I^1(\mathbf{p})) = \left(\frac{I^1(\mathbf{p})}{p_1 + \left(\frac{p_1^4}{p_2}\right)^{\frac{1}{3}}}, \frac{I^1(\mathbf{p})}{\left(\frac{p_2^4}{p_1}\right)^{\frac{1}{3}} + p_2} \right) = \left(\frac{10p_1 + 20p_2}{p_1 + \left(\frac{p_1^4}{p_2}\right)^{\frac{1}{3}}}, \frac{10p_1 + 20p_2}{\left(\frac{p_2^4}{p_1}\right)^{\frac{1}{3}} + p_2} \right)$$

$$= \left(\frac{10 + 20\frac{p_2}{p_1}}{1 + \left(\frac{p_1}{p_2}\right)^{\frac{1}{3}}}, \frac{10\frac{p_1}{p_2} + 20}{\left(\frac{p_2}{p_1}\right)^{\frac{1}{3}} + 1} \right) = \varphi^1(\mathbf{p}) = \overline{\mathbf{x}}_1(\mathbf{p})$$

$$\varphi^2(\mathbf{p}, I^2(\mathbf{p})) = \left(\frac{I^2(\mathbf{p})}{p_1 + \left(\frac{p_1^4}{p_2}\right)^{\frac{1}{3}}}, \frac{I^2(\mathbf{p})}{\left(\frac{p_2^4}{p_1}\right)^{\frac{1}{3}} + p_2} \right) = \left(\frac{20p_1 + 10p_2}{p_1 + \left(\frac{p_1^4}{p_2}\right)^{\frac{1}{3}}}, \frac{20p_1 + 10p_2}{\left(\frac{p_2^4}{p_1}\right)^{\frac{1}{3}} + p_2} \right)$$

$$= \left(\frac{20 + 10\frac{p_2}{p_1}}{1 + \left(\frac{p_1}{p_2}\right)^{\frac{1}{3}}}, \frac{20\frac{p_1}{p_2} + 10}{\left(\frac{p_2}{p_1}\right)^{\frac{1}{3}} + 1} \right) = \varphi^2(\mathbf{p}) = \overline{\mathbf{x}}_2(\mathbf{p}).$$

From Exercise 3.2, we also know that a function of global demand has a form:

$$\overline{\mathbf{x}}(\mathbf{p}) = \overline{\mathbf{x}}^1(\mathbf{p}) + \overline{\mathbf{x}}^2(\mathbf{p}) = \left(\frac{30 + 30\frac{p_2}{p_1}}{1 + \left(\frac{p_1}{p_2}\right)^{\frac{1}{3}}}, \frac{30\frac{p_1}{p_2} + 30}{\left(\frac{p_2}{p_1}\right)^{\frac{1}{3}} + 1} \right).$$

Hence, a function of excess demand has a form:

$$\mathbf{z}(\mathbf{p}) = \overline{\mathbf{x}}(\mathbf{p}) - \overline{\mathbf{a}} = \left(\frac{30 + 30\frac{p_2}{p_1}}{1 + \left(\frac{p_1}{p_2}\right)^{\frac{1}{3}}}, \frac{30\frac{p_1}{p_2} + 30}{\left(\frac{p_2}{p_1}\right)^{\frac{1}{3}} + 1} \right) - (30, 30).$$

Thus, the resulting Walrasian equilibrium price vector is given as:

$$\overline{\mathbf{p}} = \lambda(1, 1), \quad \lambda > 0.$$

A dynamic discrete-time Arrow-Hurwicz model for the data given in the exercise takes a form:

Table 3.2 Price trajectories by different values of σ (E3.6)

	1st good	2nd good
equilibrium prices:	1	1
equilibrium prices ratio p2/p1:	1	

sigma 0,05 prices	p_1	p_2	p_2/p_1	comparison with equilibrium
0	6	3	0,5	0,5
1	5,49561	4,00878	0,729451	0,270548675
2	5,224564	4,380355	0,838415	0,161584597
3	5,062887	4,573192	0,903278	0,096722427
4	4,966146	4,680292	0,94244	0,057560496
5	4,908681	4,741372	0,965935	0,034064736
6	4,874516	4,776639	0,979921	0,020079366
7	4,854436	4,79713	0,988195	0,011805017
8	4,842631	4,809076	0,993071	0,006929206
9	4,836702	4,816063	0,995937	0,00406328
10	4,831639	4,820133	0,997619	0,002381319
11	4,829258	4,82252	0,998605	0,001395111
12	4,827862	4,823917	0,999183	0,000817169
13	4,827045	4,824736	0,999521	0,000478689
14	4,826567	4,825214	0,99972	0,000280275
15	4,826286	4,825494	0,999836	0,00016413
16	4,826122	4,825658	0,999904	9,61125E-05
17	4,826026	4,825755	0,999944	5,62816E-05

sigma 0,35	p_1	p_2	p_2/p_1	comparison with equilibrium
0	6	3	0,5	0,5
1	2,46927	10,06146	4,07467	3,074669815
2	24,73749	4,596423	0,185808	0,814192022
3	18,76109	36,76079	1,959416	0,959416388
4	25,63268	33,30493	1,304409	0,304408903
5	27,66622	31,66921	1,144688	0,144688492
6	28,67939	30,78411	1,073388	0,073388052
7	29,19315	30,30547	1,038102	0,038102172
8	29,45987	30,04864	1,019982	0,019982026
9	29,59975	29,91141	1,010529	0,010529068
10	29,67345	29,83847	1,005561	0,005561149
11	29,71238	29,79976	1,002941	0,002940782
12	29,73296	29,77923	1,001556	0,001556086
13	29,74386	29,76836	1,000824	0,000823658
14	29,74962	29,7626	1,000436	0,000436049
15	29,75268	29,75964	1,000231	0,000230868
16	29,75429	29,75793	1,000122	0,00012224
17	29,75515	29,75707	1,000065	6,47252E-05

sigma 1,25	p_1	p_2	p_2/p_1	comparison with equilibrium
0	6	3	0,5	0,5
1	-6,60976	28,2196	-4,269375	5,269374801
2	-363,736	-55,429	0,1523877	0,847612264
3	-386,191	91,91994	-0,238017	1,238016801
4	-470,269	-261,282	0,5556134	0,444386618
5	-481,439	-241,16	0,5009153	0,499084704
6	-494,026	-216,034	0,4372934	0,562706562
7	-508,267	-183,464	0,3609596	0,639040447
8	-524,642	-138,377	0,2638053	0,736194666
9	-543,623	-66,4241	0,1222102	0,877789756
10	-567,066	126,2164	-0,222578	1,222577941
11	-649,411	-243,746	0,3753339	0,62466607
12	-666,299	-201,418	0,3027485	0,69725149
13	-683,173	-142,377	0,208406	0,791594045
14	-703,806	-43,372	0,0616249	0,938375128
15	-730,034	382,2287	-0,523677	1,523676579
16	-841,753	168,8622	-0,200596	1,200596874
17	-921,578	-229,086	0,248579	0,751421018

$$\begin{cases} p_1(t+1) = p_1(t) + \sigma\left(\dfrac{30+30\frac{p_2}{p_1}}{1+\left(\frac{p_1}{p_2}\right)^{\frac{1}{3}}} - 30\right) \\ p_2(t+1) = p_2(t) + \sigma\left(\dfrac{30\frac{p_1}{p_2}+30}{\left(\frac{p_2}{p_1}\right)^{\frac{1}{3}}+1} - 30\right) \end{cases}$$

where initial prices are given:

$$\begin{cases} p_1(0) = p_1^0 > 0 \\ p_2(0) = p_2^0 > 0 \end{cases}$$

and prices change over time given as a discrete variable $t = 0, 1, 2, \ldots T$.

Let us take the initial prices, for example $p_1(0) = 6$, $p_2(0) = 3$ and consider a few values for σ, for example 0.05, 0.35, 1.25. The price trajectories are obtained in an Excel file named Exercise 3.6.xlsx and presented in Table 3.2.

When $\sigma = 0.05$, the price trajectories are feasible and a structure of prices stabilizes around the equilibrium price structure in 16-th period with prices' levels $\overline{p}_1 = \overline{p}_2 \approx 4.83$. When $\sigma = 0.35$, the price trajectories are feasible and a structure of prices stabilizes around the equilibrium price structure in 17-th period with levels $\overline{p}_1 = \overline{p}_2 \approx 29.76$. When $\sigma = 1.25$, the price trajectories are infeasible.

The price trajectories in the state space and in the phase space are presented in Figs. 3.9 and 3.10.[4]

E3.7. Two traders come to a market with bundles of goods: $\mathbf{a}^1 = (10, 20)$, $\mathbf{a}^2 = (20, 10)$. Their utility functions are following:

(a) $u^1(x_{11}, x_{12}) = \ln x_{11} + \ln x_{12}$, $u^2(x_{21}, x_{22}) = \ln x_{21} + \ln x_{22}$,
(b) $u^1(x_{11}, x_{12}) = x_{11}^{1/4} + x_{12}^{1/4}$, $u^2(x_{21}, x_{22}) = x_{21}^{1/4} + x_{22}^{1/4}$,

[4] The price trajectories in the state space are obtained using an Excel file named Exercise 3.6.xlsx and a MATLAB file named Exercise_3_6_1.m. In the phase space, they are obtained using a MATLAB file named Exercise_3_6_2.m.

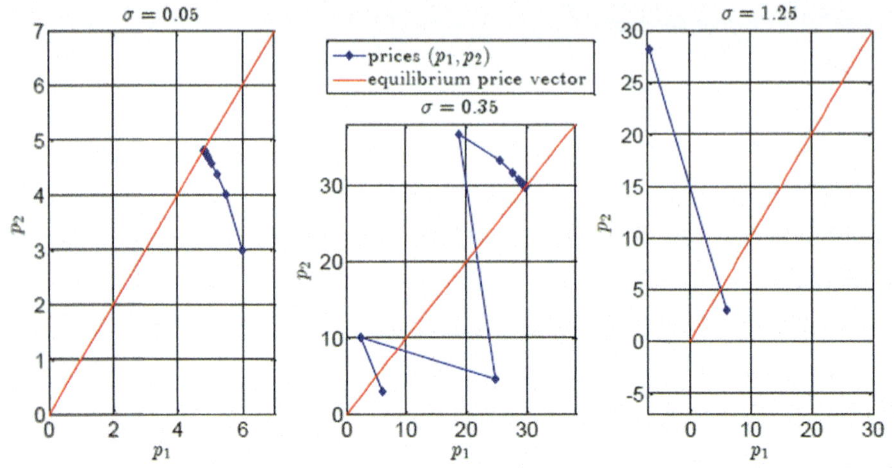

Fig. 3.9 Price trajectories in state space (E3.6)

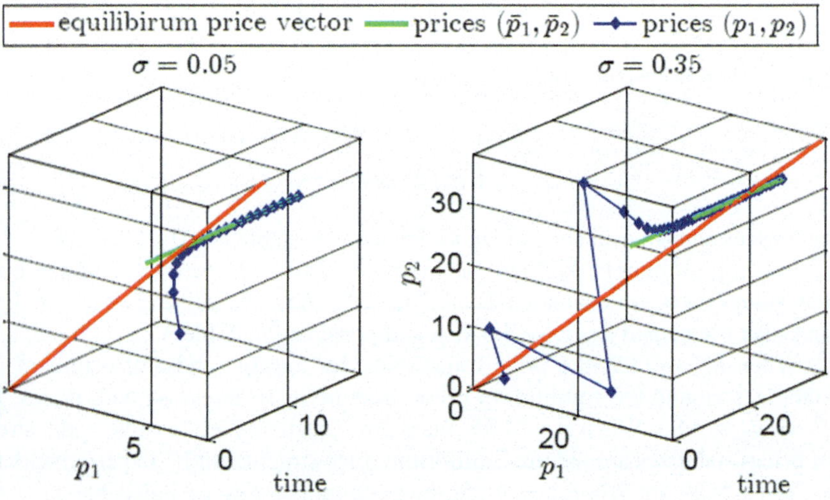

Fig. 3.10 Price trajectories in phase space (E3.6)

Consider a discrete-time version of dynamic discrete-time Arrow-Hurwicz model. A broker announces initial prices:

$$\mathbf{p}(0) = (2, 4).$$

Using a form of the excess demand function and a structure of the Walrasian equilibrium price vector found in Exercise 2 for the static Arrow-Hurwicz model:

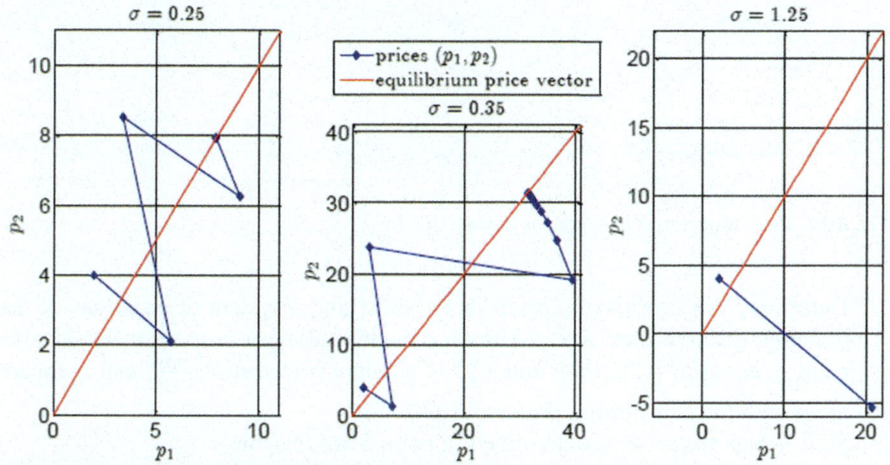

Fig. 3.11 Price trajectories in state space (E3.7 a)

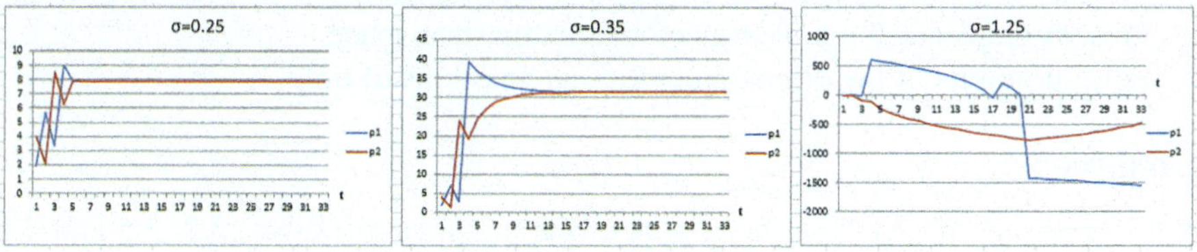

Fig. 3.12 Price trajectories as functions of time (E3.7 a)

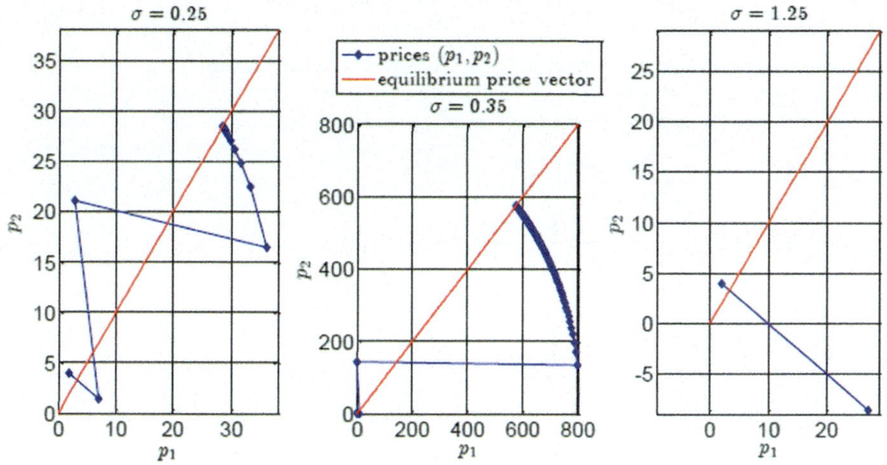

Fig. 3.13 Price trajectories in state space (E3.7 b)

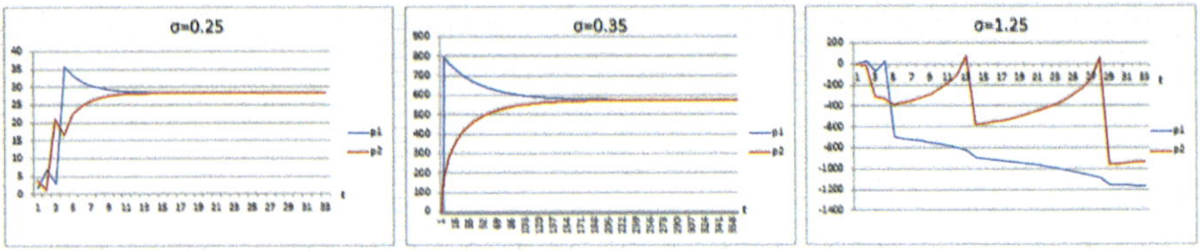

Fig. 3.14 Price trajectories as functions of time (E3.7 b)

1. Determine trajectories of a price vector satisfying a system of equations of the dynamic discrete-time Arrow-Hurwicz model, taking a proportionality coefficient σ equal to 0.25, 0.35 and 1.25. Calculate price ratios $\frac{p_2(t)}{p_1(t)}$ and compare them with the equilibrium price ratio $\frac{\overline{p}_2}{\overline{p}_1}$.
2. State which trajectories determined in point 1 are feasible.
3. State if and when (in which period) a structure of prices stabilizes around the equilibrium price structure and whether it reaches this structure in time horizon $T = 15$.
4. Present graphs of the price trajectories in the state space.
5. Present graphs of the price trajectories as functions of time.

Solutions

In this exercise, we can use the results of the previous exercises: 3.2, 3.5 and 3.6. The main results are the Walrasian equilibrium price vector:

$$\overline{\mathbf{p}} = \lambda(1, 1), \quad \lambda > 0$$

and a form of the dynamic discrete-time Arrow-Hurwicz model:

$$\text{(a)} \quad \begin{cases} p_1(t+1) = p_1(t) + \sigma\left(15\frac{p_2}{p_1} - 15\right) \\ p_2(t+1) = p_2(t) + \sigma\left(15\frac{p_1}{p_2} - 15\right) \end{cases}$$

$$\text{(b)} \quad \begin{cases} p_1(t+1) = p_1(t) + \sigma\left(\dfrac{30+30\frac{p_2}{p_1}}{1+\left(\frac{p_1}{p_2}\right)^{\frac{1}{3}}} - 30\right) \\ p_2(t+1) = p_2(t) + \sigma\left(\dfrac{30\frac{p_1}{p_2}+30}{\left(\frac{p_2}{p_1}\right)^{\frac{1}{3}}+1} - 30\right) \end{cases}$$

where prices change over time given as a discrete variable $t = 0, 1, 2, \ldots T$.

Ad 1

Initial prices announced by the broker are $p_1(0) = 2$, $p_2(0) = 4$. The price trajectories are obtained in Excel files named: Exercise 3.7 a.xlsx, Exercise 3.7 b.xlsx and presented in Tables 3.3 and 3.4.

Table 3.3 Price trajectories by different values of σ (E3.7 a)

sigma	0,25			
prices	p_1	p_2	p_2/p_1	comparison with equilibrium
0	2	4	2	1
1	5,75	2,125	0,369565	0,630434783
2	3,38587	8,52206	2,516948	1,516948352
3	9,07443	6,26196	0,690067	0,309933392
4	7,91218	7,94622	1,004302	0,004302312
5	7,92831	7,93015	1,000232	0,000232385
6	7,92918	7,92928	1,000013	1,25783E-05
7	7,92923	7,92923	1,000001	6,80891E-07
8	7,92923	7,92923	1	3,68585E-08
9	7,92923	7,92923	1	1,99525E-09
10	7,92923	7,92923	1	1,08008E-10
11	7,92923	7,92923	1	5,84666E-12
12	7,92923	7,92923	1	3,16414E-13
13	7,92923	7,92923	1	1,70974E-14
14	7,92923	7,92923	1	8,88178E-16
15	7,92923	7,92923	1	0
16	7,92923	7,92923	1	0
17	7,92923	7,92923	1	0
18	7,92923	7,92923	1	0
19	7,92923	7,92923	1	0
20	7,92923	7,92923	1	0
21	7,92923	7,92923	1	0
22	7,92923	7,92923	1	0
23	7,92923	7,92923	1	0
24	7,92923	7,92923	1	0
25	7,92923	7,92923	1	0

	0,35			
	p_1	p_2	p_2/p_1	comparison with equilibrium
0	2	4	2	1
1	7,25	1,375	0,18966	0,810344828
2	2,99569	23,8066	7,94702	6,947024199
3	39,4676	19,2174	0,48692	0,513082654
4	36,7739	24,7496	0,67302	0,326979955
5	35,0572	27,3002	0,77873	0,221267248
6	33,8956	28,7919	0,84943	0,150569556
7	33,1051	29,7226	0,89782	0,102175844
8	32,5687	30,32	0,93096	0,069043271
9	32,2062	30,7094	0,95352	0,04647586
10	31,9622	30,9653	0,96881	0,031190638
11	31,7984	31,1343	0,97911	0,020886168
12	31,6888	31,2463	0,98604	0,012964048
13	31,6155	31,3206	0,99067	0,009325909
14	31,5665	31,3701	0,99378	0,006223687
15	31,5338	31,4029	0,99585	0,004151311
16	31,5121	31,4248	0,99723	0,002768052
17	31,4975	31,4394	0,99815	0,001845296
18	31,4878	31,4491	0,99877	0,001229958
19	31,4814	31,4556	0,99918	0,000819729
20	31,4771	31,4599	0,99945	0,000546287
21	31,4742	31,4627	0,99964	0,000364042
22	31,4723	31,4647	0,99976	0,000242588
23	31,471	31,4659	0,99984	0,000161651
24	31,4702	31,4668	0,99989	0,000107716
25	31,4696	31,4673	0,99993	7,17761E-05

	1,25			
	p_1	p_2	p_2/p_1	comparison with equilibrium
0	2	4	2	1
1	20,75	-5,375	-0,259036	1,259036145
2	-2,85693	-96,5087	33,7806	32,78059605
3	611,779	-114,704	-0,187492	1,187491924
4	589,514	-233,458	-0,396018	1,396017847
5	563,338	-299,554	-0,531748	1,531748422
6	534,618	-353,566	-0,661342	1,661341852
7	503,468	-400,687	-0,795814	1,795813863
8	469,796	-442,978	-0,942914	1,942913813
9	433,367	-481,613	-1,111328	2,11132811
10	393,779	-517,224	-1,313513	2,313513106
11	350,401	-550,269	-1,570369	2,570369491
12	302,207	-580,949	-1,922357	2,92235686
13	247,412	-609,453	-2,463306	3,463306336
14	182,475	-635,814	-3,484383	4,484382931
15	98,3933	-659,946	-6,707221	7,707221335
16	-46,1171	-681,491	14,7774	13,7774008
17	212,209	-698,872	-3,293789	4,29378924
18	131,701	-723,415	-5,492873	6,492873467
19	9,96923	-746,578	-74,86307	75,86306721
20	-1412,47	-764,579	0,541305	0,458695088
21	-1421,07	-748,69	0,526848	0,473151782
22	-1429,95	-731,851	0,511804	0,488196399
23	-1439,1	-713,966	0,49612	0,503879846
24	-1448,55	-694,923	0,479738	0,520262114
25	-1458,3	-674,589	0,462585	0,537414699

Table 3.4 Price trajectories by different values of σ (E3.7 b)

sigma	0,25			
prices	p_1	p_2	p_2/p_1	comparison with equilibrium
0	2	4	2	1
1	7,0439	1,47805	0,209834	0,790165958
2	2,92605	21,1024	7,211885	6,211884772
3	36,0096	16,515	0,458627	0,54137316
4	33,2728	22,4824	0,675699	0,324301073
5	31,6467	24,889	0,786462	0,213537621
6	30,5779	26,248	0,858397	0,141602509
7	29,8696	27,0731	0,906379	0,093621183
8	29,4014	27,5897	0,938381	0,061619053
9	29,0933	27,918	0,959605	0,040394778
10	28,8913	28,1285	0,973599	0,026400801
11	28,7593	28,2641	0,982783	0,017217468
12	28,6732	28,3517	0,988788	0,011211802
13	28,6171	28,4084	0,992706	0,00729368
14	28,5807	28,4451	0,995258	0,004741645
15	28,557	28,469	0,996919	0,003081209
16	28,5415	28,4844	0,997998	0,002001651
17	28,5315	28,4944	0,9987	0,001300092
18	28,525	28,501	0,999156	0,00084432
19	28,5208	28,5052	0,999452	0,000548263
20	28,5181	28,5079	0,999644	0,000356025
21	28,5163	28,5097	0,999769	0,000231175
22	28,5151	28,5109	0,99985	0,000150104
23	28,5144	28,5116	0,999903	9,74627E-05

	0,35			
	p_1	p_2	p_2/p_1	comparison with equilibrium
0	2	4	2	1
1	9,06146	0,46927	0,05179	0,948212538
2	1,56018	145,317	93,1406	92,14063157
3	800,884	136,735	0,17073	0,82927022
4	794,77	172,545	0,2171	0,782899898
5	789,067	198,812	0,25196	0,748042087
6	783,656	220,289	0,2811	0,718896169
7	778,48	238,701	0,30663	0,693374953
8	773,506	254,925	0,32957	0,670429045
9	768,709	269,479	0,35056	0,649439778
10	764,073	282,703	0,36999	0,630005493
11	759,585	294,834	0,38815	0,611847776
12	755,232	306,047	0,40524	0,59476423
13	751,007	316,473	0,4214	0,578802274
14	746,902	326,214	0,43676	0,563243536
15	742,911	335,354	0,45141	0,54859402
16	739,026	343,959	0,46542	0,534577634
17	735,244	352,085	0,47887	0,52113177
18	731,56	359,778	0,4918	0,50820419
19	727,97	367,078	0,50425	0,495750784
20	724,47	374,019	0,51627	0,483733903
21	721,057	380,631	0,52788	0,472121115
22	717,727	386,938	0,53912	0,460884245
23	714,479	392,964	0,55	0,449966834

	1,25			
	p_1	p_2	p_2/p_1	comparison with equilibrium
0	2	4	2	1
1	27,2195	-8,60975	-0,316306	1,316308161
2	-65,1016	-300,48	4,615563	3,615562841
3	28,9631	-320,86	-11,07824	12,07824476
4	-693,924	-386,113	0,55642	0,443580273
5	-705,084	-366,067	0,519169	0,480831261
6	-717,199	-342,721	0,477861	0,52213899
7	-730,382	-315,133	0,431463	0,568536574
8	-744,778	-281,768	0,378325	0,621674979
9	-760,585	-239,987	0,31553	0,684470328
10	-778,103	-184,467	0,237072	0,762927693
11	-797,868	-101,096	0,126707	0,873292999
12	-821,242	83,3748	-0,101523	1,101522797
13	-888,204	-576,2	0,648725	0,351274788
14	-897,016	-562,617	0,627209	0,372791116
15	-906,373	-547,698	0,604274	0,395725936
16	-916,313	-531,25	0,579769	0,420231128
17	-926,876	-513,03	0,553505	0,446495381
18	-938,11	-492,734	0,525241	0,474758827
19	-950,069	-469,965	0,494664	0,505335659
20	-962,817	-444,195	0,461349	0,538650732
21	-976,43	-414,688	0,424698	0,575302068
22	-991,004	-380,372	0,383825	0,616175424
23	-1006,66	-339,573	0,337325	0,662674538

Ad 2 and 3

(a) When $\sigma = 0.25$, the price trajectories are feasible and a structure of prices stabilizes around the equilibrium price structure in sixth period with prices' levels $\overline{p}_1 = \overline{p}_2 \approx 7.93$. When $\sigma = 0.35$, the price trajectories are feasible and a structure of prices stabilizes around the equilibrium price structure in 25-th period with levels $\overline{p}_1 = \overline{p}_2 \approx 31.47$. When $\sigma = 1.25$, the price trajectories are infeasible.

(b) When $\sigma = 0.25$, the price trajectories are feasible and a structure of prices stabilizes around the equilibrium price structure in 23-rd period with prices' levels $\overline{p}_1 = \overline{p}_2 \approx 28.51$. When $\sigma = 0.35$, the price trajectories are feasible but a structure of prices approaches the equilibrium price structure very slowly, stabilizing around it in 465-th period (taking an accuracy to two decimal places in prices) with levels $\overline{p}_1 = \overline{p}_2 \approx 576.89$. When $\sigma = 1.25$, the price trajectories are infeasible.

Ad 4 and 5

a. The price trajectories in the state space and as functions of time are presented in Figs. 3.11 and 3.12.[5]
b. The price trajectories in the state space and as functions of time are presented in Figs. 3.13 and 3.14.[6]

E3.8. Consider a continuous-time version of the dynamic Arrow-Hurwicz model for the same data given as in Exercise 3.8.

1. Determine trajectories of a price vector satisfying a system of equations of the dynamic continuous-time Arrow-Hurwicz model taking a proportionality coefficient σ equal to 0.25, 0.35, 1.25 and determine whether these trajectories are feasible.
2. Determine if and when (at what moment) a structure of prices stabilizes around the equilibrium price structure.
3. Present graphs of price trajectories as functions of time.

Solution

In this exercise, we can use the results of the previous exercises: 3.2, 3.5 and 3.6. The main results are the Walrasian equilibrium price vector:

$$\overline{\mathbf{p}} = \lambda(1, 1), \quad \lambda > 0$$

and a form of the dynamic discrete-time Arrow-Hurwicz model which we can now transform to a form of the continuous-time model.

$$\text{(a)} \quad \begin{cases} \frac{dp_1(t)}{dt} = \sigma\left(15\frac{p_2}{p_1} - 15\right) \\ \frac{dp_2(t)}{dt} = \sigma\left(15\frac{p_1}{p_2} - 15\right) \end{cases}$$

$$\text{(b)} \quad \begin{cases} \frac{dp_1(t)}{dt} = \sigma\left(\frac{30+30\frac{p_2}{p_1}}{1+\left(\frac{p_1}{p_2}\right)^{\frac{1}{3}}} - 30\right) \\ \frac{dp_2(t)}{dt} = \sigma\left(\frac{30\frac{p_1}{p_2}+30}{\left(\frac{p_2}{p_1}\right)^{\frac{1}{3}}+1} - 30\right) \end{cases}$$

where prices change over time given as a discrete variable $t \in [0; T]$.

To determine approximate price trajectories, we can use a Euler method in which one approximates differential equations with difference equations. The system of the continuous-time model:

---

[5] The price trajectories in the state space are obtained using an Excel file named Exercise 3.7 a.xlsx and MATLAB file named Exercise_3_7_a.m. As functions of time, they are obtained using the Excel file Exercise 3.7 a.xlsx.

[6] The price trajectories in the state space are obtained using an Excel file named Exercise 3.7 b.xlsx and MATLAB file named Exercise_3_7_b.m. As functions of time, they are obtained using the Excel file Exercise 3.7 b.xlsx.

Table 3.5 Price trajectories by different values of σ (E3.8 a)

		1st good	2nd good											
equilibrium prices:		1	1			dt=	0,1		moment=number of steps * dt					
equilibrium prices ratio p2/p1:														
		1												
sigma	0,25					0,35					1,25			
prices	p_1	p_2	p_2/p_1	comparison with equilibrium		p_1	p_2	p_2/p_1	comparison with equilibrium		p_1	p_2	p_2/p_1	comparison with equilibrium
0	2	4	2	1	0	2	4	2	1	0	2	4	2	1
1	2,375	3,8125	1,605263	0,605263158	1	2,525	3,7375	1,4802	0,48019802	1	3,875	3,0625	0,790323	0,209677419
2	2,60197	3,67111	1,410893	0,410893038	2	2,7771	3,56718	1,2845	0,284497205	2	3,48185	3,55995	1,022429	0,02242889
3	2,75606	3,5619	1,292388	0,292387505	3	2,92646	3,4509	1,17921	0,179205122	3	3,52391	3,51882	0,998555	0,00144489
4	2,8657	3,47706	1,213334	0,213334123	4	3,02055	3,37112	1,11606	0,11606173	4	3,5212	3,52153	1,000094	9,38875E-05
5	2,9457	3,41112	1,157999	0,157998847	5	3,08148	3,31652	1,07628	0,076275576	5	3,52138	3,52135	0,999994	6,09562E-06
6	3,00495	3,35996	1,118139	0,118139194	6	3,12152	3,27932	1,05055	0,050549103	6	3,52136	3,52137	1	3,95777E-07
7	3,04926	3,32034	1,0889	0,088900132	7	3,14806	3,25405	1,03367	0,033668531	7	3,52137	3,52137	1	2,5697E-08
8	3,08259	3,28972	1,067192	0,067192092	8	3,16574	3,23695	1,0225	0,02249536	8	3,52137	3,52137	1	1,66845E-09
9	3,10779	3,26611	1,050942	0,050942391	9	3,17755	3,2254	1,01506	0,015060078	9	3,52137	3,52137	1	1,08329E-10
10	3,12689	3,24793	1,038709	0,038708537	10	3,18546	3,21761	1,0101	0,010095373	10	3,52137	3,52137	1	7,03348E-12
11	3,14141	3,23396	1,02946	0,02946035	11	3,19076	3,21237	1,00677	0,006773064	11	3,52137	3,52137	1	4,56524E-13
12	3,15246	3,22323	1,022448	0,022448494	12	3,19431	3,20883	1,00455	0,004546644	12	3,52137	3,52137	1	2,9754E-14
13	3,16088	3,21499	1,017121	0,017120692	13	3,1967	3,20646	1,00305	0,00305322	13	3,52137	3,52137	1	1,9984E-15
14	3,1673	3,20868	1,013066	0,013066012	14	3,1983	3,20486	1,00205	0,002050846	14	3,52137	3,52137	1	0
15	3,1722	3,20384	1,009977	0,009976564	15	3,19938	3,20379	1,00138	0,00137778	15	3,52137	3,52137	1	0
16	3,17594	3,20014	1,00762	0,007620474	16	3,2001	3,20306	1,00093	0,00092571	16	3,52137	3,52137	1	0
17	3,17879	3,1973	1,005822	0,005822459	17	3,20059	3,20258	1,00062	0,000622017	17	3,52137	3,52137	1	0
18	3,18098	3,19513	1,00445	0,004449636	18	3,20091	3,20225	1,00042	0,000417976	18	3,52137	3,52137	1	0
19	3,18265	3,19347	1,003401	0,003401056	19	3,20113	3,20203	1,00028	0,000280876	19	3,52137	3,52137	1	0
20	3,18392	3,1922	1,0026	0,002599904	20	3,20128	3,20189	1,00019	0,00018875	20	3,52137	3,52137	1	0
21	3,1849	3,19123	1,001988	0,00198766	21	3,20138	3,20179	1,00013	0,000126843	21	3,52137	3,52137	1	0
22	3,18564	3,19048	1,00152	0,001519701	22	3,20145	3,20172	1,00009	8,52417E-05	22	3,52137	3,52137	1	0

Table 3.6 Price trajectories by different values of σ (E3.8 b)

		1st good	2nd good											
equilibrium prices:		1	1			dt=	0,35		moment=number of steps * dt					
equilibrium prices ratio p2/p1:														
		1												
sigma	0,25					0,35					1,25			
prices	p_1	p_2	p_2/p_1	comparison with equilibrium		p_1	p_2	p_2/p_1	comparison with equilibrium		p_1	p_2	p_2/p_1	comparison with equilibrium
0	2	4	2	1	0	2	4	2	1	0	2	4	2	1
1	3,765365	3,117318	0,827893	0,172107483	1	4,471511	2,764245	0,61819	0,381809749	1	10,82682	-0,41341	-0,038184	1,038184093
2	3,463978	3,481359	1,005017	0,005017476	2	3,532096	4,283866	1,21284	0,212839893	2	-8,70734	-511,992	58,800056	57,80005556
3	3,472759	3,472622	0,999961	3,94242E-05	3	4,053912	3,853623	0,950593	0,049406584	3	602,4909	-522,386	-0,867045	1,867044575
4	3,47269	3,472691	1	3,10043E-07	4	3,932861	3,980966	1,012232	0,012231659	4	553,5363	-578,848	-1,045727	2,045727182
5	3,47269	3,47269	1	2,43823E-09	5	3,962828	3,95136	0,997106	0,002893832	5	499,8419	-630,194	-1,260787	2,260787394
6	3,47269	3,47269	1	1,91744E-11	6	3,955738	3,958471	1,000691	0,000690793	6	440,6724	-677,125	-1,536573	2,536572589
7	3,47269	3,47269	1	1,50879E-13	7	3,957431	3,95678	0,999835	0,000164531	7	374,7573	-720,023	-1,921304	2,92130356
8	3,47269	3,47269	1	1,33227E-15	8	3,957028	3,957183	1,000039	3,92083E-05	8	299,8141	-759,029	-2,531666	3,531665589

$$\begin{cases} \frac{\mathrm{d}p_1(t)}{\mathrm{d}t} = \sigma z_1(p(t)) \\ \frac{\mathrm{d}p_2(t)}{\mathrm{d}t} = \sigma z_2(p(t)) \end{cases}$$

is transformed to a system of a discrete-time model in the following way:

$$\begin{cases} p_1(t+1) - p_1(t) = \sigma z_1(p(t)) \cdot \Delta t \\ p_2(t+1) - p_2(t) = \sigma z_2(p(t)) \cdot \Delta t \end{cases}$$

where Δt denotes a time increment.[7] Let us assume that a) $\Delta t = 0.1$, b) $\Delta t = 0.35$.

Ad 1

Initial prices announced by the broker are $p_1(0) = 2$, $p_2(0) = 4$. The price trajectories are obtained in an Excel files named Exercise 3.8.xlsx and presented in Tables 3.5 and 3.6.

Ad 2

(a) We assume that $\Delta t = 0.1$. When $\sigma = 0.25$, the price trajectories are feasible and a structure of prices stabilizes around the equilibrium price structure with prices'

[7] Depending on a value of parameter Δt meaning the time increment, we observe a lack of convergence, faster or slower convergence to the equilibrium state determined as a structure of prices

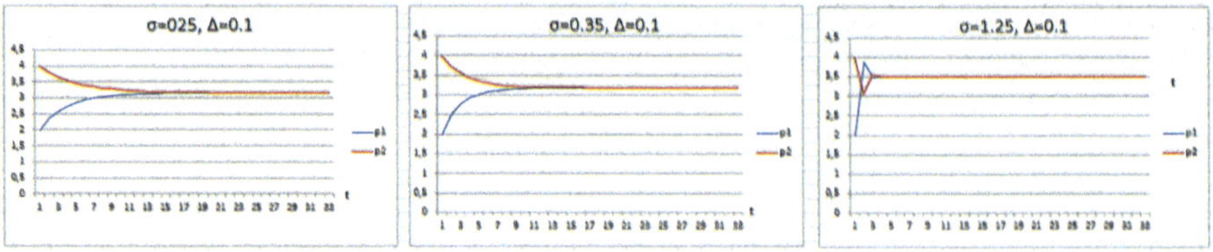

Fig. 3.15 Price trajectories as functions of time (E3.8 a)

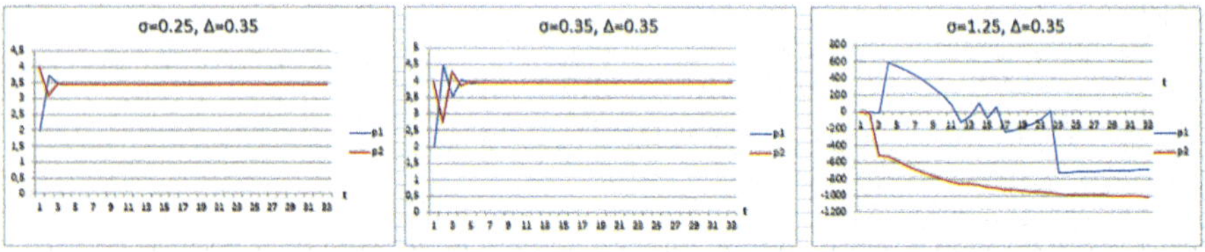

Fig. 3.16 Price trajectories as functions of time (E3.8 b)

levels $\overline{p}_1 = \overline{p}_2 \approx 3.19$, at 33-rd step which means a moment $33 \cdot 0.1 = 3.3$. When $\sigma = 0.35$, the price trajectories are feasible and a structure of prices stabilizes around the equilibrium price structure with levels $\overline{p}_1 = \overline{p}_2 \approx 3.2$, at 22-nd step, which means a moment $22 \cdot 0.1 = 2.3$. When $\sigma = 1.25$, the price trajectories are feasible and a structure of prices stabilizes around the equilibrium price structure with levels $\overline{p}_1 = \overline{p}_2 \approx 3.52$, at fourth step, which means a moment $4 \cdot 0.1 = 0.4$. Let us notice that equilibrium price levels obtained in different cases of σ value are close to each other and not far from initial price levels $p_1(0) = 2$, $p_2(0) = 4$.

(b) We assume that $\Delta t = 0.35$. When $\sigma = 0.25$, the price trajectories are feasible and a structure of prices stabilizes around the equilibrium price structure with prices' levels $\overline{p}_1 = \overline{p}_2 \approx 3.47$, at third step which means a moment $3 \cdot 0.35 = 1.05$. When $\sigma = 0.35$, the price trajectories are feasible and a structure of prices stabilizes around the equilibrium price structure with levels $\overline{p}_1 = \overline{p}_2 \approx 3.96$, at eighth step, which means a moment $8 \cdot 0.35 = 2.8$. When $\sigma = 1.25$, the price trajectories are infeasible. Let us notice that equilibrium price levels obtained in different cases of σ value (when the price trajectories are feasible) are close to each other and not far from initial price levels $p_1(0) = 2$, $p_2(0) = 4$.

Ad 3

The price trajectories as functions of time are presented in Figs. 3.15 and 3.16.[8]

[8] The price trajectories as functions of time are obtained using an Excel file named Exercise 3.8.xlsx.

Chapter 4
Rationality of Choices Made by Individual Producers

This Chapter presents 14 exercises that help in understanding the problem of describing rational behaviour of a single producer. In particular they concern: production space, a production function as a set of technologically effective processes, profit maximization problem, production total cost minimization problem under conditions of either perfect competition or monopoly, with or without constraints on resources of production factors at the disposal of an enterprise, sensitivity of supplies and prices set by a market or by a producer to changes in values of relevant parameters.

E4.1. There is a given CES production function of a form: $f(x_1, x_2) = \left(a_1 x_1^{\gamma} + a_2 x_2^{\gamma}\right)^{\frac{\theta}{\gamma}}, \theta, a_i > 0,\ i = 1, 2, \gamma \in (-\infty; 0) \cup (0; 1)$. Let us assume that a variable $u = \frac{x_2}{x_1}$ describes a quantity of the second production factor per one unit of the first production factor.

1. Justify that:
   (a) an elasticity of marginal rate of substitution of the first production factor by the second production factor is constant and equal to $E_{\sigma_{12}}(u) = 1 - \gamma$,
   (b) an elasticity of marginal rate of substitution of the second production factor by the first production factor is constant and equal to $E_{\sigma_{21}}(u) = \gamma - 1$.
2. Determine a range of variability of constant elasticities $E_{\sigma_{12}}(u)$ and $E_{\sigma_{21}}(u)$ of marginal rates of substitution.
3. Determine an elasticity of production with respect to scale of inputs and justify that it is equal to a degree $E_{\lambda}(\mathbf{x}) = \theta$ of positive homogeneity of the production function.

K. Sobczak and K. Malaga, *Workbook for Microeconomics*, Springer Texts in Business and Economics, https://doi.org/10.1007/978-3-031-41947-8_4

Solutions

Ad 1a

$$\sigma_{12}(\mathbf{x}) = \frac{\frac{\theta}{\gamma}\left(a_1x_1^\gamma + a_2x_2^\gamma\right)^{\frac{\theta}{\gamma}-1}\gamma a_1 x_1^{\gamma-1},}{\frac{\theta}{\gamma}\left(a_1x_1^\gamma + a_2x_2^\gamma\right)^{\frac{\theta}{\gamma}-1}\gamma a_2 x_2^{\gamma-1}} = \frac{a_1}{a_2}\left(\frac{x_1}{x_2}\right)^{\gamma-1}$$

$$= \frac{a_1}{a_2}\left(\frac{x_2}{x_1}\right)^{1-\gamma} = \frac{a_1}{a_2}\cdot u^{1-\gamma} = \sigma_{12}(u)$$

$$E_{\sigma_{12}(u)} = \frac{\partial\sigma_{12}(u)}{\partial u}\frac{u}{\sigma_{12}(u)} = (1-\gamma)\frac{a_1}{a_2}\cdot u^{-\gamma}\cdot\frac{u}{\frac{a_1}{a_2}\cdot u^{1-\gamma}} = 1-\gamma$$

Ad 1b

$$\sigma_{21}(\mathbf{x}) = \frac{\frac{\theta}{\gamma}\left(a_1x_1^\gamma + a_2x_2^\gamma\right)^{\frac{\theta}{\gamma}-1}\gamma a_2 x_2^{\gamma-1},}{\frac{\theta}{\gamma}\left(a_1x_1^\gamma + a_2x_2^\gamma\right)^{\frac{\theta}{\gamma}-1}\gamma a_1 x_1^{\gamma-1}} = \frac{a_2}{a_1}\left(\frac{x_2}{x_1}\right)^{\gamma-1}$$

$$= \frac{a_2}{a_1}\cdot u^{\gamma-1} = \sigma_{21}(u)$$

$$E_{\sigma_{21}(u)} = \frac{\partial\sigma_{21}(u)}{\partial u}\frac{u}{\sigma_{21}(u)}$$

$$= (\gamma-1)\frac{a_2}{a_1}\cdot u^{-\gamma}\cdot\frac{u}{\frac{a_2}{a_1}\cdot u^{\gamma-1}} = \gamma-1$$

Ad 2a

$$\gamma \in (-\infty; 0) \cup (0; 1)$$

$$-\gamma \in (-1; 0) \cup (0; +\infty)$$

$$(1-\gamma) \in (0; 1) \cup (1; +\infty)$$

Ad 2b

$$\gamma \in (-\infty; 0) \cup (0; 1)$$

$$(\gamma-1) \in (-\infty; -1) \cup (-1; 0)$$

Ad 3

$$f(\mathbf{x}) = \left(a_1x_1^\gamma + a_2x_2^\gamma\right)^{\frac{\theta}{\gamma}}$$

$$f(\lambda\mathbf{x}) = \left(a_1(\lambda x_1)^\gamma + a_2(\lambda x_2)^\gamma\right)^{\frac{\theta}{\gamma}}$$

$$= \lambda^\theta\left(a_1x_1^\gamma + a_2x_2^\gamma\right)^{\frac{\theta}{\gamma}} = \lambda^\theta f(\mathbf{x})$$

$$E_\lambda(\mathbf{x}) = \lim_{\lambda\to 1} \frac{\partial f(\lambda\mathbf{x})}{\partial\lambda}\frac{\lambda}{f(\lambda\mathbf{x})}$$
$$= \lim_{\lambda\to 1} \theta\lambda^{\theta-1} f(\mathbf{x})\frac{\lambda}{f(\mathbf{x})} = \theta$$

E4.2. For solutions of optimization problems from examples 4.3, 4.5 and 4.7 analyze sensitivity of:

1. the demand for a production factor and the maximum profit to changes in a product price and to changes in values of parameters of a production function and of a production cost function,
2. the conditional demand for a production factor and the minimum cost of producing y output units to changes in an output level and to changes in values of parameters of a production function and of a production cost function,
3. the product supply and the maximum profit to changes in a product price and to changes in values of parameters of a production function and of a production cost function.

Solutions

Example 4.3

Ad 1

See Table 4.1 and 4.2.

Table 4.1 Measures of sensitivity of demand function for production factor (E4.2)

	$\frac{\partial\psi(p,a,c_1)}{\partial a}$	$\frac{\partial\psi(p,a,c_1)}{\partial p}$	$\frac{\partial\psi(p,a,c_1)}{\partial c_1}$
$\psi(p,a,c_1) = \overline{x}^G = \left(\frac{ap}{2c_1}\right)^2$	$\frac{ap^2}{2c_1^2} > 0$	$\frac{a^2p}{2c_1^2} > 0$	$-\frac{a^2p^2}{2c_1^3} < 0$
$\overline{x}^L = b$	0	0	0

Table 4.2 **a, b** Measures of sensitivity of profit function (E4.2)

(a)

	$\frac{\partial\pi(\overline{x}^G)}{\partial a}$	$\frac{\partial\pi(\overline{x}^G)}{\partial p}$	$\frac{\partial\pi(\overline{x}^G)}{\partial c_1}$	$\frac{\partial\pi(\overline{x}^G)}{\partial b}$
$\pi(\overline{x}^G) = \frac{a^2p^2}{4c_1} - d$	$\frac{ap^2}{2c_1} > 0$	$\frac{a^2p}{2c_1} > 0$	$-\frac{a^2p^2}{4c_1^2} < 0$	0

(b)

	$\frac{\partial\pi(\overline{x}^G)}{\partial d}$	-1	-1	
$\pi(\overline{x}^L) = pab^{\frac{1}{2}} - c_1b - d$	$pb^{\frac{1}{2}} > 0$	$ab^{\frac{1}{2}} > 0$	$-b < 0$	$\frac{1}{2}pb^{-\frac{1}{2}} - c_1$

Table 4.3 Measures of sensitivity of function of conditional demand for production factor (E4.2)

	$\frac{\partial \xi(y,a)}{\partial a}$	$\frac{\partial \xi(y,a)}{\partial y}$
$\xi(\overline{y}) = \left(\frac{y}{a}\right)^2 = \tilde{x}$	$-\frac{2y^2}{a^3} < 0$	$\frac{2y}{a^2} > 0$

Table 4.4 Measures of sensitivity of function of minimum production cost of y units of product (E4.2)

	$\frac{\partial c^{tot}(y)}{\partial a}$	$\frac{\partial c^{tot}(y)}{\partial c_1}$	$\frac{\partial c^{tot}(y)}{\partial y}$	$\frac{\partial c^{tot}(y)}{\partial d}$
$c^{tot}(y) = c_1\left(\frac{y}{a}\right)^2 + d$	$-\frac{2c_1y^2}{a^3} < 0$	$\left(\frac{y}{a}\right)^2 > 0$	$\frac{2c_1y}{a^2} > 0$	1

Table 4.5 Measures of sensitivity of product supply function (E4.2)

	$\frac{\partial \eta(p,a,c_1)}{\partial a}$	$\frac{\partial \eta(p,a,c_1)}{\partial p}$	$\frac{\partial \eta(p,a,c_1)}{\partial c_1}$	$\frac{\partial \eta(p,a,c_1)}{\partial b}$
$\eta(p,a,c_1) = \overline{y}^G = \frac{pa^2}{2c_1}$	$\frac{pa}{c_1} > 0$	$\frac{a^2}{2c_1} > 0$	$-\frac{pa^2}{c_1^2} < 0$	0
$\eta(p,a,c_1) = \overline{y}^L = ab^{\frac{1}{2}}$	0	0	0	$\frac{1}{2}ab^{-\frac{1}{2}} > 0$

Table 4.6 **a, b** Measures of sensitivity of profit function (E4.2)

(a)

	$\frac{\partial \pi(\overline{y}^G)}{\partial a}$	$\frac{\partial \pi(\overline{y}^G)}{\partial p}$	$\frac{\partial \pi(\overline{y}^G)}{\partial c_1}$	$\frac{\partial \pi(\overline{y}^G)}{\partial d}$
$\pi(\overline{y}^G) = \frac{a^2p^2}{2c_1} - d$	$\frac{ap^2}{c_1} > 0$	$\frac{a^2p}{c_1} > 0$	$-\frac{a^2p^2}{c_1^2} < 0$	-1

(b)

	$\frac{\partial \pi(\overline{y}^L)}{\partial a}$	$\frac{\partial \pi(\overline{y}^L)}{\partial p}$	$\frac{\partial \pi(\overline{y}^L)}{\partial c_1}$	$\frac{\partial \pi(\overline{y}^L)}{\partial d}$
$\pi(\overline{y}^L) = pab^{\frac{1}{2}} - bc_1 - d$	$pb^{\frac{1}{2}} > 0$	$ab^{\frac{1}{2}} > 0$	$-b < 0$	-1

Ad 2

See Tables 4.3 and 4.4.

Ad 3

See Tables 4.5 and 4.6.

Example 4.5

Ad 1–3

See Tables 4.7 and 4.8.

Table 4.7 Optimal solutions to problems P1m–P3m (E4.2)

$\overline{x}^G = 2^{-\frac{12}{7}} > 0$	$\tilde{x} = \zeta(y) = \left(\frac{y}{a}\right)^2 > 0$	$\overline{y} = \mathrm{a}2^{-\frac{6}{7}} > 0$	$p(\overline{y}) = 2^{\frac{3}{7}} > 0$
$\pi\left(\overline{x}^G\right) = 7a2^{-\frac{24}{7}} - d$	$c^{\text{tot}}(y) = \frac{y^4}{a^3}$	$\pi(\overline{y}) = 7a2^{-\frac{24}{7}} - d$	$\tilde{x} = \zeta(\overline{y}) = \overline{x}^G$ $\overline{y} = a\left(\overline{x}^G\right)^{\frac{1}{2}}$

Table 4.8 Measures of sensitivity of profit function and of function of minimum production cost of y units of product (E4.2)

$\frac{\partial\pi\left(\overline{x}^G\right)}{\partial a} = 7 \cdot 2^{-\frac{24}{7}}$	$\frac{\partial\pi\left(\overline{x}^G\right)}{\partial d} = -1$
$\frac{\partial c^{\text{tot}}(y)}{\partial a} = -3\left(\frac{y}{a}\right)^4 < 0$	$\frac{\partial c^{\text{tot}}(y)}{\partial y} = 4\left(\frac{y}{a}\right)^3 > 0$

Table 4.9 Optimal solutions to problems P1m–P3m (E4.2)

$\overline{x}^G = 2^{-\frac{12}{7}} > 0$	$\tilde{x} = \zeta(y) = \left(\frac{y}{a}\right)^2 > 0$	$\overline{y} = \mathrm{a}2^{-\frac{6}{7}} > 0$	$p(\overline{y}) = 2^{\frac{3}{7}} > 0$
$\pi\left(\overline{x}^G\right) = 7a2^{-\frac{24}{7}} - d$	$c^{\text{tot}}(y) = \frac{y^4}{a^3}$	$\pi(\overline{y}) = 7a2^{-\frac{24}{7}} - d$	$\tilde{x} = \zeta(\overline{y}) = \overline{x}^G$ $\overline{y} = a\left(\overline{x}^G\right)^{\frac{1}{2}}$
$\overline{x}^L = b$	$\tilde{x} = \zeta(y) = \left(\frac{y}{a}\right)^2 > 0$	$\overline{y} = \mathrm{a}b^{\frac{1}{2}} > 0$	$p(\overline{y}) = 2^{\frac{3}{7}} > 0$
$\pi\left(\overline{x}^L\right) = ab^{\frac{1}{4}} - ab^2 - d$	$c^{\text{tot}}(y) = \frac{y^4}{a^3}$	$\pi(\overline{y}) = ab^{\frac{1}{4}} - ab^2 - d$	$\tilde{x} = \zeta(\overline{y}) = \overline{x}^L$ $\overline{y} = ab^{\frac{1}{2}}$

Table 4.10 Measures of sensitivity of profit function and of function of minimum production cost of y units of product (E4.2)

$\frac{\partial\pi\left(\overline{x}^G\right)}{\partial a} = 7 \cdot 2^{-\frac{24}{7}}$	$\frac{\partial\pi\left(\overline{x}^G\right)}{\partial d} = -1$
$\frac{\partial\pi\left(\overline{x}^L\right)}{\partial a} = b^{\frac{1}{4}} - b^2$	$\frac{\partial\pi\left(\overline{x}^L\right)}{\partial b} = \frac{1}{4}ab^{-\frac{3}{4}} - 2ab$ $\frac{\partial\pi\left(\overline{x}^L\right)}{\partial d} = \frac{\partial\pi\left(\overline{y}^G\right)}{\partial d} = -1$
$\frac{\partial c^{tot}(y)}{\partial a} = -3\left(\frac{y}{a}\right)^4 < 0$	$\frac{\partial c^{tot}(y)}{\partial y} = 4\left(\frac{y}{a}\right)^3 > 0$

Example 4.7

Ad 1–3

See Tables 4.9 and 4.10.

E4.3. There are given:

$p > 0$	a price of product manufactured by a firm,
$\mathbf{c}(\mathbf{x}) = (c_1(x_1), c_2(x_2)) > (0, 0)$	a vector of prices of production factors,
$c_i(x_i) = ax_i$	a price of i-th production factor is proportional to the demand for i-th factor,
$\mathbf{x} = (x_1, x_2) \geq (0, 0)$	a vector of inputs of production factors,

$y = f(\mathbf{x})$	an output level described by an increasing, strictly concave and twice differentiable production function,
$r(y) = py$	revenue (turnover) from sales of a manufactured product as a function of output level,
$r(\mathbf{x}) = pf(\mathbf{x})$	revenue (turnover) from sales of a manufactured product as a function of inputs of production factors,
$c^{tot}(x) = c_1(x_1)x_1 + c_2(x_2)x_2 + d$	total cost of production,
$c^v(\mathbf{x}) = c_1(x_1)x_1 + c_2(x_2)x_2$	variable cost of production,
$c^f(x) = d$	fixed cost of production,
$c(y)$	minimum cost of producing y output units, derived as an objective function corresponding to an optimal solution to problem (P2c),
$\pi(y) = r(y) - c(y) = py - c(y)$	firm profit as a function of output level,
$\pi(\mathbf{x}) = r(\mathbf{x}) - c^{tot}(\mathbf{x})$	firm profit as a function of inputs of production factors.

For a production function:

(a) power: $y = f(\mathbf{x}) = ax_1^{\alpha_1}x_2^{\alpha_2},\ a > 0,\ \alpha_i \in (0, 1),\ \alpha_1 + \alpha_2 < 1, i = 1, 2,$
(b) logarithmic: $y = f(\mathbf{x}) = a_1\ln x_1 + a_2\ln x_2,\ a_i > 0,\ i = 1, 2,$
(c) subadditive: $y = f(\mathbf{x}) = a_1x_1^{\alpha} + a_2x_2^{\alpha},\ a_i > 0,\ \alpha \in (0, 1),\ i = 1, 2.$

1. Solve the profit maximization problem (P1c).
2. Give an economic interpretation of necessary and sufficient conditions of existence of optimal solution to problem (P1c).
3. Analyze sensitivity of the demand for production factors and of the firm maximum profit to changes in a price of a product and changes in values of parameters of the cost function and of the production function.
4. Solve the cost minimization problem (P2c).
5. Give an economic interpretation of necessary and sufficient conditions of existence of optimal solution to problem (P2c).
6. Analyze sensitivity of the conditional demand for production factors and of the firm minimum cost to changes in a price of a product and changes in values of parameters of the cost function and of the production function.
7. Solve the profit maximization problem (P3c).
8. Give an economic interpretation of necessary and sufficient conditions of existence of optimal solution to problem (P3c).
9. Analyze sensitivity of the product supply and of the firm maximum profit to changes in a price of a product and changes in values of parameters of the cost function and of the production function.
10. Justify that the profit maximizations problems (P1c) and (P3c) are equivalent.

Solutions

Ad a

P1c

Let us write the problem of maximizing the firm's profit in the case of the power production function and the nonlinear function of total cost:

$$\pi(\mathbf{x}) = \left\{pax_1^{\alpha_1}x_2^{\alpha_2} - a\left(x_1^2 + x_2^2\right) - d\right\} \to \max$$

$$\mathbf{x} \geq (0, 0).$$

Then the marginal profit functions take forms:

(1) $\frac{\partial \pi(\mathbf{x})}{\partial x_1} = \alpha_1 a x_1^{\alpha_1-1} x_2^{\alpha_2} - 2ax_1,$
(2) $\frac{\partial \pi(\mathbf{x})}{\partial x_2} = \alpha_2 a x_1^{\alpha_1} x_2^{\alpha_2-1} - 2ax_2.$

It is not difficult to check that the boundary conditions for the profit function are met:

(3) $\lim_{x_1 \to 0^+} \frac{\partial \pi(\mathbf{x})}{\partial x_1} = +\infty > 0$ and $\lim_{x_1 \to +\infty} \frac{\partial \pi(\mathbf{x})}{\partial x_1} = -\infty < 0,$
(4) $\lim_{x_2 \to 0^+} \frac{\partial \pi(\mathbf{x})}{\partial x_2} = +\infty > 0$ and $\lim_{x_2 \to +\infty} \frac{\partial \pi(\mathbf{x})}{\partial x_2} = -\infty < 0.$

On this basis, we claim that $\exists_1 \overline{\mathbf{x}} > (0, 0)$, such that:

(5) $\left.\frac{\partial \pi(\mathbf{x})}{\partial x_1}\right|_{\mathbf{x}=\overline{\mathbf{x}}} = \alpha_1 pa\overline{x}_1^{\alpha_1-1}\overline{x}_2^{\alpha_2} - 2a\overline{x}_1 = 0\,,$
(6) $\left.\frac{\partial \pi(\mathbf{x})}{\partial x_2}\right|_{\mathbf{x}=\overline{\mathbf{x}}} = \alpha_2 pa\overline{x}_1^{\alpha_1}\overline{x}_2^{\alpha_2-1} - 2a\overline{x}_2 = 0.$

Let us solve the system of Eqs. (5)–(6):

(7) $\frac{\alpha_1 pa\overline{x}_1^{\alpha_1-1}\overline{x}_2^{\alpha_2}}{\alpha_2 pa\overline{x}_1^{\alpha_1}\overline{x}_2^{\alpha_2-1}} = \frac{2a\overline{x}_1}{2a\overline{x}_2},$
(8) $\frac{\alpha_1\overline{x}_2}{\alpha_2\overline{x}_1} = \frac{\overline{x}_1}{\overline{x}_2},$
(9) $\overline{x}_2 = \left(\frac{\alpha_2}{\alpha_1}\right)^{\frac{1}{2}}\overline{x}_1,$
(10) $\alpha_1 pa\overline{x}_1^{\alpha_1-1}\overline{x}_2^{\alpha_2} = 2a\overline{x}_1,$
(11) $\alpha_1 p\overline{x}_1^{\alpha_1-1}\left(\frac{\alpha_2}{\alpha_1}\right)^{\frac{\alpha_2}{2}}\overline{x}_1^{\alpha_2} = 2\overline{x}_1,$
(12) $\overline{x}_1\left(\alpha_1 p\overline{x}_1^{\alpha_1+\alpha_2-2}\left(\frac{\alpha_2}{\alpha_1}\right)^{\frac{\alpha_2}{2}} - 2\right) = 0,$
(13) $\overline{x}_1^{\alpha_1+\alpha_2-2} = \frac{2}{p\alpha_1^{\frac{2-\alpha_2}{2}}\alpha_2^{\frac{\alpha_2}{2}}},$
(14) $\overline{x}_1^{2-(\alpha_1+\alpha_2)} = \frac{p\alpha_1^{\frac{2-\alpha_2}{2}}\alpha_2^{\frac{\alpha_2}{2}}}{2},$
(15) $\overline{x}_1 = \left(\frac{p}{2}\right)^{\frac{1}{2-(\alpha_1+\alpha_2)}}\alpha_1^{\frac{2-\alpha_2}{2(2-(\alpha_1+\alpha_2))}}\alpha_2^{\frac{\alpha_2}{2(2-(\alpha_1+\alpha_2))}},$

Table 4.11 Measures of sensitivity of function of demand for production factors (E4.3a)

$\frac{\partial \overline{x}_1}{\partial a}$	0
$\frac{\partial \overline{x}_2}{\partial a}$	0
$\frac{\partial \overline{x}_1}{\partial p}$	$\frac{1}{2(2-(\alpha_1+\alpha_2)}\left(\frac{p}{2}\right)^{\frac{\alpha_1+\alpha_2-1}{2-(\alpha_1+\alpha_2)}}\alpha_1^{\frac{2-\alpha_2}{2(2-(\alpha_1+\alpha_2))}}\alpha_2^{\frac{\alpha_2}{2(2-(\alpha_1+\alpha_2))}} > 0$
$\frac{\partial \overline{x}_2}{\partial p}$	$\frac{1}{2(2-(\alpha_1+\alpha_2)}\left(\frac{p}{2}\right)^{\frac{\alpha_1+\alpha_2-1}{2-(\alpha_1+\alpha_2)}}\alpha_1^{\frac{\alpha_1}{2(2-(\alpha_1+\alpha_2))}}\alpha_2^{\frac{2-\alpha_1}{2(2-(\alpha_1+\alpha_2))}} > 0$

Table 4.12 Measures of sensitivity of profit function (E4.3a)

$\frac{\partial \pi(\overline{\mathbf{x}})}{\partial a}$	> 0
$\frac{\partial \pi(\overline{\mathbf{x}})}{\partial p}$	> 0
$\frac{\partial \pi(\overline{\mathbf{x}})}{\partial d}$	-1

(16)
$$\overline{x}_2 = \left(\frac{p}{2}\right)^{\frac{1}{2-(\alpha_1+\alpha_2)}}\left(\frac{\alpha_2}{\alpha_1}\right)^{\frac{1}{2}}\alpha_1^{\frac{2-\alpha_2}{2(2-(\alpha_1+\alpha_2))}}\alpha_2^{\frac{\alpha_2}{2(2-(\alpha_1+\alpha_2))}} = \\ = \left(\frac{p}{2}\right)^{\frac{1}{2-(\alpha_1+\alpha_2)}}\alpha_1^{\frac{\alpha_1}{2(2-(\alpha_1+\alpha_2))}}\alpha_2^{\frac{2-\alpha_1}{2(2-(\alpha_1+\alpha_2))}},$$

(17)
$$\overline{\mathbf{x}} = \left(\left(\frac{p}{2}\right)^{\frac{1}{2-(\alpha_1+\alpha_2)}}\alpha_1^{\frac{2-\alpha_2}{2(2-(\alpha_1+\alpha_2))}}\alpha_2^{\frac{\alpha_2}{2(2-(\alpha_1+\alpha_2))}}, \left(\frac{p}{2}\right)^{\frac{1}{2-(\alpha_1+\alpha_2)}}\alpha_1^{\frac{\alpha_1}{2(2-(\alpha_1+\alpha_2))}}\alpha_2^{\frac{2-\alpha_1}{2(2-(\alpha_1+\alpha_2))}}\right).$$

Let us notice that the vector of the optimal demand for production factors is determined with an accuracy of a structure or in other words with an accuracy of a multiplication by a number $\lambda > 0$.

In Tables 4.11 and 4.12 the sensitivity analysis of the demand for production factors and of the firm maximum profit is presented.

(18)
$$\overline{\mathbf{x}} = (\overline{x}_1, \overline{x}_2) = \overline{x}_1\left(1, \left(\frac{\alpha_2}{\alpha_1}\right)^{\frac{1}{2}}\right) = \lambda\left(1, \left(\frac{\alpha_2}{\alpha_1}\right)^{\frac{1}{2}}\right), \forall\lambda > 0,$$

(19)
$$\pi(\overline{\mathbf{x}}) = a\left(p\left(\frac{\alpha_2}{\alpha_1}\right)^{\frac{1}{2}} - \frac{\alpha_2}{\alpha_1} - 1\right) - d = a\left(\frac{\alpha_2}{\alpha_1}\right)^{\frac{1}{2}}\left(p - \left(\frac{\alpha_2}{\alpha_1}\right)^{\frac{1}{2}}\right) - a - d,$$

(20)
$$\pi(\overline{\mathbf{x}}) = pa\left(\frac{p}{2}\right)^{\frac{\alpha_1}{2-(\alpha_1+\alpha_2)}}\alpha_1^{\frac{(2-\alpha_2)\alpha_1}{2(2-(\alpha_1+\alpha_2))}}\alpha_2^{\frac{\alpha_2\alpha_1}{2(2-(\alpha_1+\alpha_2))}} + \left(\frac{p}{2}\right)^{\frac{\alpha_2}{2-(\alpha_1+\alpha_2)}}\alpha_1^{\frac{\alpha_1\alpha_2}{2-(\alpha_1+\alpha_2)}}\alpha_2^{\frac{2-\alpha_1}{2-(\alpha_1+\alpha_2)}} \\ -a\left(\left(\frac{p}{2}\right)^{\frac{2\alpha_1}{2-(\alpha_1+\alpha_2)}}\alpha_1^{\frac{(2-\alpha_2)\alpha_1}{2-(\alpha_1+\alpha_2)}}\alpha_2^{\frac{\alpha_2\alpha_1}{2-(\alpha_1+\alpha_2)}} + \left(\frac{p}{2}\right)^{\frac{2\alpha_2}{2-(\alpha_1+\alpha_2)}}\alpha_1^{\frac{\alpha_1\alpha_2}{2-(\alpha_1+\alpha_2)}}\alpha_2^{\frac{(2-\alpha_1)\alpha_2}{2-(\alpha_1+\alpha_2)}}\right) - d.$$

P2c

Let us write down the problem of minimizing the costs of production of y units of a product:

$$c^{\text{tot}}(\mathbf{x}) = a\left(x_1^2 + x_2^2\right) + d \to \min,$$
$$a x_1^{\alpha_1} x_2^{\alpha_2} = y,$$
$$\mathbf{x} \geq (0, 0)$$

using a the Lagrangian function:

(1) $F(\mathbf{x},\lambda) = a\left(x_1^2 + x_2^2\right) + d + \lambda\left(y - a x_1^{\alpha_1} x_2^{\alpha_2}\right).$

From the Kuhn-Tucker theorem it follows that:

(2) $\left.\frac{\partial F(\mathbf{x},\tilde{\lambda})}{\partial x_1}\right|_{\mathbf{x}=\tilde{\mathbf{x}}} = 2a\tilde{x}_1 - \tilde{\lambda}\alpha_1 a \tilde{x}_1^{\alpha_1 - 1}\tilde{x}_2^{\alpha_2} = 0$

(3) $\left.\frac{\partial F(\mathbf{x},\tilde{\lambda})}{\partial x_2}\right|_{\mathbf{x}=\tilde{\mathbf{x}}} = 2a\tilde{x}_2 - \tilde{\lambda}\alpha_2 a \tilde{x}_1^{\alpha_1}\tilde{x}_2^{\alpha_2 - 1} = 0$

(4) $\left.\frac{\partial F(\tilde{\mathbf{x}},\lambda)}{\partial \lambda}\right|_{\lambda=\tilde{\lambda}} = y - a\tilde{x}_1^{\alpha_1}\tilde{x}_2^{\alpha_2} = 0$

(5) $\frac{2a\tilde{x}_1}{2a\tilde{x}_2} = \frac{\tilde{\lambda}\alpha_1 a\tilde{x}_1^{\alpha_1-1}\tilde{x}_2^{\alpha_2}}{\tilde{\lambda}\alpha_2 a\tilde{x}_1^{\alpha_1}\tilde{x}_2^{\alpha_2-1}}$

(6) $\tilde{x}_2^2 = \left(\frac{\alpha_2}{\alpha_1}\right)\tilde{x}_1^2$

(7) $\tilde{x}_2 = \left(\frac{\alpha_2}{\alpha_1}\right)^{\frac{1}{2}}\tilde{x}_1$

(8) $a\tilde{x}_1^{\alpha_1}\tilde{x}_2^{\alpha_2} = a\tilde{x}_1^{\alpha_1}\left(\frac{\alpha_2}{\alpha_1}\right)^{\frac{\alpha_2}{2}}\tilde{x}_1^{\alpha_2} = y$

(9) $\tilde{x}_1^{\alpha_1+\alpha_2} = \frac{y}{a}\left(\frac{\alpha_1}{\alpha_2}\right)^{\frac{\alpha_2}{2}}$

(10) $\tilde{x}_1 = \left(\frac{y}{a}\right)^{\frac{1}{\alpha_1+\alpha_2}}\left(\frac{\alpha_1}{\alpha_2}\right)^{\frac{\alpha_2}{2(\alpha_1+\alpha_2)}}$

(11) $\tilde{x}_2 = \left(\frac{\alpha_2}{\alpha_1}\right)^{\frac{1}{2}}\left(\frac{y}{a}\right)^{\frac{1}{\alpha_1+\alpha_2}}\left(\frac{\alpha_1}{\alpha_2}\right)^{\frac{\alpha_2}{2(\alpha_1+\alpha_2)}} = \left(\frac{y}{a}\right)^{\frac{1}{\alpha_1+\alpha_2}}\left(\frac{\alpha_2}{\alpha_1}\right)^{\frac{\alpha_1}{2(\alpha_1+\alpha_2)}}$

(12) $\tilde{\mathbf{x}} = \left(\left(\frac{y}{a}\right)^{\frac{1}{\alpha_1+\alpha_2}}\left(\frac{\alpha_1}{\alpha_2}\right)^{\frac{\alpha_2}{2(\alpha_1+\alpha_2)}}, \left(\frac{y}{a}\right)^{\frac{1}{\alpha_1+\alpha_2}}\left(\frac{\alpha_2}{\alpha_1}\right)^{\frac{\alpha_1}{2(\alpha_1+\alpha_2)}}\right)$

(13) $\tilde{\mathbf{x}} = (\tilde{x}_1, \tilde{x}_2) = \tilde{x}_1\left(1, \left(\frac{\alpha_2}{\alpha_1}\right)^{\frac{1}{2}}\right) = \lambda\left(1, \left(\frac{\alpha_2}{\alpha_1}\right)^{\frac{1}{2}}\right) = \bar{\mathbf{x}}.$

Equation (13) shows that the function of demand for production factors and the function of conditional demand for production factors are identical in terms of a structure.

(14)
$$\begin{aligned} c^{\text{tot}}(\tilde{\mathbf{x}}) &= a\left(\left(\frac{y}{a}\right)^{\frac{2}{\alpha_1+\alpha_2}}\left(\frac{\alpha_1}{\alpha_2}\right)^{\frac{\alpha_2}{(\alpha_1+\alpha_2)}} + \left(\frac{y}{a}\right)^{\frac{2}{\alpha_1+\alpha_2}}\left(\frac{\alpha_2}{\alpha_1}\right)^{\frac{\alpha_1}{(\alpha_1+\alpha_2)}}\right) + d \\ &= a\left(\frac{y}{a}\right)^{\frac{2}{\alpha_1+\alpha_2}}\left(\frac{\alpha_1}{\alpha_2}\right)^{\frac{\alpha_2}{(\alpha_1+\alpha_2)}}\left(1 + \frac{\alpha_1}{\alpha_2}\right) + d \\ &= \frac{a(\alpha_1+\alpha_2)}{\alpha_2}\left(\frac{y}{a}\right)^{\frac{2}{\alpha_1+\alpha_2}}\left(\frac{\alpha_1}{\alpha_2}\right)^{\frac{\alpha_2}{(\alpha_1+\alpha_2)}} + d = k(y) \end{aligned}$$

Equation (14) describes the function of the minimum cost of production of y units of a product.

In Tables 4.13 and 4.14 the sensitivity analysis of the demand for production factors and of the firm maximum profit is presented.

P3c

Let us formulate the problem of maximizing the company's profit as a function of the product supply:

Table 4.13 Measures of sensitivity of function of conditional demand for production factors (E4.3a)

$\frac{\partial \tilde{x}_1}{\partial a}$	$-\frac{y}{a^2}\frac{1}{(\alpha_1+\alpha_2)}\left(\frac{y}{a}\right)^{\frac{1-\alpha_1-\alpha_2}{\alpha_1+\alpha_2}}\left(\frac{\alpha_1}{\alpha_2}\right)^{\frac{\alpha_2}{2(\alpha_1+\alpha_2)}} < 0$
$\frac{\partial \tilde{x}_2}{\partial a}$	$-\frac{y}{a^2}\frac{1}{(\alpha_1+\alpha_2)}\left(\frac{y}{a}\right)^{\frac{1-\alpha_1-\alpha_2}{\alpha_1+\alpha_2}}\left(\frac{\alpha_2}{\alpha_1}\right)^{\frac{\alpha_1}{2(\alpha_1+\alpha_2)}} < 0$
$\frac{\partial \tilde{x}_1}{\partial y}$	$\frac{1}{a(\alpha_1+\alpha_2)}\left(\frac{y}{a}\right)^{\frac{1-\alpha_1-\alpha_2}{\alpha_1+\alpha_2}}\left(\frac{\alpha_1}{\alpha_2}\right)^{\frac{\alpha_2}{2(\alpha_1+\alpha_2)}} > 0$
$\frac{\partial \tilde{x}_2}{\partial y}$	$\frac{1}{a(\alpha_1+\alpha_2)}\left(\frac{y}{a}\right)^{\frac{1-\alpha_1-\alpha_2}{\alpha_1+\alpha_2}}\left(\frac{\alpha_2}{\alpha_1}\right)^{\frac{\alpha_1}{2(\alpha_1+\alpha_2)}} > 0$

Table 4.14 Measures of sensitivity of function of minimum cost of production of y units of product (E4.3a)

$\frac{\partial c^{tot}(\tilde{\mathbf{x}})}{\partial a}$	> 0
$\frac{\partial c^{tot}(\tilde{\mathbf{x}})}{\partial y}$	> 0
$\frac{\partial c^{tot}(\tilde{\mathbf{x}})}{\partial d}$	1

$$\pi(y) = py - k(y)$$
$$= \left[py - \frac{a(\alpha_1+\alpha_2)}{\alpha_2}\left(\frac{y}{a}\right)^{\frac{2}{\alpha_1+\alpha_2}}\left(\frac{\alpha_1}{\alpha_2}\right)^{\frac{\alpha_2}{(\alpha_1+\alpha_2)}} - d\right] \to \max,$$
$$y > 0.$$

Then a function of the marginal profit takes a form:

(1) $\frac{d\pi(y)}{dy} = p - \frac{2}{\alpha_1+\alpha_2}\cdot\frac{(\alpha_1+\alpha_2)}{\alpha_2}\left(\frac{y}{a}\right)^{\frac{2-(\alpha_1+\alpha_2)}{\alpha_1+\alpha_2}}\left(\frac{\alpha_1}{\alpha_2}\right)^{\frac{\alpha_2}{(\alpha_1+\alpha_2)}}.$

It is not difficult to check that the boundary conditions for the profit function are met:

(2) $\lim_{y\to 0^+}\frac{\partial\pi(y)}{\partial y} = p > 0$ and $\lim_{y\to+\infty}\frac{\partial\pi(y)}{\partial y} = -\infty < 0.$

On this basis, we claim that $\exists_1 \overline{y} > 0$ such that:

(3) $\left.\frac{d\pi(y)}{\partial y}\right|_{y=\overline{y}} = p - \frac{2}{\alpha_1+\alpha_2}\ \frac{(\alpha_1+\alpha_2)}{\alpha_2}\left(\frac{\overline{y}}{a}\right)^{\frac{2-(\alpha_1+\alpha_2)}{\alpha_1+\alpha_2}}\left(\frac{\alpha_1}{\alpha_2}\right)^{\frac{\alpha_2}{(\alpha_1+\alpha_2)}} = 0$

(4) $\left(\frac{\overline{y}}{a}\right)^{\frac{2-(\alpha_1+\alpha_2)}{\alpha_1+\alpha_2}} = \frac{p}{2}\left(\frac{\alpha_2}{\alpha_1}\right)^{\frac{\alpha_2}{(\alpha_1+\alpha_2)}}$

(5) $\frac{\overline{y}}{a} = \left(\frac{p}{2}\right)^{\frac{(\alpha_1+\alpha_2)}{2-(\alpha_1+\alpha_2)}}\left(\frac{\alpha_2}{\alpha_1}\right)^{\frac{\alpha_2}{2-(\alpha_1+\alpha_2)}} =$

(6) $\overline{y} = a\left(\frac{p}{2}\right)^{\frac{(\alpha_1+\alpha_2)}{2-(\alpha_1+\alpha_2)}}\left(\frac{\alpha_2}{\alpha_1}\right)^{\frac{\alpha_2}{2-(\alpha_1+\alpha_2)}}$

Table 4.15 Measures of sensitivity of product supply function (E4.3a)

$\frac{\partial \overline{y}}{\partial p}$	> 0
$\frac{\partial \overline{y}}{\partial a}$	> 0
$\frac{\partial \overline{y}}{\partial d}$	0

Table 4.16 Measures of sensitivity of profit function (E4.3a)

$\frac{\partial \pi(\overline{y})}{\partial a}$	> 0
$\frac{\partial \pi(\overline{y})}{\partial p}$	> 0
$\frac{\partial \pi(\overline{y})}{\partial d}$	< 0

(7)
$$\pi(\overline{y}) = pa\left(\tfrac{p}{2}\right)^{\frac{(\alpha_1+\alpha_2)}{2-(\alpha_1+\alpha_2)}}\left(\frac{\alpha_2}{\alpha_1}\right)^{\frac{\alpha_2}{2-(\alpha_1+\alpha_2)}} - \frac{a(\alpha_1+\alpha_2)}{\alpha_2}\left(\frac{a\left(\frac{p}{2}\right)^{\frac{(\alpha_1+\alpha_2)}{2-(\alpha_1+\alpha_2)}}\left(\frac{\alpha_2}{\alpha_1}\right)^{\frac{\alpha_2}{2-(\alpha_1+\alpha_2)}}}{a}\right)^{\frac{2}{\alpha_1+\alpha_2}}\left(\frac{\alpha_1}{\alpha_2}\right)^{\frac{\alpha_2}{(\alpha_1+\alpha_2)}} - d.$$

Equation (6) describes the optimal supply of the product, and Eq. (7) the maximum profit of the company.

In Tables 4.15 and 4.16 the sensitivity analysis of the product supply and of the firm maximum profit is presented.

Ad b

P1c

Let us write the problem of maximizing the firm's profit in the case of the logarithmic production function and the nonlinear function of total cost:

$$\pi(\mathbf{x}) = \left\{p(a_1 \ln x_1 + a_2 \ln x_2) - a\left(x_1^2 + x_2^2\right) - d\right\} \to \max,$$
$$\mathbf{x} \geq (0, 0).$$

Then functions of the marginal profit take forms:

(1) $\frac{\partial \pi(\mathbf{x})}{\partial x_1} = p\frac{a_1}{x_1} - 2ax_1,$
(2) $\frac{\partial \pi(\mathbf{x})}{\partial x_2} = p\frac{a_2}{x_2} - 2ax_2.$

It is not difficult to check that the boundary conditions for the firm's profit function are met:

(3) $\lim_{x_1 \to 0^+} \frac{\partial \pi(\mathbf{x})}{\partial x_1} = +\infty > 0$ and $\lim_{x_1 \to +\infty} \frac{\partial \pi(\mathbf{x})}{\partial x_1} = -\infty < 0,$
(4) $\lim_{x_2 \to 0^+} \frac{\partial \pi(\mathbf{x})}{\partial x_2} = +\infty > 0$ and $\lim_{x_2 \to +\infty} \frac{\partial \pi(\mathbf{x})}{\partial x_2} = -\infty < 0.$

On this basis, we claim that $\exists_1 \overline{\mathbf{x}} > (0, 0)$ such that:

(5) $\left.\frac{\partial \pi(\mathbf{x})}{\partial x_1}\right|_{\mathbf{x}=\overline{\mathbf{x}}} = p\frac{a_1}{\overline{x}_1} - 2a\overline{x}_1 = 0,$

(6) $\left.\frac{\partial \pi(\mathbf{x})}{\partial x_2}\right|_{\mathbf{x}=\overline{\mathbf{x}}} = p\frac{a_2}{\overline{x}_2} - 2a\overline{x}_2 = 0.$

Let us solve the system of Eqs. (5)–(6).

(7) $\frac{\frac{a_1}{\overline{x}_1}}{\frac{a_2}{\overline{x}_2}} = \frac{2a\overline{x}_1}{2a\overline{x}_2}$

(8) $\frac{a_1\overline{x}_2}{a_2\overline{x}_1} = \frac{\overline{x}_1}{\overline{x}_2}$

(9) $\overline{x}_2 = \left(\frac{a_2}{a_1}\right)^{\frac{1}{2}}\overline{x}_1$

(10) $2a\overline{x}_1 = p\frac{a_1}{\overline{x}_1}$

(11) $\overline{x}_1^2 = \frac{pa_1}{2a}$

(12) $\overline{x}_1 = \left(\frac{pa_1}{2a}\right)^2$

(13) $2a\overline{x}_2 = p\frac{a_2}{\overline{x}_2}$

(14) $\overline{x}_2^2 = \frac{pa_2}{2a}$

(15) $\overline{x}_2 = \left(\frac{pa_2}{2a}\right)^2$

(16) $\overline{\mathbf{x}} = \left(\left(\frac{pa_1}{2a}\right)^2, \left(\frac{pa_2}{2a}\right)^2\right) = \overline{x}_1\left(1, \left(\frac{a_2}{a_1}\right)^{\frac{1}{2}}\right) = \lambda\left(1, \left(\frac{a_2}{a_1}\right)^{\frac{1}{2}}\right)$

(17)
$$\pi(\overline{\mathbf{x}}) = p\left(a_1\ln\left(\frac{pa_1}{2a}\right)^2 + a_2\ln\left(\frac{pa_2}{2a}\right)^2\right) - a\left(\left(\frac{pa_1}{2a}\right)^4 + \left(\frac{pa_2}{2a}\right)^4\right) - d$$
$$= p\cdot\ln\left(\left(\frac{p}{2a}\right)^{2(a_1+a_2)} a_1^{2a_1}a_2^{2a_2}\right) - \frac{p^4}{a^3}\left(a_1^4 + a_2^4\right) - d.$$

P2c

In Table 4.17 the sensitivity analysis of the demand for production factors is presented. Let us write down the problem of minimizing the costs of production of y units of the product:

$$c^{\text{tot}}(\mathbf{x}) = \left[a\left(x_1^2 + x_2^2\right) + d\right] \to \min,$$
$$a_1 \ln x_1 + a_2 \ln x_2 = y,$$
$$\mathbf{x} \geq (0, 0),$$

Table 4.17 Measures of sensitivity of function of demand for production factors (E4.3b)

$\frac{\partial \overline{x}_1}{\partial a_1}$	$\frac{a_1p^2}{2a^2} > 0$
$\frac{\partial \overline{x}_2}{\partial a}$	$-\frac{p^2a_1^2}{4a^3} < 0$
$\frac{\partial \overline{x}_1}{\partial p}$	$\frac{pa_1^2}{2a^2} > 0$
$\frac{\partial \overline{x}_2}{\partial a_2}$	$\frac{a_2p^2}{2a^2} > 0$
$\frac{\partial \overline{x}_1}{\partial a}$	$-\frac{p^2a_2^2}{4a^3} < 0$
$\frac{\partial \overline{x}_2}{\partial p}$	$\frac{pa_2^2}{2a^2} > 0$

using a Lagrange function:

(1) $F(\mathbf{x}, \lambda) = a\left(x_1^2 + x_2^2\right) + d + \lambda(y - a_1 \ln x_1 - a_2 \ln x_2).$

From the Kuhn-Tucker theorem it follows that:

(1) $\left.\frac{\partial F(\mathbf{x},\tilde{\lambda})}{\partial x_1}\right|_{\mathbf{x}=\tilde{\mathbf{x}}} = 2a\tilde{x}_1 - \tilde{\lambda}\frac{a_1}{\tilde{x}_1} = 0$

(2) $\left.\frac{\partial F(\mathbf{x},\tilde{\lambda})}{\partial x_2}\right|_{\mathbf{x}=\tilde{\mathbf{x}}} = 2a\tilde{x}_2 - \tilde{\lambda}\frac{a_2}{\tilde{x}_2} = 0$

(3) $\left.\frac{\partial F(\tilde{\mathbf{x}},\lambda)}{\partial \lambda}\right|_{\lambda=\tilde{\lambda}} = y - a_1 \ln \tilde{x}_1 - a_2 \ln \tilde{x}_2 = 0$

(4) $\frac{2a\tilde{x}_1}{2a\tilde{x}_2} = \frac{\tilde{\lambda}a_1\tilde{x}_2}{\tilde{\lambda}a_2\tilde{x}_1}$

(5) $\tilde{x}_2^2 = \left(\frac{a_2}{a_1}\right)\tilde{x}_1^2$

(6) $\tilde{x}_2 = \left(\frac{a_2}{a_1}\right)^{\frac{1}{2}}\tilde{x}_1$

(7) $\ln \tilde{x}_1^{a_1}\left(\frac{a_2}{a_1}\right)^{\frac{a_2}{2}}\tilde{x}_1^{a_2} = y$

(8) $\ln \tilde{x}_1^{\alpha_1+\alpha_2}\left(\frac{a_2}{a_1}\right)^{\frac{a_2}{2}} = y$

(9) $\tilde{x}_1^{a_1+a_2}\left(\frac{a_2}{a_1}\right)^{\frac{a_2}{2}} = e^y$

(10) $\tilde{x}_1^{a_1+a_2} = e^y\left(\frac{a_1}{\alpha_2}\right)^{\frac{a_2}{2}}$

(11) $\tilde{x}_1 = e^{\frac{y}{a_1+a_2}}\left(\frac{a_1}{a_2}\right)^{\frac{a_2}{2}}$

(12) $\tilde{x}_2 = \left(\frac{a_2}{a_1}\right)^{\frac{1}{2}} e^{\frac{y}{a_1+a_2}}\left(\frac{a_1}{a_2}\right)^{\frac{a_2}{2}} = e^{\frac{y}{a_1+a_2}}\left(\frac{a_2}{a_1}\right)^{\frac{1-a_2}{2}}$

(13) $\tilde{\mathbf{x}} = \left(e^{\frac{y}{a_1+a_2}}\left(\frac{a_1}{a_2}\right)^{\frac{a_2}{2}}, e^{\frac{y}{a_1+a_2}}\left(\frac{a_2}{a_1}\right)^{\frac{1-a_2}{2}}\right)$

(14) $\tilde{\mathbf{x}} = (\tilde{x}_1, \tilde{x}_2) = \tilde{x}_1\left(1, \left(\frac{a_2}{a_1}\right)^{\frac{1}{2}}\right) = \lambda\left(1, \left(\frac{a_2}{a_1}\right)^{\frac{1}{2}}\right) = \bar{\mathbf{x}}.$

Equation (14) shows that the function of demand for production factors and the function of conditional demand for production factors are identical in terms of a structure.

(15)
$$
\begin{aligned}
c^{\text{tot}}(\tilde{\mathbf{x}}) &= a\left(e^{\frac{2y}{a_1+a_2}}\left(\frac{a_1}{a_2}\right)^{a_2} + e^{\frac{2y}{a_1+a_2}}\left(\frac{a_2}{a_1}\right)^{1-a_2}\right) + d \\
&= ae^{\frac{2y}{a_1+a_2}}\left(\frac{a_1}{a_2}\right)^{a_2} \cdot \left(1 + \frac{a_1}{a_2}\right) + d \\
&= \frac{a(a_1+a_2)}{a_2} e^{\frac{2y}{a_1+a_2}}\left(\frac{a_1}{a_2}\right)^{a_2} + d = k(y).
\end{aligned}
$$

Equation (15) describes the function of the minimum cost of production of y units of a product.

In Tables 4.18 and 4.19 the sensitivity analysis of the conditional demand for production factors and of the minimum cost of production is presented.

Table 4.18 Measures of sensitivity of function of conditional demand for production factors (E4.3b)

$\frac{\partial \tilde{x}_1}{\partial y}$	> 0
$\frac{\partial \tilde{x}_2}{\partial y}$	> 0

Table 4.19 Measures of sensitivity of function of minimum cost of production of y units of product (E4.3b)

$\frac{\partial c^{\text{tot}}(\tilde{\mathbf{x}})}{\partial a}$	> 0
$\frac{\partial c^{\text{tot}}(\tilde{\mathbf{x}})}{\partial y}$	> 0
$\frac{\partial c^{\text{tot}}(\tilde{\mathbf{x}})}{\partial d}$	1

P3c

Let us formulate the problem of maximizing the company's profit as a function of the product supply:

$$\begin{aligned}\pi(y) &= py - k(y)\\ &= \left[py - \frac{a(a_1+a_2)}{a_2} e^{\frac{2y}{a_1+a_2}} \left(\frac{a_1}{a_2}\right)^{a_2} - d\right] \to \max,\\ y &> 0.\end{aligned}$$

Then a function of the marginal profit takes a form:

(1) $\frac{d\pi(y)}{dy} = p - \frac{a(a_1+a_2)}{a_2} e^{\frac{2y}{a_1+a_2}} \left(\frac{a_1}{a_2}\right)^{a_2} \frac{2}{a_1+a_2} = 0.$

It is not difficult to check that the boundary conditions for the profit function are met:

(2) $\lim\limits_{y\to 0^+} \frac{\partial\pi(y)}{\partial y} = p - \frac{2aa_1^{a_2}}{a_2^{a_2+1}} > 0$ and $\lim\limits_{y\to +\infty} \frac{\partial\pi(y)}{\partial y} = -\infty < 0.$

On this basis, we claim that $\exists_1 \overline{y} > 0$ such that:

(3) $\left.\frac{d\pi(y)}{\partial y}\right|_{y=\overline{y}} = p - \frac{a(a_1+a_2)}{a_2} e^{\frac{2\overline{y}}{a_1+a_2}} \left(\frac{a_1}{a_2}\right)^{a_2} \frac{2}{a_1+a_2} = 0$

(4) $e^{\frac{2\overline{y}}{a_1+a_2}} = \frac{pa_2}{2a}\left(\frac{a_2}{a_1}\right)^{a_2}$

(5) $\frac{2\overline{y}}{a_1+a_2} = \ln\left(\frac{pa_2}{2a}\left(\frac{a_2}{a_1}\right)^{a_2}\right)$

(6) $\overline{y} = \frac{a_1+a_2}{2} \ln\left(\frac{pa_2}{2a}\left(\frac{a_2}{a_1}\right)^{a_2}\right)$

(7) $\pi(\overline{y}) = p\frac{a_1+a_2}{2} \ln\left(\frac{pa_2}{2a}\left(\frac{a_2}{a_1}\right)^{a_2}\right) - \frac{a(a_1+a_2)}{a_2} e^{\frac{2\frac{a_1+a_2}{2} \ln \frac{pa_2}{2a}\left(\frac{a_2}{a_1}\right)^{a_2}}{a_1+a_2}} \left(\frac{a_1}{a_2}\right)^{a_2} - d.$

Equation (7) describes the optimal supply of a product, and Eq. (8) the maximum profit of a company.

Table 4.20 Measures of sensitivity of product supply function (E4.3b)

$\frac{\partial \overline{y}}{\partial p}$	> 0
$\frac{\partial \overline{y}}{\partial a}$	> 0
$\frac{\partial \overline{y}}{\partial d}$	0

Table 4.21 Measures of sensitivity of profit function (E4.3b)

$\frac{\partial \pi(\overline{y})}{\partial a}$	> 0
$\frac{\partial \pi(\overline{y})}{\partial p}$	> 0
$\frac{\partial \pi(\overline{y})}{\partial d}$	-1

In Tables 4.20 and 4.21 the sensitivity analysis of the product supply and of the firm maximum profit is presented.

Ad c

P1c

See Tables 4.22 and 4.23.

$$\pi(\mathbf{x}) = \left\{pa\left(a_1 x_1^\alpha + a_2 x_2^\alpha\right) - a\left(x_1^2 + x_2^2\right) - d\right\} \rightarrow \max$$

(1) $\left.\frac{\partial \pi(\mathbf{x})}{\partial x_1}\right|_{\mathbf{x}=\overline{\mathbf{x}}} = \alpha p a_1 \overline{x}_1^{\alpha-1} - 2a\overline{x}_1 = 0$

(2) $\left.\frac{\partial \pi(\mathbf{x})}{\partial x_2}\right|_{\mathbf{x}=\overline{\mathbf{x}}} = \alpha p a_2 \overline{x}_2^{\alpha-1} - 2a\overline{x}_2 = 0$

(3) $\overline{x}_1\left(\alpha p a_1 \overline{x}_1^{\alpha-2} - 2a\right) = 0$

(4) $\overline{x}_2\left(\alpha p a_2 \overline{x}_2^{\alpha-2} - 2a\right) = 0$

(5) $\overline{x}_1^{\alpha-2} = \left(\frac{2a}{\alpha p a_1}\right)$

(6) $\overline{x}_2^{\alpha-2} = \left(\frac{2a}{\alpha p a_2}\right)$

(7) $\overline{x}_1 = \left(\frac{\alpha p a_1}{2a}\right)^{\frac{1}{2-\alpha}}$

(8) $\overline{x}_2 = \left(\frac{\alpha p a_2}{2a}\right)^{\frac{1}{2-\alpha}}$

(9) $\overline{\mathbf{x}} = \left(\left(\frac{\alpha p a_1}{2a}\right)^{\frac{1}{2-\alpha}}, \left(\frac{\alpha p a_2}{2a}\right)^{\frac{1}{2-\alpha}}\right) = \overline{x}_1\left(1, \left(\frac{a_2}{a_1}\right)^{\frac{1}{2-\alpha}}\right) = \lambda\left(1, \left(\frac{a_2}{a_1}\right)^{\frac{1}{2-\alpha}}\right)$

(10)
$$\begin{aligned}\pi(\overline{\mathbf{x}}) = {} & pa\left(a_1\left(\frac{\alpha p a_1}{2a}\right)^{\frac{\alpha}{2-\alpha}} + a_2\left(\frac{\alpha p a_2}{2a}\right)^{\frac{\alpha}{2-\alpha}}\right) \\ & - a\left(\left(\frac{\alpha p a_1}{2a}\right)^{\frac{2}{2-\alpha}} + \left(\frac{\alpha p a_2}{2a}\right)^{\frac{2}{2-\alpha}}\right) - d.\end{aligned}$$

In Tables 4.22 and 4.23 the sensitivity analysis of the demand for production factors and of the firm maximum profit is presented.

Table 4.22 Measures of sensitivity of function of demand for production factors (E4.3c)

$\frac{\partial \overline{x}_1}{\partial a}$	< 0
$\frac{\partial \overline{x}_2}{\partial a}$	< 0
$\frac{\partial \overline{x}_1}{\partial p}$	> 0
$\frac{\partial \overline{x}_2}{\partial p}$	> 0

Table 4.23 Measures of sensitivity of profit function (E4.3c)

$\frac{\partial \pi(\overline{\mathbf{x}})}{\partial a}$	> 0
$\frac{\partial \pi(\overline{\mathbf{x}})}{\partial p}$	> 0
$\frac{\partial \pi(\overline{\mathbf{x}})}{\partial d}$	-1

P2c

Let us write down the problem of minimizing the costs of production of y units of the product:

$$c^{\text{tot}}(\mathbf{x}) = \left[a\left(x_1^2 + x_2^2\right) + d\right] \rightarrow \min,$$
$$a_1 x_1^\alpha + a_2 x_2^\alpha = y,$$
$$\mathbf{x} \geq (0, 0),$$

using a Lagrange function:

(2) $F(\mathbf{x}, \lambda) = a\left(x_1^2 + x_2^2\right) + d + \lambda\left(y - a_1 x_1^\alpha - a_2 x_2^\alpha\right).$

From the Kuhn-Tucker theorem it follows that:

(16) $\left.\frac{\partial F(\mathbf{x},\tilde{\lambda})}{\partial x_1}\right|_{\mathbf{x}=\tilde{\mathbf{x}}} = 2a\tilde{x}_1 - \tilde{\lambda}\alpha a_1 \tilde{x}_1^{\alpha-1} = 0$

(17) $\left.\frac{\partial F(\mathbf{x},\tilde{\lambda})}{\partial x_2}\right|_{\mathbf{x}=\tilde{\mathbf{x}}} = 2a\tilde{x}_2 - \tilde{\lambda}\alpha a_2 \tilde{x}_2^{\alpha-1} = 0$

(18) $\left.\frac{\partial F(\tilde{\mathbf{x}},\lambda)}{\partial \lambda}\right|_{\lambda=\tilde{\lambda}} = y - a_1\tilde{x}_1^\alpha - a_2\tilde{x}_2^\alpha = 0$

(19) $\frac{2a\tilde{x}_1}{2a\tilde{x}_2} = \frac{\tilde{\lambda}\alpha a_1 \tilde{x}_1^{\alpha-1}}{\tilde{\lambda}\alpha a_2 \tilde{x}_2^{\alpha-1}}$

(20) $\tilde{x}_2^{2-\alpha} = \left(\frac{a_2}{a_1}\right)\tilde{x}_1^{2-\alpha}$

(21) $\tilde{x}_2 = \left(\frac{a_2}{a_1}\right)^{\frac{1}{2-\alpha}}\tilde{x}_1$

(22) $a_1\tilde{x}_1^\alpha + a_2\left(\frac{a_2}{a_1}\right)^{\frac{1}{2-\alpha}}\tilde{x}_1^\alpha = y$

(23) $\tilde{x}_1^\alpha\left(\frac{a_1^{\frac{3-\alpha}{2-\alpha}} + a_2^{\frac{3-\alpha}{2-\alpha}}}{a_1^{\frac{1}{2-\alpha}}}\right) = y$

(24) $\tilde{x}_1^\alpha = \frac{a_1^{\frac{1}{2-\alpha}}\,y}{a_1^{\frac{3-\alpha}{2-\alpha}} + a_2^{\frac{3-\alpha}{2-\alpha}}}$

Table 4.24 Measures of sensitivity of function of conditional demand for production factors (E4.3c)

$\frac{\partial \tilde{x}_1}{\partial y}$	> 0
$\frac{\partial \tilde{x}_2}{\partial y}$	> 0

Table 4.25 Measures of sensitivity of function of minimum cost of production of y units of the product (E4.3c)

$\frac{\partial c^{\text{tot}}(\tilde{\mathbf{x}})}{\partial a}$	> 0
$\frac{\partial c^{\text{tot}}(\tilde{\mathbf{x}})}{\partial y}$	> 0
$\frac{\partial c^{\text{tot}}(\tilde{\mathbf{x}})}{\partial d}$	1

(25) $$\tilde{x}_1 = \frac{a_1^{\frac{1}{(2-\alpha)\alpha}} y^{\frac{1}{\alpha}}}{\left(a_1^{\frac{3-\alpha}{2-\alpha}} + a_2^{\frac{3-\alpha}{2-\alpha}}\right)^{\frac{1}{\alpha}}}$$

(26) $$\tilde{x}_2 = \left(\frac{a_2}{a_1}\right)^{\frac{1}{2}} \frac{a_1^{\frac{1}{(2-\alpha)\alpha}} y^{\frac{1}{\alpha}}}{\left(a_1^{\frac{3-\alpha}{2-\alpha}} + a_2^{\frac{3-\alpha}{2-\alpha}}\right)^{\frac{1}{\alpha}}}$$

(27) $$\tilde{\mathbf{x}} = (\tilde{x}_1, \tilde{x}_2) = \tilde{x}_1\left(1, \left(\frac{a_2}{a_1}\right)^{\frac{1}{2}}\right) = \lambda\left(1, \left(\frac{a_2}{a_1}\right)^{\frac{1}{2}}\right) = \overline{\mathbf{x}}.$$

Equation (27) shows that the function of demand for production factors and the function of conditional demand for production factorsare identical in terms of a structure.

$$c^{\text{tot}}(\tilde{\mathbf{x}}) = a\left(\frac{a_1^{\frac{2}{(2-\alpha)\alpha}} y^{\frac{2}{\alpha}}}{\left(a_1^{\frac{3-\alpha}{2-\alpha}} + a_2^{\frac{3-\alpha}{2-\alpha}}\right)^{\frac{2}{\alpha}}} + \left(\frac{a_2}{a_1}\right)\frac{a_1^{\frac{2}{(2-\alpha)\alpha}} y^{\frac{2}{\alpha}}}{\left(a_1^{\frac{3-\alpha}{2-\alpha}} + a_2^{\frac{3-\alpha}{2-\alpha}}\right)^{\frac{2}{\alpha}}}\right) + d$$

(28) $$= y^{\frac{2}{\alpha}} a \frac{a_1^{\frac{2}{(2-\alpha)\alpha}}}{\left(a_1^{\frac{3-\alpha}{2-\alpha}} + a_2^{\frac{3-\alpha}{2-\alpha}}\right)^{\frac{2}{\alpha}}}\left(1 + \frac{a_2}{a_1}\right) + d$$

$$= \frac{a(a_1 + a_2)}{a_1} y^{\frac{2}{\alpha}} \frac{a_1^{\frac{2}{(2-\alpha)\alpha}}}{\left(a_1^{\frac{3-\alpha}{2-\alpha}} + a_2^{\frac{3-\alpha}{2-\alpha}}\right)^{\frac{2}{\alpha}}} + d = k(y).$$

Equation (28) describes the function of the minimum cost of production of y units of a product.

In Tables 4.24 and 4.25 the sensitivity analysis of the conditional demand for production factors and of the minimum cost of production is presented.

P3c

Let us formulate the problem of maximizing the firm's profit as a function of the product supply:

$$\pi(y) = py - k(y)$$

$$= \left[py - \frac{a(a_1 + a_2)}{a_1} y^{\frac{2}{\alpha}} \frac{a_1^{\frac{2}{(2-\alpha)\alpha}}}{\left(a_1^{\frac{3-\alpha}{2-\alpha}} + a_2^{\frac{3-\alpha}{2-\alpha}}\right)^{\frac{2}{\alpha}}} - d \right] \to \max,$$

$$y > 0.$$

Then a function of the marginal profit takes a form:

(1) $\frac{d\pi(y)}{dy} = p - \frac{2a(a_1+a_2)}{\alpha a_1} y^{\frac{2-\alpha}{\alpha}} \frac{a_1^{\frac{2}{(2-\alpha)\alpha}}}{\left(a_1^{\frac{3-\alpha}{2-\alpha}} + a_2^{\frac{3-\alpha}{2-\alpha}}\right)^{\frac{2}{\alpha}}} = 0.$

It is not difficult to check that the boundary conditions are met for the profit function in each case of three considered production functions:

(2) $\lim\limits_{y \to 0+} \frac{d\pi(y)}{dy} = p > 0$ and $\lim\limits_{y \to +\infty} \frac{\partial \pi(y)}{\partial y} = -\infty < 0,$

on this basis, we claim that $\exists_1 \overline{y} > 0$ such that:

(3) $\left.\frac{d\pi(y)}{\partial y}\right|_{y=\overline{y}} = p - \frac{2a(a_1+a_2)}{\alpha a_1} \overline{y}^{\frac{2-\alpha}{\alpha}} \frac{a_1^{\frac{2}{(2-\alpha)\alpha}}}{\left(a_1^{\frac{3-\alpha}{2-\alpha}} + a_2^{\frac{3-\alpha}{2-\alpha}}\right)^{\frac{2}{\alpha}}} = 0,$

(4) $\overline{y}^{\frac{2-\alpha}{\alpha}} = \frac{p\alpha a_1 \left(a_1^{\frac{3-\alpha}{2-\alpha}} + a_2^{\frac{3-\alpha}{2-\alpha}}\right)^{\frac{2}{\alpha}}}{2a(a_1+a_2) a_1^{\frac{2}{(2-\alpha)\alpha}}},$

(5) $\overline{y} = \left(\frac{pa_1}{2a(a_1+a_2)}\right)^{\frac{\alpha}{(2-\alpha)}} \frac{\left(a_1^{\frac{3-\alpha}{2-\alpha}} + a_2^{\frac{3-\alpha}{2-\alpha}}\right)^{\frac{2}{2-\alpha}}}{a_1^{\frac{2}{(2-\alpha)^2}}},$

(6)
$$\pi(\overline{y}) = p^{\frac{2}{(2-\alpha)}} \left(\frac{a_1}{2a(a_1+a_2)}\right)^{\frac{\alpha}{(2-\alpha)}} \frac{\left(a_1^{\frac{3-\alpha}{2-\alpha}} + a_2^{\frac{3-\alpha}{2-\alpha}}\right)^{\frac{2}{2-\alpha}}}{a_1^{\frac{2}{(2-\alpha)^2}}}$$
$$- \frac{a(a_1+a_2)}{a_1} \left(\left(\frac{pa_1}{2a(a_1+a_2)}\right)^{\frac{\alpha}{(2-\alpha)}} \frac{\left(a_1^{\frac{3-\alpha}{2-\alpha}} + a_2^{\frac{3-\alpha}{2-\alpha}}\right)^{\frac{2}{2-\alpha}}}{a_1^{\frac{2}{(2-\alpha)^2}}} \right)^{\frac{2}{\alpha}} \frac{a_1^{\frac{2}{(2-\alpha)\alpha}}}{\left(a_1^{\frac{3-\alpha}{2-\alpha}} + a_2^{\frac{3-\alpha}{2-\alpha}}\right)^{\frac{2}{\alpha}}} - d.$$

Equation (7) describes the optimal supply of the product and Eq. (8) the maximum profit of the company.

In Tables 4.26 and 4.27 the sensitivity analysis of the product supply and of the firm maximum profit is presented.

Table 4.26 Measures of sensitivity of function of product supply (E4.3c)

$\frac{\partial \overline{y}}{\partial p}$	> 0
$\frac{\partial \overline{y}}{\partial a}$	< 0
$\frac{\partial \overline{y}}{\partial d}$	0

Table 4.27 Measures of sensitivity of profit function (E4.3c)

$\frac{\partial \pi(\overline{y})}{\partial a}$	< 0
$\frac{\partial \pi(\overline{y})}{\partial p}$	> 0
$\frac{\partial \pi(\overline{y})}{\partial d}$	-1

E4.4. Solve exercise E3, when the production total cost function has a form:

$$c^{tot}(x_1, x_2) = \alpha(f(x_1, x_2))^2 + \beta f(x_1, x_2) + \gamma,$$

or equivalently:

$$c^{tot}(y) = \alpha y^2 + \beta y + \gamma,$$

where $y = f(x_1, x_2)$ is an increasing, strictly concave and twice differentiable production function and $\Delta = \beta^2 - 4\alpha\gamma = 0,\ \alpha, \beta, \gamma > 0$.

Solutions

Let us notice that the production function $y = f(x_1, x_2)$ has the same properties as the functions:

power: $y = f(\mathbf{x}) = ax_1^{\alpha_1}x_2^{\alpha_2},\ a > 0,\ \alpha_i \in (0, 1),\ \alpha_1 + \alpha_2 < 1, i = 1, 2,$
logarithmic: $y = f(\mathbf{x}) = a_1 \ln x_1 + a_2 \ln x_2,\ a_i > 0,\ i = 1, 2,$
subadditive: $y = f(\mathbf{x}) = a_1 x_1^\alpha + a_2 x_2^\alpha,\ a_i > 0,\ \alpha \in (0, 1),\ i = 1, 2.$

(P1c)

Let us write the problem of maximizing the firm's profit in the general form:

$$\begin{aligned}\pi(\mathbf{x}) &= pf(\mathbf{x}) - \alpha(f(\mathbf{x}))^2 - \beta f(\mathbf{x}) - \gamma \\ &= \left\{-\alpha(f(\mathbf{x}))^2 + (p - \beta)(f(\mathbf{x})) - \gamma\right\} \to \max, \\ \mathbf{x} &\geq (0, 0).\end{aligned}$$

Then the marginal profit functions take forms:

(1) $\frac{\partial \pi(\mathbf{x})}{\partial x_1} = -2\alpha f(\mathbf{x})\frac{\partial f(\mathbf{x})}{\partial x_1} + (p - \beta)\frac{\partial f(\mathbf{x})}{\partial x_1},$
(2) $\frac{\partial \pi(\mathbf{x})}{\partial x_2} = -2\alpha f(\mathbf{x})\frac{\partial f(\mathbf{x})}{\partial x_2} + (p - \beta)\frac{\partial f(\mathbf{x})}{\partial x_2}.$

It is not difficult to check that the boundary conditions are met for the profit function in each case of three considered production functions:

(3) $\lim_{x_1 \to 0^+} \frac{\partial \pi(\mathbf{x})}{\partial x_1} = +\infty > 0$ and $\lim_{x_1 \to +\infty} \frac{\partial \pi(\mathbf{x})}{\partial x_1} = -\infty < 0$,
(4) $\lim_{x_2 \to 0^+} \frac{\partial \pi(\mathbf{x})}{\partial x_2} = +\infty > 0$ and $\lim_{x_2 \to +\infty} \frac{\partial \pi(\mathbf{x})}{\partial x_2} = -\infty < 0$.

On this basis, we claim that $\exists_1 \overline{\mathbf{x}} > (0, 0)$ such that:

(5) $\left.\frac{\partial \pi(\mathbf{x})}{\partial x_1}\right|_{\mathbf{x}=\overline{\mathbf{x}}} = -2\alpha f(\overline{\mathbf{x}}) \left.\frac{\partial f(\mathbf{x})}{\partial x_1}\right|_{\mathbf{x}=\overline{\mathbf{x}}} + (p - \beta) \left.\frac{\partial f(\mathbf{x})}{\partial x_1}\right|_{\mathbf{x}=\overline{\mathbf{x}}} = 0$,
(6) $\left.\frac{\partial \pi(\mathbf{x})}{\partial x_2}\right|_{\mathbf{x}=\overline{\mathbf{x}}} = -2\alpha f(\overline{\mathbf{x}}) \left.\frac{\partial f(\mathbf{x})}{\partial x_2}\right|_{\mathbf{x}=\overline{\mathbf{x}}} + (p - \beta) \left.\frac{\partial f(\mathbf{x})}{\partial x_2}\right|_{\mathbf{x}=\overline{\mathbf{x}}} = 0$.

Let us write the system of Eqs. (5)–(6) in the equivalent form:

(7) $(-2\alpha f(\overline{\mathbf{x}}) + (p - \beta)) \left.\frac{\partial f(\mathbf{x})}{\partial x_1}\right|_{\mathbf{x}=\overline{\mathbf{x}}} = 0$,
(8) $(-2\alpha f(\overline{\mathbf{x}}) + (p - \beta)) \left.\frac{\partial f(\mathbf{x})}{\partial x_2}\right|_{\mathbf{x}=\overline{\mathbf{x}}} = 0$.

It follows that:

(9) $2\alpha f(\overline{\mathbf{x}}) + (p - \beta) = 0$,
(10) $f(\overline{\mathbf{x}}) = \frac{\beta - p}{2\alpha}$.

This means that for none of the considered production functions we can give an analytical form of the demand function for both factors of production.

(P2c)

Let us write down the task of minimizing the cost of producing y units of a product:

$$\begin{aligned} &c^{\text{tot}}(f(\mathbf{x})) = \left\{\alpha(f(\mathbf{x}))^2 + \beta f(\mathbf{x}) + \gamma\right\} \to \min \\ &f(\mathbf{x}) = y, \\ &\mathbf{x} \geq (0, 0), \end{aligned}$$

using the Lagrange function:

(1) $F(\mathbf{x}, \lambda) = \alpha(f(\mathbf{x}))^2 + \beta f(\mathbf{x}) + \gamma + \lambda(y - f(\mathbf{x}))$.

From the Kuhn-Tucker theorem, it follows that:

(2) $\left.\frac{\partial F(\mathbf{x},\overline{\lambda})}{\partial x_1}\right|_{\mathbf{x}=\overline{\mathbf{x}}} = -2\alpha f(\overline{\mathbf{x}}) \left.\frac{\partial f(\mathbf{x})}{\partial x_1}\right|_{\mathbf{x}=\overline{\mathbf{x}}} + (\beta - \overline{\lambda}) \left.\frac{\partial f(\mathbf{x})}{\partial x_1}\right|_{\mathbf{x}=\overline{\mathbf{x}}} = 0$,
(3) $\left.\frac{\partial F(\mathbf{x},\overline{\lambda})}{\partial x_2}\right|_{\mathbf{x}=\overline{\mathbf{x}}} = -2\alpha f(\overline{\mathbf{x}}) \left.\frac{\partial f(\mathbf{x})}{\partial x_2}\right|_{\mathbf{x}=\overline{\mathbf{x}}} + (\beta - \overline{\lambda}) \left.\frac{\partial f(\mathbf{x})}{\partial x_2}\right|_{\mathbf{x}=\overline{\mathbf{x}}} = 0$,
(4) $\left.\frac{\partial F(\overline{\mathbf{x}},\lambda)}{\partial \lambda}\right|_{\lambda=\overline{\lambda}} = y - f(\overline{\mathbf{x}}) = 0$.

From the system of Eqs. (2)–(4) it follows that:

(5) $f(\overline{\mathbf{x}}) = \frac{\beta - p}{2\alpha}$,
(6) $f(\overline{\mathbf{x}}) = \frac{\beta - p}{2\alpha} = y$.

This means that for none of the considered production functions we can give an analytical form, neither for the conditional demand function nor for the function of the minimum cost of producing y units of a product.

(P3c)

Since we do not know the analytical form of the function of the minimum cost of production of y units of a product, we cannot find a solution to the profit maximization problem (P3c), and thus the analytical form of the product supply function and the maximum profit function.

E4.5. Solve exercise E4.3 assuming additionally that resources of production factors are limited: $\forall i = 1, 2 \quad 0 \leq x_i \leq b_i$, where $\forall i = 1, 2 \quad b_i > 0$ means the constrained resource of i-th production factor.

Solution

Based on the conclusions resulting from the solutions of the profit maximization problems in exercise E4.3, we can conclude that:

(1) If $\overline{\mathbf{x}}^G \in B = \{\mathbf{x} \in \mathbb{R}^2_+ | 0 \leq x_1 \leq b_1, 0 \leq x_2 \leq b_2\}$, then we know the analytical forms of the functions of optimal demand for factors of production, conditional demand for factors of production or optimal supply of the product. Then the optimal solutions to problems P1c, P2c and P3c in E4.3 and E.4.5 are the same.
(2) If $\overline{\mathbf{x}}^G \notin B = \{\mathbf{x} \in \mathbb{R}^2_+ | 0 \leq x_1 \leq b_1, 0 \leq x_2 \leq b_2\}$, then the function of optimal demand for factors of production has the form: $\overline{\mathbf{x}} = \overline{\mathbf{x}}^L = (b_1, b_2)$, while the optimal product supply function is given as $\overline{y} = f(b_1, b_2)$.

E4.6. Solve exercise E4.3 taking simultaneously into account the data from exercises E4.4. and E4.5.

Solution

Based on the conclusions resulting from the solutions of the profit maximization tasks in the problem E4.4. and E4.5, we can conclude that:

(1) If $\overline{\mathbf{x}}^G \in B = \{\mathbf{x} \in \mathbb{R}^2_+ | 0 \leq x_1 \leq b_1, 0 \leq x_2 \leq b_2\}$, then we do not know the analytical forms of the functions of optimal demand for factors of production, conditional demand for factors of production or optimal supply of the product.
(2) If $\overline{\mathbf{x}}^G \notin B = \{\mathbf{x} \in \mathbb{R}^2_+ | 0 \leq x_1 \leq b_1, 0 \leq x_2 \leq b_2\}$, then the function of optimal demand for factors of production has the form: $\overline{\mathbf{x}} = \overline{\mathbf{x}}^L = (b_1, b_2)$, while the optimal product supply function is given as $\overline{y} = f(b_1, b_2)$.

E4.7. There are given:

$\mathbf{x} = (x_1, x_2) \geq (0, 0)$—a vector of inputs of production factors,
$y = f(\mathbf{x})$—an output level described by an increasing, strictly concave and twice differentiable production function,
$p(y) = \left(\frac{a}{y}\right)^{\alpha} > 0$—a price of product manufactured by a monopoly as a function of product supply, set by a monopoly,
$p(f(\mathbf{x})) = \left(\frac{a}{f(\mathbf{x})}\right)^{\alpha} > 0$—a price of product manufactured by a monopoly as a function of production factors' inputs,

$c(\mathbf{x}) = (c_1(x_1), c_2(x_2)) > (0, 0)$—a vector of prices of production factors, each of whom is a function of demand reported by a monopoly for a given production factor,
$c_i(x_i) = ax_i$—a price of i-th production factor is proportional to the demand for i-th factor,
$r(y) = p(y)y$—revenue (turnover) from sales of a manufactured product as a function of product supply,
$r(\mathbf{x}) = p(f(\mathbf{x}))f(\mathbf{x})$—revenue (turnover) from sales of a manufactured product as a function of inputs of production factors,
$c^{\text{tot}}(\mathbf{x}) = c_1(x_1)x_1 + c_2(x_2)x_2 + d = a(x_1^2 + x_2^2) + d$—total cost of production,
$c^{v}(\mathbf{x}) = c_1(x_1)x_1 + c_2(x_2)x_2 = a(x_1^2 + x_2^2)$—variable cost of production,
$c^{f}(\mathbf{x}) = d$—fixed cost of production,
$k(y)$—minimum cost of producing y output units, derived as an objective function corresponding to an optimal solution to problem (P2m),
$\pi(y) = r(y) - k(y) = p(y)y - c(y)$—firm profit as a function of output level,
$\pi(\mathbf{x}) = r(\mathbf{x}) - c^{\text{tot}}(\mathbf{x})$—firm profit as a function of inputs of production factors.

For a production function:

(a) power: $y = f(\mathbf{x}) = ax_1^{\alpha_1}x_2^{\alpha_2},\ a > 0,\ \alpha_i \in (0, 1),\ \alpha_1 + \alpha_2 < 1, i = 1, 2,$
(b) logarithmic: $y = f(\mathbf{x}) = a_1 \ln x_1 + a_2 \ln x_2,\ a_i > 0,\ i = 1, 2,$
(c) subadditive: $y = f(\mathbf{x}) = a_1 x_1^{\alpha} + a_2 x_2^{\alpha},\ a_i > 0,\ \alpha \in (0, 1),\ i = 1, 2.$

1. Solve the profit maximization problem (P1m).
2. Solve the cost minimization problem (P2m).
3. Solve the profit maximization problem (P3m).
4. Determine the optimal price by which a monopoly obtains the maximum profit.
5. Justify that the profit maximizations problems (P1m) and (P3m) are equivalent.

Solutions

From the data given we get the revenue function in the following form:

$$r(y) = p(y)y = \left(\frac{a}{y}\right)^{\alpha} \cdot y = a^{\alpha} y^{1-\alpha} = a^{\alpha} y = a^{\alpha} f(\mathbf{x})^{1-\alpha} = r(\mathbf{x}).$$

Then:

(a) For the power production function: $y = f(\mathbf{x}) = ax_1^{\alpha_1}x_2^{\alpha_2},\ a > 0,\ \alpha_i \in (0, 1),\ \alpha_1 + \alpha_2 < 1, i = 1, 2,$

$$r(\mathbf{x}) = a^{\alpha} a^{1-\alpha} x_1^{\alpha_1(1-\alpha)} x_2^{\alpha_2(1-\alpha)} = ax_1^{\beta_1}x_2^{\beta_2},$$
$$\beta_1 = \alpha_1(1-\alpha) < 1,\ \beta_2 = \alpha_2(1-\alpha) < 1.$$

(b) For the logarithmic production function: $y = f(\mathbf{x}) = a_1 \ln x_1 + a_2 \ln x_2,\ a_1, a_2 > 0,$

$$r(\mathbf{x}) = a^{\alpha}(a_1 \ln x_1 + a_2 \ln x_2)^{1-\alpha}.$$

(c) For the subadditive production function: $y = f(\mathbf{x}) = a_1 x_1^{\alpha} + a_2 x_2^{\alpha},\ a_1, a_2 > 0, 0 < \alpha < 1$,

$$r(\mathbf{x}) = a^{\alpha}\left(a_1 x_1^{\alpha} + a_2 x_2^{\alpha}\right)^{1-\alpha}.$$

Ad a

P1m

Let us write the problem (P1m) of maximizing the firm's profit in the case of the power production function and the nonlinear function of total cost:

$$\pi(\mathbf{x}) = \left\{a x_1^{\beta_1} x_2^{\beta_2} - a\left(x_1^2 + x_2^2\right) - d\right\} \to \max,$$
$$\mathbf{x} \geq (0, 0).$$

Then the marginal profit functions take forms:

(1) $\frac{\partial \pi(\mathbf{x})}{\partial x_1} = \beta_1 a x_1^{\beta_1 - 1} x_2^{\beta_2} - 2a x_1,$

(2) $\frac{\partial \pi(\mathbf{x})}{\partial x_2} = \beta_2 a x_1^{\beta_1} x_2^{\beta_2 - 1} - 2a x_2.$

It is not difficult to check that the boundary conditions for the profit function are met:

(3) $\lim\limits_{x_1 \to 0^+} \frac{\partial \pi(\mathbf{x})}{\partial x_1} = +\infty > 0$ and $\lim\limits_{x_1 \to \infty} \frac{\partial \pi(\mathbf{x})}{\partial x_1} = -\infty < 0,$

(4) $\lim\limits_{x_2 \to 0^+} \frac{\partial \pi(\mathbf{x})}{\partial x_2} = +\infty > 0$ and $\lim\limits_{x_2 \to \infty} \frac{\partial \pi(\mathbf{x})}{\partial x_2} = -\infty < 0.$

On this basis, we claim that $\exists_1 \overline{\mathbf{x}} > (0, 0)$ such that:

(5) $\left.\frac{\partial \pi(\mathbf{x})}{\partial x_1}\right|_{\mathbf{x}=\overline{\mathbf{x}}} = \beta_1 a \overline{x}_1^{\beta_1 - 1} \overline{x}_2^{\beta_2} - 2a\overline{x}_1 = 0,$

(6) $\left.\frac{\partial \pi(\mathbf{x})}{\partial x_2}\right|_{\mathbf{x}=\overline{\mathbf{x}}} = \beta_2 a \overline{x}_1^{\beta_1} \overline{x}_2^{\beta_2 - 1} - 2a\overline{x}_2 = 0.$

Let us solve the system of Eqs. (5)–(6):

(7) $\frac{\beta_1}{\beta_2}\frac{\overline{x}_2}{\overline{x}_1} = \frac{\overline{x}_1}{\overline{x}_2}$

(8) $\overline{x}_2^2 = \frac{\beta_2}{\beta_1}\overline{x}_1^2$

(9) $\overline{x}_2 = \left(\frac{\beta_2}{\beta_1}\right)^{\frac{1}{2}} \overline{x}_1$

(10) $a\overline{x}_1\left(\beta_1 \overline{x}_1^{\beta_1 - 2}\left(\frac{\beta_2}{\beta_1}\right)^{\frac{\beta_2}{2}} \overline{x}_1^{\beta_2} - 2\right) = 0$

(11) $\overline{x}_1^{\beta_1 + \beta_2 - 2} \beta_1^{\frac{2-\beta_2}{2}} \beta_2^{\frac{\beta_2}{2}} = 2$

(12) $\overline{x}_1^{\beta_1 + \beta_1 - 2} \beta_1^{\frac{2-\beta_2}{2}} \beta_2^{\frac{\beta_2}{2}} = \frac{2}{\beta_1^{\frac{2-\beta_2}{2}} \beta_2^{\frac{\beta_2}{2}}}$

(13) $\overline{x}_1^{2 - \beta_1 - \beta_2} = \frac{\beta_1^{\frac{2-\beta_2}{2}} \beta_2^{\frac{\beta_2}{2}}}{2}$

(14) $\overline{x}_1 = \dfrac{\beta_1^{\frac{2-\beta_2}{2(2-\beta_1-\beta_2)}} \beta_2^{\frac{\beta_2}{2(2-\beta_1-\beta_2)}}}{2^{\frac{1}{2-\beta_1-\beta_2}}}$

(15) $\overline{x}_2 = \left(\frac{\beta_2}{\beta_1}\right)^{\frac{1}{2}} \dfrac{\beta_1^{\frac{2-\beta_2}{2(2-\beta_1-\beta_2)}} \beta_2^{\frac{\beta_2}{2(2-\beta_1-\beta_2)}}}{2^{\frac{1}{2-\beta_1-\beta_2}}} = \dfrac{\beta_1^{\frac{\beta_1}{2(2-\beta_1-\beta_2)}} \beta_2^{\frac{2-\beta_1}{2(2-\beta_1-\beta_2)}}}{2^{\frac{1}{2-\beta_1-\beta_2}}}$

(16)
$$\overline{\mathbf{x}} = \left(\frac{\beta_1^{\frac{2-\beta_2}{2(2-\beta_1-\beta_2)}} \beta_2^{\frac{\beta_2}{2(2-\beta_1-\beta_2)}}}{2^{\frac{1}{2-\beta_1-\beta_2}}}, \frac{\beta_1^{\frac{\beta_1}{2(2-\beta_1-\beta_2)}} \beta_2^{\frac{2-\beta_1}{2(2-\beta_1-\beta_2)}}}{2^{\frac{1}{2-\beta_1-\beta_2}}} \right) = \overline{x}_1 \left(1, \left(\frac{\beta_2}{\beta_1}\right)^{\frac{1}{2}}\right)$$
$$= \lambda \left(1, \left(\frac{\beta_2}{\beta_1}\right)^{\frac{1}{2}}\right), \forall \lambda > 0$$

(17) $\pi(\overline{\mathbf{x}}) = a\left(\left(\frac{\beta_2}{\beta_1}\right)^{\frac{\beta_2}{2}} - \frac{\beta_2}{\beta_1}\right) - (a + d).$

P2m

We have the problem of minimizing the cost of production of y units of a product:

$$c^{\text{tot}}(\mathbf{x}) = \{a(x_1^2 + x_2^2) + d\} \to \min,$$
$$a x_1^{\alpha_1} x_2^{\alpha_2} = y > 0,$$
$$x_1, x_2 \geq 0.$$

Let us write it down using Lagrange function:

(1) $F(x_1, x_2, \lambda) = a(x_1^2 + x_2^2) + d + \lambda(y - a x_1^{\alpha_1} x_2^{\alpha_2}).$

From the Kuhn-Tucker theorem it follows that:

(2) $\left.\frac{\partial F(\mathbf{x},\tilde{\lambda})}{\partial x_1}\right|_{\mathbf{x}=\tilde{\mathbf{x}}} = 2a\tilde{x}_1 - \tilde{\lambda}\alpha_1 a \tilde{x}_1^{\alpha_1 - 1}\tilde{x}_2^{\alpha_2} = 0$

(3) $\left.\frac{\partial F(\mathbf{x},\tilde{\lambda})}{\partial x_2}\right|_{\mathbf{x}=\tilde{\mathbf{x}}} = 2a\tilde{x}_2 - \tilde{\lambda}\alpha_2 a \tilde{x}_1^{\alpha_1}\tilde{x}_2^{\alpha_2 - 1}\alpha = 0$

(4) $\left.\frac{\partial F(\tilde{\mathbf{x}},\lambda)}{\partial \lambda}\right|_{\lambda=\tilde{\lambda}} = y - a\tilde{x}_1^{\alpha_1}\tilde{x}_2^{\alpha_2} = 0$

(5) $\frac{2a\tilde{x}_1}{2a\tilde{x}_2} = \frac{\tilde{\lambda}\alpha_1 a \tilde{x}_1^{\alpha_1 - 1}\tilde{x}_2^{\alpha_2}}{\tilde{\lambda}\alpha_2 a \tilde{x}_1^{\alpha_1}\tilde{x}_2^{\alpha_2 - 1}}$

(6) $\tilde{x}_2^2 = \left(\frac{\alpha_2}{\alpha_1}\right)\tilde{x}_1^2$

(7) $\tilde{x}_2 = \left(\frac{\alpha_2}{\alpha_1}\right)^{\frac{1}{2}}\tilde{x}_1$

(8) $a\tilde{x}_1^{\alpha_1}\tilde{x}_2^{\alpha_2} = a\tilde{x}_1^{\alpha_1}\left(\frac{\alpha_2}{\alpha_1}\right)^{\frac{\alpha_2}{2}}\tilde{x}_1^{\alpha_2} = y$

(9) $\tilde{x}_1^{\alpha_1+\alpha_2} = \frac{y}{a}\left(\frac{\alpha_1}{\alpha_2}\right)^{\frac{\alpha_2}{2}}$

(10) $\tilde{x}_1 = \left(\frac{y}{a}\right)^{\frac{1}{\alpha_1+\alpha_2}}\left(\frac{\alpha_1}{\alpha_2}\right)^{\frac{\alpha_2}{2(\alpha_1+\alpha_2)}}$

(11) $\tilde{x}_2 = \left(\frac{\alpha_2}{\alpha_1}\right)^{\frac{1}{2}}\left(\frac{y}{a}\right)^{\frac{1}{\alpha_1+\alpha_2}}\left(\frac{\alpha_1}{\alpha_2}\right)^{\frac{\alpha_2}{2(\alpha_1+\alpha_2)}} = \left(\frac{y}{a}\right)^{\frac{1}{\alpha_1+\alpha_2}}\left(\frac{\alpha_2}{\alpha_1}\right)^{\frac{\alpha_1}{2(\alpha_1+\alpha_2)}}$

(12) $\tilde{\mathbf{x}} = \left(\left(\frac{y}{a}\right)^{\frac{1}{\alpha_1+\alpha_2}}\left(\frac{\alpha_1}{\alpha_2}\right)^{\frac{\alpha_2}{2(\alpha_1+\alpha_2)}}, \left(\frac{y}{a}\right)^{\frac{1}{\alpha_1+\alpha_2}}\left(\frac{\alpha_2}{\alpha_1}\right)^{\frac{\alpha_1}{2(\alpha_1+\alpha_2)}}\right)$

$$(13)\quad \widetilde{\mathbf{x}} = (\tilde{x}_1 \tilde{x}_2) = \tilde{x}_1\left(1, \left(\frac{\alpha_2}{\alpha_1}\right)^{\frac{1}{2}}\right) = \lambda\left(1, \left(\frac{\alpha_2}{\alpha_1}\right)^{\frac{1}{2}}\right) = \overline{\mathbf{x}}.$$

Equation (13) shows that the function of demand for production factors and the function of conditional demand for production factors are identical in terms of a structure.

The function of the minimum cost of production of y units of a product is:

$$\begin{aligned} c^{\mathrm{tot}}(\widetilde{\mathbf{x}}) &= a\left(\left(\frac{y}{a}\right)^{\frac{2}{\alpha_1+\alpha_2}}\left(\frac{\alpha_1}{\alpha_2}\right)^{\frac{\alpha_2}{(\alpha_1+\alpha_2)}} + \left(\frac{y}{a}\right)^{\frac{2}{\alpha_1+\alpha_2}}\left(\frac{\alpha_2}{\alpha_1}\right)^{\frac{\alpha_1}{(\alpha_1+\alpha_2)}}\right) + d \\ (14)\qquad &= a\left(\frac{y}{a}\right)^{\frac{2}{\alpha_1+\alpha_2}}\left(\frac{\alpha_1}{\alpha_2}\right)^{\frac{\alpha_2}{(\alpha_1+\alpha_2)}}\left(1+\frac{\alpha_1}{\alpha_2}\right) + d \\ &= \frac{a(\alpha_1+\alpha_2)}{\alpha_2}\left(\frac{y}{a}\right)^{\frac{2}{\alpha_1+\alpha_2}}\left(\frac{\alpha_1}{\alpha_2}\right)^{\frac{\alpha_2}{(\alpha_1+\alpha_2)}} + d = k(y) \end{aligned}$$

P3m

The problem of maximizing the profit with regard to the supply of the product has the following form:

$$\pi(y) = \left\{a^{\alpha} y^{1-\alpha} - \frac{a(\alpha_1+\alpha_2)}{\alpha_2}\left(\frac{y}{a}\right)^{\frac{2}{\alpha_1+\alpha_2}}\left(\frac{\alpha_1}{\alpha_2}\right)^{\frac{\alpha_2}{(\alpha_1+\alpha_2)}} - d\right\} \to \max$$

$$y \geq 0.$$

Then a function of the marginal profit takes a form:

$$\begin{aligned} \frac{d\pi(y)}{dy} &= (1-\alpha)a^{\alpha}y^{-\alpha} - \frac{2}{\alpha_1+\alpha_2}\frac{a(\alpha_1+\alpha_2)}{a\alpha_2}\left(\frac{y}{a}\right)^{\frac{2-\alpha_1-\alpha_2}{\alpha_1+\alpha_2}}\left(\frac{\alpha_1}{\alpha_2}\right)^{\frac{\alpha_2}{(\alpha_1+\alpha_2)}} \\ (1)\qquad &= (1-\alpha)a^{\alpha}y^{-\alpha} - \frac{2}{\alpha_2}\left(\frac{y}{a}\right)^{\frac{2-\alpha_1-\alpha_2}{\alpha_1+\alpha_2}}\left(\frac{\alpha_1}{\alpha_2}\right)^{\frac{\alpha_2}{(\alpha_1+\alpha_2)}}. \end{aligned}$$

It is not difficult to check that the boundary conditions for the profit function are met:

$$(2)\quad \lim_{y\to 0^+}\frac{d\pi(y)}{dy} = +\infty > 0 \text{ and } \lim_{y\to +\infty}\frac{\partial\pi(y)}{\partial y} = -\infty < 0.$$

On this basis, we claim that $\exists_1 \overline{y} > 0$ such that:

$$(3)\quad \left.\frac{d\pi(y)}{\partial y}\right|_{y=\overline{y}} = (1-\alpha)a^{\alpha}\overline{y}^{-\alpha} - \frac{2}{\alpha_2}\left(\frac{\overline{y}}{a}\right)^{\frac{2-\alpha_1-\alpha_2}{\alpha_1+\alpha_2}}\left(\frac{\alpha_1}{\alpha_2}\right)^{\frac{\alpha_2}{(\alpha_1+\alpha_2)}} = 0$$

$$(4)\quad \overline{y}^{-\alpha}\left((1-\alpha)a^{\alpha} - \frac{2}{\alpha_2}\left(\frac{1}{a}\right)^{\frac{2-\alpha_1-\alpha_2}{\alpha_1+\alpha_2}}\overline{y}^{\frac{2+(\alpha-1)(\alpha_1+\alpha_2)}{\alpha_1+\alpha_2}}\left(\frac{\alpha_1}{\alpha_2}\right)^{\frac{\alpha_2}{(\alpha_1+\alpha_2)}}\right) = 0$$

$$(5)\quad \overline{y}^{\frac{2+(\alpha-1)(\alpha_1+\alpha_2)}{\alpha_1+\alpha_2}} = \frac{(1-\alpha)a^{\frac{2+}{\alpha_1+\alpha_2}}}{2}\alpha_1^{\frac{\alpha_2}{(\alpha_1+\alpha_2)}}$$

$$(6)\quad \overline{y} = a\left(\frac{\alpha_2(1-\alpha)}{2}\right)^{\frac{\alpha_1+\alpha_2}{2+(\alpha-1)(\alpha_1+\alpha_2)}}\alpha_1^{\frac{\alpha_2}{2+(\alpha-1)(\alpha_1+\alpha_2)}}$$

(7) $\overline{y} = a\left(\frac{\alpha_2}{\alpha_1}\right)^{\frac{\alpha_2}{2}}$

(8) $p(\overline{y}) = \left(\frac{a}{\overline{y}}\right)^{\alpha} = \left(\frac{\alpha_1}{\alpha_2}\right)^{\frac{\alpha\alpha_2}{2}} = \left(\frac{\alpha_1}{\alpha_2}\right)^{\frac{\beta_2}{2}} > 0.$

Problems P1m and P3m are equivalent because:

$\overline{\mathbf{x}} = \lambda\left(1, \left(\frac{\alpha_2}{\alpha_1}\right)^{\frac{1}{2}}\right) = \tilde{\mathbf{x}}$ and $\overline{y} = a\left(\frac{\alpha_2}{\alpha_1}\right)^{\frac{\alpha_2}{2}}$ $\pi(\overline{\mathbf{x}}) = \pi(\overline{y}).$

Ad b

P1m

Let us write the problem (P1m) of maximizing the firm's profit in case of the logarithmic production function and the nonlinear function of total cost:

$$\pi(\mathbf{x}) = \left\{a^{\alpha}(a_1 \ln x_1 + a_2 \ln x_2)^{1-\alpha} - a\left(x_1^2 + x_2^2\right) - d\right\} \to \max$$
$$\mathbf{x} \geq (0, 0).$$

Then functions of the marginal profit take forms:

(1) $\frac{\partial \pi(\mathbf{x})}{\partial x_1} = (1-\alpha)a^{\alpha}(a_1 \ln x_1 + a_2 \ln x_2)^{-\alpha}\frac{a_1}{x_1} - 2ax_1,$

(2) $\frac{\partial \pi(\mathbf{x})}{\partial x_2} = (1-\alpha)a^{\alpha}(a_1 \ln x_1 + a_2 \ln x_2)^{-\alpha}\frac{a_2}{x_2} - 2ax_2.$

It is not difficult to check that the boundary conditions for the profit function are met:

(3) $\lim_{x_1 \to 0^+} \frac{\partial \pi(\mathbf{x})}{\partial x_1} = +\infty > 0$ and $\lim_{x_1 \to +\infty} \frac{\partial \pi(\mathbf{x})}{\partial x_1} = -\infty < 0,$

(4) $\lim_{x_2 \to 0^+} \frac{\partial \pi(\mathbf{x})}{\partial x_2} = +\infty > 0$ and $\lim_{x_2 \to +\infty} \frac{\partial \pi(\mathbf{x})}{\partial x_2} = -\infty < 0.$

On this basis, we claim that $\exists_1 \overline{\mathbf{x}} > (0, 0)$ such that:

(5) $\left.\frac{\partial \pi(\mathbf{x})}{\partial x_1}\right|_{\mathbf{x}=\overline{\mathbf{x}}} = (1-\alpha)a^{\alpha}(a_1 \ln \overline{x}_1 + a_2 \ln \overline{x}_2)^{-\alpha}\frac{a_1}{\overline{x}_1} - 2a\overline{x}_1 = 0,$

(6) $\left.\frac{\partial \pi(\mathbf{x})}{\partial x_2}\right|_{\mathbf{x}=\overline{\mathbf{x}}} = (1-\alpha)a^{\alpha}(a_1 \ln \overline{x}_1 + a_2 \ln \overline{x}_2)^{-\alpha}\frac{a_2}{\overline{x}_2} - 2a\overline{x}_2 = 0.$

Let us solve the system of Eqs. (5)–(6):

(7) $\frac{a_1}{a_2}\frac{\overline{x}_2}{\overline{x}_1} = \frac{\overline{x}_1}{\overline{x}_2}$

(8) $\overline{x}_2^2 = \frac{a_2}{a_1}\overline{x}_1^2$

(9) $\overline{x}_2 = \left(\frac{a_2}{a_1}\right)^{\frac{1}{2}}\overline{x}_1$

(10) $\overline{\mathbf{x}} = \left(\overline{x}_1, \left(\frac{a_2}{a_1}\right)^{\frac{1}{2}}\overline{x}_1\right) = \overline{x}_1\left(1, \left(\frac{a_2}{a_1}\right)^{\frac{1}{2}}\right) = \lambda\left(1, \left(\frac{a_2}{a_1}\right)^{\frac{1}{2}}\right), \forall\lambda > 0$

(11) $\pi(\overline{\mathbf{x}}) = a^{\alpha}\left(\frac{1}{2}a_2 \ln\left(\frac{a_2}{a_1}\right)\right)^{1-\alpha} - a\left(1 + \left(\frac{a_2}{a_1}\right)\right) - d.$

P2m

The problem of minimizing the cost of production of y units of the product takes a form:

$$c^{\text{tot}}(\mathbf{x}) = \{a(x_1^2 + x_2^2) + d\} \to \min,$$
$$a_1 \ln x_1 + a_2 \ln x_2 = y > 0,$$
$$x_1, x_2 \geq 0.$$

Let us write it down using the Lagrange function:

(1) $F(x_1, x_2, \lambda) = a(x_1^2 + x_2^2) + d + \lambda(y - a_1 \ln x_1 + a_2 \ln x_2).$

From the Kuhn-Tucker theorem it follows that:

(2) $\left.\frac{\partial F(\mathbf{x},\tilde{\lambda})}{\partial x_1}\right|_{\mathbf{x}=\tilde{\mathbf{x}}} = 2a\tilde{x}_1 - \tilde{\lambda}\frac{a_1}{\tilde{x}_1} = 0$

(3) $\left.\frac{\partial F(\mathbf{x},\tilde{\lambda})}{\partial x_2}\right|_{\mathbf{x}=\tilde{\mathbf{x}}} = 2a\tilde{x}_2 - \tilde{\lambda}\frac{a_2}{\tilde{x}_2} = 0$

(4) $\left.\frac{\partial F(\tilde{\mathbf{x}},\lambda)}{\partial \lambda}\right|_{\lambda=\tilde{\lambda}} = y - a_1 \ln \tilde{x}_1 - a_2 \ln \tilde{x}_2 = 0$

(5) $\frac{2a\tilde{x}_1}{2a\tilde{x}_2} = \frac{\tilde{\lambda}\frac{a_1}{\tilde{x}_1}}{\tilde{\lambda}\frac{a_2}{\tilde{x}_2}}$

(6) $\tilde{x}_2^2 = \left(\frac{a_2}{a_1}\right)\tilde{x}_1^2$

(7) $\tilde{x}_2 = \left(\frac{a_2}{a_1}\right)^{\frac{1}{2}}\tilde{x}_1$

(8) $a_1 \ln \tilde{x}_1 + a_2 \ln\left(\frac{a_2}{a_1}\right)^{\frac{1}{2}}\tilde{x}_1 = y$

(9) $\ln \tilde{x}_1^{a_1}\left(\frac{a_2}{a_1}\right)^{\frac{a_2}{2}}\tilde{x}_1^{a_2} = y$

(10) $\tilde{x}_1^{a_1+a_2}\left(\frac{a_2}{a_1}\right)^{\frac{a_2}{2}} = e^y$

(11) $= e^{\frac{y}{a_1+a_2}}\left(\frac{a_1}{a_2}\right)^{\frac{a_2}{2(\alpha_1+a_2)}}$

(12) $\tilde{x}_2 = \left(\frac{a_2}{a_1}\right)^{\frac{1}{2}} e^{\frac{y}{a_1+a_2}}\left(\frac{a_1}{a_2}\right)^{\frac{a_2}{2(\alpha_1+a_2)}}$

(12) $\tilde{\mathbf{x}} = \left(e^{\frac{y}{a_1+a_2}}\left(\frac{a_1}{a_2}\right)^{\frac{a_2}{2(\alpha_1+a_2)}}, \left(\frac{a_2}{a_1}\right)^{\frac{1}{2}} e^{\frac{y}{a_1+a_2}}\left(\frac{a_1}{a_2}\right)^{\frac{a_2}{2(\alpha_1+a_2)}}\right)$

(13) $\tilde{\mathbf{x}} = (\tilde{x}_1, \tilde{x}_2) = \tilde{x}_1\left(1, \left(\frac{\alpha_2}{\alpha_1}\right)^{\frac{1}{2}}\right) = \lambda\left(1, \left(\frac{\alpha_2}{\alpha_1}\right)^{\frac{1}{2}}\right) = \overline{\mathbf{x}}, \quad \forall\lambda > 0.$

Equation (13) shows that the function of demand for production factors and the function of conditional demand for production factors are identical in terms of a structure.

The function of the minimum cost of production of y units of a product is:

$$c^{tot}(\widetilde{\mathbf{x}}) = a\left(e^{\frac{2y}{a_1+a_2}}\left(\frac{a_1}{a_2}\right)^{\frac{a_2}{(\alpha_1+a_2)}} + \left(\frac{a_2}{a_1}\right)e^{\frac{2y}{a_1+a_2}}\left(\frac{a_1}{a_2}\right)^{\frac{a_2}{(\alpha_1+a_2)}}\right) + d$$

(14) $$= ae^{\frac{2y}{a_1+a_2}}\left(\frac{a_1}{a_2}\right)^{\frac{a_2}{(\alpha_1+a_2)}}\left(1+\frac{a_2}{a_1}\right) + d$$

$$= \frac{a(a_1+a_2)}{a_1}ae^{\frac{2y}{a_1+a_2}}\left(\frac{a_1}{a_2}\right)^{\frac{a_2}{(\alpha_1+a_2)}} + d = k(y)$$

P3m

The problem of maximizing the profit with regard to the supply of a product has the following form:

$$\pi(y) = \left\{a^\alpha y^{1-\alpha} - \frac{a(a_1+a_2)}{a_1}e^{\frac{2y}{a_1+a_2}}\left(\frac{a_1}{a_2}\right)^{\frac{a_2}{(\alpha_1+a_2)}} + d\right\} \to \max$$

$$y \geq 0.$$

Then a function of the marginal profit takes a form:

(1) $$\frac{d\pi(y)}{dy} = (1-\alpha)a^\alpha y^{-\alpha} - \frac{2}{a_1+a_2}\frac{a(a_1+a_2)}{aa_2}e^{\frac{2y}{a_1+a_2}}\left(\frac{a_1}{a_2}\right)^{\frac{a_2}{(\alpha_1+a_2)}}$$
$$= (1-\alpha)a^\alpha y^{-\alpha} - \frac{2}{a}e^{\frac{2y}{a_1+a_2}}\left(\frac{\alpha_1}{\alpha_2}\right)^{\frac{a_2}{(a_1+a_2)}}.$$

It is not difficult to check that the boundary conditions for the profit function are met:

(2) $\lim_{y\to 0+}\frac{d\pi(y)}{dy} = +\infty > 0$ and $\lim_{y\to+\infty}\frac{\partial\pi(y)}{\partial y} = -\infty < 0.$

On this basis, we claim that $\exists_1 \overline{y} > 0$ such that:

(3) $\left.\frac{d\pi(y)}{dy}\right|_{y=\overline{y}} = (1-\alpha)a^\alpha\overline{y}^{-\alpha} - \frac{2}{a}e^{\frac{2\overline{y}}{a_1+a_2}}\left(\frac{\alpha_1}{\alpha_2}\right)^{\frac{a_2}{(a_1+a_2)}} = 0$

(4) $\overline{y} = a_2\ln\left(\frac{\alpha_2}{\alpha_1}\right)^{\frac{1}{2}}$

(5) $p(\overline{y}) = \left(\frac{a}{a_2\ln\left(\frac{a_2}{a_1}\right)^{\frac{1}{2}}}\right)^\alpha.$

Problems P1m and P3m are equivalent because:
$\overline{\mathbf{x}} = \lambda\left(1, \left(\frac{\alpha_2}{\alpha_1}\right)^{\frac{1}{2}}\right) = \widetilde{\mathbf{x}}$ and $\overline{y} = a_2\ln\left(\frac{\alpha_2}{\alpha_1}\right)^{\frac{1}{2}}$ $\pi(\overline{\mathbf{x}}) = \pi(\overline{y}).$

Ad c

P1m

Let us write the problem (P1m) of maximizing the firm's profit in case of the subadditive production function and the nonlinear function of total cost:

$$\pi(\mathbf{x}) = \left\{a^{\alpha}\left(a_1 x_1^{\alpha} + a_2 x_2^{\alpha}\right)^{1-\alpha} - a\left(x_1^2 + x_2^2\right) - d\right\} \to \max,$$
$$\mathbf{x} \geq (0, 0).$$

Then the marginal profit functions take forms:

(1) $\frac{\partial \pi(\mathbf{x})}{\partial x_1} = (1-\alpha)a^{\alpha}\left(a_1 x_1^{\alpha} + a_2 x_2^{\alpha}\right)^{-\alpha} \alpha a_1 x_1^{\alpha-1} - 2a x_1,$
(2) $\frac{\partial \pi(\mathbf{x})}{\partial x_2} = (1-\alpha)a^{\alpha}\left(a_1 x_1^{\alpha} + a_2 x_2^{\alpha}\right)^{-\alpha} \alpha a_2 x_2^{\alpha-1} - 2a x_2.$

It is not difficult to check that the boundary conditions for the profit function are met:

(3) $\lim\limits_{x_1 \to 0+} \frac{\partial \pi(\mathbf{x})}{\partial x_1} = +\infty > 0$ and $\lim\limits_{x_1 \to +\infty} \frac{\partial \pi(\mathbf{x})}{\partial x_1} = -\infty < 0,$
(4) $\lim\limits_{x_2 \to 0+} \frac{\partial \pi(\mathbf{x})}{\partial x_2} = +\infty > 0$ and $\lim\limits_{x_2 \to +\infty} \frac{\partial \pi(\mathbf{x})}{\partial x_2} = -\infty < 0.$

On this basis, we claim that $\exists_1 \overline{\mathbf{x}} > (0, 0)$ such that:

(5) $\left.\frac{\partial \pi(\mathbf{x})}{\partial x_1}\right|_{\mathbf{x}=\overline{\mathbf{x}}} = (1-\alpha)a^{\alpha}\left(a_1 \overline{x}_1^{\alpha} + a_2 \overline{x}_2^{\alpha}\right)^{-\alpha} \alpha a_1 \overline{x}_1^{\alpha-1} - 2a\overline{x}_1 = 0,$
(6) $\left.\frac{\partial \pi(\mathbf{x})}{\partial x_2}\right|_{\mathbf{x}=\overline{\mathbf{x}}} = (1-\alpha)a^{\alpha}\left(a_1 \overline{x}_1^{\alpha} + a_2 \overline{x}_2^{\alpha}\right)^{-\alpha} \alpha a_2 \overline{x}_2^{\alpha-1} - 2a\overline{x}_2 = 0.$

Letus solve the system of Eqs. (5)–(6):

(7) $\frac{a_1 \overline{x}_1^{\alpha-1}}{a_2 \overline{x}_2^{\alpha-1}} = \frac{\overline{x}_1}{\overline{x}_2}$
(8) $\overline{x}_2^{\alpha-2} = \frac{a_1}{a_2} \overline{x}_1^{\alpha-2}$
(9) $\overline{x}_2 = \left(\frac{a_2}{a_1}\right)^{\frac{1}{2-\alpha}} \overline{x}_1$
(10) $\overline{\mathbf{x}} = \overline{x}_1\left(1, \left(\frac{a_2}{a_1}\right)^{\frac{1}{2-\alpha}}\right) = \lambda\left(1, \left(\frac{a_2}{a_1}\right)^{\frac{1}{2-\alpha}}\right), \forall \lambda > 0$
(11) $\pi(\overline{\mathbf{x}}) = a^{\alpha}\left(a_1 + a_2\left(\frac{a_2}{a_1}\right)^{\frac{1}{2-\alpha}}\right)^{1-\alpha} - a\left(1 + \left(\frac{a_2}{a_1}\right)^{\frac{2}{2-\alpha}}\right) - d.$

P2m

The problem of minimizing the cost of production of y units of a product takes a form:

$$c^{\text{tot}}(\mathbf{x}) = \left\{a\left(a_1 x_1^{\alpha} + a_2 x_2^{\alpha}\right) + d\right\} \to \min$$
$$a_1 x_1^{\alpha} + a_2 x_2^{\alpha} = y > 0,$$
$$x_1, x_2 \geq 0.$$

Let us write it down using a Lagrange function:

(1) $F(x_1, x_2, \lambda) = a\left(x_1^2 + x_2^2\right) + d + \lambda\left(y - a_1 x_1^\alpha + a_2 x_2^\alpha\right).$

From the Kuhn-Tucker theorem it follows that:

(2) $\left.\frac{\partial F(\mathbf{x},\tilde{\lambda})}{\partial x_1}\right|_{\mathbf{x}=\tilde{\mathbf{x}}} = 2a\tilde{x}_1 - \tilde{\lambda}\alpha a_1 \tilde{x}_1^{\alpha-1} = 0$

(3) $\left.\frac{\partial F(\mathbf{x},\tilde{\lambda})}{\partial x_2}\right|_{\mathbf{x}=\tilde{\mathbf{x}}} = 2a\tilde{x}_2 - \tilde{\lambda}\alpha a_2 \tilde{x}_2^{\alpha-1} = 0$

(4) $\left.\frac{\partial F(\tilde{\mathbf{x}},\lambda)}{\partial \lambda}\right|_{\lambda=\tilde{\lambda}} = y - a_1\overline{x}_1^\alpha - a_2\overline{x}_2^\alpha = 0$

(5) $\frac{2a\tilde{x}_1}{2a\tilde{x}_2} = \frac{\tilde{\lambda}\alpha 1\tilde{x}_2^{\alpha-1}}{\tilde{\lambda}\alpha a_2\tilde{x}_2^{\alpha-1}}$

(6) $\tilde{x}_2^{2-\alpha} = \left(\frac{a_2}{a_1}\right)\tilde{x}_1^{2-\alpha}$

(7) $\tilde{x}_2 = \left(\frac{a_2}{a_1}\right)^{\frac{1}{2-\alpha}}\tilde{x}_1$

(8) $a_1\tilde{x}_1^\alpha + a_2\left(\frac{a_2}{a_1}\right)^{\frac{\alpha}{2-\alpha}}\tilde{x}_1^\alpha = \tilde{x}_1^\alpha\left(a_1 + a_2\left(\frac{a_2}{a_1}\right)^{\frac{\alpha}{2-\alpha}}\right) = \tilde{x}_1^\alpha\left(\frac{a_1^{\frac{2}{2-\alpha}} + a_2^{\frac{2}{2-\alpha}}}{a_1^{\frac{\alpha}{2-\alpha}}}\right) = y$

(9) $\tilde{x}_1^\alpha = y\left(\frac{a_1^{\frac{\alpha}{2-\alpha}}}{a_1^{\frac{2}{2-\alpha}} + a_2^{\frac{2}{2-\alpha}}}\right)$

(10) $\tilde{x}_1 = \left(\frac{y a_1^{\frac{\alpha}{2-\alpha}}}{a_1^{\frac{2}{2-\alpha}} + a_2^{\frac{2}{2-\alpha}}}\right)^{\frac{1}{\alpha}}$

(11) $\tilde{x}_2 = \left(\frac{a_2}{a_1}\right)^{\frac{1}{2-\alpha}}\left(\frac{y a_1^{\frac{\alpha}{2-\alpha}}}{a_1^{\frac{2}{2-\alpha}} + a_2^{\frac{2}{2-\alpha}}}\right)^{\frac{1}{\alpha}}$

(12) $\tilde{\mathbf{x}} = \left(\left(\frac{y a_1^{\frac{\alpha}{2-\alpha}}}{a_1^{\frac{2}{2-\alpha}} + a_2^{\frac{2}{2-\alpha}}}\right)^{\frac{1}{\alpha}}, \left(\frac{a_2}{a_1}\right)^{\frac{1}{2-\alpha}}\left(\frac{y a_1^{\frac{\alpha}{2-\alpha}}}{a_1^{\frac{2}{2-\alpha}} + a_2^{\frac{2}{2-\alpha}}}\right)^{\frac{1}{\alpha}}\right)$

(13) $\tilde{\mathbf{x}} = (\tilde{x}_1, \tilde{x}_2) = \tilde{x}_1\left(1, \left(\frac{a_2}{a_1}\right)^{\frac{1}{2-\alpha}}\right) = \lambda\left(1, \left(\frac{a_2}{a_1}\right)^{\frac{1}{2-\alpha}}\right) = \overline{\mathbf{x}}.$

Equation (13) shows that the function of demand for production factors and the function of conditional demand for production factors are identical in terms of a structure.

The function of the minimum cost of production of y units of a product is:

$$c^{\text{tot}}(\widetilde{\mathbf{x}}) = a\left(\left(\frac{ya_1^{\frac{\alpha}{2-\alpha}}}{a_1^{\frac{2}{2-\alpha}} + a_2^{\frac{2}{2-\alpha}}}\right)^{\frac{2}{\alpha}} + \left(\frac{a_2}{a_1}\right)^{\frac{2}{2-\alpha}}\left(\frac{ya_1^{\frac{\alpha}{2-\alpha}}}{a_1^{\frac{2}{2-\alpha}} + a_2^{\frac{2}{2-\alpha}}}\right)^{\frac{2}{\alpha}}\right) + d$$

$$(14)\quad = a\left(\frac{ya_1^{\frac{\alpha}{2-\alpha}}}{a_1^{\frac{2}{2-\alpha}} + a_2^{\frac{2}{2-\alpha}}}\right)^{\frac{2}{\alpha}}\left(1 + \left(\frac{a_2}{a_1}\right)^{\frac{2}{2-\alpha}}\right) + d$$

$$= a\left(\frac{ya_1^{\frac{\alpha}{2-\alpha}}}{a_1^{\frac{2}{2-\alpha}} + a_2^{\frac{2}{2-\alpha}}}\right)^{\frac{2}{\alpha}}\left(\frac{a_1^{\frac{2}{2-\alpha}} + a_2^{\frac{2}{2-\alpha}}}{a_1^{\frac{2}{2-\alpha}}}\right) + d$$

$$= ay^{\frac{2}{\alpha}}\left(a_1^{\frac{2}{2-\alpha}} + a_2^{\frac{2}{2-\alpha}}\right)^{\frac{\alpha-2}{\alpha}} + d = k(y).$$

P3m

The problem of maximizing the profit with regard to the supply of a product has the following form:

$$\pi(y) = \left\{a^\alpha y^{1-\alpha} - ay^{\frac{2}{\alpha}}\left(a_1^{\frac{2}{2-\alpha}} + a_2^{\frac{2}{2-\alpha}}\right)^{\frac{\alpha-2}{\alpha}} - d\right\} \to \max$$

$$y \geq 0.$$

Then a function of the marginal profit takes a form:

(1) $\frac{d\pi(y)}{dy} = (1-\alpha)a^\alpha y^{-\alpha} - \frac{2}{\alpha}ay^{\frac{2-\alpha}{\alpha}}\left(a_1^{\frac{2}{2-\alpha}} + a_2^{\frac{2}{2-\alpha}}\right)^{\frac{\alpha-2}{\alpha}}.$

It is not difficult to check that the boundary conditions for the profit function are met:

(2) $\lim\limits_{y\to 0^+} \frac{d\pi(y)}{dy} = +\infty > 0$ and $\lim\limits_{y\to +\infty} \frac{d\pi(y)}{dy} = -\infty < 0.$

On this basis, we claim that $\exists_1 \overline{y} > 0$ such that:

(3) $\left.\frac{d\pi(y)}{\partial y}\right|_{y=\overline{y}} = (1-\alpha)a^\alpha \overline{y}^{-\alpha} - \frac{2}{\alpha}a\overline{y}^{\frac{2-\alpha}{\alpha}}\left(a_1^{\frac{2}{2-\alpha}} + a_2^{\frac{2}{2-\alpha}}\right)^{\frac{\alpha-2}{\alpha}} = 0$

(4) $\overline{y} = \frac{a_1^{\frac{2}{2-\alpha}} + a_2^{\frac{2}{2-\alpha}}}{a_1^{\frac{\alpha}{2-\alpha}}}$

(5) $p(\overline{y}) = \left(\frac{a}{\overline{y}}\right)^\alpha = \left(\frac{aa_1^{\frac{\alpha}{2-\alpha}}}{a_1^{\frac{2}{2-\alpha}} + a_2^{\frac{2}{2-\alpha}}}\right)^\alpha > 0.$

Problems P1m and P3m are equivalent because:

$\overline{\mathbf{x}} = \lambda\left(1, \left(\frac{\alpha_2}{\alpha_1}\right)^{\frac{1}{2}}\right) = \widetilde{\mathbf{x}}$ and $\overline{y} = a\left(\frac{\alpha_2}{\alpha_1}\right)^{\frac{\alpha_2}{2}}$ $\pi(\overline{\mathbf{x}}) = \pi(\overline{y}).$

E4.8.*[1] Solve exercise E4.7, when the production total cost function has a form:

$$c^{\text{tot}}(x_1, x_2) = \alpha(f(x_1, x_2))^2 + \beta f(x_1, x_2) + \gamma,$$

or equivalently:

$$c^{\text{tot}}(y) = \alpha y^2 + \beta y + \gamma,$$

where $y = f(x_1, x_2)$ is an increasing, strictly concave and twice differentiable production function and $\Delta = \beta^2 - 4\alpha\gamma = 0,\ \alpha, \beta, \gamma > 0$.

Solutions

The data given are:
a production function:

(a) power function: $y = f(\mathbf{x}) = ax_1^{\alpha_1}x_2^{\alpha_2},\ a > 0,\ \alpha_i \in (0, 1),\ \alpha_1 + \alpha_2 < 1, i = 1, 2$,
(b) logarithmic: $y = f(\mathbf{x}) = a_1 \ln x_1 + a_2 \ln x_2,\ a_i > 0,\ i = 1, 2$,
(c) subadditive: $y = f(\mathbf{x}) = a_1 x_1^{\alpha} + a_2 x_2^{\alpha},\ a_i > 0,\ \alpha \in (0, 1),\ i = 1, 2$,

and

$p(y) = \left(\frac{a}{y}\right)^{\alpha} > 0$ a price of product manufactured by a monopoly as a function of product supply, set by a monopoly.

Ad 1

Solve the profit maximization problem (P1m).

The profit function with inputs of production factors as arguments has a form:

$$\pi(\mathbf{x}) = p(f(\mathbf{x})) \cdot f(\mathbf{x}) - c^{\text{tot}}(\mathbf{x}) = \left(\frac{a}{f(\mathbf{x})}\right)^{\alpha} f(\mathbf{x})$$
$$- \left(\alpha(f(\mathbf{x}))^2 + \beta f(\mathbf{x}) + \gamma\right)$$
$$= a^{\alpha} f(\mathbf{x})^{1-\alpha} - \alpha(f(\mathbf{x}))^2 - \beta f(\mathbf{x}) - \gamma.$$

A necessary condition for existence of a maximum of this function takes the following form:

$$\frac{\partial \pi(\mathbf{x})}{\partial x_i} = a^{\alpha}(1-\alpha) f(\mathbf{x})^{-\alpha} \cdot \frac{\partial f(\mathbf{x})}{\partial x_i} - 2\alpha f(\mathbf{x}) \frac{\partial f(\mathbf{x})}{\partial x_i} - \beta \frac{\partial f(\mathbf{x})}{\partial x_i} = 0 \quad i = 1, 2,$$

---

[1] This exercise is not a standard one due to a form of the production total cost function resulting in a not standard necessary condition for existence of a profit function's maximum. Thus, one needs to take into account that solutions and answers to the subsequent tasks neither do have standard forms.

where $\frac{\partial f(\mathbf{x})}{\partial x_i} > 0$ since function $f(\mathbf{x})$ is increasing.

Simplifying the necessary condition to:

$$a^{\alpha}(1-\alpha)f(\mathbf{x})^{-\alpha} - 2\alpha f(\mathbf{x}) - \beta = 0$$

we can notice that in fact we are left with only one equation while there are two variables x_1, x_2 for which we would like to find their optimal values. Having one equation it is not possible. Instead we can determine an optimal level of output and then a relationship between inputs of production factors for a given level of output.

Using the fact that $y = f(\mathbf{x})$ the necessary condition can be written as:

$$a^{\alpha}(1-\alpha)y^{-\alpha} - 2\alpha y - \beta = 0.$$

This is a nonlinear equation and n be solved by numerical methods.[2] For a given optimal output level $\overline{y}$ the relationship between inputs of production factors results from the form of production function:

(a) $ax_1^{\alpha_1}x_2^{\alpha_2} = \overline{y}$ $x_2 = \left(\frac{\overline{y}}{ax_1^{\alpha_1}}\right)^{\frac{1}{\alpha_2}}$ $\overline{\mathbf{x}} = \left(x_1, \left(\frac{\overline{y}}{ax_1^{\alpha_1}}\right)^{\frac{1}{\alpha_2}}\right)$, $x_1 > 0$

(b) $a_1 \ln x_1 + a_2 \ln x_2 = \overline{y}$ $x_2 = \left(\frac{e^{\overline{y}}}{x_1^{a_1}}\right)^{\frac{1}{a_2}}$ $\overline{\mathbf{x}} = \left(x_1, \left(\frac{e^{\overline{y}}}{x_1^{a_1}}\right)^{\frac{1}{a_2}}\right)$, $x_1 > 0$

(c) $a_1x_1^{\alpha} + a_2x_2^{\alpha} = \overline{y}$ $x_2 = \left(\frac{\overline{y}-a_1x_1^{\alpha}}{a}\right)^{\frac{1}{\alpha}}$ $\overline{\mathbf{x}} = \left(x_1, \left(\frac{\overline{y}-a_1x_1^{\alpha}}{a}\right)^{\frac{1}{\alpha}}\right)$, $0 \le x_1 \le \left(\frac{\overline{y}}{a_1}\right)^{\frac{1}{\alpha}}$.

Ad 2

Present a geometric illustration of the profit maximization problem (P1m).

Taking for example $a = 10$, $\alpha = 0.75$, $\gamma = 1$ (which gives $\beta \approx 1.73$) we get the optimal output $\overline{y}$ equal to about 0.4773.

The geometric illustration of the problem is presented in Fig. 4.1. We can notice that the necessary condition determines the optimal output level for which the profit reaches its maximum. On the right-hand side of Fig. 4.1, we present graphs of the function resulting from the relationship $f(x_1, x_2) = \overline{y}$ in cases (a)–(c), taking $\overline{y} \approx 0.4773$. The green curve is a graph in the case of the power production function ($\alpha_1 = \alpha_2 = 0.75$), the pink one—in the case of the logarithmic function ($a_1 = a_2 = 0.75$) and the black one—in the case of the subadditive production function ($a_1 = a_2 = 0.75$). One can notice that taking specified values for parameters we bound a set of solutions, that is the set combinations of inputs that satisfy the condition $f(x_1, x_2) = \overline{y}$. But in every case (a)–(c) the number of solutions is uncountably infinite. There is no uniquely determined solution. Here the solution is determined with an accuracy of a relationship between inputs of production factors.

---

[2] MATLAB files to find the optimal value of output using numerical methods are called myfun_E4_8.m and solvery_E4_8.m. The latter is the file to be run. Taking for example $a = 10$, $\alpha = 0.75$, $\gamma = 1$ (which gives $\beta \approx 1.73$) we get the optimal output $\overline{y}$ equal to about 0.4773.

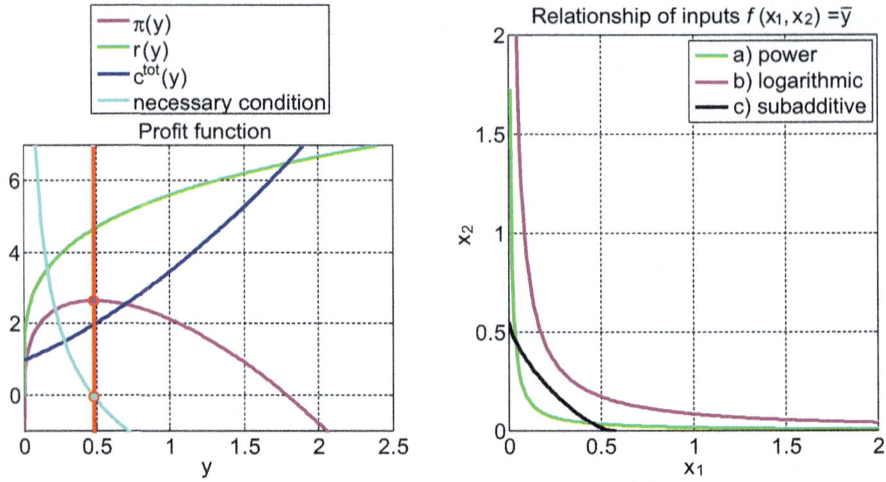

Fig. 4.1 Profit maximization problem (P1m, P3m) (E4.8)

Ad 3

Give an economic interpretation of the necessary and sufficient conditions of the existence of an optimal solution to problem (P1m).

- For the necessary condition

If by given values of parameters the profit function $\pi(\mathbf{x})$ has a maximum value obtained for an optimal level $\overline{y}$ of output, then the necessary condition is satisfied for this level of output. Inputs of production factors should then satisfy a condition $f(x_1, x_2) = \overline{y}$.

- For the sufficient condition

If by some values of parameters the profit function is strictly concave[3] then there exists the maximum of this function.

[3] Let us recall that strict concavity in the case of a function of many variables requires that the Hessian matrix of the profit function is negative definite. Here, it depends on values of parameters of the production function and of the production total cost function. Let us assume that these values are such that the profit function is strictly concave, which requires, among others that $\alpha \in (0; 1)$.

Ad 4

Solve the cost minimization problem (P2m).

The problem has the following form:

$$c^{\text{tot}}(\mathbf{x}) = \{\alpha(f(\mathbf{x}))^2 + \beta f(\mathbf{x}) + \gamma\} \to \min$$
$$y = f(\mathbf{x}) = \text{const.} > 0,$$
$$x_1, x_2 \geq 0.$$

The problem can be expressed using a Lagrange function:

$$L(\mathbf{x}, \lambda) = c^{\text{tot}}(\mathbf{x}) + \lambda(y - f(\mathbf{x})) = \alpha(f(\mathbf{x}))^2 + \beta f(\mathbf{x}) + \gamma + \lambda(y - f(\mathbf{x}))$$

for which a necessary condition for existence of a minimum takes a form of the following system:

$$\begin{cases} \frac{\partial L(\mathbf{x},\lambda)}{\partial x_i} = 2\alpha f(\mathbf{x}) \cdot \frac{\partial f(\mathbf{x})}{\partial x_i} + \beta \frac{\partial f(\mathbf{x})}{\partial x_i} - \lambda \frac{\partial f(\mathbf{x})}{\partial x_i} = 0 \;\; i = 1, 2 \\ \frac{\partial L(\mathbf{x},\lambda)}{\partial \lambda} = y - f(\mathbf{x}) = 0 \end{cases},$$

where $\frac{\partial f(\mathbf{x})}{\partial x_i} > 0$ since function $f(\mathbf{x})$ is increasing. The system can be simplified to:

$$\begin{cases} 2\alpha f(\mathbf{x}) + \beta - \lambda = 0 \\ y = f(\mathbf{x}) \end{cases}$$

and then to:

$$\begin{cases} 2\alpha y + \beta - \lambda = 0 \\ y = f(\mathbf{x}) \end{cases}.$$

We can notice that by a given level y of output and given values of parameters using this system one can find a value of λ and only a relationship between inputs of production factors. But determining optimal inputs is not possible since there is only one equation for two variables x_1, x_2.

For a given output level y the relationship between inputs of production factors results from the form of a production function:

(a) $ax_1^{\alpha_1}x_2^{\alpha_2} = y \quad x_2 = \left(\frac{y}{ax_1^{\alpha_1}}\right)^{\frac{1}{\alpha_2}} \quad \tilde{\mathbf{x}} = \left(x_1, \left(\frac{y}{ax_1^{\alpha_1}}\right)^{\frac{1}{\alpha_2}}\right), \quad x_1 > 0$

(b) $a_1 \ln x_1 + a_2 \ln x_2 = y \quad x_2 = \left(\frac{e^y}{x_1^{a_1}}\right)^{\frac{1}{a_2}} \quad \tilde{\mathbf{x}} = \left(x_1, \left(\frac{e^y}{x_1^{a_1}}\right)^{\frac{1}{a_2}}\right), \quad x_1 > 0$

(c) $a_1x_1^\alpha + a_2x_2^\alpha = y \quad x_2 = \left(\frac{y - a_1x_1^\alpha}{a}\right)^{\frac{1}{\alpha}} \quad \tilde{\mathbf{x}} = \left(x_1, \left(\frac{y - a_1x_1^\alpha}{a}\right)^{\frac{1}{\alpha}}\right), \quad 0 \leq x_1 \leq \left(\frac{y}{a_1}\right)^{\frac{1}{\alpha}}$.

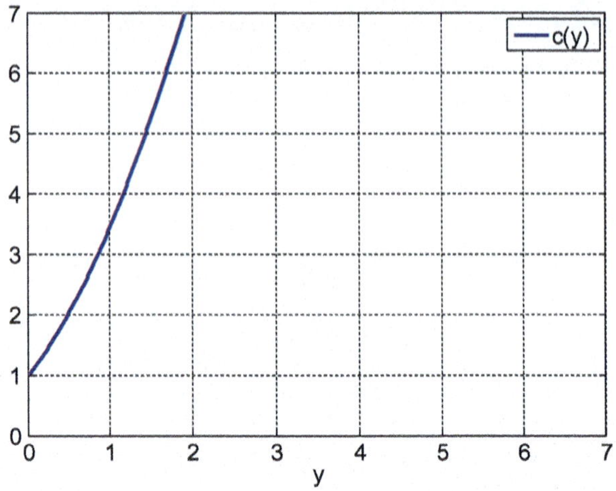

Fig. 4.2 Firm's minimal cost function of producing y output units (E4.8)

Ad 5

Present a geometric illustration of the cost minimization problem (P2m).

Taking for example $\alpha = 0.75, \gamma = 1$ (which gives $\beta \approx 1.73$) we get a monopoly's minimal cost function of producing y output units in the following form (Fig. 4.2).

$$c^{\text{tot}}(y) = \alpha y^2 + \beta y + \gamma = c(y),$$
$$c^{\text{tot}}(y) = 0.75y^2 + 1.73y + 1 = c(y).$$

Ad 6

Give an economic interpretation of the necessary and sufficient conditions of the existence of an optimal solution to problem (P2m).

Any inputs of production factors satisfying a condition resulting from the production function $f(x_1, x_2) = y$ are the solution to the problem. The solution is determined with an accuracy of a relationship between the inputs.

Ad 7

Solve the profit maximization problem (P3m).

The profit function with output level as an argument has a form:

$$\pi(y) = p(y) \cdot y - c(y) = \left(\frac{a}{y}\right)^{\alpha} y - c(y) = a^{\alpha} y^{1-\alpha} - \left(\alpha y^2 + \beta y + \gamma\right).$$

A necessary condition for existence of a maximum of this function takes the following form:

$$\frac{\partial \pi(y)}{\partial y} = a^{\alpha}(1-\alpha)y^{-\alpha} - 2\alpha y - \beta = 0.$$

This is a nonlinear equation and can be solved by numerical methods.[4]

Let us check if and when the profit function $\pi(y)$ is strictly concave:

$$\frac{\partial^2 \pi(y)}{\partial y^2} = -a^{\alpha}(1-\alpha)\alpha y^{-\alpha-1} - 2\alpha < 0.$$

One can notice that the inequality above is satisfied for example when $\alpha \in (0; 1)$.

Ad 8

Present a geometric illustration of the profit maximization problem (P3m).

The geometric illustration of the problem is presented in Fig. 4.1 on its left-hand side. This is the same figure as for the problem (P1m). Taking for example $a = 10$, $\alpha = 0.75$, $\gamma = 1$ (which gives $\beta \approx 1.73$) we get the optimal output $\overline{y}$ equal to about 0.4773.

Ad 9

Give an economic interpretation of the necessary and sufficient conditions of the existence of an optimal solution to problem (P3m).

- For the necessary condition

If by given values of parameters the profit function $\pi(y)$ has a maximum value obtained for an optimal level $\overline{y}$ of output, then the necessary condition is satisfied for this level of output.

- For the sufficient condition

If by some values of parameters the profit function is strictly concave, then there exists the maximum of this function.

Ad 10

Justify that the profit maximizations problems (P1m) and (P3m) are equivalent.

The solutions to problems (P1m) and (P3m) indicate the same optimal level $\overline{y}$ of output (found using numerical methods from the nonlinear equation). To have this level of output, a producer has to combine production factors in the amounts resulting from the production function formula. This means that he/she is able to determine the optimal level of output and then to use the proper inputs of production factors.

Ad 11

Determine the optimal price by which a monopoly obtains the maximum profit.

---

[4] MATLAB files to find the optimal value of output using numerical methods are called myfun_E4_8.m and solvery_E4_8.m. The latter is the file to be run. Taking for example, $a = 10$, $\alpha = 0.75$, $\gamma = 1$ (which gives $\beta \approx 1.73$) we get the optimal output $\overline{y}$ equal to about 0.4773.

The optimal level of a price results from a relation between the price and the supply:

$$p(\overline{y}) = \left(\frac{a}{\overline{y}}\right)^{\alpha}.$$

We can notice that here the optimal price does not depend on the form of the production function. It depends on the form of the production total cost function and its parameters since the optimal level $\overline{y}$ of output is determined from an equation:

$$a^{\alpha}(1-\alpha)y^{-\alpha} = 2\alpha y + \beta,$$

where the right-hand side of the equation (the necessary condition in problems (P1m) and (P3m) results from the total cost function.

E4.9. Solve exercise E4.7 assuming additionally that resources of production factors are limited: $\forall i = 1, 2 \quad 0 \le x_i \le b_i$, where $\forall i = 1, 2 \quad b_i > 0$ means the constrained resource of i-th production factor.

Solutions

The data given are:
a production function:

(a) power function: $y = f(\mathbf{x}) = ax_1^{\alpha_1}x_2^{\alpha_2},\ a > 0,\ \alpha_i \in (0, 1),\ \alpha_1 + \alpha_2 < 1, i = 1, 2,$
(b) logarithmic: $y = f(\mathbf{x}) = a_1\ln x_1 + a_2\ln x_2,\ a_i > 0,\ i = 1, 2,$
(c) subadditive: $y = f(\mathbf{x}) = a_1x_1^{\alpha} + a_2x_2^{\alpha},\ a_i > 0,\ \alpha \in (0, 1),\ i = 1, 2,$

and

$p(y) = \left(\frac{a}{y}\right)^{\alpha} > 0$ a price of product manufactured by a monopoly as a function of product supply, set by a monopoly.

Ad 1

Solve the profit maximization problem (P1m).

The profit function with inputs of production factors as arguments has a general form:

$$\pi(\mathbf{x}) = p(f(\mathbf{x}))\cdot f(\mathbf{x}) - c^{\text{tot}}(\mathbf{x}) = \left(\frac{a}{f(\mathbf{x})}\right)^{\alpha} f(\mathbf{x})$$
$$- \left(a\left(x_1^2 + x_2^2\right) + d\right) = a^{\alpha} f(\mathbf{x})^{1-\alpha} - a\left(x_1^2 + x_2^2\right) - d.$$

In this exercise one imposes the additional constraints on inputs of production factors:

$$x_i \leq b_i \quad i = 1, 2.$$

necessary condition for existence of a maximum of the profit function takes the following form:

$$\begin{cases} \frac{\partial \pi(\mathbf{x})}{\partial x_1} = a^{\alpha}(1-\alpha) f(\mathbf{x})^{-\alpha} \cdot \frac{\partial f(\mathbf{x})}{\partial x_1} - 2ax_1 = 0 \\ \frac{\partial \pi(\mathbf{x})}{\partial x_2} = a^{\alpha}(1-\alpha) f(\mathbf{x})^{-\alpha} \cdot \frac{\partial f(\mathbf{x})}{\partial x_2} - 2ax_2 = 0. \end{cases}$$

Transforming the necessary condition leads to:

$$x_2 = \frac{\frac{\partial f(\mathbf{x})}{\partial x_2}}{\frac{\partial f(\mathbf{x})}{\partial x_1}} x_1$$

which gives the following relationships between inputs of production factors:

$$\text{(a) } x_2 = \sqrt{\tfrac{\alpha_2}{\alpha_1}} x_1 \quad \text{(b) } x_2 = \sqrt{\tfrac{a_2}{a_1}} x_1 \quad \text{(c) } x_2 = \left(\tfrac{\alpha_2}{\alpha_1}\right)^{\frac{1}{2-\alpha}} x_1.$$

Substituting this relationship into one of the equations of the necessary condition gives the global solution that is a solution obtained when the constraints on inputs of production factors are not binding:

(a)

$$\overline{x}_1^G = \left[\frac{2}{1-\alpha} \alpha_1^{\frac{1}{2}\alpha_2(1-\alpha)-1} \alpha_2^{\frac{1}{2}\alpha_2(\alpha-1)}\right]^{\frac{1}{(\alpha_1+\alpha_2)(1-\alpha)-2}}$$

$$\overline{x}_2^G = \left[\frac{2}{1-\alpha} \alpha_1^{\frac{1}{2}\alpha_1(\alpha-1)} \alpha_2^{\frac{1}{2}\alpha_1(1-\alpha)-1}\right]^{\frac{1}{(\alpha_1+\alpha_2)(1-\alpha)-2}}$$

(b) $\overline{\mathbf{x}}^G = \left(\overline{x}_1^G, \overline{x}_2^G\right)$ can be found using numerical methods from a system:

$$\begin{cases} a^{\alpha-1}(1-\alpha)a_1 = 2x_1^2 \left(\ln x_1^{a_1} x_2^{a_2}\right)^{\alpha} \\ x_2 = \sqrt{\frac{a_2}{a_1}} x_1 \end{cases},$$

if values of parameters are given

(c)

$$\overline{x}_1^G = \left(\frac{1}{2} a^{\alpha-1} \alpha(1-\alpha) a_1\right)^{\frac{1}{\alpha^2-\alpha+2}} \left(a_1 + a_2 \left(\frac{a_2}{a_1}\right)^{\frac{\alpha}{2-\alpha}}\right)^{\frac{-\alpha}{\alpha^2-\alpha+2}},$$

$$\overline{x}_2^G = \left(\frac{1}{2} a^{\alpha-1} \alpha(1-\alpha) a_2\right)^{\frac{1}{\alpha^2-\alpha+2}} \left(a_2 + a_1 \left(\frac{a_1}{a_2}\right)^{\frac{\alpha}{2-\alpha}}\right)^{\frac{-\alpha}{\alpha^2-\alpha+2}}$$

Let us assume that $a = 1$, $\alpha = 0.75$ and that parameters of the production function have the following values:

(a) $\alpha_1 = \alpha_2 = 0.75$
(b) $a_1 = a_2 = 5$
(c) $a_1 = a_2 = 3$.

Then the optimal inputs as the global solution are:

(a) $\overline{\boldsymbol{x}}^G = \left(\overline{x}_1^G, \overline{x}_2^G\right) \approx (0.233, 0.233)$
(b) $\overline{\boldsymbol{x}}^G = \left(\overline{x}_1^G, \overline{x}_2^G\right) \approx (1.0483, 1.0483)$—found using numerical methods[5]
(c) $\overline{\boldsymbol{x}}^G = \left(\overline{x}_1^G, \overline{x}_2^G\right) \approx (0.2366, 0.2366)$,

which gives the optimal output as the global solution[6]:

(a) $\overline{y}^G = f\left(\overline{x}_1^G, \overline{x}_2^G\right) \approx 0.1125$
(b) $\overline{y}^G = f\left(\overline{x}_1^G, \overline{x}_2^G\right) \approx 0.4713$
(c) $\overline{y}^G = f\left(\overline{x}_1^G, \overline{x}_2^G\right) \approx 2.0356$.

Now we can consider a few cases depending on whether the constraints are binding or not:

(1) None of the constraints is binding

if $\overline{x}_i^G \leq b_i, \quad i = 1, 2$ then $\overline{x}_i = \overline{x}_i^G$. The solution takes the following form:

$$\overline{\mathbf{x}} = \left(\overline{x}_1^G, \overline{x}_2^G\right),$$

which means that the firm can use the production factors in quantities resulting from the global solution. Using less than available resources is optimal.

(2) The constraint on resource of the first production factor is binding

if $\overline{x}_1^G > b_1$ and $\overline{x}_2^G \leq b_2$ then $\overline{x}_1 = b_1$ while $\overline{x}_1 = \overline{x}_2^G$. The solution takes the following form:

$$\overline{\mathbf{x}} = \left(b_1, \overline{x}_2^G\right).$$

(3) The constraint on resource of the second production factor is binding

if $\overline{x}_1^G \leq b_1$ and $\overline{x}_2^G > b_2$ then $\overline{x}_1 = \overline{x}_1^G$ while $\overline{x}_2 = b_2$. The solution takes the following form:

$$\overline{\mathbf{x}} = \left(\overline{x}_1^G, b_2\right).$$

(4) The constraints on quantities of both goods are binding

if $\overline{x}_1^G > b_1$ and $\overline{x}_2^G > b_2$ then $\overline{x}_1 = b_1$ and $\overline{x}_2 = b_2$. The solution takes the following form:

$$\overline{\mathbf{x}} = (b_1, b_2),$$

[5] MATLAB files to find the optimal value of output using numerical methods are called myfun_E4_9_1.m and solvery_E4_9_1.m. The latter is the file to be run.

[6] These are the same values as obtained in task 7 (ad 7).

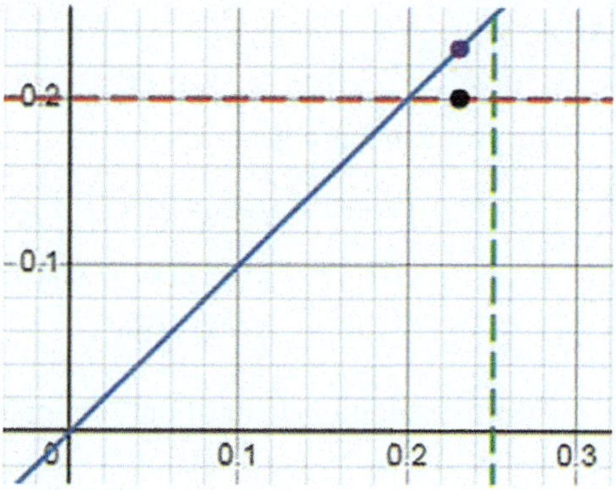

Fig. 4.3 Profit maximization problem (P1m) (E4.9)

which means that the firm can use the production factors only in quantities constrained by the resources. Using all available resources is optimal.

Ad 2

Present a geometric illustration of the profit maximization problem (P1m).

Taking for example $\alpha = 0.75$, $\alpha_1 = \alpha_2 = 0.75$ in the example (a) we get the global solution $\overline{\mathbf{x}}^G = \left(\overline{x}_1^G, \overline{x}_2^G\right) \approx (0.23, 0.23)$. The global solution has to be compared with the resources of production factors b_1 and b_2 (Fig. 4.3).

Let us assume that the constrained resources of production factors are $(b_1, b_2) = (0.25, 0.2)$. Because of these constraints the global solution $(0.23, 0.23)$ can't be used by the firm—the firm has to use inputs $(0.23, 0.2)$. The constraint on the first production factor is not binding, the constraint on the second factor is binding.

Ad 3

Give an economic interpretation of the necessary and sufficient conditions of the existence of an optimal solution to problem (P1m).

- For the necessary condition

If by given values of parameters the profit function $\pi(\mathbf{x})$ has a maximum value obtained for optimal inputs $\overline{\mathbf{x}}^G = \left(\overline{x}_1^G, \overline{x}_2^G\right)$ of production factors, then the necessary condition is satisfied for these inputs. From the necessary condition it results that when the inputs are optimal as the global solution to the problem, then the marginal revenue equals the marginal cost of production.

- For the sufficient condition

If by some values of parameters the profit function is strictly concave[7] then there exists the maximum of this function obtained for the global solution $\overline{\mathbf{x}}^G = \left(\overline{x}_1^G, \overline{x}_2^G\right)$.

[7] Let us recall that strict concavity in case of a function of many variables requires that the Hessian matrix of the profit function is negative definite. Here, it depends on values of parameters of the production function. Let us assume that these values are such that the profit function is strictly concave, which requires, among others that $\alpha \in (0; 1)$.

Ad 4

Solve the cost minimization problem (P2m).

The problem has a general form:

$$\begin{aligned} & c^{\text{tot}}(\mathbf{x}) = \{a(x_1^2 + x_2^2) + d\} \rightarrow \min \\ & y = f(\mathbf{x}) = \text{const.} > 0, \\ & x_1, x_2 \geq 0. \end{aligned}$$

There are additional constraints on inputs of production factors:

$$x_i \leq b_i \quad i = 1, 2.$$

The problem can be expressed using a Lagrange function:

$$L(\mathbf{x}, \lambda) = c^{\text{tot}}(\mathbf{x}) + \lambda(y - f(\mathbf{x})) = a(x_1^2 + x_2^2) + d + \lambda(y - f(\mathbf{x}))$$

for which a necessary condition for existence of a minimum takes a form of the following system:

$$\begin{cases} \frac{\partial L(\mathbf{x},\lambda)}{\partial x_i} = 2ax_i - \lambda \frac{\partial f(\mathbf{x})}{\partial x_i} = 0 \ \ i = 1, 2 \\ \frac{\partial L(\mathbf{x},\lambda)}{\partial \lambda} = y - f(\mathbf{x}) = 0. \end{cases}$$

Transforming the necessary condition leads to:

$$\begin{cases} x_2 = \frac{\frac{\partial f(\mathbf{x})}{\partial x_2}}{\frac{\partial f(\mathbf{x})}{\partial x_1}} x_1 \\ y = f(\mathbf{x}), \end{cases}$$

which gives the following relationships between inputs of production factors:

$$\text{(a) } x_2 = \sqrt{\tfrac{\alpha_2}{\alpha_1}} x_1 \quad \text{(b) } x_2 = \sqrt{\tfrac{a_2}{a_1}} x_1 \quad \text{(c) } x_2 = \left(\frac{\alpha_2}{\alpha_1}\right)^{\frac{1}{2-\alpha}} x_1.$$

Substituting this relationship into the third equation of the necessary condition gives the global solution that is a solution obtained when the constraints on inputs of production factors are not binding:

$$\text{(a)} \ \ \widetilde{\mathbf{x}}^G = (\widetilde{x}_1^G, \widetilde{x}_2^G) = \left(\left[\frac{y}{a}\left(\frac{\alpha_1}{\alpha_2}\right)^{\frac{1}{2}\alpha_2}\right]^{\frac{1}{\alpha_1+\alpha_2}}, \left[\frac{y}{a}\left(\frac{\alpha_2}{\alpha_1}\right)^{\frac{1}{2}\alpha_1}\right]^{\frac{1}{\alpha_1+\alpha_2}}\right)$$

$$\text{(b)} \ \ \widetilde{\mathbf{x}}^G = (\widetilde{x}_1^G, \widetilde{x}_2^G) = \left(\left[e^y\left(\frac{a_1}{a_2}\right)^{\frac{1}{2}a_2}\right]^{\frac{1}{a_1+a_2}}, \left[e^y\left(\frac{a_2}{a_1}\right)^{\frac{1}{2}a_1}\right]^{\frac{1}{a_1+a_2}}\right)$$

$$\text{(c)} \ \ \widetilde{\mathbf{x}}^G = (\widetilde{x}_1^G, \widetilde{x}_2^G) = \left(\left[a_1 + a_2\left(\frac{a_2}{a}\right)^{\frac{\alpha}{2-\alpha}}\right]^{-\frac{1}{\alpha}} y^{\frac{1}{\alpha}}, \left[a_1\left(\frac{a_1}{a_2}\right)^{\frac{\alpha}{2-\alpha}} + a_2\right]^{-\frac{1}{\alpha}} y^{\frac{1}{\alpha}}\right).$$

Now we can consider a few cases depending on whether the constraints on production factors are binding or not:

(1) None of the constraints is binding

if $\tilde{x}_i^G \leq b_i, \quad i = 1, 2$ then $\tilde{x}_i = \tilde{x}_i^G$.

(2) The constraint on quantity of the first good is binding

if $\tilde{x}_1^G > b_1$ and $\tilde{x}_2^G \leq b_2$ then $\tilde{x}_1 = b_1$ while

$$\text{(a) } \tilde{x}_2^L = \left(\tfrac{y}{a} b_1^{-\alpha_1}\right)^{\frac{1}{\alpha_2}} \quad \text{(b) } \tilde{x}_2^L = \left(e^y b_1^{-a_1}\right)^{\frac{1}{a_2}} \quad \text{(c) } \tilde{x}_2^L = \left(y - a_1 b_1^{\alpha}\right)^{\frac{1}{\alpha}} a_2^{-\frac{1}{\alpha}}.$$

If now $\tilde{x}_2^L \leq b_2$ then the solution is $\tilde{\mathbf{x}} = \left(b_1, \tilde{x}_2^L\right)$.

Because of the constraint on resource of the first production factor a producer chooses bigger input of the second factor than it results from the optimization problem with no constraints on inputs of production factors.

If $\tilde{x}_2^L > b_2$ then there is no solution satisfying $f(\mathbf{x}) = y$.

(3) The constraint on quantity of the second good is binding

if $\tilde{x}_2^G > b_2$ and $\tilde{x}_1^G \leq b_1$ then $\tilde{x}_2 = b_2$ while

$$\text{(a) } \tilde{x}_1^L = \left(\tfrac{y}{a} b_2^{-\alpha_2}\right)^{\frac{1}{\alpha_1}} \quad \text{(b) } \tilde{x}_1^L = \left(e^y b_2^{-a_2}\right)^{\frac{1}{a_1}} \quad \text{(c) } \tilde{x}_1^L = \left(y - a_2 b_2^{\alpha}\right)^{\frac{1}{\alpha}} a_1^{-\frac{1}{\alpha}}.$$

If now $\tilde{x}_1^L \leq b_1$ then the solution is $\tilde{\mathbf{x}} = \left(\tilde{x}_1^L, b_2\right)$.

Because of the constraint on resource of the second production factor a producer chooses bigger input of the first factor than it results from the optimization problem with no constraints on inputs of production factors.

If $\tilde{x}_1^L > b_1$ then there is no solution satisfying $f(\mathbf{x}) = y$.

(4) The constraints on quantities of both goods are binding

if $\tilde{x}_1^G > b_1$ and $\tilde{x}_2^G > b_2$ then there is no solution satisfying $f(\mathbf{x}) = y$.

Ad 5

Present a geometric illustration of the cost minimization problem (P2m).

Taking for example:

(a) $a = 1, \alpha_1 = \alpha_2 = 0.75$
(b) $a_1 = a_2 = 5$
(c) $a_1 = a_2 = 3, \alpha = 0.75$,

we get the global solution:

(a) $\tilde{\mathbf{x}}^G = \left(\tilde{x}_1^G, \tilde{x}_2^G\right) = \left(\left(\frac{y}{10}\right)^{\frac{2}{3}}, \left(\frac{y}{10}\right)^{\frac{2}{3}}\right)$
(b) $\tilde{\mathbf{x}}^G = \left(\tilde{x}_1^G, \tilde{x}_2^G\right) = \left(e^{0.1y}, e^{0.1y}\right)$
(c) $\tilde{\mathbf{x}}^G = \left(\tilde{x}_1^G, \tilde{x}_2^G\right) = \left(\left(\frac{y}{6}\right)^{\frac{4}{3}}, \left(\frac{y}{6}\right)^{\frac{4}{3}}\right)$.

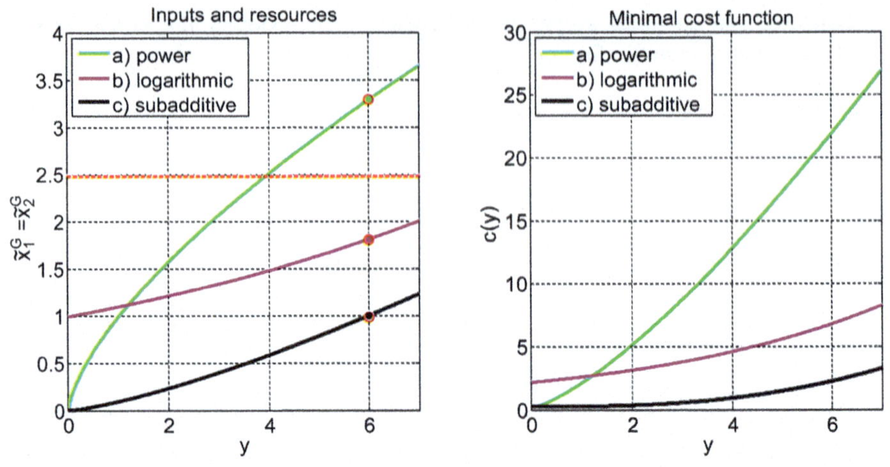

Fig. 4.4 Cost minimization problem (P2m) (E4.9)

Taking for example $a = 1, \alpha = 0.75, d = 0.25$ we get a monopoly's minimal cost function of producing y output units in the following form:

$$c^{\text{tot}}\left(\tilde{x}_1^G, \tilde{x}_2^G\right) = a\left[\left(\tilde{x}_1^G\right)^2 + \left(\tilde{x}_2^G\right)^2\right] + d = c(y),$$
$$c^{\text{tot}}\left(\tilde{x}_1^G, \tilde{x}_2^G\right) = \left(\tilde{x}_1^G\right)^2 + \left(\tilde{x}_2^G\right)^2 + 0.25 = c(y).$$

The global solution has to be compared with the resources of production factors b_1 and b_2 (Fig. 4.4).

Let us assume that $b_1 = b_2 = 2.5$ and that the producer wants to have an output level $y = 6$. In the case of the logarithmic and the subadditive production functions the resources are sufficient to obtain this output and the producer can use the optimal inputs $\overset{\sim G}{\mathbf{x}} = \left(\tilde{x}_1^G, \tilde{x}_2^G\right)$ that are smaller than resources and guarantee the minimal cost of production. In the case of the power production function, the resources are not sufficient to obtain an output level $y = 6$. We can state that there is no optimal solution in such case and that the producer has to change an output level he/she wants to obtain choosing a smaller one.

Ad 6

Give an economic interpretation of the necessary and sufficient conditions of the existence of an optimal solution to problem (P2m).

An optimal Lagrange multiplier $\tilde{\lambda}$ and optimal inputs $\overset{\sim G}{\mathbf{x}} = \left(\tilde{x}_1^G, \tilde{x}_2^G\right)$ of production factors satisfying the necessary condition are the global solution to the problem. The inputs which satisfy the necessary condition guarantee the desired output level and in the same time minimal cost of production.

Ad 7

Solve the profit maximization problem (P3m).

From point 5 we know that the minimal cost function has the following form:

$$c(y) = a\left[\left(\tilde{x}_1^G\right)^2 + \left(\tilde{x}_2^G\right)^2\right] + d.$$

The profit function with output level as an argument has a form:

$$\pi(y) = r(y) - c(y) = p(y)\cdot y - c(y) = \left(\frac{a}{y}\right)^{\alpha} y - c(y) = a^{\alpha} y^{1-\alpha} - c(y).$$

There is an additional constraint on output level resulting from the constraints on inputs of production factors:

$$y \leq f(b_1, b_2)$$

A necessary condition for existence of a maximum of the profit function takes the following form:

$$\frac{\partial \pi(y)}{\partial y} = \frac{\partial r(y)}{\partial y} - \frac{\partial c(y)}{\partial y} = a^{\alpha}(1-\alpha)y^{-\alpha} - \frac{\partial c(y)}{\partial y} = 0.$$

Let us assume that $a = 1, \alpha = 0.75, d = 0.25$ and that parameters of the production function have the following values:

(a) $\alpha_1 = \alpha_2 = 0.75$
(b) $a_1 = a_2 = 5$
(c) $a_1 = a_2 = 3$.

Then the profit function takes a form:

(a) $\pi(y) = y^{0.25} - 2y^{\frac{4}{3}} - 0.25$
(b) $\pi(y) = y^{0.25} - 2e^{0.2y} - 0.25$
(c) $\pi(y) = y^{0.25} - 2\left(\frac{y}{6}\right)^{\frac{8}{3}} - 0.25$.

The necessary condition gives the global solution,[8] that is a solution obtained when the constraints on inputs of production factors are not binding:

(a) $\overline{y}^G = \left(\frac{3}{32}\right)^{\frac{12}{13}} \approx 0.1125$
(b) $\overline{y}^G \approx 0.4713$—found using numerical methods[9] from an equation: $0.25y^{-0.75} - 0.4e^{0.2y} = 0$
(c) $\overline{y}^G = \left(6^{\frac{8}{3}} \cdot \frac{3}{64}\right)^{\frac{12}{29}} \approx 2.0356$.

---

[8] These are the same values as obtained in task 1 (ad 1).

[9] MATLAB files to find the optimal value of output using numerical methods are called myfun_E4_9_2.m and solvery_E4_9_2.m. The latter is the file to be run.

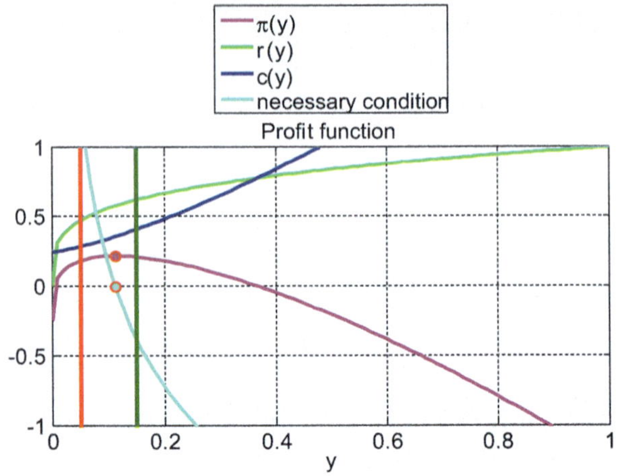

Fig. 4.5 Profit maximization problem (P3m) (E4.9)

Now we can consider a few cases depending on whether the constraint $y \leq f(b_1, b_2)$ is binding or not:

(1) The constraint is not binding:

if $\overline{y}^G \leq f(b_1, b_2)$ then the solution is $\overline{y} = \overline{y}^G$, which means that the firm can use the production factors in quantities resulting from the global solution. Using less than available resources is optimal.

(2) The constraint is binding which means that the firm can use the production factors only in quantities constrained by the resources:

- if $\overline{y}^G > f(b_1, b_2)$ and $\overline{x}_1^G \leq b_1$ while $\overline{x}_2^G > b_2$ then the solution is $\overline{y} = f\left(\overline{x}_1^G, b_2\right)$,
- if $\overline{y}^G > f(b_1, b_2)$ and $\overline{x}_1^G > b_1$ while $\overline{x}_2^G \leq b_2$ then the solution is $\overline{y} = f\left(b_1, \overline{x}_2^G\right)$,
- if $\overline{y}^G > f(b_1, b_2)$ and $\overline{x}_1^G > b_1, \overline{x}_2^G > b_2$ then the solution is $\overline{y} = f(b_1, b_2)$.

Ad 8

Present a geometric illustration of the profit maximization problem (P3m).

In Fig. 4.5, the problem is presented for point (a) assuming $a = 1, \alpha = 0.75, d = 0.25, \alpha_1 = \alpha_2 = 0.75$.

When the constraint $y \leq f(b_1, b_2)$ on the output resulting from the constraints on the production factors is binding, for example having $f(b_1, b_2) = 0.05$, then the optimal supply equal to $\overline{y}^G = 0.11$ can't be used by the firm. The firm has to use the supply 0.05, so the maximum supply can be obtained from the resources of production factors. When the constraint on the output is not binding, for example having $f(b_1, b_2) = 0.15$, then the firm uses the supply resulting from the global solution that is $\overline{y} = \overline{y}^G = 0.11$ which is less than the output resulting from the usage of all available resources.

Ad 9

Give an economic interpretation of the necessary and sufficient conditions of the existence of an optimal solution to problem (P3m).

- For the necessary condition

If by given values of parameters the profit function $\pi(y)$ has a maximum value obtained for an optimal level $\overline{y}$ of output, then the necessary condition is satisfied for this level of output. From the necessary condition it results that when the output is optimal as the global solution to the problem, then the marginal revenue equals the marginal minimal cost of production.

- For the sufficient condition

If by some values of parameters the profit function is strictly concave, then there exists the maximum of this function obtained for the global solution $\overline{y}^G$.

Ad 10

Justify that the profit maximizations problems (P1m) and (P3m) are equivalent.

The solutions to problems (P1m) and (P3m) indicate the same optimal level $\overline{y}^G$ of output.[10] If we substitute the optimal inputs of production factors obtained as the global solution to the problem (P1m) into the production function:

$$f\left(\overline{\mathbf{x}}^G\right) = f\left(\overline{x}_1^G, \overline{x}_2^G\right) = \overline{y}^G,$$

we get the same value of the optimal supply obtained as the global solution to the problem (P3m). Moreover the maximum profit is the same in both problems, (P1m) and (P3m).

Ad 11

Determine the optimal price by which a monopoly obtains the maximum profit.

The optimal price in a general form is given as:

$$p(\overline{y}) = \left(\frac{a}{\overline{y}}\right)^{\alpha} \quad \text{or} \quad p(\overline{\mathbf{x}}) = \left(\frac{a}{f(\overline{\mathbf{x}})}\right)^{\alpha},$$

- if $\overline{x}_i^G \le b_i, \quad i = 1, 2$ then $p(\overline{\mathbf{x}}) = p\left(\overline{\mathbf{x}}^G\right)$
- if $\overline{x}_1^G > b_1$ and $\overline{x}_2^G \le b_2$ then $p(\overline{\mathbf{x}}) = p\left(b_1, \overline{x}_2^G\right)$
- if $\overline{x}_1^G \le b_1$ and $\overline{x}_2^G > b_2$ then $p(\overline{\mathbf{x}}) = p\left(\overline{x}_1^G, b_2\right)$
- if $\overline{x}_1^G > b_1$ and $\overline{x}_2^G > b_2$ then $p(\overline{\mathbf{x}}) = p(b_1, b_2)$.

[10] One can compare values obtained in tasks 1 and 7 (ad 1 and ad 7).

The producer determines the price of her/his product on the basis of inputs that she/he uses in the production.

E4.10.*[11] Solve exercise E4.7 taking simultaneously into account the data from exercises E4.8 and E4.9.

Solutions

The data given are:

- a production function:
  (a) power function: $y = f(\mathbf{x}) = ax_1^{\alpha_1}x_2^{\alpha_2},\ a > 0,\ \alpha_i \in (0, 1),\ \alpha_1 + \alpha_2 < 1, i = 1, 2,$
  (b) logarithmic: $y = f(\mathbf{x}) = a_1\ln x_1 + a_2\ln x_2,\ a_i > 0,\ i = 1, 2,$
  (c) subadditive: $y = f(\mathbf{x}) = a_1x_1^{\alpha} + a_2x_2^{\alpha},\ a_i > 0,\ \alpha \in (0, 1),\ i = 1, 2,$

- a price of product manufactured by a monopoly as a function of product supply, set by a monopoly:

$$p(y) = \left(\frac{a}{y}\right)^{\alpha} > 0,$$

- a production total cost function of a form

$$c^{\text{tot}}(x_1, x_2) = \alpha(f(x_1, x_2))^2 + \beta f(x_1, x_2) + \gamma$$
$$\Delta = \beta^2 - 4\alpha\gamma = 0,\ \alpha, \beta, \gamma > 0,$$

- and constraints on inputs of production factors

$$x_i \leq b_i \quad i = 1, 2.$$

Ad 1

Solve the profit maximization problem (P1m).

In exercise E4.8 we found that there exists the optimal output guaranteeing the maximum profit. But this optimal output can be obtained by infinitely many combinations of inputs of production factors. In other words, the optimal output is uniquely determined but the inputs are not uniquely determined. The production factors have to be used in amount that result from the optimal output and the production function. The relationship between the inputs obtained in exercise E4.8 can be treated now as

[11] This exercise is not a standard one (see exercise E4.8) due to a form of the production total cost function resulting in a not standard necessary condition for existence of a profit function's maximum. Thus, one needs to take into account that solutions and answers to the subsequent tasks neither do have standard forms.

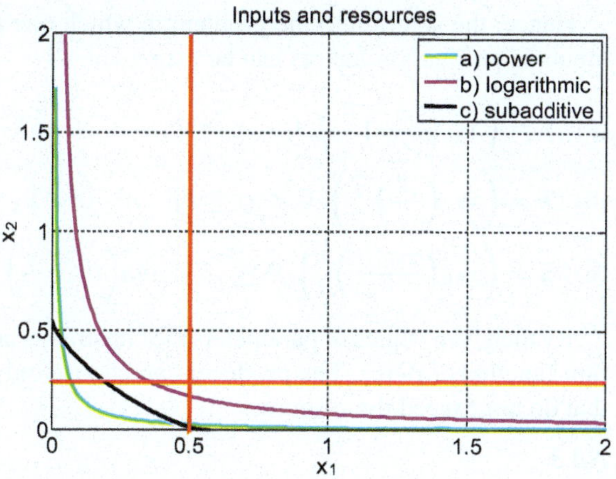

Fig. 4.6 Profit maximization problem (P1m) (E4.10)

the global solution that is a solution that would be if there were no constraints on inputs of production factors:

(a) $ax_1^{\alpha_1}x_2^{\alpha_2} = \overline{y}$ $x_2^G = \left(\frac{\overline{y}}{ax_1^{\alpha_1}}\right)^{\frac{1}{\alpha_2}}$ $\overline{\mathbf{x}}^G = \left(x_1, \left(\frac{\overline{y}}{ax_1^{\alpha_1}}\right)^{\frac{1}{\alpha_2}}\right)$, $x_1 > 0$

(b) $a_1 \ln x_1 + a_2 \ln x_2 = \overline{y}$ $x_2^G = \left(\frac{e^{\overline{y}}}{x_1^{a_1}}\right)^{\frac{1}{a_2}}$ $\overline{\mathbf{x}}^G = \left(x_1, \left(\frac{e^{\overline{y}}}{x_1^{a_1}}\right)^{\frac{1}{a_2}}\right)$, $x_1 > 0$

(c) $a_1x_1^\alpha + a_2x_2^\alpha = \overline{y}$ $x_2^G = \left(\frac{\overline{y}-a_1x_1^\alpha}{a}\right)^{\frac{1}{\alpha}}$ $\overline{\mathbf{x}}^G = \left(x_1, \left(\frac{\overline{y}-a_1x_1^\alpha}{a}\right)^{\frac{1}{\alpha}}\right)$, $0 \le x_1 \le \left(\frac{\overline{y}}{a_1}\right)^{\frac{1}{\alpha}}$.

Now there are additional constraints on inputs of production factors:

$$x_i \le b_i i = 1, 2.$$

Among combinations of inputs of production factors that give the maximum profit, a producer has to choose such amounts that do not exceed available resources.

Ad 2

Present a geometric illustration of the profit maximization problem (P1m).

Taking for example $a = 10$, $\alpha = 0.75$, $\gamma = 1$ (which gives $\beta \approx 1.73$) we get the optimal output $\overline{y}$ equal to about 0.4773. Let us assume that the resources of production factors are $b_1 = 0.5$ and $b_2 = 0.25$. The problem is presented in Fig. 4.6. It can be noticed that among all combinations guaranteeing the optimal output $\overline{y}$ only part of them satisfy the conditions:

$$x_i \le b_i \quad i = 1, 2.$$

Hence, the solution to the problem in which one accounts for the constraints on inputs of production factors can be expressed as:

(a) $\overline{\mathbf{x}} = \left(x_1, \left(\frac{\overline{y}}{ax_1^{\alpha_1}}\right)^{\frac{1}{\alpha_2}}\right), 0 < x_1 \leq b_1 \quad \wedge \quad 0 < \overline{x}_2 \leq b_2$

(b) $\overline{\mathbf{x}} = \left(x_1, \left(\frac{e^{\overline{y}}}{x_1^{a_1}}\right)^{\frac{1}{a_2}}\right), 0 < x_1 \leq b_1 \quad \wedge \quad 0 < \overline{x}_2 \leq b_2$

(c) $\overline{\mathbf{x}} = \left(x_1, \left(\frac{\overline{y} - a_1 x_1^{\alpha}}{a}\right)^{\frac{1}{\alpha}}\right), 0 \leq x_1 \leq \min\left(b_1, \left(\frac{\overline{y}}{a_1}\right)^{\frac{1}{\alpha}}\right) \quad \wedge \quad 0 < \overline{x}_2 \leq b_2,$

By the given values of parameters the constraints are binding in case of all production functions (a)–(c). The producer can choose only these combinations of inputs that do not exceed the resources.

Ad 3

Give an economic interpretation of the necessary and sufficient conditions of the existence of an optimal solution to problem (P1m).

- For the necessary condition

If by given values of parameters the profit function $\pi(\mathbf{x})$ has a maximum value obtained for an optimal level $\overline{y}$ of output, then the necessary condition is satisfied for this level of output. Inputs of production factors should then satisfy a condition $f(x_1, x_2) = \overline{y}$. Because of the constraints on inputs of production factors, the set of inputs treated as the global solution is now bounded by b_1 and b_2.

- For the sufficient condition

If by some values of parameters the profit function is strictly concave,[12] then there exists the maximum of this function obtained for the global solution $\overline{\mathbf{x}}^G$.

Ad 4

Solve the cost minimization problem (P2m).

The relationship between the inputs obtained in exercise E4.8 can be treated now as the global solution that is a solution that would be if there were no constraints on inputs of production factors:

(a) $ax_1^{\alpha_1} x_2^{\alpha_2} = y \quad x_2 = \left(\frac{y}{ax_1^{\alpha_1}}\right)^{\frac{1}{\alpha_2}} \quad \widetilde{\mathbf{x}}^G = \left(x_1, \left(\frac{y}{ax_1^{\alpha_1}}\right)^{\frac{1}{\alpha_2}}\right), \quad x_1 > 0$

(b) $a_1 \ln x_1 + a_2 \ln x_2 = y \quad x_2 = \left(\frac{e^y}{x_1^{a_1}}\right)^{\frac{1}{a_2}} \quad \widetilde{\mathbf{x}}^G = \left(x_1, \left(\frac{e^y}{x_1^{a_1}}\right)^{\frac{1}{a_2}}\right), \quad x_1 > 0$

---

[12] Let us recall that strict concavity in case of a function of many variables requires that the Hessian matrix of the profit function is negative definite. Here it depends on values of parameters of the production function and of the production total cost function. Let us assume that these values are such that the profit function is strictly concave, which requires, among others that $\alpha \in (0; 1)$.

(c) $a_1 x_1^\alpha + a_2 x_2^\alpha = y$ $x_2 = \left(\frac{y - a_1 x_1^\alpha}{a}\right)^{\frac{1}{\alpha}}$ $\tilde{\mathbf{x}}^G = \left(x_1, \left(\frac{y - a_1 x_1^\alpha}{a}\right)^{\frac{1}{\alpha}}\right)$, $0 \leq x_1 \leq \left(\frac{y}{a_1}\right)^{\frac{1}{\alpha}}$.

Now there are additional constraints on inputs of production factors:

$$x_i \leq b_i i = 1, 2.$$

Among combinations of inputs of production factors that allow to obtain a given output level y, a producer has to choose such amounts that do not exceed available resources. The solution to the problem in which one accounts for the constraints on inputs of production factors can be expressed as:

(a) $\tilde{\mathbf{x}} = \left(x_1, \left(\frac{y}{a x_1^{\alpha_1}}\right)^{\frac{1}{\alpha_2}}\right)$, $0 < x_1 \leq b_1 \quad \wedge \quad 0 < \tilde{x}_2 \leq b_2$

(b) $\tilde{\mathbf{x}} = \left(x_1, \left(\frac{e^y}{x_1^{\alpha_1}}\right)^{\frac{1}{\alpha_2}}\right)$, $0 < x_1 \leq b_1 \quad \wedge \quad 0 < \tilde{x}_2 \leq b_2$

(c) $\tilde{\mathbf{x}} = \left(x_1, \left(\frac{y - a_1 x_1^\alpha}{a}\right)^{\frac{1}{\alpha}}\right)$, $0 \leq x_1 \leq \min\left(b_1, \left(\frac{y}{a_1}\right)^{\frac{1}{\alpha}}\right) \quad \wedge \quad 0 < \tilde{x}_2 \leq b_2$.

Ad 5

Present a geometric illustration of the cost minimization problem (P2m).

Taking for example $\alpha = 0.75$, $\gamma = 1$ (which gives $\beta \approx 1.73$) we get a monopoly's minimal cost function of producing y output units in the following form:

$$c^{\text{tot}}(y) = \alpha y^2 + \beta y + \gamma = c(y),$$
$$c^{\text{tot}}(y) = 0.75 y^2 + 1.73 y + 1 = c(y).$$

Let us assume that the resources of production factors are $b_1 = 0.5$ and $b_2 = 0.25$ which gives a constraint on the output level $y \leq f(b_1, b_2) = f(0.5, 0.25)$. In the case of the power production function from point (a), taking $a = 10$, $\alpha_1 = \alpha_2 = 0.75$, the constraint is $y \leq 2.1$. In Fig. 4.7, a firm's minimal cost function is presented in comparison with this constraint.

Ad 6

Give an economic interpretation of the necessary and sufficient conditions of the existence of an optimal solution to problem (P2m).

Any inputs of production factors satisfying a condition resulting from the production function $f(x_1, x_2) = y$ are the global solution to the problem. The solution is determined with an accuracy of a relationship between the inputs.

Ad 7

Solve the profit maximization problem (P3m).

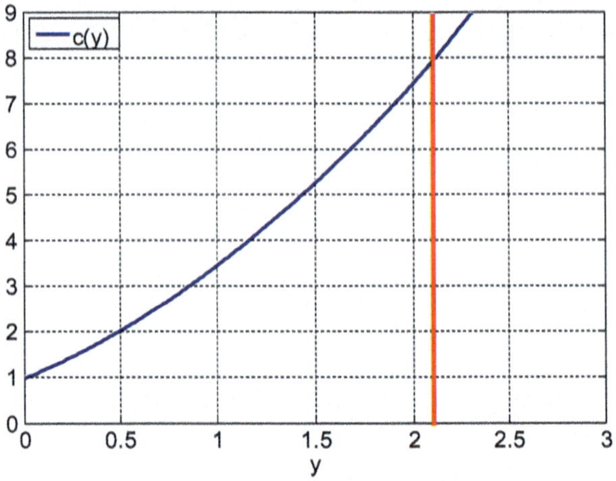

Fig. 4.7 Firm's minimal cost function of producing y output units (E4.10)

In exercise E4.8 we found that there exists the optimal output guaranteeing the maximum profit. It is derived from a necessary condition for existence of a maximum of the profit function:

$$\frac{\partial \pi(y)}{\partial y} = a^{\alpha}(1-\alpha)y^{-\alpha} - 2\alpha y - \beta = 0$$

and treated as the global solution $\overline{y}^G$. When one accounts for the constraint on the output level $y \leq f(b_1, b_2)$ resulting from the constraints on inputs of production factors, then the solution takes a form:

$$\overline{y} = \min(f(b_1, b_2), \overline{y}^G).$$

Ad 8

Present a geometric illustration of the profit maximization problem (P3m).

Taking for example $a = 10$, $\alpha = 0.75$, $\gamma = 1$ (which gives $\beta \approx 1.73$), we get the optimal output $\overline{y}$ equal to about 0.4773. Let us first assume that the resources of production factors are $b_1 = 0.5$ and $b_2 = 0.25$ which gives a constraint on the output level $y \leq f(b_1, b_2) = f(0.5, 0.25)$. In the case of the power production function from point a), taking $a = 10$, $\alpha_1 = \alpha_2 = 0.75$, the constraint is $y \leq 2.1$ and is not binding. When the resources of production factors are $b_1 = \frac{1}{8}$ and $b_2 = \frac{1}{16}$, the constraint is $y \leq 0.26$ and is binding. In this case, the profit corresponding to the output level $f(0.5, 0.25)$ is smaller than the profit corresponding to the optimal output as the global solution. In Fig. 4.8, the optimal output as the global solution is presented in comparison with the constraints on output level.

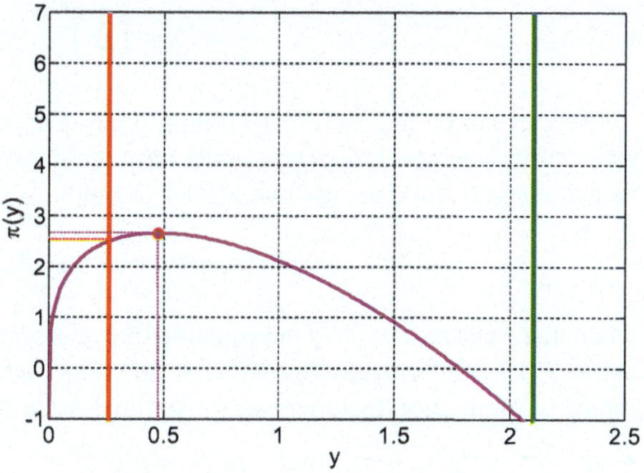

Fig. 4.8 Profit maximization problem (P3m) (E4.10)

Ad 9

Give an economic interpretation of the necessary and sufficient conditions of the existence of an optimal solution to problem (P3m).

- For the necessary condition

If by given values of parameters, the profit function $\pi(y)$ has a maximum value obtained for an optimal level $\overline{y}^G$ of output treated as the global solution, then the necessary condition is satisfied for this level of output.

- For the sufficient condition

If by some values of parameters the profit function is strictly concave, then there exists the maximum of this function obtained for the global solution $\overline{y}^G$.

Ad 10

The solutions to problems (P1m) and (P3m) indicate the same optimal level $\overline{y}$ of output (found using numerical methods from the nonlinear equation). To have this level of output a producer has to combine production factors in the amounts resulting from the production function formula. This means that he/she is able to determine the optimal level of output and then to use the proper inputs of production factors. If the producer has limited resources of production factors he/she has to compare the optimal inputs obtained as the global solution with the maximization problems with the resources. If the constraints on inputs are not binding then using less than resources is optimal. If the constraints are binding then using all available resources in the proper relationship resulting from the production function is optimal.

Ad 11

The optimal level of a price results from a relation between the price and the supply:

$$p(\overline{y}) = \left(\frac{a}{\overline{y}}\right)^{\alpha}.$$

We can notice that here the optimal price does not depend on the form of the production function. It depends on the form of the production total cost function and its parameters, since the optimal level $\overline{y}$ of output is determined from an equation:

$$a^{\alpha}(1-\alpha)y^{-\alpha} = 2\alpha y + \beta,$$

where the right-hand side of the equation (the necessary condition in problems (P1m) and (P3m)) results from the total cost function. Accounting for the constraints on inputs of production factors gives the optimal price as:

- if $\overline{y}^{G} \leq f(b_1, b_2)$, then $p(\overline{y}) = p(\overline{y}^{G})$,
- if $\overline{y}^{G} > f(b_1, b_2)$, then $p(\overline{y}) = p(f(b_1, b_2))$.

E4.11. A production process in some firm acting in the perfect competition is described by a one-variable production function of a form:

$$f(x(t)) = x(t)^{0.25}.$$

In periods $t = 0, 1, 2, \ldots, 20$ the price of a production factor, the product price and the production fixed cost evolve according to the following equations:

$$C(t) = 4 \cdot 0.98^{-t},$$

$$p(t) = -0.006t^2 + 0.1t + 3,$$

$$d(t) = \frac{(-0.006t^2 + 0.1t + 3)^2 t}{480 \cdot 0.98^{-t}} + \frac{t}{30} + 1.$$

Using the dynamic approach:

1. Solve the profit maximization problem with regard to an input of a production factor.
2. Present a trajectory of the demand for a production factor and a trajectory of the firm's maximum profit.
3. Solve the production cost minimization problem assuming that the fixed output level $y(t)$ that the firm wants to achieve in subsequent periods is given by a formula:

$$y(t) = 0.00035(t + 15)^2 + 1.25.$$

4. Present a trajectory of the conditional demand for a production factor and a trajectory of the production minimum cost.

5. Solve the profit maximization problem with regard to output level.
6. Present a trajectory of the product optimal supply and a trajectory of the firm's maximum profit.

Solution

Ad 1

Solve the profit maximization problem with regard to an input of a production factor.

The profit function with inputs of production factors as arguments has a form:

$$\begin{aligned}\pi(x(t)) &= r(x(t)) - c^{\text{tot}}(x(t))\\ &= p(t)f(x(t)) - (C(t)x(t) + d(t))\\ &= p(t)x(t)^{0.25} - c(t)x(t) - d(t).\end{aligned}$$

A necessary condition for existence of a maximum of this function takes the following form:

$$\frac{\mathrm{d}\pi(x(t))}{\mathrm{d}x(t)} = 0.25p(t)x(t)^{-0.75} - C(t) = 0$$

and gives an optimal input of the production factor:

$$\overline{x}(t) = \left(\frac{p(t)}{4C(t)}\right)^{\frac{4}{3}}$$

and the optimal supply:

$$\overline{y}(t) = \left(\frac{p(t)}{4C(t)}\right)^{\frac{1}{3}}.$$

The optimal input and the optimal supply depend positively on the price $p(t)$ of the product and negatively on the price $C(t)$ of the production factor.

A sufficient condition for existence of the maximum of the profit function has a form:

$$\frac{\mathrm{d}^2\pi(x(t))}{\mathrm{d}x(t)^2} = -0.25 \cdot 0.75p(t)x(t)^{-1.75} < 0$$

and is satisfied since the price of the product and an input of the production factor have positive values.

The maximum profit function then takes the following form:

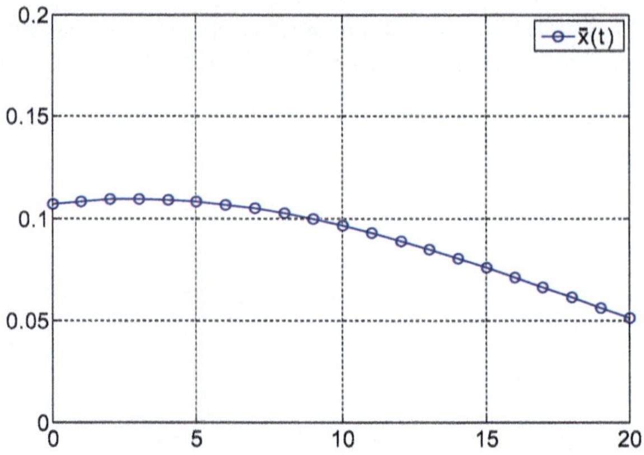

Fig. 4.9 Demand for production factor (E4.11)

$$\begin{aligned}\Pi(p(t), C(t), d(t)) &= \max \pi(x(t)) = \pi(\overline{x}(t))\\ &= p(t)\overline{x}(t)^{0.25} - C(t)\overline{x}(t) - d(t)\\ &= p(t)\left(\frac{p(t)}{4C(t)}\right)^{\frac{1}{3}} - C(t)\left(\frac{p(t)}{4C(t)}\right)^{\frac{4}{3}} - d(t)\\ &= 3\left(\frac{p(t)}{4c(t)}\right)^{\frac{1}{3}} - d(t)\end{aligned}$$

The maximum profit depends positively on the price $p(t)$ of the product and negatively on the price $C(t)$ of the production factor and on the production fixed cost $d(t)$. Whether it is positive, equal to 0 or negative depends ultimately on the production fixed cost.

Ad 2

Present a trajectory of the demand for a production factor (Fig. 4.9) and a trajectory of the firm's maximum profit (Fig. 4.10).

It can be seen in Fig. 4.10 that the maximum profit is negative from 12th period to the last 20th period. The firm should decide whether to continue the production activity or to leave the market. It can try to lower the production fixed cost. When it is not possible, the firms should quit its production activity.

Ad 3

Solve the production cost minimization problem assuming that the fixed output level $y(t)$ that the firm wants to achieve in subsequent periods is given by a formula:

$$y(t) = 0.00035(t + 15)^2 + 1.25.$$

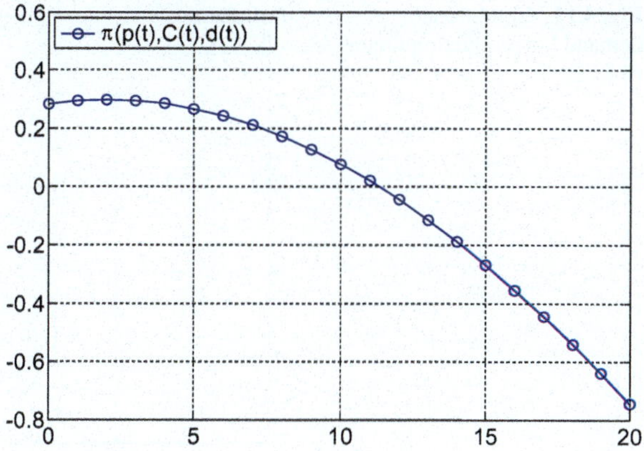

Fig. 4.10 Maximum profit of firm (P1c) (E4.11)

The problem has the following form:

$$c^{\text{tot}}(x(t)) = \{C(t)x(t) + d(t)\} \to \min$$
$$y(t) = f(x(t)) = \text{const.} > 0,$$
$$x \geq 0.$$

Because there is only one production factor its optimal input $\tilde{x}(t)$ can be found directly from an equation:

$$y(t) = x(t)^{0.25},$$

which gives

$$\tilde{x}(t) = y(t)^4.$$

Hence the minimal cost function takes a form:

$$c^{\text{tot}}(\tilde{x}(t)) = C(t)\tilde{x}(t) + d(t) = C(t)y(t)^4 + d(t) = c(y(t)).$$

Ad 4

Present a trajectory of the conditional demand for a production factor (Fig. 4.11) and a trajectory of the production minimum cost (Fig. 4.12).

Ad 5

Solve the profit maximization problem with regard to output level.

The profit function with output level as an argument has a form:

$$\pi(y(t)) = r(t) - c(y(t)) = p(t)y(t) - c(y(t)) = p(t)y(t) - C(t)y(t)^4 - d(t).$$

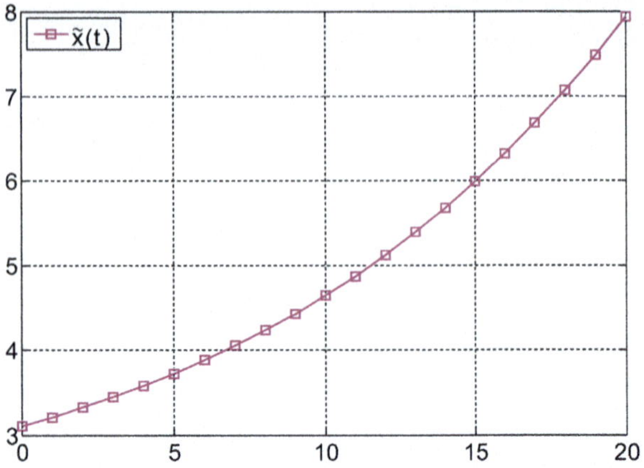

Fig. 4.11 Conditional demand for production factor (E4.11)

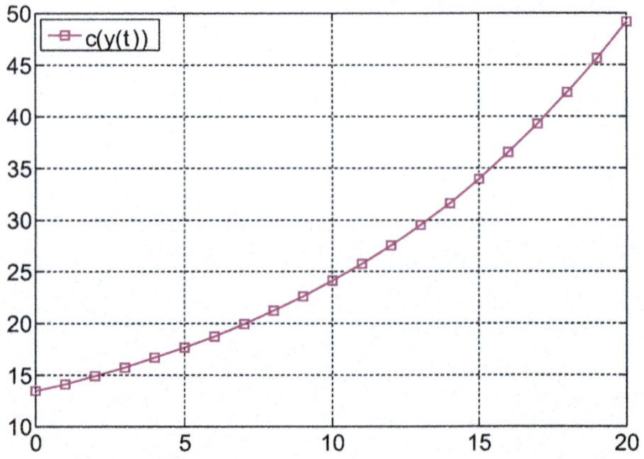

Fig. 4.12 Production minimum cost (E4.11)

A necessary condition for existence of a maximum of this function takes the following form:

$$\frac{\mathrm{d}\pi(y(t))}{\mathrm{d}y(t)} = p(t) - 4C(t)y(t)^3 = 0$$

and gives the optimal output level:

$$\overline{y}(t) = \left(\frac{p(t)}{4C(t)}\right)^{\frac{1}{3}}.$$

The optimal supply depends positively on the price $p(t)$ of the product and negatively on the price $C(t)$ of the production factor. We can notice that the solution to the profit maximization problem with regard to output level is the same as optimal output level that results from the solution to the profit maximization problem with regard to an input of a production factor.

A sufficient condition for existence of the maximum of the profit function has a form:

$$\frac{d^2\pi(y(t))}{dy(t)^2} = -12C(t)y(t)^2 < 0,$$

and is satisfied since the price of the production factor and an output have positive values.

The maximum profit function then takes the following form:

$$\begin{aligned}\Pi(p(t), C(t), d(t)) &= \max \pi(y(t)) = \pi(\overline{y}(t)) = p(t)\overline{y}(t) - C(t)\overline{y}(t)^4 - d(t) \\ &= p(t)\left(\frac{p(t)}{4C(t)}\right)^{\frac{1}{3}} - C(t)\left(\frac{p(t)}{4C(t)}\right)^{\frac{4}{3}} - d(t) \\ &= 3\left(\frac{p(t)}{4c(t)}\right)^{\frac{1}{3}} - d(t)\end{aligned}$$

The maximum profit depends positively on the price $p(t)$ of the product and negatively on the price $C(t)$ of the production factor and on the production fixed cost $d(t)$. Whether it is positive, equal to 0 or negative depends ultimately on the production fixed cost. We can notice that the maximum profit obtained from the solution to the profit maximization problem with regard to output level is the same as the maximum profit obtained from the solution to the profit maximization problem with regard to an input of a production factor. This shows that these two problems are equivalent.

Ad 6

Present a trajectory of the product optimal supply (Fig. 4.13) and a trajectory of the firm's maximum profit (Fig. 4.14).

It can be seen in Fig. 4.14 that the maximum profit is negative from 12th period to the last 20th period. The firm should decide whether to continue the production activity or to leave the market. It can try to lower the production fixed cost. When it is not possible the firms should quit its production activity.

E4.12. At any moment $t \in [0; 20]$ a firm and conditions in which it acts are described as in exercise E4.11, except additional constraint in a form of a production factor resource:

$$b(t) = 0.01(t + 1).$$

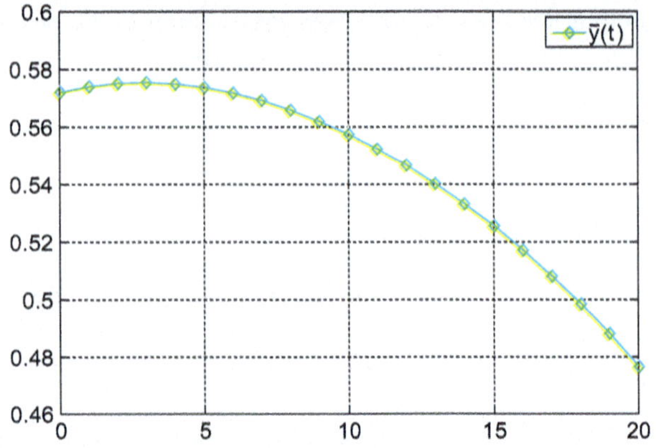

Fig. 4.13 Optimal supply of product (E4.11)

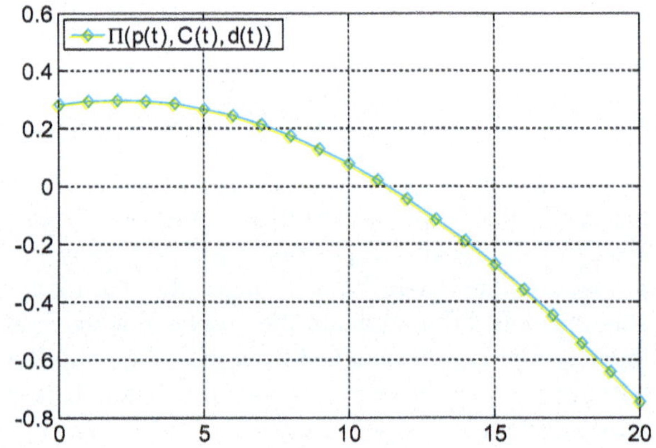

Fig. 4.14 Maximum profit of firm (P3c) (E4.11)

Using the dynamic approach:

1. Solve the profit maximization problem with regard to an input of a production factor and determine time intervals in which the constraint on the production factor resource is binding.
2. Present a trajectory of the demand for a production factor and a trajectory of the firm's maximum profit.
3. Solve the production cost minimization problem assuming that the fixed output level $y(t)$ that the firm wants to achieve in subsequent periods is given by a formula:

$$y(t) = 0.00035(t + 15)^2 + 1.25.$$

Determine time intervals in which the constraint on the production factor resource is binding.

4. Present a trajectory of the conditional demand for a production factor and a trajectory of the production minimum cost.
5. Solve the profit maximization problem with regard to output level and determine time intervals in which a constraint on output level resulting from the constraint on the production factor resource is binding.
6. Present a trajectory of the product optimal supply and a trajectory of the firm's maximum profit.

Solution

Ad 1

Solve the profit maximization problem with regard to an input of a production factor and determine time intervals in which the constraint on the production factor resource is binding.

The global solution obtained in exercise E4.11:

$$\overline{x}^G(t) = \left(\frac{p(t)}{4C(t)}\right)^{\frac{4}{3}}$$

needs to be compared with the constraint on input of the production factor:

$$b(t) = 0.01(t+1).$$

When $\overline{x}^G(t) \le b(t)$ then the constraint is not binding and the solution is $\overline{x}(t) = \overline{x}^G(t)$.

When $\overline{x}^G(t) > b(t)$ then the constraint is binding and the solution is $\overline{x}(t) = b(t)$.

Summing up $\overline{x}(t) = \min(\overline{x}^G(t), b(t))$.

Time intervals in which the constraint on the production factor resource is binding can be found from an equation[13]:

$$\overline{x}^G(t) = b(t)$$

that gives $t \in [0; 9)$.

Ad 2

Present a trajectory of the demand for a production factor (Fig. 4.15) and a trajectory of the firm's maximum profit (Fig. 4.16).

---

[13] In a MATLAB file called Exercise_4_12.m the intervals are found using commands:

```
T1=find(xG>b,1,'first')/100-0.01 and T2=find(xG>b,1,'last')/100-
0.01.
```

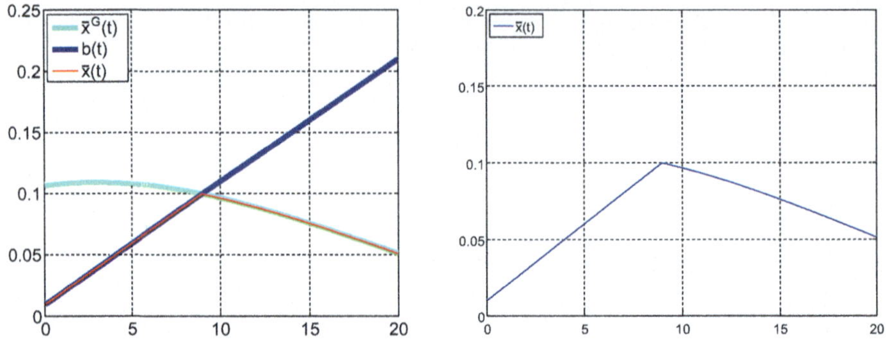

Fig. 4.15 Demand for production factor (E4.12)

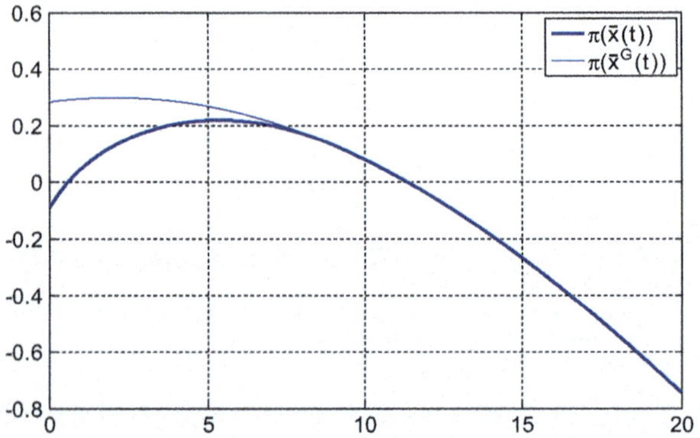

Fig. 4.16 Maximum profit of firm (P1c) (E4.12)

It can be seen in Fig. 4.16 that the maximum profit is negative at the beginning of the time horizon and from moment $t \approx 11.4$ to the end of the time horizon $T = 20$. The firm should decide whether to continue the production activity or to leave the market. It can try to lower the production fixed cost. When it is not possible the firms should quit its production activity.

Ad 3

Solve the production cost minimization problem assuming that the fixed output level $y(t)$ that the firm wants to achieve in subsequent periods is given by a formula:

$$y(t) = 0.00035(t + 15)^2 + 1.25.$$

Determine time intervals in which the constraint on the production factor resource is binding.

The global solution obtained in exercise E4.11:

$$\tilde{x}^G(t) = y(t)^4$$

needs to be compared with the constraint on input of the production factor:

$$b(t) = 0.01(t + 1).$$

When $\tilde{x}^G(t) \leq b(t)$ then the constraint is not binding and the solution is $\tilde{x}(t) = \tilde{x}^G(t)$.

When $\tilde{x}^G(t) > b(t)$ then the constraint is binding and the solution is $\tilde{x}(t) = b(t)$.

Summing up $\tilde{x}(t) = \min(\tilde{x}^G(t), b(t))$.

Time intervals in which the constraint on the production factor resource is binding can be found from an equation[14]:

$$\tilde{x}^G(t) = b(t)$$

that gives $t \in [0; 20]$. It means that in the whole time interval, the constraint on input of the production factor is binding when one regards the cost minimization problem and the conditional demand for the production factor. The firm can't produce the desired amount of its product because it has the limited resource of the production factor. The firm has to decide whether to continue the production activity taking into account the maximum profit it can achieve over time.

Let us recall, from exercise E4.11 that the minimal cost function is:

$$c^{\text{tot}}(\tilde{x}(t)) = C(t)\tilde{x}(t) + d(t) = C(t)y(t)^4 + d(t) = c(y(t)),$$

where $C(t)$ is an increasing function given as:

$$C(t) = 4 \cdot 0.98^{-t}.$$

Ad 4

Present a trajectory of the conditional demand for a production factor and a trajectory of the production minimum cost (Figs. 4.17 and 4.18).

Ad 5

Solve the profit maximization problem with regard to output level and determine time intervals in which a constraint on output level resulting from the constraint on the production factor resource is binding.

The global solution obtained in exercise E4.11:

$$\overline{y}^G(t) = \left(\frac{p(t)}{4C(t)}\right)^{\frac{1}{3}}$$

[14] In a MATLAB file called Exercise_4_12.m the intervals are found using commands: T1=find(xGG>b,1,'first')/100-0.01 and T2=find(xGG>b,1,'last')/100-0.01.

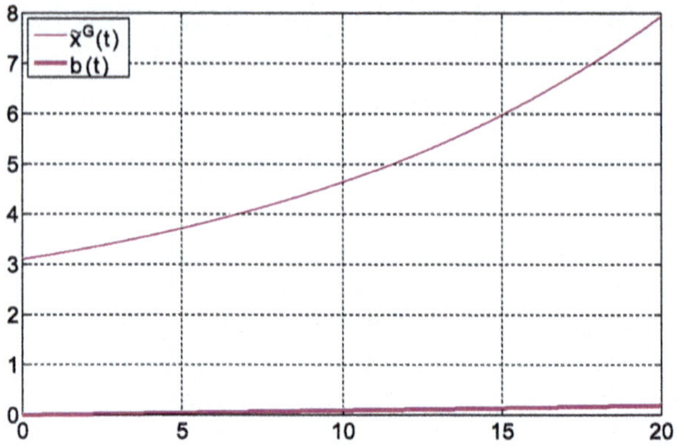

Fig. 4.17 Conditional demand for production factor (E4.12)

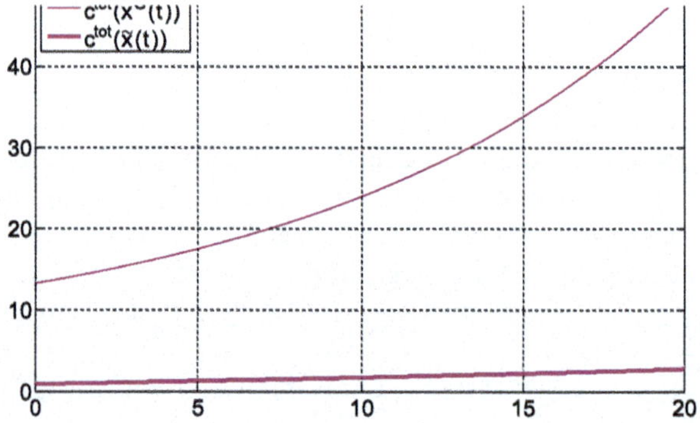

Fig. 4.18 Minimum cost of production (E4.12)

needs to be compared with a constraint resulting from the constraint on input of the production factor:

$$f(b(t)) = b(t)^{0.25} = (0.01(t+1))^{0.25}.$$

When $\overline{y}^G(t) \leq f(b(t))$ then the constraint is not binding and the solution is $\overline{y}(t) = \overline{y}^G(t)$.

When $\overline{y}^G(t) > f(b(t))$ then the constraint is binding and the solution is $\overline{y}(t) = f(b(t))$.

Summing up $\overline{y}(t) = \min(\overline{y}^G(t), f(b(t)))$.

Time intervals in which the constraint on the production factor resource is binding can be found from an equation[15]:

$$\overline{y}^G(t) = f(b(t))$$

[15] In a MATLAB file called Exercise_4_12.m the intervals are found using commands: T1=find(yG>yL,1,'first')/100-0.01 and T2=find(yG>yL,1,'last')/100-0.01.

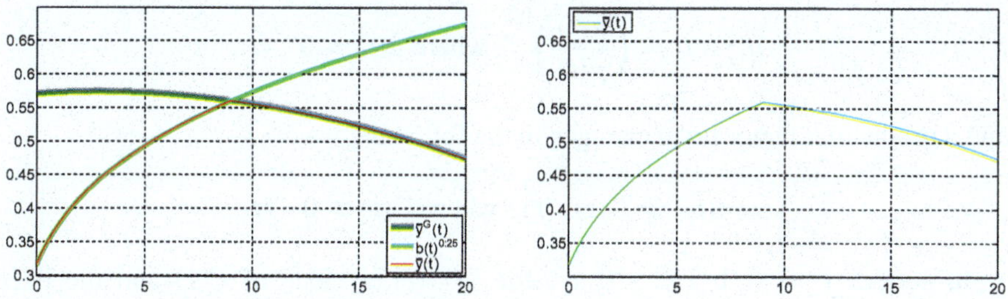

Fig. 4.19 Optimal supply of product (E4.12)

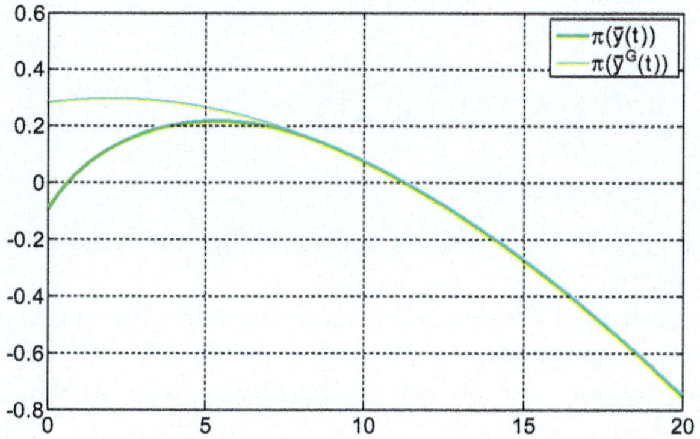

Fig. 4.20 Maximum profit of firm (P3c) (E4.12)

that gives $t \in [0; 9)$.

Ad 6

Present a trajectory of the product optimal supply (Fig. 4.19) and a trajectory of the firm's maximum profit (Fig. 4.20).

It can be seen in Fig. 4.20 that the maximum profit is negative at the beginning of the time horizon and from moment $t \approx 11.4$ to the end of the time horizon $T = 20$. The firm should decide whether to continue the production activity or to leave the market. It can try to lower the production fixed cost. When it is not possible the firms should quit its production activity.

E4.13. A production process in a firm acting as a monopoly is described by a one-variable production function of a form:

$$f(x(t)) = x(t)^{0.25}.$$

The price of a product manufactured by this monopoly changes according to a function of a form:

$$p(y(t)) = \left(\frac{a(t)}{y(t)}\right)^{0.5}, \text{ where } a(t) > 0 \quad \forall t,$$

and a production factor price changes in the following way:

$$c(x(t)) = C(t)x(t), \text{ where } C(t) > 0 \quad \forall t.$$

In periods $t = 0, 1, 2, ..., 20$ a value of $a(t)$, a value of $C(t)$ and the fixed production cost change according to equations:

$$a(t) = 3^{0.1t} + 3,$$
$$C(t) = 3^{-0.1t},$$
$$d(t) = \frac{(-0.006t^2 + 0.1t + 3)^2 t}{480 \cdot 0.98^{-t}} + \frac{t}{30} + 1.$$

Using the dynamic approach:

1. Solve the monopoly profit maximization problem with regard to an input of a production factor.
2. Present a trajectory of the demand for a production factor and a trajectory of the monopoly maximum profit.
3. Solve the production cost minimization problem assuming that the fixed output level $y(t)$ that the monopoly wants to achieve in subsequent periods is given by a formula:

$$y(t) = 0.00035(t + 15)^2 + 1.25.$$

4. Present a trajectory of the conditional demand for a production factor and a trajectory of the production minimum cost.
5. Solve the monopoly profit maximization problem with regard to output level.
6. Present a trajectory of the product optimal supply and a trajectory of the monopoly maximum profit.
7. Determine the product optimal price and present its trajectory.

Solution

Ad 1

Solve the monopoly profit maximization problem with regard to an input of a production factor.

The profit function with inputs of production factors as arguments has a form:

$$
\begin{aligned}
\pi(x(t)) &= r(x(t)) - c^{\mathrm{tot}}(x(t)) \\
&= p(t)f(x(t)) - (c(x(t))x(t) + d(t)) \\
&= a(t)^{0.5} f(x(t))^{-0.5} f(x(t)) - C(t)x(t)x(t) - d(t) \\
&= a(t)^{0.5} f(x(t))^{0.5} - C(t)x(t)^2 - d(t) \\
&= a(t)^{0.5}(x(t)^{0.25})^{0.5} - C(t)x(t)^2 - d(t) \\
&= a(t)^{0.5}x(t)^{0.125} - C(t)x(t)^2 - d(t)
\end{aligned}
$$

A necessary condition for existence of a maximum of this function takes the following form:

$$
\frac{\mathrm{d}\pi(x(t))}{\mathrm{d}x(t)} = 0.125a(t)^{0.5}x(t)^{-0.875} - 2C(t)x(t) = 0
$$

and gives an optimal input of the production factor:

$$
\overline{x}(t) = \left(\frac{a(t)^{0.5}}{16C(t)}\right)^{\frac{8}{15}}
$$

and the optimal supply:

$$
\overline{y}(t) = \left(\frac{a(t)^{0.5}}{16C(t)}\right)^{\frac{2}{15}}.
$$

A sufficient condition for existence of the maximum of the profit function has a form:

$$
\frac{\mathrm{d}^2\pi(x(t))}{\mathrm{d}x(t)^2} = -0.875 \cdot 0.125a(t)^{0.5}x(t)^{-1.875} - 2C(t) < 0
$$

and is satisfied.

The maximum profit is:

$$
\max\pi(x(t)) = \pi(\overline{x}(t)) = a(t)^{0.5}\overline{x}(t)^{0.125} - C(t)\overline{x}(t)^2 - d(t)
$$

and whether it is positive, equal to 0 or negative depends ultimately on the production fixed cost $d(t)$.

Ad 2

Present a trajectory of the demand for a production factor (Fig. 4.21) and a trajectory of the monopoly maximum profit (Fig. 4.22).

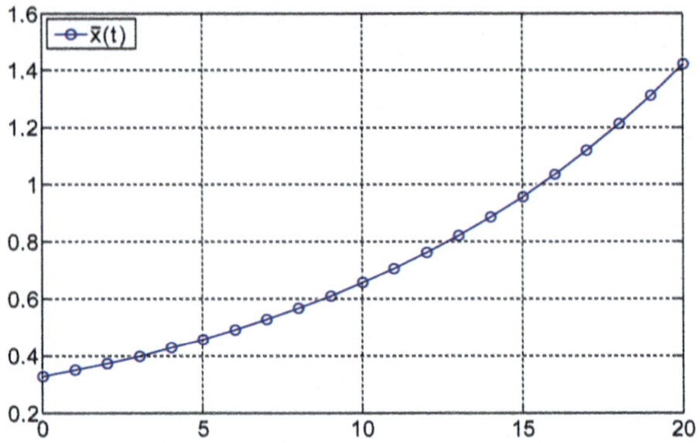

Fig. 4.21 Demand for production factor (E4.13)

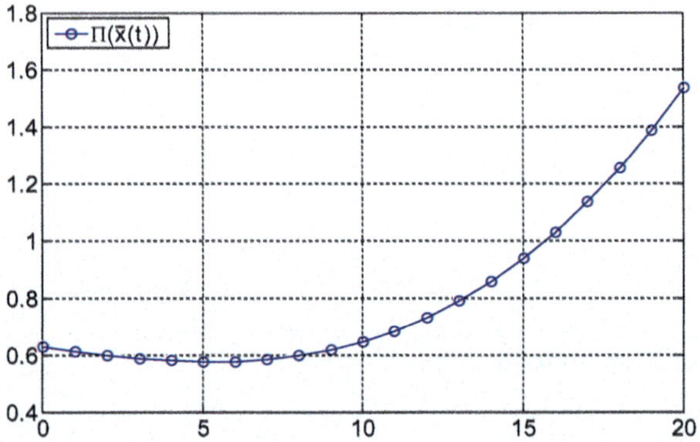

Fig. 4.22 Maximum profit of monopoly (P1m) (E4.13)

It can be seen in Fig. 4.22 that the maximum profit of the monopoly is positive in all considered periods. It results from sufficiently low production fixed cost $d(t)$ and the fact that a monopoly sets the highest price among all forms of market that firm can operate on. Generally, it can happen that the maximum profit of a monopoly is negative, but only due to very high production fixed cost.

Ad 3

Solve the production cost minimization problem assuming that the fixed output level $y(t)$ that the monopoly wants to achieve in subsequent periods is given by a formula:

$$y(t) = 0.00035(t + 15)^2 + 1.25.$$

The problem has the following form:

$$\begin{aligned} &c^{\text{tot}}(x(t)) = \left\{C(t)x(t)^2 + d(t)\right\} \to \min \\ &y(t) = f(x(t)) = \text{const.} > 0, \\ &x \geq 0. \end{aligned}$$

Because there is only one production factor its optimal input $\tilde{x}(t)$ can be found directly from an equation:

$$y(t) = x(t)^{0.25},$$

which gives

$$\tilde{x}(t) = y(t)^4.$$

Hence, the minimal cost function takes a form:

$$c^{\text{tot}}(\tilde{x}(t)) = C(t)\tilde{x}(t)^2 + d(t) = C(t)y(t)^8 + d(t) = c(y(t)).$$

Ad 4

Present a trajectory of the conditional demand for a production factor and a trajectory of the production minimum cost (Figs. 4.23 and 4.24).

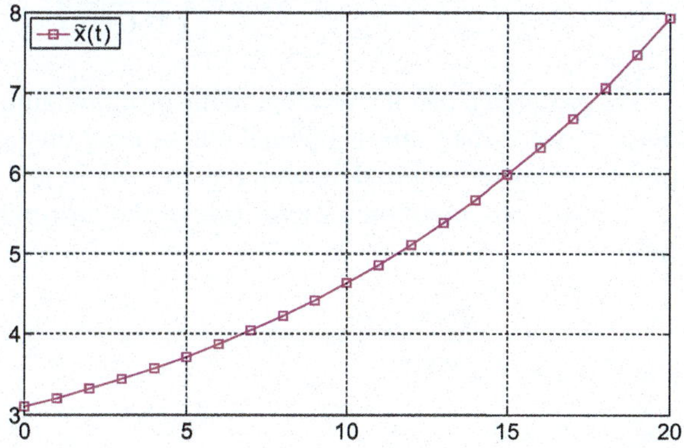

Fig. 4.23 Conditional demand for production factor (E4.13)

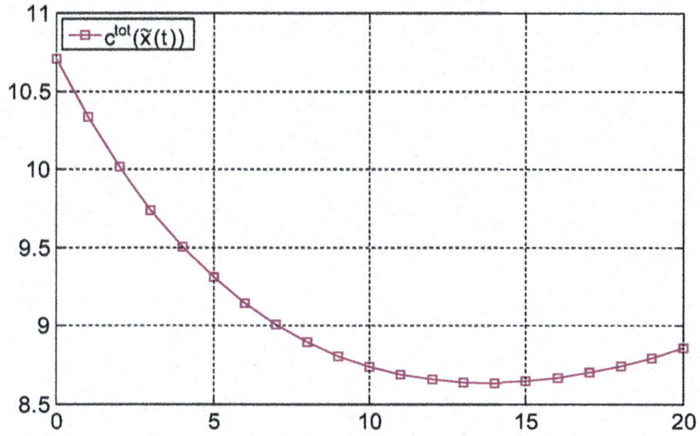

Fig. 4.24 Minimum cost of production (E4.13)

Ad 5

Solve the monopoly profit maximization problem with regard to output level.

The profit function with output level as an argument has a form:

$$\begin{aligned}\pi(y(t)) &= r(y(t)) - c(y(t)) = p(y(t))y(t)\\ &- C(t)y(t)^8 - d(t) = a(t)^{0.5}y(t)^{-0.5}y(t)\\ &- C(t)y(t)^8 - d(t) = a(t)^{0.5}y(t)^{0.5} - C(t)y(t)^8 - d(t).\end{aligned}$$

A necessary condition for existence of a maximum of this function takes the following form:

$$\frac{\mathrm{d}\pi(y(t))}{\mathrm{d}y(t)} = 0.5a(t)^{0.5}y(t)^{-0.5} - 8C(t)y(t)^7 = 0$$

and gives the optimal output level:

$$\overline{y}(t) = \left(\frac{a(t)^{0.5}}{16C(t)}\right)^{\frac{2}{15}}.$$

We can notice that the solution to the profit maximization problem with regard to output level is the same as optimal output level that results from the solution to the profit maximization problem with regard to an input of a production factor.

A sufficient condition for existence of the maximum of the profit function has a form:

$$\frac{\mathrm{d}^2\pi(y(t))}{\mathrm{d}y(t)^2} = -0.25a(t)y(t)^{-1.5} - 56C(t)y(t)^6 < 0$$

and is satisfied.

The maximum profit is:

$$\max\pi(y(t)) = \pi(\overline{y}(t)) = a(t)^{0.5}\overline{y}(t)^{0.5} - C(t)\overline{y}(t)^8 - d(t)$$

and whether it is positive, equal to 0 or negative depends ultimately on the production fixed cost $d(t)$. We can notice that the maximum profit obtained from the solution to the profit maximization problem with regard to output level is the same as the maximum profit obtained from the solution to the profit maximization problem with regard to an input of a production factor. This shows that these two problems are equivalent.

Ad 6

Present a trajectory of the product optimal supply and a trajectory of the monopoly maximum profit (Figs. 4.25 and 4.26).

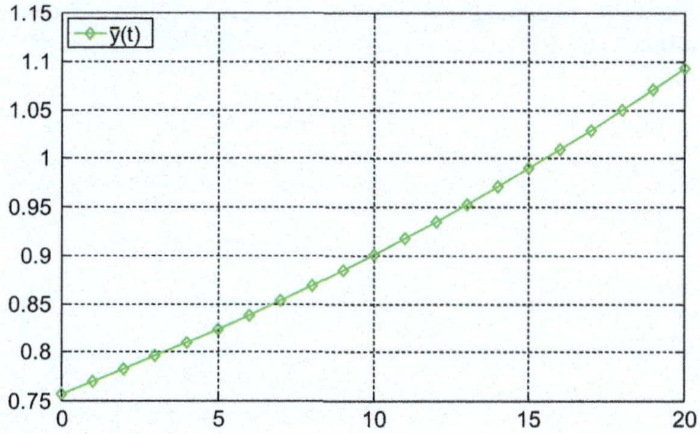

Fig. 4.25 Optimal supply of product (E4.13)

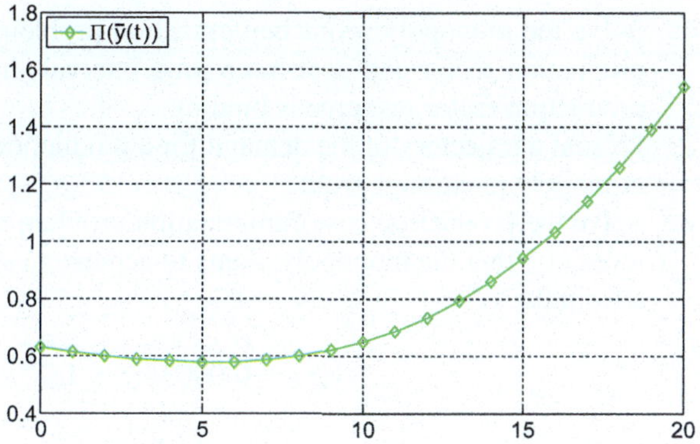

Fig. 4.26 Maximum profit of monopoly (P3m) (E4.13)

Ad 7

Determine the product optimal price and present its trajectory (Fig. 4.27).

The optimal price of the product is

$$p(\overline{y}(t)) = \left(\frac{a(t)}{\overline{y}(t)}\right)^{0.5} = \left(a(t) \cdot \left(\frac{a(t)^{0.5}}{16C(t)}\right)^{-\frac{2}{15}}\right)^{0.5} = \left(16a(t)^7 C(t)\right)^{\frac{1}{15}}.$$

E4.14. At any moment $t \in [0; 20]$ a monopoly and conditions in which it acts are described as in exercise E4.13, except for an additional constraint in a form of a production factor resource:

$$b(t) = 0.01t + 1.$$

Using the dynamic approach:

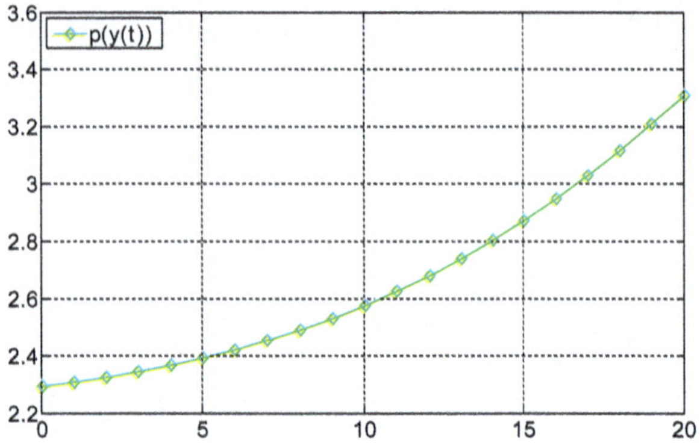

Fig. 4.27 Optimal price of product (E4.13)

1. Solve the monopoly profit maximization problem with regard to an input of a production factor and determine time intervals in which the constraint on the production factor resource is binding.
2. Present a trajectory of the demand for a production factor and a trajectory of the monopoly maximum profit.
3. Solve the production cost minimization problem assuming that the fixed output level $y(t)$ that the monopoly wants to achieve in subsequent periods is given by a formula:

$$y(t) = 0.00035(t + 15)^2 + 1.25.$$

   Determine time intervals in which the constraint on the production factor resource is binding.
4. Present a trajectory of the conditional demand for a production factor and a trajectory of the production minimum cost.
5. Solve the monopoly profit maximization problem with regard to output level and determine time intervals in which a constraint on output level resulting from the constraint on the production factor resource is binding.
6. Present a trajectory of the product optimal supply and a trajectory of the monopoly maximum profit.
7. Determine the product optimal price and present its trajectory in comparison with a trajectory of a price which would be set by the monopoly if there was no constraint on the production factor resource.

Solution

Ad 1

Solve the monopoly profit maximization problem with regard to an input of a production factor and determine time intervals in which the constraint on the production factor resource is binding.

The global solution obtained in exercise E4.13:

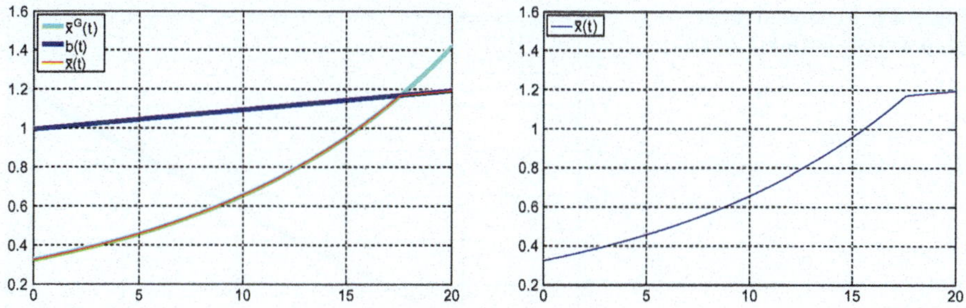

Fig. 4.28 Demand for production factor (E4.14)

$$\overline{x}^G(t) = \left(\frac{a(t)^{0.5}}{16C(t)}\right)^{\frac{8}{15}}$$

needs to be compared with the constraint on input of the production factor:

$$b(t) = 0.01t + 1.$$

When $\overline{x}^G(t) \leq b(t)$ then the constraint is not binding and the solution is $\overline{x}(t) = \overline{x}^G(t)$.

When $\overline{x}^G(t) > b(t)$ then the constraint is binding and the solution is $\overline{x}(t) = b(t)$.

Summing up $\overline{x}(t) = \min(\overline{x}^G(t), b(t))$.

Time intervals in which the constraint on the production factor resource is binding can be found from an equation[16]:

$$\overline{x}^G(t) = b(t)$$

that gives $t \in (17.6; 20]$.

Ad 2

Present a trajectory of the demand for a production factor and a trajectory of the monopoly maximum profit (Figs. 4.28 and 4.29).

Ad 3

Solve the production cost minimization problem assuming that the fixed output level $y(t)$ that the monopoly wants to achieve in subsequent periods is given by a formula:

$$y(t) = 0.00035(t + 15)^2 + 1.25.$$

[16] In a MATLAB file called Exercise_4_14.m the intervals are found using commands: T1=find(xG>b,1,'first')/100-0.01 and T2=find(xG>b,1,'last')/100-0.01.

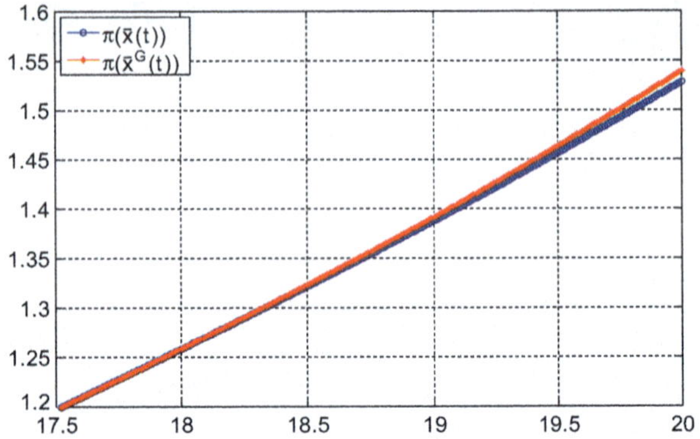

Fig. 4.29 Maximum profit of monopoly (P1m) (E4.14)

Determine time intervals in which the constraint on the production factor resource is binding.

The global solution obtained in exercise E4.13:

$$\tilde{x}^G(t) = y(t)^4$$

needs to be compared with the constraint on input of the production factor:

$$b(t) = 0.01t + 1.$$

When $\tilde{x}^G(t) \leq b(t)$ then the constraint is not binding and the solution is $\tilde{x}(t) = \tilde{x}^G(t)$.

When $\tilde{x}^G(t) > b(t)$ then the constraint is binding and the solution is $\tilde{x}(t) = b(t)$.

Summing up $\tilde{x}(t) = \min(\tilde{x}^G(t), b(t))$.

Time intervals in which the constraint on the production factor resource is binding can be found from an equation[17]:

$$\tilde{x}^G(t) = b(t)$$

that gives $t \in [0; 20]$. It means that in the whole time interval the constraint on input of the production factor is binding when one regards the cost minimization problem and the conditional demand for the production factor. The firm can't produce the desired amount of its product because it has the limited resource of the production factor.

Let us recall, from exercise E4.13 that the minimal cost function is:

$$c^{\text{tot}}(\tilde{x}(t)) = C(t)\tilde{x}(t)^2 + d(t) = C(t)y(t)^8 + d(t) = c(y(t)),$$

where $C(t)$ is a decreasing function given as:

[17] In a MATLAB file called Exercise_4_14.m the intervals are found using commands: T1=find(xGG>b,1,'first')/100-0.01 and T2=find(xGG>b,1,'last')/100-0.01.

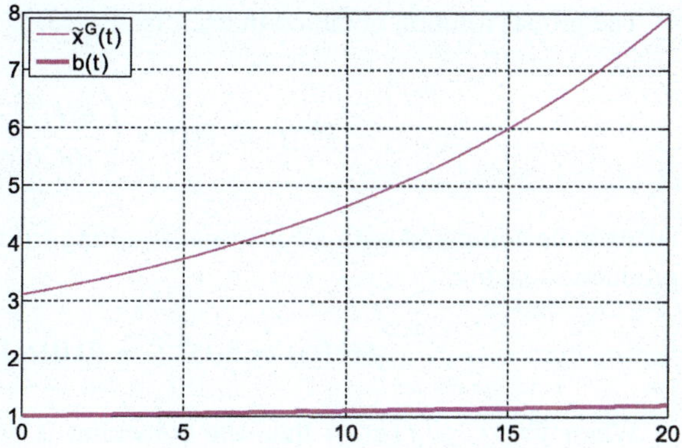

Fig. 4.30 Conditional demand for production factor (E4.14)

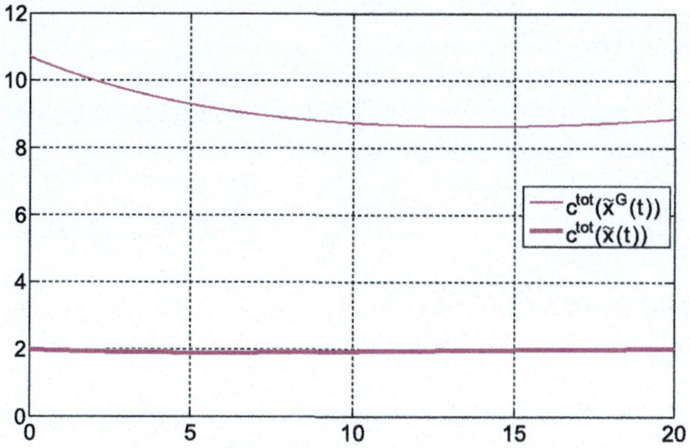

Fig. 4.31 Minimum cost of production (E4.14)

$$C(t) = 3^{-0.1t}.$$

Ad 4

Present a trajectory of the conditional demand for a production factor and a trajectory of the production minimum cost (Figs. 4.30 and 4.31).

Ad 5

Solve the monopoly profit maximization problem with regard to output level and determine time intervals in which a constraint on output level resulting from the constraint on the production factor resource is binding.

The global solution obtained in exercise E4.13:

$$\overline{y}^G(t) = \overline{y}(t) = \left(\frac{a(t)^{0.5}}{16C(t)}\right)^{\frac{2}{15}}$$

needs to be compared with a constraint resulting from the constraint on input of the production factor:

$$f(b(t)) = b(t)^{0.25} = (0.01t + 1)^{0.25}.$$

When $\overline{y}^G(t) \leq f(b(t))$ then the constraint is not binding and the solution is $\overline{y}(t) = \overline{y}^G(t)$.

When $\overline{y}^G(t) > f(b(t))$ then the constraint is binding and the solution is $\overline{y}(t) = f(b(t))$.

Summing up $\overline{y}(t) = \min(\overline{y}^G(t), f(b(t)))$.

Time intervals in which the constraint on the production factor resource is binding can be found from an equation[18]:

$$\overline{y}^G(t) = f(b(t))$$

that gives $t \in (17.6; 20]$.

Ad 6

Present a trajectory of the product optimal supply and a trajectory of the monopoly maximum profit (Figs. 4.32 and 4.33).

Ad 7

Determine the product optimal price and present its trajectory in comparison with a trajectory of a price which would be set by the monopoly if there was no constraint on the production factor resource.

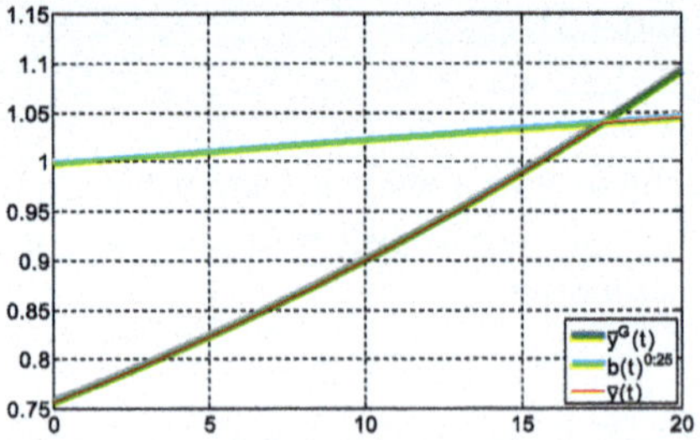

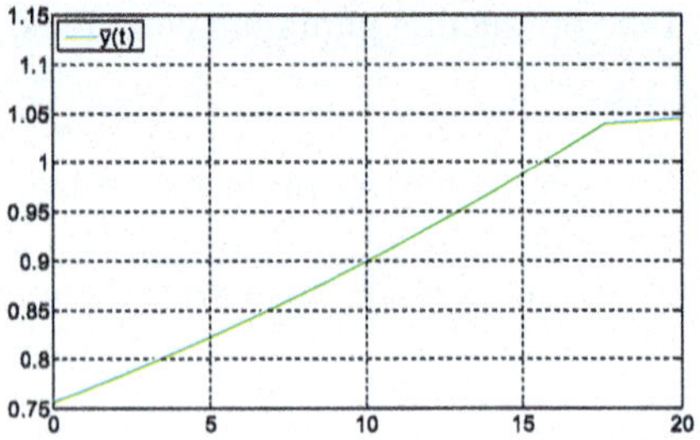

Fig. 4.32 Optimal supply of product (E4.14)

[18] In a MATLAB file called Exercise_4_14.m the intervals are found using commands: T1=find(yG>yL,1,'first')/100-0.01 and T2=find(yG>yL,1,'last')/100-0.01.

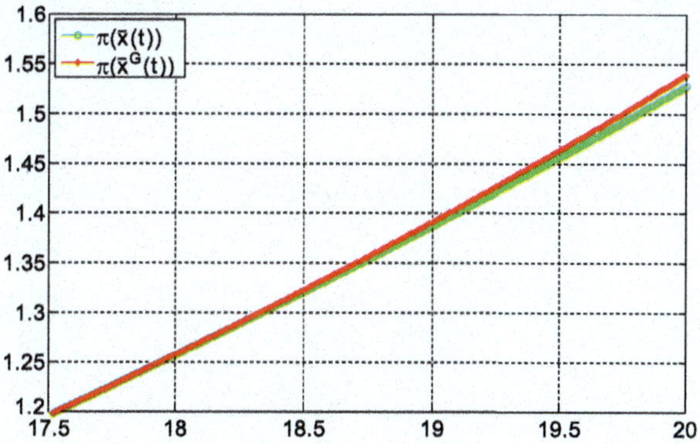

Fig. 4.33 Maximum profit of monopoly (P3m) (E4.14)

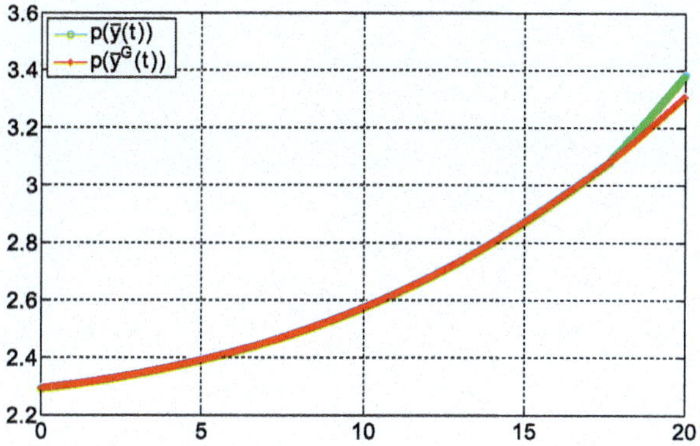

Fig. 4.34 Optimal price of product (E4.14)

The optimal price of the product is:

$$p(\overline{y}(t)) = \left(\frac{a(t)}{\overline{y}(t)}\right)^{0.5},$$

where $\overline{y}(t) = \min(\overline{y}^G(t), f(b(t)))$ (Fig. 4.34).

Chapter 5
Rationality of Choices Made by a Group of Producers by Exogenously Determined Function of Demand for a Product

This Chapter presents 18 exercises that help in understanding the problem of describing rational decisions made by individual producers in the conditions of perfect competition, monopoly or duopoly with exogenously defined demand functions. In particular they concern following problems: determining the supply by an enterprise operating in perfect competition, setting a price of a product and the supply by a monopolist, price discrimination by a monopolist when the supply of a product is intended for two markets. Part of the exercises deals with the issues of quantitative competition, on the basis of the Cournot and Stackelberg duopoly models and with the issues of price competition, on the basis of the Bertrand duopoly model. These exercises are presented in the static and the dynamic context. The focus is to consider problems of a partial equilibrium of an enterprise and a general equilibrium of a market.

E5.1. Determine an inverse function of demand and a function inverse to a given demand function: $y^d(p) = -ap^\alpha + b,\ a, b > 0$. Draw graphs of these functions in the case when:

A. $\alpha \in (0; 1)$,
B. $\alpha > 1$.

Solutions

Ad A

$$\alpha \in (0; 1)$$
$$y^d(p) = -ap^\alpha + b,\ a, b > 0$$
$$p(y^d) = \left(\frac{b - y^d(p)}{a}\right)^{\frac{1}{\alpha}}$$
$$y^i(p) = \left(\frac{b - p}{a}\right)^{\frac{1}{\alpha}}.$$

K. Sobczak and K. Malaga, *Workbook for Microeconomics*, Springer Texts in Business and Economics, https://doi.org/10.1007/978-3-031-41947-8_5

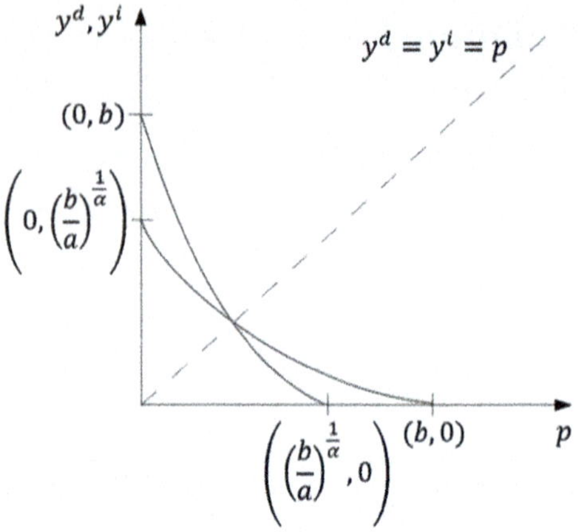

Fig. 5.1 Function of demand and function inverse to demand function when $\alpha \in (0; 1)$ (E5.1 A)

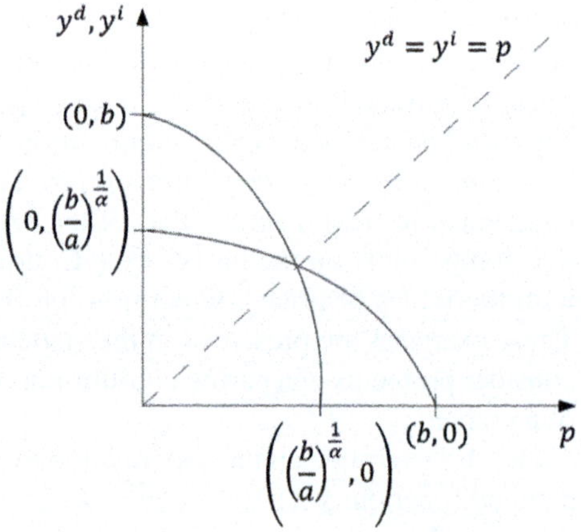

Fig. 5.2 Function of demand and function inverse to demand function when $\alpha > 1$ (E5.1 B)

See Fig. 5.1.

Ad B

$$\alpha > 1$$

$$y^d(p) = -ap^{\alpha} + b, \; a, b > 0$$

$$p(y^d) = \left(\frac{b - y^d(p)}{a}\right)^{\frac{1}{\alpha}}$$

$$y^i(p) = \left(\frac{b - p}{a}\right)^{\frac{1}{\alpha}}.$$

See Fig. 5.2.

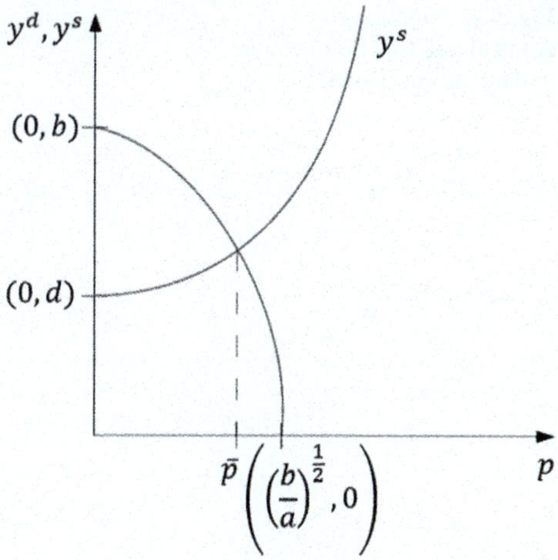

Fig. 5.3 Demand function and supply function in space $\mathbb{R}^2_+$ (E5.2 A)

E5.2. There is a market of a product with exogenously determined demand function and product supply function:

A. $y^d(p) = -ap^2 + b,\ a, b > 0,\quad y^s(p) = cp^2 + d,\ c, d > 0,\ b > d,$
B. $y^d(p) = -ap^{\frac{1}{2}} + b,\ a, b > 0,\quad y^s(p) = cp^{\frac{1}{2}} + d,\ c, d > 0,\ b > d.$

1. Determine ranges of: a product price, demand for the product, the product supply.
2. Draw graphs of the demand function and the supply function in space $\mathbb{R}^2_+$.
3. Determine an inverse function of demand and a function inverse to a given demand function. Draw their graphs in space $\mathbb{R}^2_+$.

Solutions

Ad A

1.
$$y^d(p) = -ap^2 + b,\ a, b > 0,$$
$$y^d(p) \in [0; b]$$
$$y^s(p) = cp^2 + d,\ c, d > 0,\ b > d$$
$$p \in \left[0; \left(\frac{b}{a}\right)^{\frac{1}{2}}\right]$$
$$y^s(p) \in [d; +\infty).$$

2. Figure 5.3.

3.
$$p^2 = \frac{b - y^d}{a},\ \text{then } p = \left(\frac{b - y^d}{a}\right)^{\frac{1}{2}}$$
$$y^i = \left(\frac{b - p}{a}\right)^{\frac{1}{2}}.$$

See Fig. 5.4.

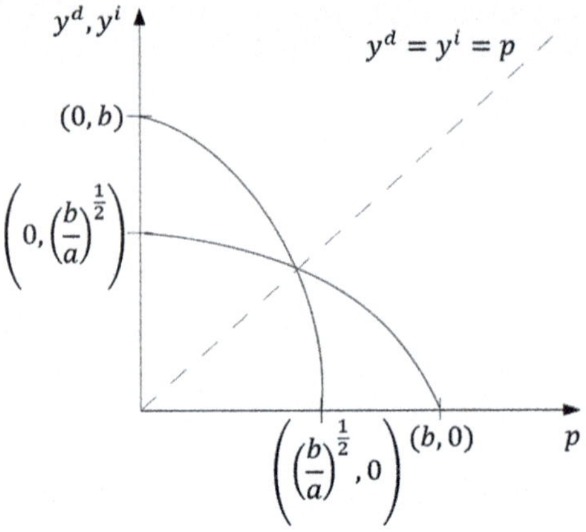

Fig. 5.4 Function of demand and function inverse to demand function (E5.2 A)

$$y^d(\overline{p}) = y^s(\overline{p})$$
$$-a\overline{p}^2 + b = c\overline{p}^2 + d$$

4. $\overline{p}^2(a + c) = b - d$

$$\overline{p} = \left(\frac{b-d}{a+c}\right)^{\frac{1}{2}} > 0.$$

Ad B

1.
$$y^d(p) = -ap^{\frac{1}{2}} + b,\ a, b > 0,$$
$$y^d(p) \in [0; b]$$
$$y^s(p) = cp^{\frac{1}{2}} + d,\ c, d > 0,\ b > d$$
$$p \in \left[0; \left(\frac{b}{a}\right)^2\right]$$
$$y^s(p) \in [d; +\infty).$$

2. Figure 5.5.

3.
$$p^{\frac{1}{2}} = \frac{b - y^d}{a},\ \text{then}\ p = \left(\frac{b - y^d}{a}\right)^2$$
$$y^i = p = \left(\frac{b-p}{a}\right)^2.$$

See Fig. 5.6.

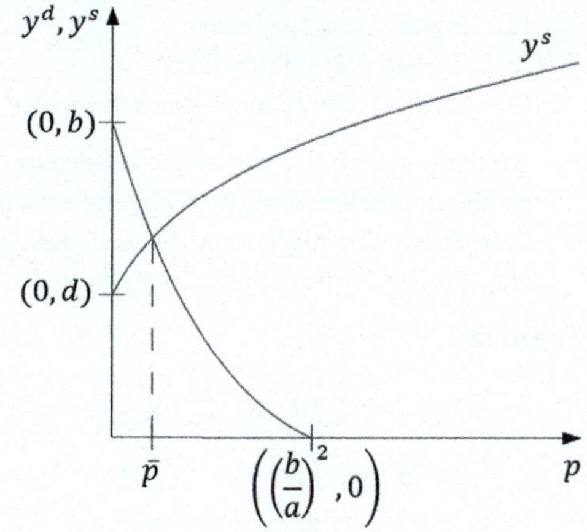

Fig. 5.5 Demand function and supply function in space $\mathbb{R}_+^2$ (E5.2 B)

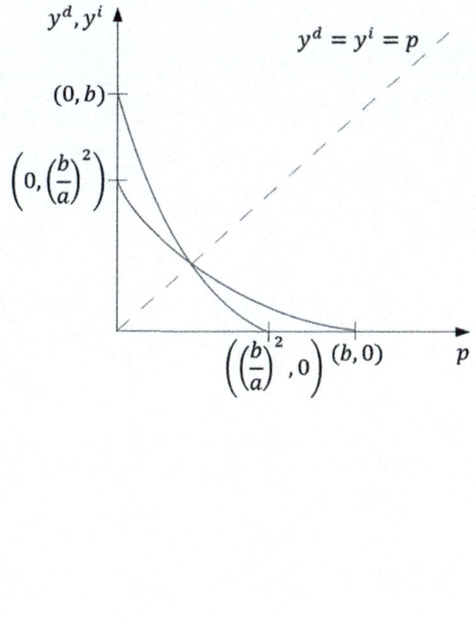

Fig. 5.6 Function of demand and function inverse to demand function (E5.2 B)

$$y^d(\overline{p}) = y^s(\overline{p})$$

$$-a\overline{p}^{\frac{1}{2}} + b = c\overline{p}^{\frac{1}{2}} + d$$

4. $$\overline{p}^{\frac{1}{2}}(a + c) = b - d$$

$$\overline{p} = \left(\frac{b-d}{a+c}\right)^2 > 0.$$

E5.3. Two producers act in perfect competition on a market described in Sect. 5.1[1], supplying one homogenous product. A function of demand for the product is linear: $y^d(p) = -ap + b,\ a, b > 0$, while functions of production total costs are nonlinear and of a form: $c_j^{tot}(y_j) = cy_j^2 + d_j,\ c_j, d_j > 0,\ j = 1, 2.$

1. Determine the optimal supply of a product:

[1] See a textbook Malaga K., Sobczak K, *Microeconomics. Static and Dynamic Analysis*, Springer Nature Switzerland, 2022.

(a) By the first producer,
(b) By the second producer,
(c) By both producers—the total supply.

2. Analyse sensitivity of the optimal supply by the first producer, by the second producer and the total supply by both producers to changes in values of parameters describing the market: a market capacity, strength of consumers' reaction to changes in a product price, production marginal cost of each producer.

Solutions

$$y^d(p) = -ap + b, \quad a, b > 0,$$
$$c_j^{tot}(y_j) = c_j y_j^2 + d_j, \quad c_j, d_j > 0,\ j = 1, 2.$$
$$p = \frac{b - y^d(p)}{a} = \frac{b - (y_1 + y_2)}{a} = \alpha - \beta(y_1 + y_2), \quad \alpha = \frac{b}{a}, \beta = \frac{1}{a}$$

Ad 1a

$$\Pi_1(y_1, y_2) = py_1 - \left(c_1 y_1^2 + d_1\right) = (\alpha - \beta(y_1 + y_2))y_1 - \left(c_1 y_1^2 + d_1\right)$$
$$= \left\{(\alpha - c_1)y_1^2 - \beta y_1 y_2 - d_1\right\} \to \max$$

Ad 1b

$$\Pi_2(y_1, y_2) = py_2 - \left(c_2 y_2^2 + d_2\right) = (\alpha - \beta(y_1 + y_2))y_2 - \left(c_2 y_2^2 + d_1\right)$$
$$= \left\{(\alpha - c_2)y_2^2 - \beta y_1 y_2 - d_2\right\} \to \max$$

Ad 1c

(1) $\left.\frac{\partial \Pi_1(y_1, y_2)}{\partial y_1}\right|_{y=\overline{y}} = 2(\alpha - c_1)\overline{y}_1 - \beta\overline{y}_2 = 0.$

(2) $\left.\frac{\partial \Pi_1(y_1, y_2)}{\partial y_2}\right|_{y=\overline{y}} = 2(\alpha - c_2)\overline{y}_2 - \beta\overline{y}_1 = 0.$

Let us divide Eq. (1) by Eq. (2):

(3) $\frac{(\alpha - c_1)\overline{y}_1}{(\alpha - c_2)\overline{y}_2} = \frac{\overline{y}_2}{\overline{y}_1}.$

(4) $\overline{y}_1^2 = \left(\frac{\alpha - c_2}{\alpha - c_1}\right)\overline{y}_2^2 = \left(\frac{b - ac_2}{b - ac_1}\right)\overline{y}_2^2.$

(5) Then $\overline{y}_1 = \left(\frac{b - ac_2}{b - ac_1}\right)^{\frac{1}{2}}\overline{y}_2$

or

(6) $\overline{y}_2 = \left(\frac{b - ac_1}{b - ac_2}\right)^{\frac{1}{2}}\overline{y}_1,$

(7) $\overline{\mathbf{y}} = \overline{y}_2\left(\frac{b - ac_2}{b - ac_1}, 1\right) = \lambda\left(\frac{b - ac_2}{b - ac_1}, 1\right) > (0, 0), \quad \lambda > 0,\ c_1 < \frac{b}{a},\ c_2 < \frac{b}{a},$

or

Table 5.1 (a) Measures of sensitivity of product supply of two producers to changes in parameters of demand function and cost function, (b) Measures of sensitivity of total supply of product of two producers to changes in parameters of demand function and cost function

(a)	
$\overline{y}_1 = \left(\frac{b-ac_2}{b-ac_1}\right)^{\frac{1}{2}} \overline{y}_2$	$\overline{y}_2 = \left(\frac{b-ac_1}{b-ac_2}\right)^{\frac{1}{2}} \overline{y}_1$
$\frac{\partial \overline{y}_1}{\partial a} = -\frac{1}{2}\left(\frac{b-ac_2}{b-ac_1}\right)^{-\frac{1}{2}} \frac{2b-a(c_1+c_2)}{(b-ac_1)^2} \overline{y}_2 < 0$	$\frac{\partial \overline{y}_2}{\partial a} = -\frac{1}{2}\left(\frac{b-ac_1}{b-ac_2}\right)^{-\frac{1}{2}} \frac{2b-a(c_1+c_2)}{(b-ac_2)^2} \overline{y}_1 < 0$
$\frac{\partial \overline{y}_1}{\partial b} = \frac{1}{2}\left(\frac{b-ac_2}{b-ac_1}\right)^{-\frac{1}{2}} \frac{a(c_2-c_1)}{(b-ac_1)^2} \overline{y}_2 > 0$	$\frac{\partial \overline{y}_2}{\partial b} = \frac{1}{2}\left(\frac{b-ac_1}{b-ac_2}\right)^{-\frac{1}{2}} \frac{a(c_1-c_2)}{(b-ac_2)^2} \overline{y}_1 > 0$
$\frac{\partial \overline{y}_1}{\partial c_1} = \frac{1}{2}\left(\frac{b-ac_2}{b-ac_1}\right)^{-\frac{1}{2}} \frac{a(b-ac_2)}{(b-ac_1)^2} \overline{y}_2 > 0$	$\frac{\partial \overline{y}_2}{\partial c_1} = -\frac{1}{2}\left(\frac{b-ac_1}{b-ac_2}\right)^{-\frac{1}{2}} \frac{a(b-ac_2)}{(b-ac_2)^2} \overline{y}_2 < 0$
$\frac{\partial \overline{y}_1}{\partial c_2} = -\frac{1}{2}\left(\frac{b-ac_2}{b-ac_1}\right)^{-\frac{1}{2}} \frac{a(b-ac_1)}{(b-ac_1)^2} \overline{y}_2 < 0$	$\frac{\partial \overline{y}_1}{\partial c_2} = \frac{1}{2}\left(\frac{b-ac_1}{b-ac_2}\right)^{-\frac{1}{2}} \frac{a(b-ac_1)}{(b-ac_1)^2} \overline{y}_2 > 0$
$\frac{\partial \overline{y}_1}{\partial \overline{y}_2} = \frac{b-ac_1}{b-ac_2} > 0$	$\frac{\partial \overline{y}_2}{\partial \overline{y}_1} = \frac{b-ac_2}{b-ac_1} > 0$
(b)	
$\overline{y} = \lambda \frac{2b-a(c_1+c_2)}{b-ac_1}$	$\overline{y} = \lambda \frac{2b-a(c_1+c_2)}{b-ac_2}$
$\frac{\partial \overline{y}}{\partial a} = \lambda \frac{b(c_1-c_2)(c_1^2+c_1c_2)}{(b-ac_1)^2} \in \mathbb{R}$	$\frac{\partial \overline{y}}{\partial a} = \lambda \frac{b(c_2-c_1)(c_2^2+c_1c_2)}{(b-ac_2)^2} \in \mathbb{R}$
$\frac{\partial \overline{y}}{\partial b} = \lambda \frac{a(c_2-c_1)}{(b-ac_1)^2} \in \mathbb{R}$	$\frac{\partial \overline{y}_2}{\partial b} = \lambda \frac{a(c_1-c_2)}{(b-ac_2)^2} \in \mathbb{R}$
$\frac{\partial \overline{y}}{\partial c_1} = \lambda \frac{a(b-ac_2)}{(b-ac_1)^2} > 0$	$\frac{\partial \overline{y}}{\partial c_1} = -\lambda \frac{a}{b-ac_2} < 0$
$\frac{\partial \overline{y}}{\partial c_2} = -\lambda \frac{a}{b-ac_1} < 0$	$\frac{\partial \overline{y}}{\partial c_2} = \lambda \frac{a(b-ac_1)}{(b-ac_2)^2} > 0$

(8) $\overline{\mathbf{y}} = \overline{y}_1\left(1, \frac{b-ac_1}{b-ac_2}\right) = \lambda\left(1, \frac{b-ac_1}{b-ac_2}\right) > (0,0), \quad \lambda > 0, \quad c_1 < \frac{b}{a}, \quad c_2 < \frac{b}{a},$

(9) $\overline{y} = \overline{y}_1 + \overline{y}_2 = \lambda \frac{2b-a(c_1+c_2)}{b-ac_1} > 0,$

or

(10) $\overline{y} = \overline{y}_1 + \overline{y}_2 = \lambda \frac{2b-a(c_1+c_2)}{b-ac_2} > 0.$

Ad 2

In Table 5.1, the sensitivity analysis of the product supplies is presented.

E5.4. Three producers act in conditions of an oligopoly on a market of one homogenous product, having equal positions on the market. A function of demand for the product is linear $y^d(p) = -ap + b,\ a, b > 0$, functions of production total costs are also linear: $c_i^{tot}(y_i) = c_i y_i + d_i,\ c_i, d_i > 0, i = 1, 2, 3$.

1. Determine the optimal supply of a product by each of three producers.
2. Determine the optimal total supply by all three producers.
3. Analyse sensitivity of the optimal supply by each producer and the total supply by all three producers to changes in values of parameters describing the market:

a market capacity, strength of consumers' reaction to changes in a product price, production marginal cost of each producer.

4. Generalize conclusions derived in points 1–3 to the case of r producers ($r \in \mathbb{N}, r \geq 3$).

Solution

Ad 1

We have:

- Functions of the total production costs of three producers:

(1) $\forall i = 1, 2, 3 \quad c_i^{tot}(y_i) = c_i^v(y_i) + c_i^f(y_i) = c_i y_i + d_i, \quad c_i, d_i > 0.$

being sums of variable cost functions:

(2) $\forall i = 1, 2, 3 \quad c_i^v(y_i) = c_i y_i, \quad c_i > 0,$

and the fixed cost functions:

(3) $\forall i = 1, 2, 3 \quad c_i^f(y_i) = d_i > 0.$

Since the total cost functions are linear functions of output, then:

(1) $\forall i = 1, 2, 3 \quad \frac{dc_i^{tot}(y_i)}{dy_i} = \frac{dc_i^v(y_i)}{dy_i} = c_i > 0,$

the marginal total and variable costs of the i-th producer are increasing functions of output.

The function of demand for a product reported by consumers, depending on its price set by producers, is:

(5) $y^d(p) = -ap + b, \quad a, b > 0,$

where:

a A measure of consumer reaction to a change in the price of a product,
b Measure of market capacity.

Since the demand function must take non-negative values, so:

(6) $p \in \left[0; \frac{b}{a}\right].$

The total supply by the three producers adjusts to the demand that is reported by consumers by the given price of the product:

(7) $y_1 + y_2 + y_3 = y^d(p) = -ap + b, \quad a, b > 0.$

The first producer wants to determine such a quantity of output that, given the output of the second and third producers, guarantees her/him the maximum profit:

(8) $$\begin{array}{c} \Pi_1(y_1)|_{y_2, y_3 = \text{const.} \geq 0} \rightarrow \max \\ y_1 \geq 0. \end{array}$$

The second producer wants to determine such a quantity of output that, given the output of the first and third producers, guarantees her/him the maximum profit:

$$\text{(9)}\quad \begin{array}{l} \Pi_2(y_2)|_{y_1,y_3=\text{const.}\geq 0} \to \max \\ \qquad\qquad\qquad y_2 \geq 0. \end{array}.$$

The third producer wants to determine such a quantity of output that, given the production volumes of the first and second producers, guarantees her/him the maximum profit:

$$\text{(10)}\quad \begin{array}{l} \Pi_3(y_3)|_{y_1,y_2=\text{const.}\geq 0} \to \max \\ \qquad\qquad\qquad y_3 \geq 0. \end{array}.$$

The profit function of i-th producer can be expressed as the difference between its revenue function from the sale of the product and the function of the total cost of production:

$$\text{(11)}\quad \forall i = 1, 2, 3 \quad \Pi_i(y_i) = p(y)y_i - c_i y_i - d_i = (p(y) - c_i)y_i - d_i,$$

Substituting into the system of Eqs. (11) an inverse demand function $p(y) = \frac{b-y}{a} = \alpha - \beta(y_1 + y_2 + y_3)$ where: $\alpha = \frac{b}{a}, \beta = \frac{1}{a}$, we get the profit functions of the three producers as functions of their output:

- For the first producer:

$$\text{(12)}\quad \begin{aligned} &\Pi_1(y_1, y_2, y_3) = [\alpha - \beta(y_1 + y_2 + y_3)]y_1 \\ &\quad - c_1 y_1 - d_1 = [\alpha - c_1]y_1 - \beta\left(y_1^2 + y_1 y_2 + y_1 y_3\right) - d_1, \end{aligned}$$

- For the second producer:

$$\text{(13)}\quad \begin{aligned} &\Pi_2(y_1, y_2, y_3) = [\alpha - \beta(y_1 + y_2 + y_3)]y_2 - c_2 y_2 \\ &\quad - d_2 = [\alpha - c_2]y_2 - \beta(y_2^2 + y_1 y_2 + y_2 y_3) - d_2, \end{aligned}$$

- For the third producer:

$$\text{(14)}\quad \begin{aligned} &\Pi_3(y_1, y_2, y_3) = [\alpha - \beta(y_1 + y_2 + y_3)]y_3 - c_3 y_3 \\ &\quad - d_3 = [\alpha - c_3]y_3 - \beta(y_3^2 + y_1 y_3 + y_2 y_3) - d_3. \end{aligned}$$

The necessary and sufficient conditions for the profit maximization problem for the first producer, taking levels of production of the second and third producers as given, are[2]:

$$\text{(15)}\quad \left.\frac{\partial \Pi_1(y_1, y_2, y_3)}{\partial y_1}\right|_{y_1=\overline{y}_1, y_2, y_3=\text{const.}\geq 0} = 0 \quad \text{—necessary condition,}$$

[2] The profit function of the first (second, third) producer with a given supply of a product of the other two enterprises is a one-variable function. In conditions (15)–(20), we use notations appropriate for first- and second-order partial derivatives, but the necessary and sufficient conditions for the existence of an optimum refer in fact to one-variable functions.

(16) $\left.\frac{\partial^2\Pi_1(y_1,y_2,y_3)}{\partial y_1^2}\right|_{y_1=\overline{y}_1,y_2,y_3=\text{const.}\geq 0} < 0$ —sufficient condition.

The necessary and sufficient conditions for the profit maximization problem for the second producer, taking levels of production of the second and third producers as given, are:

(17) $\left.\frac{\partial\Pi_2(y_1,y_2,y_3)}{\partial y_2}\right|_{y_2=\overline{y}_2,y_1,y_3=\text{const.}\geq 0} = 0$ – necessary condition,

(18) $\left.\frac{\partial^2\Pi_2(y_1,y_2,y_3)}{\partial y_2^2}\right|_{y_2=\overline{y}_2,y_1,y_3=\text{const.}\geq 0} < 0$ – sufficient condition.

The necessary and sufficient conditions for the profit maximization problem for the third producer, taking levels of production of the first and second producers as given, are:

(19) $\left.\frac{\partial\Pi_3(y_1,y_2,y_3)}{\partial y_3}\right|_{y_3=\overline{y}_3,y_1,y_2=\text{const.}\geq 0} = 0$ – necessary condition,

(20) $\left.\frac{\partial^2\Pi_3(y_1,y_2,y_3)}{\partial y_3^2}\right|_{y_3=\overline{y}_3,y_1,y_2=\text{const.}\geq 0} < 0$ – sufficient condition.

Considering the necessary and sufficient conditions for the profit functions described by Eqs. (12)–(14), we obtain:

- For the first producer:

(21) $\left.\frac{\partial\Pi_1(y_1,y_2,y_3)}{\partial y_1}\right|_{y_1=\overline{y}_1,\ y_2,y_3=\text{const.}\geq 0} = \alpha - c_1 - 2\beta\,\overline{y}_1 - \beta(y_2 + y_3) = 0,$

(22) $\left.\frac{\partial^2\Pi_1(y_1,y_2,y_3)}{\partial y_1^2}\right|_{y_1=\overline{y}_1,\ y_2,y_3=\text{const.}\geq 0} = -2\beta < 0,,$

which means that for any (given) levels of production of the second and third producers, the first producer obtains a maximum profit for $y_1 = \overline{y}_1$.

- For the second producer:

(23) $\left.\frac{\partial\Pi_2(y_1,y_2,y_3)}{\partial y_2}\right|_{y_2=\overline{y}_2,\ y_1,y_3=\text{const.}\geq 0} = \alpha - c_2 - 2\beta\,\overline{y}_2 - \beta(y_1 + y_3) = 0,$

(24) $\left.\frac{\partial^2\Pi_2(y_1,y_2,y_3)}{\partial y_2^2}\right|_{y_2=\overline{y}_2,\ y_1,y_3=\text{const.}\geq 0} = -2\beta < 0,$

which means that for any (given) levels of production of the first and third producers, the second producer obtains a maximum profit for $y_2 = \overline{y}_2$:

- For the third producer:

(25) $\left.\frac{\partial\Pi(y_1,y_2,y_3)}{\partial y_3}\right|_{y_3=\overline{y}_3,\ y_1,y_2=\text{const.}\geq 0} = \alpha - c_3 - 2\beta\,\overline{y}_3 - \beta(y_1 + y_2) = 0,$

(26) $\left.\frac{\partial^2\Pi_3(y_1,y_2,y_3)}{\partial y_3^2}\right|_{y_3=\overline{y}_3,\ y_1,y_2=\text{const.}\geq 0} = -2\beta < 0,$

which means that for any (given) levels of production of the first and second producers, the third producer obtains a maximum profit for $y_3 = \overline{y}_3$.

In order to find the equilibrium state in the Cournot oligopoly model, one needs to solve the following system of equations:

(27) $\alpha - c_1 - 2\beta\,\overline{y}_1 - \beta\,\overline{y}_2 - \beta\,\overline{y}_3 = 0,$
(28) $\alpha - c_2 - 2\beta\,\overline{y}_2 - \beta\,\overline{y}_1 - \beta\,\overline{y}_3 = 0,$
(29) $\alpha - c_3 - 2\beta\,\overline{y}_3 - \beta\,\overline{y}_1 - \beta\,\overline{y}_2 = 0,$

equivalent to the system of equations:

(30) $2\,\overline{y}_1 + \overline{y}_2 + \overline{y}_3 = \frac{\alpha - c_1}{\beta} = b - ac_1,$
(31) $2\,\overline{y}_2 + \overline{y}_1 + \overline{y}_3 = \frac{\alpha - c_2}{\beta} = b - ac_2,$
(32) $2\,\overline{y}_3 + \overline{y}_1 + \overline{y}_2 = \frac{\alpha - c_3}{\beta} = b - ac_3.$

Finally, after simple transformations, the equilibrium state in the Cournot oligopoly model is described by a vector[3]:

(30) $\overline{\mathbf{y}}^{(C)} = \left(\overline{y}_1^{(C)}, \overline{y}_2^{(C)}, \overline{y}_3^{(C)}\right) = \left(\frac{b - a(3c_1 - (c_2 + c_3))}{4}, \frac{b - a(3c_2 - (c_1 + c_3))}{4}, \frac{b - a(3c_3 - (c_1 + c_2))}{4}\right).$

This is the optimal state of equilibrium in the sense of Nash.

It follows that the optimal total supply of a product in the Cournot oligopoly market is:

(31) $\overline{y} = \overline{y}_1^{(C)} + \overline{y}_2^{(C)} + \overline{y}_3^{(C)} = \frac{3b - a(c_1 + c_2 + c_3)}{4},$

and the Walrasian equilibrium price takes the value:

(32) $\overline{p} = \frac{b + a(c_1 + c_2 + c_3)}{4a}.$

The maximum profits of enterprises are at the following levels:

(33) $\Pi_1(\overline{y}_1, \overline{y}_2, \overline{y}_3) = \frac{(b - a(3c_1 - (c_2 + c_3))(b + a(c_1 + c_2 + c_3) - 4c_1)}{16} - d_1.$
(34) $\Pi_2(\overline{y}_1, \overline{y}_2, \overline{y}_3) = \frac{(b - a(3c_2 - (c_1 + c_3))(b + a(c_1 + c_2 + c_3) - 4c_2)}{16} - d_2.$
(35) $\Pi_3(\overline{y}_1, \overline{y}_2, \overline{y}_3) = \frac{(b - a(3c_3 - (c_2 + c_3))(b + a(c_1 + c_2 + c_3) - 4c_3)}{16} - d_3.$

Ad 3

See Table 5.2.

Ad 4

In case of four producers:

$$\overline{y}_1 = \frac{b - a(4c_1 - (c_2 + c_3 + c_4))}{5} \quad \overline{y}_2 = \frac{b - a(4c_2 - (c_1 + c_3 + c_4))}{5}$$
$$\overline{y}_3 = \frac{b - a(4c_3 - (c_1 + c_1 + c_4))}{5} \quad \overline{y}_4 = \frac{b - a(4c_4 - (c_1 + c_2 + c_3))}{5}$$
$$\overline{y} = \frac{4b - a(c_1 + c_2 + c_3 + c_4)}{5}$$
$$\overline{p} = \frac{b + a(c_1 + c_2 + c_3 + c_4)}{5a}.$$

[3] The Reader interested in a specific solution by specific values of parameters can exploit an Excel file called Exercise 5.4.xlsx.

Table 5.2 Measures of sensitivity to changes in parameters of demand function and cost function for: (a) supply of first producer's product, (b) supply of second producer's product, (c) supply of third producer's product, (d) total supply of a product, (e) Walrasian equilibrium price

(a)

$\overline{y}_1$	$\frac{\partial \overline{y}_1}{\partial a}$	$\frac{\partial \overline{y}_1}{\partial b}$	$\frac{\partial \overline{y}_1}{\partial c_1}$	$\frac{\partial \overline{y}_1}{\partial c_2}$	$\frac{\partial \overline{y}_1}{\partial c_3}$
$\frac{b-a(3c_1-(c_2+c_3))}{4}$	$\frac{-3c_1+(c_2+c_3)}{4}$	$\frac{1}{4}$	$-\frac{3a}{4}$	$\frac{a}{4}$	$\frac{a}{4}$

(b)

$\overline{y}_2$	$\frac{\partial \overline{y}_2}{\partial a}$	$\frac{\partial \overline{y}_2}{\partial b}$	$\frac{\partial \overline{y}_2}{\partial c_1}$	$\frac{\partial \overline{y}_2}{\partial c_2}$	$\frac{\partial \overline{y}_2}{\partial c_3}$
$\frac{b-a(3c_2-(c_1+c_3))}{4}$	$\frac{-3c_2+(c_1+c_3)}{4}$	$\frac{1}{4}$	$\frac{a}{4}$	$-\frac{3a}{4}$	$\frac{a}{4}$

(c)

$\overline{y}_3$	$\frac{\partial \overline{y}_3}{\partial a}$	$\frac{\partial \overline{y}_3}{\partial b}$	$\frac{\partial \overline{y}_3}{\partial c_1}$	$\frac{\partial \overline{y}_3}{\partial c_2}$	$\frac{\partial \overline{y}_3}{\partial c_3}$
$\frac{b-a(3c_3-(c_1+c_2))}{4}$	$\frac{-3c_3+(c_1+c_2)}{4}$	$\frac{1}{4}$	$\frac{a}{4}$	$\frac{a}{4}$	$-\frac{3a}{4}$

(d)

$\overline{y}$	$\frac{\partial \overline{y}}{\partial a}$	$\frac{\partial \overline{y}}{\partial b}$	$\frac{\partial \overline{y}}{\partial c_1}$	$\frac{\partial \overline{y}}{\partial c_2}$	$\frac{\partial \overline{y}}{\partial c_3}$
$\frac{3b-a(c_1+c_2+c_3)}{4}$	$\frac{-(c_1+c_2+c_3)}{4}$	$\frac{3}{4}$	$-\frac{a}{4}$	$-\frac{a}{4}$	$-\frac{a}{4}$

(e)

$\overline{p}$	$\frac{\partial \overline{p}}{\partial a}$	$\frac{\partial \overline{p}}{\partial b}$	$\frac{\partial \overline{p}}{\partial c_1}$	$\frac{\partial \overline{p}}{\partial c_2}$	$\frac{\partial \overline{p}}{\partial c_3}$
$\frac{b+a(c_1+c_2+c_3)}{4a}$	$-\frac{b}{4a^2}$	$\frac{1}{4a}$	$\frac{1}{4}$	$\frac{1}{4}$	$\frac{1}{4}$

In case of r producers ($r \geq 3$):

$$\overline{y}_i = \frac{b - a\left(r \cdot c_i - \sum_{j=1, j\neq i}^{r} c_i\right)}{r+1} \qquad i = 1, 2, \ldots, r$$

$$\overline{y} = \frac{r \cdot b - a(c_1 + c_2 + \cdots + c_r)}{r+1}$$

$$\overline{p} = \frac{b + a(c_1 + c_2 + \cdots + c_r)}{(r+1)a}.$$

E5.5. Consider two markets of one homogenous product. The first one is a perfect competition market described in Sect. 5.1[4], the second one is a monopolistic market (a monopoly) presented in Sect. 5.2[5]. Determine conditions by which the optimal supply of a product on the perfect competition market is:

(a) bigger than,
(b) equal to,

[4] See a textbook Malaga K., Sobczak K, *Microeconomics. Static and Dynamic Analysis*, Springer Nature Switzerland, 2022.

[5] See a textbook Malaga K., Sobczak K, *Microeconomics. Static and Dynamic Analysis*, Springer Nature Switzerland, 2022.

(c) smaller than

the optimal supply of a product on the monopolistic market.

Solutions

Perfect competition market

$$y_1^d(p) = -a_1 p_1 + b_1$$

$$p_1 = \frac{b_1 - y_1^d(p)}{a_1} = \alpha_1 - \beta_1 y_1^d(p), \quad \text{where} \quad \alpha_1 = \frac{b_1}{a_1}, \beta_1 = \frac{1}{a_1}$$

$$\text{If } y_1^d(p) = y_1^s(p) = y_1, \quad \text{then} \quad p_1 y_1 = (\alpha_1 - \beta_1 y_1) y_1$$

$$\Pi_1(y_1) = p_1 y_1 - c_1^{tot}(y_1) = \{(\alpha_1 - \beta_1 y_1) y_1 - (c_1 y_1 + d_1)\} \to \max$$

$$\frac{\mathrm{d}\Pi_1(y_1)}{\mathrm{d}y_1} = -2\beta_1 y_1 + (\alpha_1 - c_1)$$

$$\lim_{y_1 \to 0^+} \frac{\mathrm{d}\Pi_1(y_1)}{\mathrm{d}y_1} = \alpha_1 - c_1 > 0 \quad \text{for} \quad c_1 < \alpha_1 = \frac{b_1}{a_1}$$

$$\lim_{y_1 \to +\infty} \frac{\mathrm{d}\Pi_1(y_1)}{\mathrm{d}y_1} = -\infty$$

$$\left.\frac{\mathrm{d}\Pi_1(y_1)}{\mathrm{d}y_1}\right|_{y_1 = \overline{y}_1} = -2\beta_1 \overline{y}_1 + (\alpha_1 - c_1) = 0$$

$$\overline{y}_1 = \frac{\alpha_1 - c_1}{2\beta} = \frac{b_1 - a_1 c_1}{2} > 0 \quad \text{for} \quad c_1 < \frac{b_1}{a_1}.$$

Monopolistic market—monopoly

$$y_2^d(p) = -a_2 p_2 + b_2$$

$$p_2 = \frac{b_2 - y_2^d(p)}{a_2} = \alpha_2 - \beta_2 y_2^d(p), \quad \text{where} \quad \alpha_2 = \frac{b_2}{a_2}, \beta_2 = \frac{1}{a_2}$$

$$\text{If } y_2^d(p) = y_2^s(p) = y_2, \quad \text{then} \quad p_2 y_2 = (\alpha_2 - \beta_2 y_2) y_2$$

$$\Pi_2(y_2) = p_2 y_2 - c_2^{tot}(y_2) = \{(\alpha_2 - \beta_2 y_2) y_2 - (c_2 y_2 + d_2)\} \to \max$$

$$\frac{\mathrm{d}\Pi_2(y_2)}{\mathrm{d}y_2} = -2\beta_2 y_2 + (\alpha_2 - c_2)$$

$$\lim_{y_2 \to 0^+} \frac{\mathrm{d}\Pi_2(y_2)}{\mathrm{d}y_2} = \alpha_2 - c_2 > 0 \quad \text{for} \quad c_2 < \alpha_2 = \frac{b_2}{a_2}$$

$$\lim_{y_2 \to +\infty} \frac{\mathrm{d}\Pi_2(y_2)}{\mathrm{d}y_2} = -\infty$$

$$\left.\frac{\mathrm{d}\Pi_2(y_2)}{\mathrm{d}y_2}\right|_{y_2 = \overline{y}_2} = -2\beta_2 \overline{y}_2 + (\alpha_2 - c_2) = 0$$

$$\overline{y}_2 = \frac{\alpha_2 - c_2}{2\beta_2} = \frac{b_2 - a_2 c_2}{2} > 0 \quad \text{for} \quad c_2 < \frac{b_2}{a_2}.$$

Ad a

$$\bar{y}_1 > \bar{y}_2 \quad \Leftrightarrow \quad b_1 > b_2 \quad \wedge \quad a_1c_1 > a_2c_2$$

Ad b

$$\bar{y}_1 = \bar{y}_2 \quad \Leftrightarrow \quad b_1 = b_2 \quad \wedge \quad a_1c_1 = a_2c_2$$

Ad c

$$\bar{y}_1 < \bar{y}_2 \quad \Leftrightarrow \quad b_1 < b_2 \quad \wedge \quad a_1c_1 < a_2c_2.$$

E5.6. Formulate and solve a problem of choice of the optimal supply and of the optimal price set by a monopolistic company considered in Example 5.3. Assume a nonlinear function of production total cost of a form: $c^{tot}(y) = cy^2 + d, \ c, d > 0$. Analyse sensitivity of the optimal supply and of a product optimal price to changes in values of parameters describing the market: a market capacity, strength of consumers' reaction to changes in a product price, production marginal cost.

Solution

Following functions are given:

- A linear function of demand for a product:

$$y^d = -ap + b, \quad a, b > 0,$$

- A linear inverse function of demand for a product:

$$p\left(y^d\right) = \frac{b - y^d}{a} = \alpha - \beta y^d, \quad a, b > 0, \alpha = \frac{b}{a} > 0, \beta = \frac{1}{a} > 0,$$

- A nonlinear function of total cost of production:

$$c^{tot}\left(y^s(p)\right) = cy^{s2} + d, \quad c, d > 0$$

- $r(y^s) = p(y^s)y^s$—revenue (turnover) from sales of a product.

We assume that the supply of a product is equal to the demand reported by consumers:

$$y^s = y^d = y.$$

Then the profit maximization problem for a monopolist takes the form:

$$\begin{aligned}
&\Pi(y) = r(y) - c^{tot}(y) = p(y)y - c^{tot}(y) = (\alpha - \beta y)y - cy^2 - d \\
&= \{-(\beta + c)y^2 + \alpha y - d\} \to \max \\
&y \geq 0. \\
&\left.\frac{d\Pi(y)}{dy}\right|_{y=\overline{y}} = -2(\beta + c)\overline{y} + \alpha = 0 \Leftrightarrow \\
&\Leftrightarrow \overline{y} = \frac{\alpha}{2(\beta + c)} = \frac{\frac{b}{a}}{2\frac{1+ac}{a}} = \frac{b}{2(1 + ac)} > 0,
\end{aligned}$$

which means that an output level guaranteeing the maximum profit for a monopolist is positive.

Then a level of a product price set by a monopolist is:

$$p(\overline{y}) = \frac{b - \overline{y}}{a} = \frac{b - \frac{b}{2(1+ac)}}{a} = \frac{b(1 + 2ac)}{2a(1 + ac)} > 0.$$

The monopolist's maximum profit at the equilibrium price is:

$$\Pi(\overline{y}) = p(\overline{y})\overline{y} - c\overline{y}^2 - d = \frac{b^2}{4a(1 + ac)} - d.$$

If in addition:

$$\frac{b^2}{4a(1 + ac)} > d,$$

then the monopolist's maximum profit is positive.

Let us notice that the product price and the product supply set by a monopolist, which by given demand for a product guarantee the maximum profit, depend on: a market capacity b, the strength a of consumers' reaction to changes in a product price, the production marginal total (variable) cost c. The maximum profit of a monopolist depends also on the fixed cost of production d.

Let us analyse sensitivity of the product optimal supply by a monopolist and of the product price to changes of values of parameters that describe the considered model of a monopolistic market. Values of adequate measures are presented in Table 5.3a, b.

From Table 5.3a and b, it follows that a unit increase in market capacity b results in an increase in the optimal supply and in the product price. A unit increase in the marginal variable cost of production c results in a decrease in the product optimal supply and an increase in the product optimal price. A unit increase in the strength a of consumers' reaction to changes in the price of a product set by a monopolist results in a decrease in the product price and in the product optimal supply.

Table 5.3 Measures of response to changes in parameters' values for: (a) product supply by monopolist, (b) product price set by monopolist

(a)			
Characteristic $\overline{y} = \frac{b}{2(1+ac)}$	$\frac{\partial \overline{y}}{\partial a}$	$\frac{\partial \overline{y}}{\partial b}$	$\frac{\partial \overline{y}}{\partial c}$
Value	$\frac{-bc}{2(1+ac)^2} < 0$	$\frac{1}{2(1+ac)} > 0$	$\frac{-ab}{2(1+ac)^2} < 0$
(b)			
Characteristic $p(\overline{y}) = \frac{b(1+2ac)}{2a(1+ac)}$	$\frac{\partial p(\overline{y})}{\partial a}$	$\frac{\partial p(\overline{y})}{\partial b}$	$\frac{\partial p(\overline{y})}{\partial c}$
Value	$\frac{-4a^2bc^2-2b-4abc}{4a^2(1+ac)^2} < 0$	$\frac{1+2ac}{2a(1+ac)} > 0$	$\frac{b}{2(1+ac)^2} > 0$

E5.7. Formulate and solve a problem of choice of the optimal supply and of the optimal price set by a monopolistic company considered in Example 5.4[6]. Assume that the monopolist can supply her/his product to two different markets, thus regards discriminatory pricing. Assume a nonlinear function of production total cost: $c^{tot}(y) = cy^2 + d,\ c, d > 0$. Analyse how the optimal supply and a product optimal price react to changes in values of parameters describing the markets: market capacities, consumers' sensitivities to changes in a product price, production marginal cost.

Solution

Let us take following notation:

y_1—an output level intended for the first market,

y_2—an output level intended for the second market,

$y = \xi(y_1, y_2) = y_1 + y_2$—total quantity of the product manufactured by the monopolist supplied to both markets,

$c^{tot}(y) = c^v(y) + c^f(y)$—production total cost,

$c^v(y)$—production variable cost,

$c^f(y)$—production fixed cost,

$p_1(y_1) > 0$—a product price set by the monopolist on the first market,

$p_2(y_2) > 0$—a product price set by the monopolist on the second market,

$y_1^d = y_1^d(p_1)$—the demand reported by consumers for a product on the first market,

$y_2^d = y_2^d(p_2)$—the demand reported by consumers for a product on the second market,

$y_1^s = y_1^s(p_1)$—the supply of the product intended for the first market,

$y_2^s = y_2^s(p_2)$—the supply of the product intended for the second market,

$r_1(y_1) = p_1(y_1)y_1$—revenue from sales of the product on the first market,

$r_2(y_2) = p_2(y_2)y_2$—revenue from sales of the product on the second market.

[6] See a textbook Malaga K., Sobczak K, *Microeconomics. Static and Dynamic Analysis*, Springer Nature Switzerland, 2022.

From now on it is assumed that:

(1) $\forall i = 1, 2 \;\; y_i^d = y_i^d(p_i) = y_i^s(p_i) = y_i,$

which means that the output level on each market matches the demand reported for the product on this market. We assume also that is not possible to resell the product between the markets.

There are given:

A production total cost function:

(2) $c^{tot}(y) = c^v(y) + c^f(y) = cy^2 + d = c(y_1 + y_2)^2 + d, \quad c, d > 0,$

according to which the production total cost depends on the total output, regardless it is intended for the first or for the second market.

A function of demand reported for a product on the first market:

(3) $y_1^d(p_1) = -a_1 p_1 + b_1,$

such that:

(4) $\frac{dy_1^d(p_1)}{dp_1} = -a_1 < 0,$

and is decreasing in a price of a product price set on the first market.

An inverse function of consumer demand reported for a product on the first market:

(5) $p_1\left(y_1^d\right) = \frac{b_1}{a_1} - \frac{y_1^d}{a_1} = \alpha_1 - \beta_1 y_1^d, \quad a_1, b_1 > 0 \Rightarrow \alpha_1, \beta_1 > 0.$

A function of revenue from sales of a product one the first market:

(6) $r_1(y_1) = p_1(y_1)y_1 = (\alpha_1 - \beta_1 y_1)y_1 = \alpha_1 y_1 - \beta_1 y_1^2.$

A function of demand reported for a product on the second market:

(7) $y_2^d(p_2) = -a_2 p_2 + b_2,$

such that:

(7) $\frac{dy_2^d(p_2)}{dp_2} = -a_2 < 0.$

and is decreasing in a price of a product price set on the second market.

An inverse function of consumer demand reported for a product on the second market:

(8) $p_2\left(y_2^d\right) = \frac{b_2}{a_2} - \frac{y_2^d}{a_2} = \alpha_2 - \beta_2 y_2^d, \quad a_2, b_2 > 0 \Rightarrow \alpha_2, \beta_2 > 0.$

A function of revenue from sales of a product one the second market:

(9) $r_2(y_2) = p_2(y_2)y_2 = (\alpha_2 - \beta_2 y_2)y_2 = \alpha_2 y_2 - \beta_2 y_2^2.$

A monopolist's profit function of a form:

$$\begin{aligned} &\Pi(y_1, y_2) = r_1(y_1) + r_2(y_2) - c^{tot}(y_1, y_2) \\ (10) \quad &= \alpha_1 y_1 - \beta_1 y_1^2 + \alpha_2 y_2 - \beta_2 y_2^2 - c(y_1 + y_2)^2 - d \\ &y_1, y_2 \geq 0. \end{aligned}$$

Formulate and solve a problem of choice of the optimal supply and of the optimal price set by a monopolistic company.

The necessary condition for existence of an optimal solution to the monopolist's profit maximization problem has a form of two equations:

(11) $\left.\frac{\partial \Pi(y_1,y_2)}{\partial y_1}\right|_{y=\overline{y}} = \alpha_1 - (2\beta_1 + c)\overline{y}_1 = 0,$

(12) $\left.\frac{\partial \Pi(y_1,y_2)}{\partial y_2}\right|_{y=\overline{y}} = \alpha_2 - (2\beta_2 + c)\overline{y}_2 = 0,$

which gives:

- For the first market:

(13) $\overline{y}_1 = \frac{\alpha_1}{2\beta_1+c} = \frac{b_1}{2(1+a_1c)} > 0$, where $\alpha_1 = \frac{b_1}{a_1}$, $\beta_1 = \frac{1}{a_1}$,

- For the second market:

(14) $\overline{y}_2 = \frac{\alpha_2}{2\beta_2+c_2} = \frac{b_2}{2(1+a_2c)} > 0$, where $\alpha_2 = \frac{b_2}{a_2}$, $\beta_2 = \frac{1}{a_2}$,

The sufficient condition for existence of an optimal solution to the monopolist's profit maximization problem has a form of two inequalities:

(15) $\left.\frac{\partial^2 \Pi(y_1,y_2)}{\partial y_1^2}\right|_{y=\overline{y}} = -(2\beta_1 + c) < 0,$

(16) $\left.\frac{\partial^2 \Pi(y_1,y_2)}{\partial y_2^2}\right|_{y=\overline{y}} = -(2\beta_2 + c) < 0,$

(17) $\left.\frac{\partial^2 \Pi(y_1,y_2)}{\partial y_1^2}\right|_{y=\overline{y}} \cdot \left.\frac{\partial^2 \Pi(y_1,y_2)}{\partial y_2^2}\right|_{y=\overline{y}} - \left.\frac{\partial^2 \Pi(y_1,y_2)}{\partial y_1 \partial y_2}\right|_{y=\overline{y}} \cdot \left.\frac{\partial^2 \Pi(y_1,y_2)}{\partial y_2 \partial y_1}\right|_{y=\overline{y}} > 0.$

The Hessian of the profit function has a form:

(18) $H(y_1, y_2) = \begin{bmatrix} -2\beta_1 - c & 0 \\ 0 & -2\beta_2 - c \end{bmatrix}.$

Since a condition $\det H(y_1, y_2) = 4\beta_1\beta_2 + 2c(\beta_1 + \beta_2) + c^2 > 0$ is satisfied, then for the output levels, the monopolist obtains the maximum profit.

Let us notice that the optimal supply of a product intended for each of the markets depends on: i-th's market capacity $b_i > 0$ (the demand for a product by zero price), the strength $a_i > 0$ of consumers' reaction to changes in a product price on i-th market and on the production marginal total (variable) cost $c > 0$.

The optimal total supply of a product supplied for both market is:

(19) $\overline{y} = \overline{y}_1 + \overline{y}_2 = \frac{b_1}{2(1+a_1c)} + \frac{b_2}{2(1+a_2c)} = \frac{b_1(1+a_2c)+b_2(1+a_1c)}{2(1+a_1c)(1+a_2c)} > 0.$

Let us notice that the optimal total supply of a product intended for both markets depends on: market capacities $b_1, b_2 > 0$, the strength $a_1, a_2 > 0$ of consumers' reaction to changes in product prices on both markets, the production marginal total cost $c > 0$.

From the assumption, it is known that the output level on i-th market ($i = 1, 2$), including the optimal level, matches the demand reported for the product on this market. On the basis of conditions describing, the inverse demand functions one can determine the optimal levels of a product price on two markets that a monopolist wants to set to maximize her/his profit.

The product price on the first market is:

$$p_1(\overline{y}_1) = \frac{b_1}{a_1} - \frac{\overline{y}_1}{a_1} = \frac{b_1(1 + 2a_1c)}{2a_1(1 + a_1c)},$$

and on the second market:

$$p_2(\overline{y}_2) = \frac{b_2}{a_2} - \frac{\overline{y}_2}{a_2} = \frac{b_2(1 + 2a_2c)}{2a_2(1 + a_2c)}.$$

Let us notice that the optimal price of a product on i-th market ($i = 1, 2$) depends on: i-th's market capacity $b_i > 0$, the strength $a_i > 0$ of consumers' reaction to changes in a product price on i-th market and on the production marginal total (variable) cost $c > 0$.

Analyse how the optimal supply and a product optimal price react to changes in values of parameters describing the markets: market capacities, consumers' sensitivities to changes in a product price, production marginal cost.

Table 5.4a–d present measures of sensitivity of the optimal supply and optimal prices on each market to changes of values of parameters.

E5.8. Consider the Cournot duopoly model when a production total cost function for i-th producer ($i = 1, 2$) is nonlinear and of a form: $c_i^{tot}(y) = c_i y_i^2 + d_i,\ c_i, d_i > 0$. Determine optimal levels of: the product supply by each producer, the total supply by both producers, an equilibrium price. Analyse how these levels react to changes in values of parameters describing the market: a market capacity, strength of consumers' reaction to changes in a product price, production marginal costs.

Solution

Let us apply a following set of assumptions:

Two producers ($i = 1, 2$) act on a market of a homogeneous (undifferentiated) product. Functions of their production total cost are as follows:

(1) $\forall i = 1, 2\ \ c_i^{tot}(y_i) = c_i^v(y_i) + c_i^f(y_i) = c_i y_i^2 + d_i,\quad c_i, d_i > 0,$

being the sum of variable cost functions:

(2) $\forall i = 1, 2\ \ c_i^v(y_i) = c_i y_i^2,\quad c_i > 0.$

and the fixed costs:

(3) $\forall i = 1, 2\ \ c_i^f(y_i) = d_i > 0.$

Since the total cost functions are nonlinear functions of output levels, then:

(4) $\forall i = 1, 2\ \ \frac{dc_i^{tot}(y_i)}{dy_i} = \frac{dc_i^v(y_i)}{dy_i} = 2c_i y_i > 0,$

Table 5.4 Measures of response to changes in parameters' values for: (a) first market's optimal supply, (b) second market's optimal supply, (c) optimal price on first market, (d) optimal price on second market

(a)					
Characteristic $\overline{y}_1 = \frac{b_1}{2(1+a_1c)}$	$\frac{\partial \overline{y}_1}{\partial c}$	$\frac{\partial \overline{y}_1}{\partial a_1}$	$\frac{\partial \overline{y}_1}{\partial b_1}$	$\frac{\partial \overline{y}_1}{\partial a_2}$	$\frac{\partial \overline{y}_1}{\partial b_2}$
Value	$-\frac{a_1b_1}{2(1+a_1c)^2} < 0$	$-\frac{b_1c}{2(1+a_1c)^2} < 0$	$\frac{1}{2(1+a_1c)} > 0$	0	0
(b)					
Characteristic $\overline{y}_1 = \frac{b_2}{2(1+a_2c)}$	$\frac{\partial \overline{y}_2}{\partial c}$	$\frac{\partial \overline{y}_2}{\partial a_1}$	$\frac{\partial \overline{y}_2}{\partial b_1}$	$\frac{\partial \overline{y}_2}{\partial a_2}$	$\frac{\partial \overline{y}_2}{\partial b_2}$
Value	$-\frac{a_2b_2}{2(1+a_2c)^2} < 0$	0	0	$-\frac{b_1c}{2(1+a_2c)^2} < 0$	$\frac{1}{2(1+a_2c)} > 0$
(c)					
Characteristic $p_1(\overline{y}_1) = \frac{b_1(1+2a_1c)}{2a_1(1+a_1c)}$	$\frac{\partial p_1(\overline{y}_1)}{\partial c}$	$\frac{\partial p_1(\overline{y}_1)}{\partial a_1}$	$\frac{\partial p_1(\overline{y}_1)}{\partial b_1}$	$\frac{\partial p_1(\overline{y}_1)}{\partial a_2}$	$\frac{\partial p_1(\overline{y}_1)}{\partial b_2}$
Value	$\frac{b_1}{2(1+a_1c)^2} > 0$	$\frac{-4a_1^2b_1c^2-2b_1-4a_1b_1c}{4a_1^2(1+a_1c)^2} < 0$	$\frac{1+2a_1c}{2a_1(1+a_1c)} > 0$	0	0
(d)					
Characteristic $p_2(\overline{y}_2) = \frac{b_2(1+2a_2c)}{2a_2(1+a_2c)}$	$\frac{\partial p_2(\overline{y}_2)}{\partial c}$	$\frac{\partial p_2(\overline{y}_2)}{\partial a_1}$	$\frac{\partial p_2(\overline{y}_2)}{\partial b_1}$	$\frac{\partial p_2(\overline{y}_2)}{\partial a_2}$	$\frac{\partial p_2(\overline{y}_2)}{\partial b_2}$
Value	$\frac{b_2}{2(1+a_2c)^2} < 0$	0	0	$\frac{-4a_2^2b_2c^2-2b_2-4a_2b_2c}{4a_2^2(1+a_2c)^2} < 0$	$\frac{1+2a_2c}{2a_2(1+a_2c)} > 0$

that is: the marginal total cost and the marginal variable cost for the i-th producer are equal and increasing in an output level.

A function of demand reported for a product by consumers, depending on its price set by producers, is as follows:

(5) $y^d(p) = -ap + b, \quad a, b > 0,$

where a denotes a measure of the consumers' reaction strength to an unit increase in a price of a product and b denotes a measure of a market capacity.

Since values of the demand function have to be non-negative then:

(6) $p \in \left[0; \frac{b}{a}\right].$

The total output by both producers matches the demand that consumers report by a given price of a product:

(7) $y_1 + y_2 = y^d(p) = -ap + b, \quad a, b > 0.$

The first producer wants to determine such an output level that guarantees the maximum profit for her/him taking an output level of the second producer as given:

(8) $\Pi_1(y_1)|_{y_2=\text{const.}\geq 0} \to \max \quad y_1 \geq 0.$

The second producer wants to determine such an output level that guarantees the maximum profit for her/him taking an output level of the first producer as given:

(9) $\Pi_2(y_2)|_{y_1=\text{const.}\geq 0} \to \max \quad y_2 \geq 0.$

A profit function of i-th producer ($i = 1, 2$) can be expressed as the difference between revenue from sales of a product and total cost of production:

(10) $\forall i = 1, 2 \quad \Pi_i(y_i) = p(y)y_i - \left[c_i y_i^2 + d_i\right].$

Substituting an inverse function of demand $p(y) = \frac{b-y}{a} = \alpha - \beta(y_1 + y_2)$, where: $\alpha = \frac{b}{a}$, $\beta = \frac{1}{a}$, into Eq. (1), one obtains the profit functions of both producers as functions of their output levels:

- For the first producer:

(11) $\Pi_1(y_1, y_2) = [\alpha - \beta(y_1 + y_2)]y_1 - \left[c_1 y_1^2 + d_1\right] = \alpha y_1 - (\beta + c_1)y_1^2 - \beta y_1 y_2 - d_1,$

- For the second producer:

(12) $\Pi_2(y_1, y_2) = [\alpha - \beta(y_1 + y_2)]y_2 - \left[c_2 y_2^2 + d_2\right] = \alpha y_2 - (\beta + c_2)y_2^2 - \beta y_1 y_2 - d_2.$

When the output level of the second producer is taken as given, thus treated as a parameter, the necessary condition and the sufficient condition for the profit maximization problem of the first producer are following[7]:

---

[7] The profit function of the first (second) producer is an one-variable function when the supply of a product by the second (first) producer is set. In conditions, we do use notions appropriate for the first- and second-order partial derivatives, but the necessary and sufficient conditions of the optimum existence refer actually to one-variable functions.

(13) $\left.\frac{\partial \Pi_1(y_1, y_2)}{\partial y_1}\right|_{y_1=\overline{y}_1,\ y_2=\text{const.}\geq 0} = 0$ – the necessary condition,

(14) $\left.\frac{\partial^2 \Pi_1(y_1, y_2)}{\partial y_1^2}\right|_{y_1=\overline{y}_1,\ y_2=\text{const.}\geq 0} < 0$ – the sufficient condition.

When the output level of the first producer is taken as given, thus treated as a parameter, the necessary condition and the sufficient condition for the profit maximization problem of the second producer are following:

(15) $\left.\frac{\partial \Pi_2(y_1, y_2)}{\partial y_2}\right|_{y_2=\overline{y}_2,\ y_1=\text{const.}\geq 0} = 0$ – the necessary condition,

(16) $\left.\frac{\partial^2 \Pi_2(y_1, y_2)}{\partial y_2^2}\right|_{y_2=\overline{y}_2,\ y_1=\text{const.}\geq 0} < 0$ – the sufficient condition.

Deriving the necessary and sufficient conditions for the profit functions described we get:

- For the first producer:

(17) $\left.\frac{\partial \Pi_1(y_1, y_2)}{\partial y_1}\right|_{y_1=\overline{y}_1,\ y_2=\text{const.}\geq 0} = \alpha - 2(\beta + c_1)\overline{y}_1 - \beta y_2 = 0,$

(18) $\left.\frac{\partial^2 \Pi_1(y_1, y_2)}{\partial y_1^2}\right|_{y_1=\overline{y}_1,\ y_2=\text{const.}\geq 0} = -2(\beta + c_1) < 0,$

which means that for any (given) output level $y_2 \geq 0$ set by the second producer, the first producer obtains the maximum profit when $y_1 = \overline{y}_1$:

- For the second producer:

(19) $\left.\frac{\partial \Pi_2(y_1, y_2)}{\partial y_2}\right|_{y_2=\overline{y}_2,\ y_1=\text{const.}\geq 0} = \alpha - 2(\beta + c_2)\overline{y}_2 - \beta y_1 = 0,$

(20) $\left.\frac{\partial^2 \Pi_2(y_1, y_2)}{\partial y_2^2}\right|_{y_2=\overline{y}_2,\ y_1=\text{const.}\geq 0} = -2(\beta + c_2) < 0,$

which means that for any (given) output level $y_1 \geq 0$ set by the first producer, the second producer obtains the maximum profit when $y_2 = \overline{y}_2$.

From necessary conditions, it results that:

(21) $\overline{y}_1 = \frac{\alpha - \beta y_2}{2(\beta + c_1)} = \frac{b - y_2}{2(1 + ac_1)} \quad RL_1,$

and this equation is called a reaction line equation of the first producer; similarly.

(22) $\overline{y}_2 = \frac{\alpha - \beta y_1}{2(\beta + c_2)} = \frac{b - y_1}{2(1 + ac_2)} \quad RL_2;$

and this equation is called a reaction line equation of the second producer.

The respective reaction line equation describes the output level of the first (second) producer which, by the output level of the second (first) producer taken as given, guarantees the maximum profit for the first (second) producer.

In order to find the equilibrium state in the Cournot duopoly model, one should solve following system of equations:

(23) $\alpha - 2(\beta + c_1)\overline{y}_1 - \beta \overline{y}_2 = 0,$

(24) $\alpha - 2(\beta + c_2)\overline{y}_2 - \beta \overline{y}_1 = 0.$

From Eq. (23), we derive an expression:

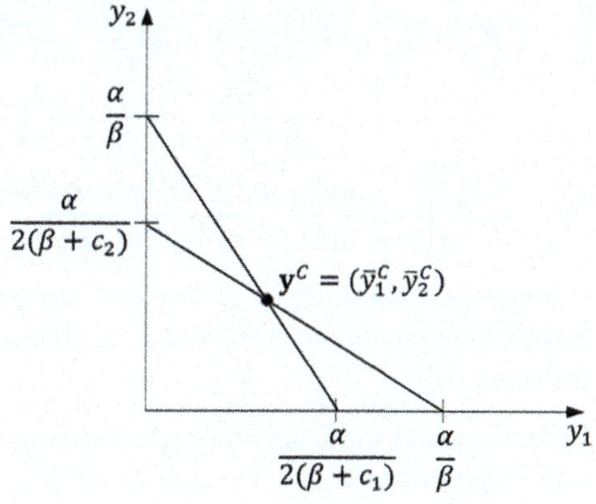

Fig. 5.7 Equilibrium state in Cournot duopoly model

(25) $\overline{y}_2 = \frac{\alpha - 2(\beta + c_1)\overline{y}_1}{\beta}$,

which we substitute into (24) expression getting:

(26) $\alpha - 2(\beta + c_2)\frac{\alpha - 2(\beta + c_1)\overline{y}_1}{\beta} - \beta\overline{y}_1 = 0,$

(27) $\alpha\beta - 2(\beta + c_2)\alpha + \left(4\beta^2 + 4\beta c_1 + 4\beta c_2 + 4c_1c_2 - \beta^2\right)\overline{y}_1 = 0.$

Then

(28) $\overline{y}_1 = \frac{\alpha(\beta + 2c_2)}{3\beta^2 + 4\beta(c_1 + c_2) + 4c_1c_2} = \frac{b(1 + 2ac_2)}{3 + 4a(c_1 + c_2) + 4a^2c_1c_2}$,

(29) $\overline{y}_2 = \frac{\alpha(\beta + 2c_1)}{3\beta^2 + 4\beta(c_1 + c_2) + 4c_1c_2} = \frac{b(1 + 2ac_1)}{3 + 4a(c_1 + c_2) + 4a^2c_1c_2}$,

(30) $\overline{y} = \overline{y}_1 + \overline{y}_2 = \frac{2b[1 + a(c_1 + c_2)]}{3 + 4a(c_1 + c_2) + 4a^2c_1c_2}$,

(31) $\overline{\mathbf{y}}^{(C)} = \left(\overline{y}_1^{(C)}, \overline{y}_2^{(C)}\right) = \left(\frac{b(1 + 2ac_2)}{3 + 4a(c_1 + c_2) + 4a^2c_1c_2}, \frac{b(1 + 2ac_1)}{3 + 4a(c_1 + c_2) + 4a^2c_1c_2}\right).$

Figure 5.7 presents a mechanism of reaching the equilibrium state in the Cournot duopoly model. It is not difficult to notice that each producer aiming at the maximization of her/his own profit and taking the output level set by the competitor as given will seek to have the output in her/his own firm on a level resulting from his/her reaction line. Accepting an output level different than the one resulting from his/her reaction line would be inconsistent with the profit maximization aim. As a consequence, both producers will accept as optimal these output levels which are indicated by the intersection of their reaction lines.

The equilibrium state exists, there is exactly one such state and it is globally stable. This means that if the parameters of the profit function of each producer do not change, then as a result of rational behaviour of both producers, the supply of the product is shared between both producers and equal to the demand reported for this product by consumers. These shares in the product supply provide the maximum profit for each producer.

On the basis of condition (7) and (30), one can determine the equilibrium price in the Cournot duopoly model:

$$\overline{p}^{(C)}\left(\overline{y}_1^{(C)}, \overline{y}_2^{(C)}\right) = \alpha - \beta\left(\overline{y}_1^{(C)} + \overline{y}_2^{(C)}\right)$$

(31)
$$= \frac{b}{a} - \frac{1}{a} \cdot \frac{2b[1 + a(c_1 + c_2)]}{3 + 4a(c_1 + c_2) + 4a^2 c_1 c_2}$$
$$= \frac{b\left[1 + 2a(c_1 + c_2) + 4a^2 c_1 c_2\right]}{a\left[3 + 4a(c_1 + c_2) + 4a^2 c_1 c_2\right]}.$$

Optimal quantities of producers' supply, total supply and prices in Walrasian equilibrium and their responses to changes in parameters' values are presented in Table 5.5.

E5.9. Consider the Stackelberg duopoly model when a production total cost function for i-th producer ($i = 1, 2$) is nonlinear and of a form: $c_i^{tot}(y) = c_i y_i^2 + d_i, \; c_i, d_i > 0$. Determine the product optimal supply by: a leader, a follower, both producers and an equilibrium price. Analyse how these levels react to changes in values of parameters describing the market: a market capacity, strength of consumers' reaction to changes in a product price, production marginal costs.

Solution

Let us apply a following set of assumptions:

(S1) Two producers ($i = 1, 2$) act on a market of a homogeneous (undifferentiated) product. The first producer is a **leader** and the second is a **follower**.
(S2) Functions of production total cost for producers are as follows:

(1) $\forall i = 1, 2 \quad c_i^{tot}(y_i) = c_i^v(y_i) + c_i^f(y_i) = c_i y_i^2 + d_i, \quad c_i, d_i > 0,$

being the sum of variable cost functions:

(2) $\forall i = 1, 2 \quad c_i^v(y_i) = c_i y_i^2, \quad c_i > 0,$

and the fixed costs:

(3) $\forall i = 1, 2 \quad c_i^f(y_i) = d_i > 0.$

Since the total cost functions are nonlinear functions of output levels, then:

(4) $\forall i = 1, 2 \quad \frac{\mathrm{d}c_i^{tot}(y_i)}{\mathrm{d}y_i} = \frac{\mathrm{d}c_i^v(y_i)}{\mathrm{d}y_i} = 2c_i y_i > 0,$

that is: the marginal total cost and the marginal variable cost for the i-th producer are equal and increasing in an output level.

(S3) A function of demand reported for a product by consumers, depending on its price set by producers, is as follows:

(5) $y^d(p) = -ap + b \quad a, b > 0,$

where a denotes a measure of the consumers' reaction strength to an unit increase in a price of a product and b denotes a measure of a market capacity.

Since values of the demand function have to be non-negative then:

(6) $p \in \left[0; \frac{b}{a}\right].$

Table 5.5 (a) Optimal quantities of producers' supply, total supply and prices in Walrasian equilibrium; Sensitivity measures of: (b) first producer's supply, (c) second producer's supply, (d) of both producers' total supply, (e) Walrasian equilibrium price

Characteristic	Value
(a)	
$\overline{y}_1^{(C)}$	$\frac{b(1+2ac_2)}{3+4a(c_1+c_2)+4a^2c_1c_2}$
$\overline{y}_2^{(C)}$	$\frac{b(1+2ac_1)}{3+4a(c_1+c_2)+4a^2c_1c_2}$
$\overline{y}^{(C)}$	$\frac{2b[1+a(c_1+c_2)]}{3+4a(c_1+c_2)+4a^2c_1c_2}$
$p(\overline{y}^{(C)})$	$\frac{b[1+2a(c_1+c_2)+4a^2c_1c_2]}{a[3+4a(c_1+c_2)+4a^2c_1c_2]} = \frac{b}{a} - \frac{2b[1+a(c_1+c_2)]}{a[3+4a(c_1+c_2)+4a^2c_1c_2]}$
(b)	
$\frac{\partial \overline{y}_1^{(C)}}{\partial a}$	$\frac{2b[c_2-2c_1-4ac_1c_2(1+ac_2)]}{[3+4a(c_1+c_2)+4a^2c_1c_2]^2} < 0$ when $c_2 < 2c_1 + 4ac_1c_2(1+ac_2)$
$\frac{\partial \overline{y}_1^{(C)}}{\partial b}$	$\frac{1+2ac_2}{3+4a(c_1+c_2)+4a^2c_1c_2} > 0$
$\frac{\partial \overline{y}_1^{(C)}}{\partial c_1}$	$-\frac{8ab(1+2ac_2)(1+ac_2)}{[3+4a(c_1+c_2)+4a^2c_1c_2]^2} < 0$
$\frac{\partial \overline{y}_1^{(C)}}{\partial c_2}$	$\frac{2ab(1+2ac_1)}{[3+4a(c_1+c_2)+4a^2c_1c_2]^2} > 0$
(c)	
$\frac{\partial \overline{y}_2^{(C)}}{\partial a}$	$\frac{2b[c_1-2c_2-4ac_1c_2(1+ac_1)]}{[3+4a(c_1+c_2)+4a^2c_1c_2]^2} < 0$ when $c_1 < 2c_2 + 4ac_1c_2(1+ac_1)$
$\frac{\partial \overline{y}_2^{(C)}}{\partial b}$	$\frac{1+2ac_1}{3+4a(c_1+c_2)+4a^2c_1c_2} > 0$
$\frac{\partial \overline{y}_2^{(C)}}{\partial c_1}$	$\frac{2ab(1+2ac_2)}{[3+4a(c_1+c_2)+4a^2c_1c_2]^2} > 0$
$\frac{\partial \overline{y}_2^{(C)}}{\partial c_2}$	$-\frac{8ab(1+2ac_1)(1+ac_1)}{[3+4a(c_1+c_2)+4a^2c_1c_2]^2} < 0$
(d)	
$\frac{\partial \overline{y}^{(C)}}{\partial a}$	$\frac{-2b(c_1+c_2)[1+4a^2c_1c_2]-16abc_1c_2}{[3+4a(c_1+c_2)+4a^2c_1c_2]^2} < 0$
$\frac{\partial \overline{y}^{(C)}}{\partial b}$	$\frac{2[1+a(c_1+c_2)]}{3+4a(c_1+c_2)+4a^2c_1c_2} > 0$
$\frac{\partial \overline{y}^{(C)}}{\partial c_1}$	$\frac{-2ab(1+2ac_2)(3+4ac_2)}{[3+4a(c_1+c_2)+4a^2c_1c_2]^2} < 0$
$\frac{\partial \overline{y}^{(C)}}{\partial c_2}$	$\frac{-2ab(1+2ac_1)(3+4ac_1)}{[3+4a(c_1+c_2)+4a^2c_1c_2]^2} < 0$
(e)	

(continued)

Table 5.5 (continued)

Characteristic	Value
$\frac{\partial p\left(\overline{y}^{(C)}\right)}{\partial a}$	$\frac{-3b-8ab(c_1+c_2)\left[1+a(c_1+c_2)+a^2c_1c_2\right]-16a^4bc_1^2c_2^2}{a^2\left[3+4a(c_1+c_2)+4a^2c_1c_2\right]^2}<0$
$\frac{\partial p\left(\overline{y}^{(C)}\right)}{\partial b}$	$\frac{1+2a(c_1+c_2)+4a^2c_1c_2}{a\left[3+4a(c_1+c_2)+4a^2c_1c_2\right]}>0$
$\frac{\partial p\left(\overline{y}^{(C)}\right)}{\partial c_1}$	$\frac{2b+8abc_2[1+ac_2]}{\left[3+4a(c_1+c_2)+4a^2c_1c_2\right]^2}>0$
$\frac{\partial p\left(\overline{y}^{(C)}\right)}{\partial c_2}$	$\frac{2b+8abc_1[1+ac_1]}{\left[3+4a(c_1+c_2)+4a^2c_1c_2\right]^2}>0$

(S4) The total output by both producers matches the demand that consumers report by a given price of a product:

(7) $y_1 + y_2 = y^d(p) = -ap + b, \quad a, b > 0.$

(S5) An inverse function of consumer demand for a product manufactured by producers has a form:

(8) $p(y_1, y_2) = \frac{b}{a} - \frac{1}{a}(y_1 + y_2) = \alpha - \beta(y_1 + y_2), \quad \alpha, \beta > 0,\ \alpha = \frac{b}{a},\ \beta = \frac{1}{a}.$

Let us notice that:

(9) $\frac{\partial p(y_1, y_2)}{\partial y_1} = \frac{\partial p(y_1, y_2)}{\partial y_2} = -\beta = -\frac{1}{a} < 0,$

thus, no matter which producer increases the output by one physical unit, it leads to a decrease in a product price by $\beta = \frac{1}{a}$ money units.

(S6) The first producer (the leader) wants to determine such an output level that guarantees the maximum profit for her/him:

(10) $\Pi_1(y_1) \rightarrow \max \quad y_1 \geq 0.$

A profit function of the first producer can be expressed as the difference between her/his revenue from sales of a product and total cost of production:

(11) $\Pi_1(y_1) = p(y_1, y_2)y_1 - c_1y_1^2 - d_1.$

Substituting the inverse function of demand (8) into Eq. (11), one obtains the profit function of the first producer as:

$$
(12) \quad \begin{aligned} \Pi_1(y_1, y_2) &= [\alpha - \beta(y_1 + y_2)]y_1 - \left[c_1y_1^2 + d_1\right] \\ &= \alpha y_1 - (\beta + c_1)y_1^2 - \beta y_1y_2 - d_1 \end{aligned} .
$$

(S7) The second producer (the follower) wants to determine such an output level that guarantees the maximum profit for her/him taking an output level of the first producer as given:

(13) $\Pi_2(y_2)\big|_{y_1=\text{const.}\geq 0} \rightarrow \max \quad y_2 \geq 0.$

A profit function of the second producer can be expressed as the difference between her/his revenue from sales of a product and total cost of production:

(14) $\Pi_2(y_2) = p(y_1, y_2)y_2 - c_2 y_2^2 - d_2.$

Substituting the inverse function of demand (8) into Eq. (14), one obtains the profit function of the second producer as:

(15) $\Pi_2(y_1, y_2) = [\alpha - \beta(y_1 + y_2)]y_2 - \left[c_2 y_2^2 + d_2\right] = \alpha y_2 - (\beta + c_2)y_2^2 - \beta y_1 y_2 - d_2.$

Let us now derive optimal solutions to the profit maximization problems of both producers in a duopoly in the Stackelberg model.

The necessary condition and the sufficient condition for the profit maximization problem of the first producer are following:

(16) $\left.\frac{\partial \Pi_1(y_1, y_2)}{\partial y_1}\right|_{y_1=\overline{y}_1} = 0$ – the necessary condition,

(17) $\left.\frac{\partial^2 \Pi_1(y_1, y_2)}{\partial y_1^2}\right|_{y_1=\overline{y}_1} < 0$ – the sufficient condition.

When the output level of the first producer is taken as given, thus treated as a parameter, the necessary condition and the sufficient condition for the profit maximization problem of the second producer are following:

(18) $\left.\frac{\partial \Pi_2(y_1, y_2)}{\partial y_2}\right|_{y_2=\overline{y}_2,\ y_1=\text{const.}\geq 0} = 0$ – the necessary condition,

(19) $\left.\frac{\partial^2 \Pi_2(y_1, y_2)}{\partial y_2^2}\right|_{y_2=\overline{y}_2,\ y_1=\text{const.}\geq 0} < 0$ – the sufficient condition.

Deriving the necessary condition and the sufficient condition for the profit function of the second producer (the follower), we get:

(20) $\left.\frac{\partial \Pi_2(y_1, y_2)}{\partial y_2}\right|_{y_2=\overline{y}_2,\ y_1=\text{const.}\geq 0} = \alpha - 2(\beta + c_2)\overline{y}_2 - \beta y_1 = 0,$

(21) $\left.\frac{\partial^2 \Pi_2(y_1, y_2)}{\partial y_2^2}\right|_{y_2=\overline{y}_2,\ y_1=\text{const.}\geq 0} = -2(\beta + c_2) < 0,$

which means that for any (given) output level $y_1 \geq 0$ set by the first producer, the second producer obtains the maximum profit when $y_2 = \overline{y}_2$.

From condition (20), it results that:

(22) $\overline{y}_2 = \frac{\alpha}{2(\beta+c_2)} - \frac{\beta y_1}{2(\beta+c_2)}$ $\boldsymbol{RL_2}$.

Equation (22) is called a **reaction line of the follower**. From perspective of the follower, it describes her/his output level which, by the output level of the leader taken as given, guarantees the maximum profit for the follower. From perspective of the leader, the equation describes a share of the market which, by a given output level of the leader, is to be captured by the follower.

Substituting expression (22) into the leader's profit function, one gets:

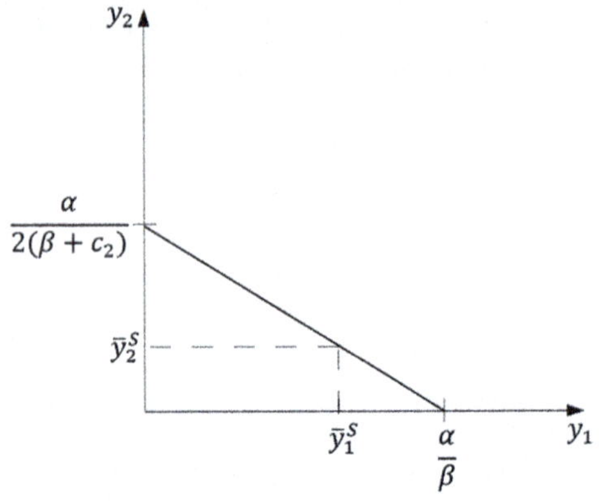

Fig. 5.8 Equilibrium state in the Stackelberg duopoly model

$$\begin{aligned}\Pi_1(y_1, y_2) &= \alpha y_1 - (\beta + c_1)y_1^2 - \beta y_1\left(\frac{\alpha}{2(\beta+c_2)} - \frac{\beta y_1}{2(\beta+c_2)}\right) - d_1 \\ &= \frac{\alpha(\beta+2c_2)y_1 - \left[\beta^2 + 2\beta(c_1+c_2) + 2c_1c_2\right]y_1^2}{2(\beta+c_2)} - d_1.\end{aligned} \tag{23}$$

Then the necessary condition for the leader's profit function takes a form:

$$\left.\frac{\partial\Pi_1(y_1,y_2)}{\partial y_1}\right|_{y_1=\bar{y}_1} = \frac{\alpha(\beta+2c_2) - 2\left[\beta^2+2\beta(c_1+c_2)+2c_1c_2\right]\bar{y}_1}{2(\beta+c_2)} = 0, \tag{24}$$

and the sufficient condition for the leader's profit function is:

$$\left.\frac{\partial^2\Pi_1(y_1,y_2)}{\partial y_1^2}\right|_{y_1=\bar{y}_1} = -\frac{\beta^2+2\beta(c_1+c_2)+2c_1c_2}{\beta+c_2} < 0. \tag{25}$$

From conditions (24) and (25), it results that for an output level:

$$\begin{aligned}\bar{y}_1^{(S)} &= \frac{\alpha(\beta+2c_2)}{2\left[\beta^2+2\beta(c_1+c_2)+2c_1c_2\right]} = \frac{b(1+2ac_2)}{2\left[1+2a(c_1+c_2)+2a^2c_1c_2\right]} \\ &= \frac{abc_2}{1+2a(c_1+c_2)+2a^2c_1c_2} + \frac{b}{2\left[1+2a(c_1+c_2)+2a^2c_1c_2\right]},\end{aligned} \tag{26}$$

the leader obtains the maximum profit.

Substituting expression (26) into Eq. (22):

$$\begin{aligned}\bar{y}_2^{(S)} &= \frac{\alpha}{2(\beta+c_2)} - \frac{\beta}{2(\beta+c_2)} \cdot \frac{\alpha(\beta+2c_2)}{2\left[\beta^2+2\beta(c_1+c_2)+2c_1c_2\right]} \\ &= \frac{\alpha c_1}{\beta^2+2\beta(c_1+c_2)+2c_1c_2} = \frac{abc_1}{1+2a(c_1+c_2)+2a^2c_1c_2},\end{aligned} \tag{27}$$

one derives the optimal output level of the follower.

When we compare the optimal output levels of the leader and of the follower, assuming the same value of $c_1 = c_2 = c$, we can notice that the leader's output level is bigger.

The equilibrium state in the Stackelber duopoly model is presentedin Fig. 5.8. Let us notice that in the Stackelberg duopoly model, there is only the reaction line of the follower, who has to accept unconditionally the choice made by the leader. On the other hand the leader, when deciding her/his optimal output level, does not have to take into account the decisions made by the follower. The product supply by the leader is determined by her/his profit function which depends on revenue from sales and on production total cost. The equilibrium state in the Stackelberg duopoly model exists, there is exactly one such state and it is determined uniquely by the product supplies by the leader and by the follower. Deciding her/his output level, the follower relies on the choice made by the leader as well as on the maximum profit that can be obtained when the leader has made decision to manufacture $\overline{y}_1^{(S)}$ units of a product.

As a result, in the equilibrium state, the optimal supply of the product by the leader and by the follower in the Stackelberg duopoly model is given as:

$$\text{(28)}\quad \overline{\mathbf{y}}^{(S)} = \left(\overline{y}_1^{(S)}, \overline{y}_2^{(S)}\right) = \left(\frac{b(1+2ac_2)}{2\left[1+2a(c_1+c_2)+2a^2c_1c_2\right]}, \frac{abc_1}{1+2a(c_1+c_2)+2a^2c_1c_2}\right).$$

Then the total supply of the product equals:

$$\text{(29)}\quad \overline{y}^{(S)} = \overline{y}_1^{(S)} + \overline{y}_2^{(S)} = \frac{b[1+2a(c_1+c_2)]}{2\left[1+2a(c_1+c_2)+2a^2c_1c_2\right]};$$

hence, the equilibrium price in the Stackelberg duopoly model is:

$$\text{(30)}\quad \begin{aligned} \overline{p}^{(S)}\left(\overline{y}_1^{(S)}, \overline{y}_2^{(S)}\right) &= \alpha - \beta\left(\overline{y}_1^{(S)} + \overline{y}_2^{(S)}\right) \\ &= \frac{b}{a} - \frac{1}{a}\cdot\frac{b[1+2a(c_1+c_2)]}{2\left[1+2a(c_1+c_2)+2a^2c_1c_2\right]} \\ &= \frac{b\left[1+2a(c_1+c_2)+4a^2c_1c_2\right]}{2a\left[1+2a(c_1+c_2)+2a^2c_1c_2\right]} \\ &= \frac{b}{2a} + \frac{abc_1c_2}{\left[1+2a(c_1+c_2)+2a^2c_1c_2\right]} \end{aligned},$$

which means that the total supply of a product by both producers and the equilibrium price set by them depend on: the market capacity $b > 0$, the strength of consumers' reaction $a > 0$ to changes in a product price and on the marginal (variable or total) costs of production $c_1, c_2 > 0$.

Let us analyse the sensitivity of the product optimal supply and of the equilibrium price to changes in values of the parameters of the Stackelberg duopoly model (Table 5.6).

E5.10. Compare conclusions drawn from solutions to exercises E5.6, E5.8 and E5.9 assuming they relate to a market of one homogenous product in cases of the: pure monopoly, Cournot duopoly, the Stackelberg duopoly.

Solution

Let us compare the supply of a product by a monopolist with the total supply of the product by both producers in the Cournot duopoly and the total supply by the leader and the follower in the Stackelberg duopoly. Let us also compare optimal prices set by the producers. For this purpose, let us assume that in each case the same value of the parameter c is used in the function of the production total cost:

Table 5.6 (a) Optimal quantities of producers' supply, total supply and prices in Walrasian equilibrium; Sensitivity measures to changes in parameters' values for: (a) leader's optimal supply, (c) follower's optimal supply, (d) total optimal supply from both producers, (e) Walrasian equilibrium price

Characteristic	Value
(a)	
$\overline{y}_1^{(S)}$	$\frac{b(1+2ac_2)}{2[1+2a(c_1+c_2)+2a^2c_1c_2]}$
$\overline{y}_2^{(S)}$	$\frac{abc_1}{1+2a(c_1+c_2)+2a^2c_1c_2}$
$\overline{y}^{(S)}$	$\frac{b[1+2a(c_1+c_2)]}{2[1+2a(c_1+c_2)+2a^2c_1c_2]}$
$p\left(\overline{y}^{(S)}\right)$	$\frac{b[1+2a(c_1+c_2)+4a^2c_1c_2]}{2a[1+2a(c_1+c_2)+2a^2c_1c_2]} = \frac{b}{2a} + \frac{abc_1c_2}{[1+2a(c_1+c_2)+2a^2c_1c_2]}$
(b)	
$\frac{\partial\overline{y}_1^{(S)}}{\partial a}$	$\frac{-2abc_1c_2(1+ac_2)-bc_1}{[1+2a(c_1+c_2)+2a^2c_1c_2]^2} < 0$
$\frac{\partial\overline{y}_1^{(S)}}{\partial b}$	$\frac{1+2ac_2}{2[1+2a(c_1+c_2)+2a^2c_1c_2]} > 0$
$\frac{\partial\overline{y}_1^{(S)}}{\partial c_1}$	$-\frac{ab(1+2ac_2)(1+ac_2)}{[1+2a(c_1+c_2)+2a^2c_1c_2]^2} < 0$
$\frac{\partial\overline{y}_1^{(S)}}{\partial c_2}$	$\frac{a^2bc_1}{[1+2a(c_1+c_2)+2a^2c_1c_2]^2} > 0$
(c)	
$\frac{\partial\overline{y}_2^{(S)}}{\partial a}$	$\frac{bc_1(1-2a^2c_1c_2)}{[1+2a(c_1+c_2)+2a^2c_1c_2]^2} < 0$ when $2a^2c_1c_2 > 1$
$\frac{\partial\overline{y}_2^{(S)}}{\partial b}$	$\frac{ac_1}{1+2a(c_1+c_2)+2a^2c_1c_2} > 0$
$\frac{\partial\overline{y}_2^{(S)}}{\partial c_1}$	$\frac{ab(1+2ac_2)}{[1+2a(c_1+c_2)+2a^2c_1c_2]^2} > 0$
$\frac{\partial\overline{y}_2^{(S)}}{\partial c_2}$	$-\frac{2a^2bc_1(1+ac_1)}{[1+2a(c_1+c_2)+2a^2c_1c_2]^2} < 0$
(d)	
$\frac{\partial\overline{y}^{(S)}}{\partial a}$	$-\frac{2abc_1c_2[1+a(c_1+c_2)]}{[1+2a(c_1+c_2)+2a^2c_1c_2]^2} < 0$
$\frac{\partial\overline{y}^{(S)}}{\partial b}$	$\frac{1+2a(c_1+c_2)}{2[1+2a(c_1+c_2)+2a^2c_1c_2]} > 0$
$\frac{\partial\overline{y}^{(S)}}{\partial c_1}$	$-\frac{a^2bc_2[1+2ac_2]}{[1+2a(c_1+c_2)+2a^2c_1c_2]^2} < 0$
$\frac{\partial\overline{y}^{(S)}}{\partial c_2}$	$-\frac{a^2bc_1[1+2ac_1]}{[1+2a(c_1+c_2)+2a^2c_1c_2]^2} < 0$
(e)	
$\frac{\partial p\left(\overline{y}^{(S)}\right)}{\partial a}$	$-\frac{b+4ab[a(c_1^2+c_2^2)+c_1+c_2]+2a^2bc_1c_2[3+4a(c_1+c_2)+4a^2c_1c_2]}{2a^2[1+2a(c_1+c_2)+2a^2c_1c_2]^2} < 0$

(continued)

Table 5.6 (continued)

Characteristic	Value
$\frac{\partial p\left(\overline{y}^{(S)}\right)}{\partial b}$	$\frac{1+2a(c_1+c_2)+4a^2c_1c_2}{2a\left[1+2a(c_1+c_2)+2a^2c_1c_2\right]} > 0$
$\frac{\partial p\left(\overline{y}^{(S)}\right)}{\partial c_1}$	$\frac{abc_2(1+2ac_2)}{\left[1+2a(c_1+c_2)+2a^2c_1c_2\right]^2} > 0$
$\frac{\partial p\left(\overline{y}^{(S)}\right)}{\partial c_2}$	$\frac{abc_1(1+2ac_1)}{\left[1+2a(c_1+c_2)+2a^2c_1c_2\right]^2} > 0$

Table 5.7 Comparison of total supplies and optimal prices between models of: monopoly, Cournot duopoly, Stackelberg duopoly

	Monopoly	Cournot duopoly	Stackelberg duopoly
Total supply	$\overline{y} = \frac{b}{2(1+ac)} = \frac{b+4abc}{2+10ac+8a^2c^2} = \frac{2b+4abc}{4+12ac+8a^2c^2}$	$\overline{y}^{(C)} = \frac{2b+4abc}{3+8ac+4a^2c^2}$	$\overline{y}^{(S)} = \frac{b+4abc}{2+8ac+4a^2c^2}$
Price	$p(\overline{y}) = \frac{b(1+2ac)}{2a(1+ac)} = \frac{b\left[1+4ac+4a^2c^2\right]}{2a+4a^2c+4a^3c^2}$	$p\left(\overline{y}^{(C)}\right) = \frac{b\left[1+4ac+4a^2c^2\right]}{3a+8a^2c+4a^3c^2}$	$p\left(\overline{y}^{(S)}\right) = \frac{b\left[1+4ac+4a^2c^2\right]}{2a+8a^2c+4a^3c^2}$

$$c^{tot}(y) = cy^2 + d$$
$$c_i^{tot}(y_i) = cy_i^2 + d_i.$$

Then we can make the comparison. It is presented in Table 5.7.

We can notice that the monopoly's supply is smaller than the total supply by both producers in the Stackelberg duopoly as well as in the Cournot duopoly. We can also notice that the monopoly's optimal price is the highest one of all considered cases.

Analysing responses of total supplies and optimal prices to changes in values of parameters of the demand function and of the production total cost function, one can notice that in each model, the responses have the same sign. They are presented in Table 5.8. Particularly, an increase in sensitivity a of consumers to changes in a price of a product always leads to a decrease in the total supply and in the optimal price.[8] An increase in the market capacity b leads always to an increase in the total supply and in the optimal price. An increase in the production total cost c always leads to a decrease in the total supply and to an increase in the optimal price.

[8] Let us recall that we consider ordinary goods, hence the demand decreases when the price of a product increases.

Table 5.8 Comparison of responses of total supplies and optimal prices to changes in values of parameters

	Parameter whose value is changed	Monopoly	Cournot duopoly	Stackelberg duopoly
Response of total supply	a	<0	<0	<0
	b	>0	>0	>0
	c	<0	<0	<0
Response of price	a	<0	<0	<0
	b	>0	>0	>0
	c	>0	>0	>0

E5.11. In Table 5.9a and b, there are given measures of reaction of the optimal supplies of two substitute products to changes in values of parameters of demand functions and of production total cost functions. The functions are linear and given in the same forms as in Sect. 5.4.4.1[9] where the Bertrand duopoly model is presented. Check if the given results are correct and on their basis formulate conclusions about the reactions.

Solution

Let us recall the basic standard assumptions of the Bertrand duopoly model:

- Functions of producers' production total cost are as follows[10]:

$$\forall i = 1, 2 \quad c_i^{tot}(y_i) = c_i^v(y_i) + c_i^f(y_i) = c_i y_i + d_i, \quad c_i, d_i > 0,$$

- The supply of each product matches the demand that consumers report for this product

$$y_1^s(p_1, p_2) = y_1^d(p_1, p_2) = y_1 = b_1 - a_1 p_1 + \gamma_1 p_2,$$
$$y_2^s(p_1, p_2) = y_2^d(p_1, p_2) = y_2 = b_2 - a_2 p_2 + \gamma_2 p_1.$$

By this assumptions, we get following optimal supplies of substitute products offered by the producers in the Bertrand duopoly:

$$\overline{y}_1^{(B)} = \frac{a_1\left[2a_2(b_1 - a_1 c_1) + \gamma_1(b_2 + a_2 c_2 + \gamma_2 c_1)\right]}{4a_1 a_2 - \gamma_1 \gamma_2}$$

[9] See a textbook Malaga K., Sobczak K, *Microeconomics. Static and Dynamic Analysis*, Springer Nature Switzerland, 2022.

[10] For the sake of simplicity, it is assumed that functions of production total costs are linear functions of output levels. One can take as well into account some nonlinear functions of output levels, getting different results.

Table 5.9 Measures of response to changes in parameters' values for: (a) first product's optimal suppply, (b) second product's optimal supply

Characteristic	Value
(a)	
$\frac{\partial \overline{y}_1^{(B)}}{\partial c_1}$	$\frac{-a_1(2a_1a_2-\gamma_1\gamma_2)}{4a_1a_2-\gamma_1\gamma_2} < 0$
$\frac{\partial \overline{y}_1^{(B)}}{\partial c_2}$	$\frac{a_1a_2\gamma_1}{4a_1a_2-\gamma_1\gamma_2} > 0$
$\frac{\partial \overline{y}_1^{(B)}}{\partial b_1}$	$\frac{2a_1a_2}{4a_1a_2-\gamma_1\gamma_2} > 0$
$\frac{\partial \overline{y}_1^{(B)}}{\partial b_2}$	$\frac{a_1\gamma_1}{4a_1a_2-\gamma_1\gamma_2} > 0$
$\frac{\partial \overline{y}_1^{(B)}}{\partial \gamma_1}$	$\frac{2a_1a_2[\gamma_2(b_1+a_1c_1)+2a_1(b_2+a_2c_2)]}{(4a_1a_2-\gamma_1\gamma_2)^2} > 0$
$\frac{\partial \overline{y}_1^{(B)}}{\partial \gamma_2}$	$\frac{a_1\gamma_1[2a_2(b_1+a_1c_1)+\gamma_1(b_2+a_2c_2)]}{(4a_1a_2-\gamma_1\gamma_2)^2} > 0$
$\frac{\partial \overline{y}_1^{(B)}}{\partial a_1}$	$-\frac{\gamma_1\gamma_2[2a_2(b_1-2a_1c_1)+\gamma_1(b_2+a_2c_2+\gamma_2c_1)]+8a_1^2a_2^2c_1}{(4a_1a_2-\gamma_1\gamma_2)^2} < 0$
$\frac{\partial \overline{y}_1^{(B)}}{\partial a_2}$	$-\frac{a_1\gamma_1[\gamma_2(2b_1+2a_1c_1+\gamma_1c_2)+4a_1b_2]}{(4a_1a_2-\gamma_1\gamma_2)^2} < 0$
(b)	
$\frac{\partial \overline{y}_2^{(B)}}{\partial c_1}$	$\frac{a_1a_2\gamma_2}{4a_1a_2-\gamma_1\gamma_2} > 0$
$\frac{\partial \overline{y}_2^{(B)}}{\partial c_2}$	$\frac{-a_2(2a_1a_2-\gamma_1\gamma_2)}{4a_1a_2-\gamma_1\gamma_2} < 0$
$\frac{\partial \overline{y}_2^{(B)}}{\partial b_1}$	$\frac{a_2\gamma_2}{4a_1a_2-\gamma_1\gamma_2} > 0$
$\frac{\partial \overline{y}_2^{(B)}}{\partial b_2}$	$\frac{2a_1a_2}{4a_1a_2-\gamma_1\gamma_2} > 0$
$\frac{\partial \overline{y}_2^{(B)}}{\partial \gamma_1}$	$\frac{a_2\gamma_2[2a_1(b_2+a_2c_2)+\gamma_2(b_1+a_1c_1)]}{(4a_1a_2-\gamma_1\gamma_2)^2} > 0$
$\frac{\partial \overline{y}_2^{(B)}}{\partial \gamma_2}$	$\frac{2a_1a_2[\gamma_1(b_2+a_2c_2)+2a_2(b_1+a_1c_1)]}{(4a_1a_2-\gamma_1\gamma_2)^2} > 0$
$\frac{\partial \overline{y}_2^{(B)}}{\partial a_1}$	$-\frac{a_2\gamma_2[\gamma_1(2b_2+2a_2c_2+\gamma_2c_1)+4a_2b_1]}{(4a_1a_2-\gamma_1\gamma_2)^2} < 0$
$\frac{\partial \overline{y}_2^{(B)}}{\partial a_2}$	$-\frac{\gamma_1\gamma_2[2a_1(b_2-2a_2c_2)+\gamma_2(b_1+a_1c_1+\gamma_1c_2)]+8a_1^2a_2^2c_2}{(4a_1a_2-\gamma_1\gamma_2)^2} < 0$

$$\overline{y}_2^{(B)} = \frac{a_2[2a_1(b_2 - a_2c_2) + \gamma_2(b_1 + a_1c_1 + \gamma_1c_2)]}{4a_1a_2 - \gamma_1\gamma_2},$$

where the parameters mean:

c_i Marginal total (variable) cost of production of i-th product,

b_i Capacity of i-th product's market,

γ_i Sensitivity of i-th ($i = 1, 2$) product's consumers to changes in a price of j-th ($j = 1, 2,\ j \neq i$) product,

a_i Sensitivity of i-th ($i = 1, 2$) product's consumers to changes in a price of i-th product,

and there is an assumption used that $a_i > \gamma_i$ which has an economic reason and allows to state what is a sign of reaction.

Let us focus on reactions for the first product's optimal supply noticing that due to the symmetry in results (presented in Table 5.9a and b) reactions and conclusions for the second product's optimal supply are analogous.

Reaction of the first product's optimal supply to a change in the marginal total cost of production of the first product is expressed as:

$$\frac{\partial \overline{y}_1^{(B)}}{\partial c_1} = \frac{-a_1(2a_1a_2 - \gamma_1\gamma_2)}{4a_1a_2 - \gamma_1\gamma_2} < 0$$

and means that when this marginal cost increases $c.p.$ (*ceteris paribus*), then the optimal supply of the first product decreases.

Reaction of the first product's optimal supply to a change in the marginal total cost of production of the second product is expressed as:

$$\frac{\partial \overline{y}_1^{(B)}}{\partial c_2} = \frac{a_1a_2\gamma_1}{4a_1a_2 - \gamma_1\gamma_2} > 0$$

and means that when this marginal cost increases $c.p.$ (*ceteris paribus*) then the optimal supply of the first product increases.

Reaction of the first product's optimal supply to a change in the capacity of the first product's market is expressed as:

$$\frac{\partial \overline{y}_1^{(B)}}{\partial b_1} = \frac{2a_1a_2}{4a_1a_2 - \gamma_1\gamma_2} > 0$$

and means that when this capacity increases $c.p.$ (*ceteris paribus*), then the optimal supply of the first product increases.

Reaction of the first product's optimal supply to a change in the capacity of the second product's market is expressed as:

$$\frac{\partial \overline{y}_1^{(B)}}{\partial b_2} = \frac{a_1\gamma_1}{4a_1a_2 - \gamma_1\gamma_2} > 0$$

and means that when this capacity increases $c.p.$ (*ceteris paribus*), then the optimal supply of the first product increases.

Reaction of the first product's optimal supply to a change in the sensitivity of the first product's consumers to changes in the price of the second product is expressed as:

$$\frac{\partial \overline{y}_1^{(B)}}{\partial \gamma_1} = \frac{2a_1a_2\left[\gamma_2(b_1 + a_1c_1) + 2a_1(b_2 + a_2c_2)\right]}{(4a_1a_2 - \gamma_1\gamma_2)^2} > 0$$

and means that when this sensitivity increases *c.p.* (*ceteris paribus*), then the optimal supply of the first product increases.

Reaction of the first product's optimal supply to a change in the sensitivity of the second product's consumers to changes in the price of the first product is expressed as:

$$\frac{\partial \overline{y}_1^{(B)}}{\partial \gamma_2} = \frac{a_1\gamma_1\left[2a_2(b_1 + a_1c_1) + \gamma_1(b_2 + a_2c_2)\right]}{(4a_1a_2 - \gamma_1\gamma_2)^2} > 0$$

and means that when this sensitivity increases *c.p.* (*ceteris paribus*), then the optimal supply of the first product increases.

Reaction of the first product's optimal supply to a change in the sensitivity of the first product's consumers to changes in the price of the first product is expressed as:

$$\frac{\partial \overline{y}_1^{(B)}}{\partial a_1} = -\frac{\gamma_1\gamma_2\left[2a_2(b_1 - 2a_1c_1) + \gamma_1(b_2 + a_2c_2 + \gamma_2c_1)\right] + 8a_1^2a_2^2c_1}{(4a_1a_2 - \gamma_1\gamma_2)^2} < 0$$

and means that when this sensitivity increases *c.p.* (*ceteris paribus*), then the optimal supply of the first product decreases.

Reaction of the first product's optimal supply to a change in the sensitivity of the second product's consumers to changes in the price of the second product is expressed as:

$$\frac{\partial \overline{y}_1^{(B)}}{\partial a_2} = -\frac{a_1\gamma_1\left[\gamma_2(2b_1 + 2a_1c_1 + \gamma_1c_2) + 4a_1b_2\right]}{(4a_1a_2 - \gamma_1\gamma_2)^2} < 0$$

and means that when this sensitivity increases *c.p.* (*ceteris paribus*), then the optimal supply of the first product decreases.

Reactions and conclusions for the second product's optimal supply are analogous.

E5.12. Two producers act on a market of two heterogeneous substitute products. The first producer (leader) can set an optimal price of her/his product on a level that guarantees her/him the maximum profit regardless a price level of a product supplied by the competitor. The second producer (follower) decides a price level of her/his product depending on the other product's price set by the leader. There are given functions of:

(a) Production total costs for both producers:

$$\forall i = 1, 2 \quad c_i^{tot}(y_i) = c_i^v(y_i) + c_i^f(y_i) = c_i y_i + d_i, \quad c_i, d_i > 0,$$

(b) Demand for the first producer's (leader) product:

$$y_1^d(p_1, p_2) = b_1 - a_1 p_1, \quad a_1, b_1, > 0,$$

(c) Demand for the second producer's (follower) product:

$$y_2^d(p_1, p_2) = b_2 - a_2 p_2 + \gamma_2 p_1, \quad a_2, b_2, \gamma_2 > 0.$$

The supply of each producer's product is assumed to match the demand reported for this product:

$$y_1^s(p_1, p_2) = y_1^d(p_1, p_2) = y_1 = b_2 - a_1 p_1,$$
$$y_2^s(p_1, p_2) = y_2^d(p_1, p_2) = y_2 = b_2 - a_2 p_2 + \gamma_2 p_1.$$

1. Formulate the profit maximization problem for:
   - The first producer: $\Pi_1(p_1) \to \max \quad p_1 \geq 0$
   - The second producer: $\Pi_2(p_1, p_2)|_{p_1=\text{const.}\geq 0} \to \max \quad p_1, p_2 \geq 0.$
2. Solve the profit maximization problems for both producers determining optimal levels of prices of both products and maximum profits of both producers.
3. Analyse how optimal prices of both products react to changes in values of parameters describing the market: market capacities, consumers' sensitivities to changes in prices of products, production marginal costs.
4. Draw reaction lines of both producers and illustrate an equilibrium state of this modified Bertrand duopoly model.
5. Determine the optimal supply of each product manufactured by a given producer.
6. State which of the strategies of setting an optimal price level of a product is more rational and more beneficial: the one of the leader or the one of the follower?

Solutions

Ad 1

Formulate the profit maximization problem for:

- The first producer: $\Pi_1(p_1) \to \max \quad p_1 \geq 0$
- The second producer: $\Pi_2(p_1, p_2)|_{p_1=\text{const.}\geq 0} \to \max \quad p_1, p_2 \geq 0.$

The task is to determine the profit functions of the leader and the follower. The leader's revenue, production total cost and profit are described by functions:

$$r_1(p_1) = p_1 y_1 = p_1(b_1 - a_1 p_1) = b_1 p_1 - a_1 p_1^2$$
$$c_1^{tot}(y_1) = c_1 y_1 + d_1 = c_1(b_1 - a_1 p_1) + d_1 = b_1 c_1 - a_1 c_1 p_1 + d_1 = c_1^{tot}(p_1)$$
$$\Pi_1(p_1) = r_1(p_1) - c^{tot}(p_1) = -(b_1 c_1 + d_1) + (b_1 + a_1 c_1) p_1 - a_1 p_1^2.$$

The follower's revenue, production total cost and profit are described by functions:

$$r_2(p_1, p_2) = p_2 y_2 = p_2(b_2 - a_2 p_2 + \gamma_2 p_1) = b_2 p_2 - a_2 p_2^2 + \gamma_2 p_1 p_2$$
$$c_2^{tot}(y_2) = c_2 y_2 + d_2 = c_2(b_2 - a_2 p_2 + \gamma_2 p_1) + d_1 = c_2^{tot}(p_1, p_2)$$
$$\Pi_2(p_1, p_2) = r_2(p_1, p_2) - c_2^{tot}(p_1, p_2) = -(b_2 c_2 + d_2)$$
$$+ (b_2 + a_2 c_2) p_2 + \gamma_2 p_1 (p_2 - c_2) - a_2 p_2^2.$$

Ad 2

Solve the profit maximization problems for both producers determining optimal levels of prices of both products and maximum profits of both producers.

The necessary and the sufficient conditions for existence of a maximum of the profit function in case of the follower take the following form:

$$\left.\frac{\partial \Pi_2(p_1, p_2)}{\partial p_2}\right|_{p_2=\overline{p}_2,\, p_1=\text{const.}\geq 0} = b_2 + a_2 c_2 + \gamma_2 p_1 - 2a_2 \overline{p}_2 = 0$$
$$\left.\frac{\partial^2 \Pi_2(p_1, p_2)}{\partial p_2^2}\right|_{p_2=\overline{p}_2,\, p_1=\text{const.}\geq 0} = -2a_2 \overline{p}_2 < 0,$$

which gives a line of the follower's reaction to changes in the price of a product of the leader:

$$\overline{p}_2 = \frac{b_2 + a_2 c_2}{2a_2} + \frac{\gamma_2}{2a_2} p_1 \quad RL_2.$$

The necessary and the sufficient conditions for existence of a maximum of the profit function in case of the leader take the following form:

$$\left.\frac{d\Pi_1(p_1)}{dp_1}\right|_{p_1=\overline{p}_1} = b_1 + a_1 c_1 - 2a_1 \overline{p}_1 = 0$$
$$\left.\frac{d^2\Pi_1(p_1)}{dp_1^2}\right|_{p_1=\overline{p}_1} = -2a_1 < 0$$

which gives the optimal price of the leader's product:

$$\overline{p}_1 = \frac{b_1 + a_1 c_1}{2a_1}.$$

Substituting this price into the follower's reaction line equation, we get the optimal price of the follower's product:

$$\overline{p}_2 = \frac{b_2 + a_2 c_2}{2a_2} + \frac{\gamma_2}{2a_2} \overline{p}_1 = \frac{b_2 + a_2 c_2}{2a_2} + \frac{\gamma_2}{2a_2} \cdot \frac{b_1 + a_1 c_1}{2a_1}$$

$$= \frac{2a_1(b_2 + a_2c_2) + \gamma_2(b_1 + a_1c_1)}{4a_1a_2} = \frac{b_2 + a_2c_2}{2a_2} + \frac{\gamma_2(b_1 + a_1c_1)}{4a_1a_2}$$

We can notice that by the assumption $a_1 = a_2, b_1 = b_2, c_1 = c_2$, the optimal price of the follower's product is bigger than the optimal price of the leader's product.

Having optimal prices of both products, we can determine maximum profit of the leader:

$$\begin{aligned}\max \Pi_1(p_1) &= \Pi_1(\overline{p}_1) = -(b_1c_1 + d_1) + (b_1 + a_1c_1)\overline{p}_1 - a_1\overline{p}_1^2 \\ &= -(b_1c_1 + d_1) + (b_1 + a_1c_1)\frac{b_1 + a_1c_1}{2a_1} - a_1\left(\frac{b_1 + a_1c_1}{2a_1}\right)^2 \\ &= \frac{1}{4}c_1(a_1c_1 - 2b_1) + \frac{b_1^2}{4a_1} - d_1\end{aligned}$$

and of the follower

$$\begin{aligned}&\max \Pi_2(p_1, p_2) = \Pi_2(\bar{p}_1, \bar{p}_2) \\ &= -(b_2c_2 + d_2) + (b_2 + a_2c_2)\bar{p}_2 + \gamma_2\bar{p}_1(\bar{p}_2 - c_2) - a_2\bar{p}_2^2 \\ &= -(b_2c_2 + d_2) + \bar{p}_2(b_2 + a_2c_2 + \gamma_2\bar{p}_1 - a_2\bar{p}_2) - c_2\gamma_2\bar{p}_1 \\ &= -(b_2c_2 + d_2) + \bar{p}_2 \cdot \frac{2a_1(b_2 + a_2c_2) + \gamma_2(b_1 + a_1c_1)}{4a_1} - \frac{c_2\gamma_2(b_1 + a_1c_1)}{2a_1} \\ &= -(b_2c_2 + d_2) + \frac{[2a_1(b_2 + a_2c_2) + \gamma_2(b_1 + a_1c_1)]^2}{16a_1^2a_2} - \frac{c_2\gamma_2(b_1 + a_1c_1)}{2a_1} \\ &= -(b_2c_2 + d_2) + \frac{(b_2 + a_2c_2)^2}{4a_2} + \frac{(b_2 + a_2c_2)^2}{4a_2} \\ &+ \frac{\gamma_2(b_1 + a_1c_1)(b_2 + a_2c_2)}{4a_1a_2} + \frac{\gamma_2^2(b_1 + a_1c_1)}{16a_1^2a_2} - \frac{c_2\gamma_2(b_1 + a_1c_1)}{2a_1}.\end{aligned}$$

Ad 3

Analyse how optimal prices of both products react to changes in values of parameters describing the market: market capacities, consumers' sensitivities to changes in prices of products, production marginal costs.

From point 2, we know the optimal prices' forms:

$$\begin{aligned}\overline{p}_1 &= \frac{b_1 + a_1c_1}{2a_1} = \frac{1}{2}a_1^{-1}b_1 + \frac{1}{2}c_1 \\ \overline{p}_2 &= \frac{b_2 + a_2c_2}{2a_2} + \frac{\gamma_2(b_1 + a_1c_1)}{4a_1a_2} \\ &= \frac{1}{2}a_2^{-1}b_2 + \frac{1}{2}c_2 + \frac{\gamma_2b_1}{4a_1a_2} + \frac{\gamma_2c_1}{4a_2}.\end{aligned}$$

Let us recall the meaning of the parameters:

c_i Marginal total (variable) cost of production of i-th product ($i = 1, 2$),
b_i Capacity of i-th product's market ($i = 1, 2$),
γ_2 Sensitivity of consumers of the second product (offered by the follower) to changes in a price of the first product (offered by the leader),
a_i Sensitivity of i-th ($i = 1, 2$) product's consumers to changes in a price of i-th product ($a_2 > \gamma_2$).

Reaction of i-th product's optimal price to a change in the marginal total cost of production of this product is expressed as:

$$\frac{\partial \overline{p}_i}{\partial c_i} = \frac{1}{2} \quad i = 1, 2$$

and means that when this marginal cost increases $c.p.$ (*ceteris paribus*) by one money unit, then the optimal price of i-th product increases by 0.5 of money unit.

Reaction of i-th ($i = 1, 2$) product's optimal price to a change in the marginal total cost of production of j-th ($j \neq i$) product is expressed as:

$$\frac{\partial \overline{p}_1}{\partial c_2} = 0, \quad \frac{\partial \overline{p}_2}{\partial c_1} = \frac{\gamma_2}{4a_2} > 0$$

and means that when the marginal cost of production of the follower's product increases $c.p.$ (*ceteris paribus*), then the optimal price of the leader's product does not change while the optimal price of the follower's product increases when the marginal cost of production of the leader's product increases $c.p.$ This shows that the marginal cost of production for the follower does not affect the optimal price of the leader's product. In contrast, the marginal cost of production for the leader affects the optimal price of the follower's product

Reaction of i-th product's optimal price to a change in the capacity of the first product's market is expressed as:

$$\frac{\partial \overline{p}_i}{\partial b_i} = \frac{1}{2} a_1^{-1} > 0 \quad i = 1, 2$$

and means that when this capacity increases $c.p.$ (*ceteris paribus*), then the optimal price of i-th product increases.

Reaction of i-th ($i = 1, 2$) product's optimal price to a change in the capacity of j-th ($j \neq i$) product's market is expressed as:

$$\frac{\partial \overline{p}_1}{\partial b_2} = 0, \quad \frac{\partial \overline{p}_2}{\partial b_1} = \frac{\gamma_2}{4a_1 a_2} > 0$$

and means that when the capacity of the market for the follower's product increases $c.p.$ (*ceteris paribus*), then the optimal price of the leader's product does not change while the optimal price of the follower's product increases when the capacity of the market for the leader's product increases $c.p.$ This shows that the capacity of the market of the follower's product does not affect the optimal price of the leader's product. In contrast, the capacity of the market of the leader's product affects the optimal price of the follower's product.

Reaction of i-th product's optimal price to a change in the sensitivity of i-th product's consumers to changes in the price of i-th product is expressed as:

$$\frac{\partial \overline{p}_1}{\partial a_1} = -\frac{1}{2} a_1^{-2} b_1 < 0, \qquad \frac{\partial \overline{p}_2}{\partial a_2} = -\frac{1}{2} a_2^{-2} b_2 - \frac{\gamma_2 b_1}{4 a_1 a_2^2} - \frac{\gamma_2 c_1}{4 a_2^2} < 0$$

and means that when this sensitivity increases $c.p.$ (*ceteris paribus*), then the optimal price of i-th product decreases. Assuming $a_1 = b_1$ and $b_1 = b_2$ the reaction of the optimal price of the follower's product is stronger than of the optimal price of the leader's product.

Reaction of i-th ($i = 1, 2$) product's optimal price to a change in sensitivity of j-th ($j \neq i$) product's consumers to changes in the price of j-th product is expressed as:

$$\frac{\partial \overline{p}_1}{\partial a_2} = 0, \qquad \frac{\partial \overline{p}_2}{\partial a_1} = -\frac{\gamma_2 b_1}{4 a_1^2 a_2} < 0$$

and means that when the sensitivity of the consumers of the follower's product to changes in the price of the follower's product increases $c.p.$ (*ceteris paribus*), then the optimal price of the leader's product does not change while the optimal price of the follower's product decreases when the sensitivity of the consumers of the leader's product to changes in the price of the leader's product increases $c.p.$ This shows that the sensitivity of consumers of the follower's product does not affect the optimal price of the leader's product. In contrast, the sensitivity of consumers of the leader's product affects the optimal price of the follower's product.

Reaction of i-th ($i = 1, 2$) product's optimal price to a change in sensitivity of consumers of the follower's product to changes in the price of the leader's product is expressed as:

$$\frac{\partial \overline{p}_1}{\partial \gamma_2} = 0, \qquad \frac{\partial \overline{p}_2}{\partial \gamma_2} = \frac{b_1}{4 a_1 a_2} + \frac{c_1}{4 a_2} > 0$$

and means that when the sensitivity of the consumers of the follower's product to changes in the price of the leader's product increases $c.p.$ (*ceteris paribus*), then the optimal price of the leader's product does not change while the optimal price of the follower's product increases This shows that the sensitivity of consumers of the follower's product does not affect the optimal price of the leader's product. But it affects the optimal price of the follower's product.

Summing up, the optimal price of the leader's product depends only on three parameters—those related to her/his production and the demand for her/his product.

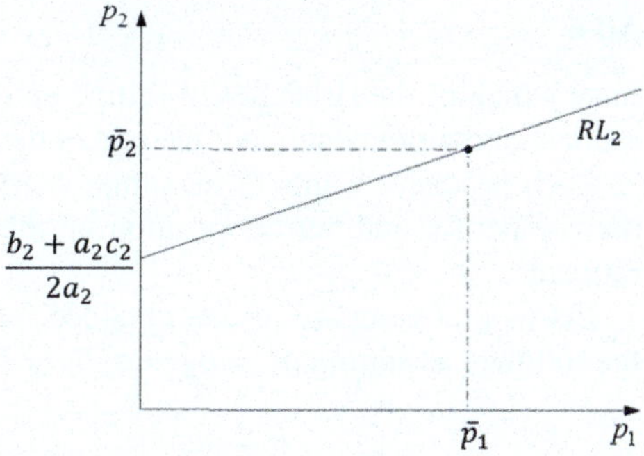

Fig. 5.9 Reaction line of follower and equilibrium state of modified Bertrand duopoly model (E5.12)

The optimal price of the follower's product depends on all parameters of the model (except for the production fixed cost d_i), not only those related to her/his production and the demand for her/his product but also those related to her/his competitor's (the leader's) production and the demand for her/his competitor's product.

Ad 4

Draw reaction lines of both producers and illustrate an equilibrium state of this modified Bertrand duopoly model (Fig. 5.9).

Ad 5

Determine the optimal supply of each product manufactured by a given producer.

The optimal supply by the leader takes a form:

$$\overline{y}_1 = b_1 - a_1\overline{p}_1 = b_1 - a_1\frac{b_1 + a_1c_1}{2a_1} = \frac{b_1 - a_1c_1}{2}.$$

The optimal supply by the follower takes a form

$$\begin{aligned}\bar{y}_2 &= b_2 - a_2\bar{p}_2 + \gamma_2\bar{p}_1 = b_2 - a_2\frac{2a_1(b_2 + a_2c_2) + \gamma_2(b_1 + a_1c_1)}{4a_1a_2} + \gamma_2\frac{b_1 + a_1c_1}{2a_1}\\ &= \frac{4a_1b_2 - 2a_1b_2 - 2a_1a_2c_2 - \gamma_2(b_1 + a_1c_1) + 2\gamma_2(b_1 + a_1c_1)}{4a_1}\\ &= \frac{2a_1b_2 - 2a_1a_2c_2 + \gamma_2(b_1 + a_1c_1)}{4a_1}\\ &= \frac{2a_1(b_2 - a_2c_2) + \gamma_2(b_1 + a_1c_1)}{4a_1} = \frac{b_2 - a_2c_2}{2} + \frac{\gamma_2(b_1 + a_1c_1)}{4a_1}\end{aligned}$$

We can notice that by the assumption $a_1 = a_2, b_1 = b_2, c_1 = c_2$, the optimal supply of the follower's product is bigger than the optimal supply of the leader's product.

Ad 6

State which of the strategies of setting an optimal price level of a product are more rational and more beneficial: the one of the leader or the one of the follower?

Each producer wants to maximize her/his profit taking into account he/she has the competitor and her/his position on the market. In this sense, each producer is rational.

Let us first compare results obtained for the leader with the results obtained for the follower assuming $a_1 = a_2 = a, b_1 = b_2 = b, c_1 = c_2 = c$:

$$\overline{p}_1 = \frac{b+ac}{2a} < \overline{p}_2 = \frac{b+ac}{2a} + \frac{\gamma_2(b+ac)}{4a^2}$$
$$\overline{y}_1 = \frac{b-ac}{2} < \overline{y}_2 = \frac{b-ac}{2} + \frac{\gamma_2(b+ac)}{4a}$$

where $b > ac$ is an assumption that has to be satisfied. Otherwise, the optimal supply by the leader would be negative which has no economic sense.

Now, assuming moreover that $d_1 = d_2 = d$, we get the maximum profits for producers as follows:

$$\max \Pi_1 = \bar{p}_1\bar{y}_1 - c\bar{y}_1 - d_1 = \frac{b+ac}{2a} \cdot \frac{b-ac}{2} - c\frac{b-ac}{2} - d$$

$$\max \Pi_2 = \bar{p}_2\bar{y}_2 - c\bar{y}_2 - d_2 = \left(\frac{b+ac}{2a} + \frac{\gamma_2(b+ac)}{4a^2}\right) \cdot \left(\frac{b-ac}{2} + \frac{\gamma_2(b+ac)}{4a}\right)$$
$$- c\left(\frac{b-ac}{2} + \frac{\gamma_2(b+ac)}{4a}\right) - d = \frac{b+ac}{2a} \cdot \frac{b-ac}{2} - c\frac{b-ac}{2}$$
$$- d + \frac{b+ac}{2a} \cdot \frac{\gamma_2(b+ac)}{4a} + \frac{\gamma_2(b+ac)}{4a^2} \cdot \frac{b-ac}{2} - c\frac{\gamma_2(b+ac)}{4a}$$
$$= \max \Pi_1 + \frac{\gamma_2(b+ac)^2}{8a^2} + \frac{\gamma_2(b^2-a^2c^2)}{8a^2} - c\frac{\gamma_2(b+ac)}{4a}$$
$$= \max \Pi_1 + \frac{\gamma_2(b^2+2abc+a^2c^2+b^2-a^2c^2)}{8a^2} - \frac{\gamma_2(bc+ac^2)}{4a}$$
$$= \max \Pi_1 + \frac{\gamma_2(2b^2+2abc)}{8a^2} - c\frac{\gamma_2(2abc+2a^2c^2)}{8a^2}$$
$$= \max \Pi_1 + \frac{\gamma_2(2b^2-2a^2c^2)}{8a^2} = \max \Pi_1 + \frac{2\gamma_2(b^2-a^2c^2)}{8a^2}.$$

One can notice that the maximum profit for the follower is bigger whenever $b^2 > a^2c^2$, thus always by the required assumption that $b > ac$. This shows that the follower's strategy of setting an optimal price level of her/his product is more rational and beneficial than the leader's strategy.

E5.13. Compare the original and the modified (E5.12) Bertrand duopoly models.[11] State if the leader position in the modified Bertrand duopoly model is more beneficial for the first producer than a market position equal to the one of the second producer when these two producers compete on prices.

Solution

For the sake of simplicity, let us assume that $a_1 = a_2 = a$, $b_1 = b_2 = b$, $c_1 = c_2 = c$ and $\gamma_1 = \gamma_2 = \gamma$. Then the optimal price and optimal supply of the leader's product in both models are:

$$\overline{p}_1^{(B)} = \frac{2a(b+ac)+\gamma(b+ac)}{4a^2-\gamma^2} = \frac{(b+ac)(2a+\gamma)}{4a^2-\gamma^2}$$
$$= \frac{(b+ac)(2a+\gamma)}{(2a-\gamma)(2a+\gamma)} = \frac{b+ac}{2a-\gamma} > \frac{b+ac}{2a} = \overline{p}_1$$
$$\overline{y}_1^{(B)} = \frac{a\left[2a(b-ac)+\gamma(b+ac+\gamma c)\right]}{4a^2-\gamma^2} = \left\| \frac{:2a^2}{:2a^2} \right\|$$
$$= \frac{b-ac}{2-\frac{\gamma^2}{2a^2}} + \frac{\frac{1}{2a}\gamma(b+ac+\gamma c)}{2-\frac{\gamma^2}{2a^2}} > \frac{b-ac}{2} = \overline{y}_1.$$

One can notice that the optimal price and the optimal supply of the leader's product are bigger in the standard Bertrand duopoly model than in the modified model. This shows again that the leader's strategy is less rational and less beneficial than the follower's strategy. It is also less rational and less beneficial than the one he/she would have in case of the equivalent market position. The leader would benefit if he/she decided to take market position equivalent to her/his competitor. The leader position in the market conditions described in exercise E5.12 results in a situation in which the leader does not take into account the consumers of her/his competitor's product and the fact their products are substitutes for each other.

If we again assume (for the sake of simplicity) that $a_1 = a_2 = a$, $b_1 = b_2 = b$, $c_1 = c_2 = c$ and $\gamma_1 = \gamma_2 = \gamma$, then the optimal price and optimal supply of the follower's product in both models are:

$$\overline{p}_2^{(B)} = \frac{2a(b+ac)+\gamma(b+ac)}{4a^2-\gamma^2} > \frac{2a(b+ac)+\gamma(b+ac)}{4a^2} = \overline{p}_2$$
$$\overline{y}_2^{(B)} = \frac{a\left[2a(b-ac)+\gamma(b+ac+\gamma c)\right]}{4a^2-\gamma^2} = \left\| \frac{:a}{:a} \right\|$$
$$= \frac{2a(b-ac)+\gamma(b+ac+\gamma c)}{4a-\frac{\gamma^2}{a}} > \frac{2a(b-ac)+\gamma(b+ac)}{4a} = \overline{y}_2$$

[11] The reference for the comparison can be the comparative analysis, presented in Sect. 5.4.3 (See a textbook Malaga K., Sobczak K, Microeconomics. Static and Dynamic Analysis, Springer Nature Switzerland, 2022.), of Cournot and Stackelberg duopoly models.

One can notice that the optimal price and the optimal supply of the follower's product are bigger in the standard Bertrand duopoly model than in the modified model. This shows that if the leader decided to take equivalent position to her/his competitor, then not only he/she would benefit but also the follower.

E5.14. The demand for a product of a monopolistic company evolves according to a linear function of a form:

$$y^d(t) = -a(t)p(t) + b(t), \quad a(t), b(t) > 0, \quad \forall t = 0, 1, \ldots, 20.$$

A function of production total cost is given as:

$$c^{tot}\left(y^s(t)\right) = c(t)y^s(t) + d(t), \quad c(t), d(t) > 0, \quad \forall t = 0, 1, \ldots, 20.$$

1. Solve the profit maximization problem determining the optimal supply and an optimal price level by the following assumptions:
   (a) $a(t) = -\frac{1}{t+1} + 2, \quad b(t) = 10, \quad c(t) = 2,$
   (b) $a(t) = 1, \quad b(t) = -0.025t^2 + 0.75t + 10, \quad c(t) = 2,$
   (c) $a(t) = 1, \quad b(t) = 10, \quad c(t) = \frac{1}{t+1} + 1.$
2. Present trajectories of the optimal supply and of the optimal price.
3. Analyse how the optimal supply and the optimal price react to changes (*ceteris paribus*) in values of parameters describing the market: market capacity, consumers' sensitivity to changes in a product price, production marginal costs.

Solutions

Ad 1

Solve the profit maximization problem determining the optimal supply and an optimal price level.

The profit function takes a form:

$$\pi(y(t)) = r(y(t)) - c^{tot}(y(t)) = p(y(t)) \cdot y(t) - c^{tot}(y(t)).$$

We need first to derive an inverted function $p(y(t))$ of the consumer demand:

$$y(t) = -a(t)p(t) + b(t)$$
$$a(t)p(t) = -y(t) + b(t)$$
$$p(t) = -\frac{1}{a(t)}y(t) + \frac{b(t)}{a(t)}.$$

Substituting this function into the profit function and using the form of the production total cost function we get:

$$\pi(y(t)) = \left(-\frac{1}{a(t)}y(t) + \frac{b(t)}{a(t)}\right)y(t) - (c(t)y(t) + d(t))$$
$$= -\frac{1}{a(t)}y(t)^2 + \left(\frac{b(t)}{a(t)} - c(t)\right)y(t) - d(t).$$

The necessary condition for existence of a maximum of this function is following:

$$\frac{\mathrm{d}\pi(y(t))}{\mathrm{d}y(t)} = -\frac{2}{a(t)}y(t) + \frac{b(t)}{a(t)} - c(t) = 0$$

and gives the optimal supply:

$$\overline{y}(t) = \frac{b(t) - a(t)c(t)}{2}.$$

The sufficient condition for existence of a maximum of the profit function is following:

$$\frac{\mathrm{d}^2\pi(y(t))}{\mathrm{d}y(t)^2} = -\frac{2}{a(t)} < 0$$

and is satisfied.

The optimal price set by the monopoly takes a form:

$$\overline{p}(t) = p(\overline{y}(t)) = -\frac{1}{a(t)}\overline{y}(t) + \frac{b(t)}{a(t)} = \frac{-b(t) + a(t)c(t)}{2a(t)}$$
$$+ \frac{b(t)}{a(t)} = \frac{b(t) + a(t)c(t)}{2a(t)} = \frac{1}{2}\left(\frac{b(t)}{a(t)} + c(t)\right).$$

(a) $a(t) = -\frac{1}{t+1} + 2, \quad b(t) = 10, \quad c(t) = 2,$

$$\overline{y}(t) = 5 - \frac{1}{2}\left(-\frac{1}{t+1} + 2\right) \cdot 2 = \frac{1}{t+1} + 3$$
$$\overline{p}(t) = \frac{1}{2}\left(\frac{10(t+1)}{-1 + 2t + 2} + 2\right) = \frac{5(t+1)}{2t+1} + 1.$$

(b) $a(t) = 1, \quad b(t) = -0.025t^2 + 0.75t + 10, \quad c(t) = 2,$

$$\overline{y}(t) = -0.0125t^2 + 0.375t + 5 - \frac{1}{2}(1 \cdot 2) = -0.0125t^2 + 0.375t + 4$$
$$\overline{p}(t) = -0.0125t^2 + 0.375t + 5 + \frac{1}{2} \cdot 2 = -0.0125t^2 + 0.375t + 6.$$

(c) $a(t) = 1, \quad b(t) = 10, \quad c(t) = \frac{1}{t+1} + 1$

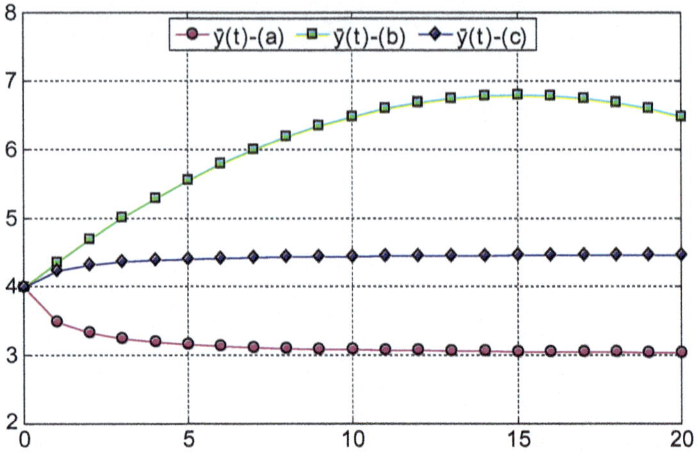

Fig. 5.10 Optimal supply (E5.14)

$$\overline{y}(t) = 5 - \frac{1}{2}\left(\frac{1}{t+1} + 1\right) = \frac{4.5t + 4}{t+1}$$
$$\overline{p}(t) = 5 + \frac{1}{2}\left(\frac{1}{t+1} + 1\right) = \frac{5.5t + 6}{t+1}.$$

Ad 2

Present trajectories[12] of the optimal supply and of the optimal price (Figs. 5.10 and 5.11).

Ad 3

Analyse how the optimal supply and the optimal price react to changes (*ceteris paribus*) in values of parameters describing the market: market capacity, consumers' sensitivity to changes in a product price, production marginal costs.

Reactions of the optimal supply and of the optimal price to a change in the market capacity are expressed as:

$$\frac{\partial \overline{y}(t)}{\partial b(t)} = \frac{1}{2}, \qquad \frac{\partial \overline{p}(t)}{\partial b(t)} = \frac{1}{2a(t)} > 0$$

and mean that when the capacity increases *c.p.* (*ceteris paribus*) by one physical unit, then the optimal supply increases by 0.5 of the physical unit and the optimal price increases.

Reactions of the optimal supply and of the optimal price to a change in the sensitivity of consumers to changes in a price of the product are expressed as:

[12] A MATLAB file to obtain these trajectories is called Exercise_5_14.m.

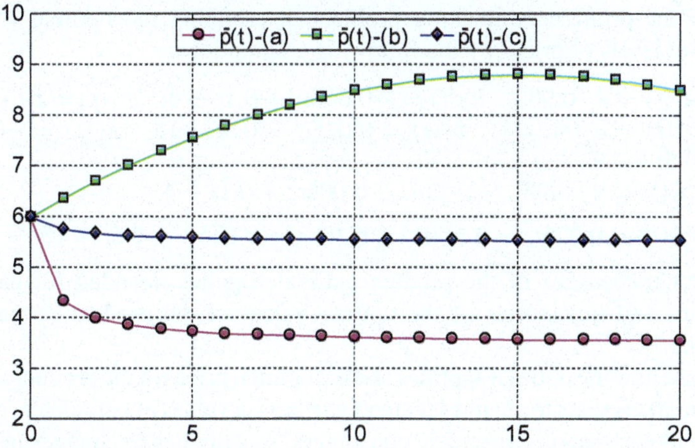

Fig. 5.11 Optimal price (E5.14)

$$\frac{\partial \overline{y}(t)}{\partial a(t)} = -\frac{1}{2}c(t) < 0, \qquad \frac{\partial \overline{p}(t)}{\partial a(t)} = -\frac{b(t)}{2(a(t))^2} < 0$$

and mean that when the sensitivity increases $c.p.$ (*ceteris paribus*), then the optimal supply and the optimal price decrease.

Reactions of the optimal supply and of the optimal price to a change in the production marginal cost are expressed as:

$$\frac{\partial \overline{y}(t)}{\partial c(t)} = -\frac{1}{2}a(t) < 0, \qquad \frac{\partial \overline{p}(t)}{\partial c(t)} = \frac{1}{2}$$

and mean that when the marginal cost increases $c.p.$ (*ceteris paribus*) by one money unit, then the optimal supply decreases and the optimal price increases by 0.5 of the money unit.

E5.15. Some monopolistic company considers discriminatory pricing for its product supplied to two different markets. The demand reported by consumers for i-th product ($i = 1, 2$) evolves according to a linear function of a form:

$$y_i^d(t) = -a_i(t)p_i(t) + b_i(t), \quad a_i(t), b_i(t) > 0, \quad i = 1, 2, \quad \forall t \in [0; 20].$$

A function of production total cost is given as:

$$c^{tot}\left(y^s(t)\right) = c(t)y^s(t) + d(t), \quad c(t), d(t) > 0, \quad t \in [0; 20],$$

where

$$c(t) = \frac{1}{t+1} + 1.$$

1. Solve the profit maximization problem determining the optimal supply and optimal levels of prices by the following assumptions:
   (a) $a_1(t) = 4 \cdot 0.98^t$, $a_2(t) = -0.006t^2 + 0.1t + 4$, $b_1(t) = b_2(t) = 15$,
   (b) $a_1(t) = a_2(t) = 4$, $b_1(t) = 0.025t^2 - 0.5t + 15$, $b_2(t) = -0.025t^2 + 0.5t + 15$,
   (c) $a_1(t) = 4 \cdot 0.98^t$, $a_2(t) = -0.006t^2 + 0.1t + 4$,
   $b_1(t) = 0.025t^2 - 0.5t + 15$, $b_2(t) = -0.025t^2 + 0.5t + 15$.
2. Present trajectories of the product optimal supplies intended for each of the markets and trajectories of the optimal prices of the product on each of the market.
3. Analyse how the optimal supplies and the optimal prices of the product supplied to both markets react to changes (*ceteris paribus*) in values of parameters describing the markets: market capacities, consumers' sensitivities to changes in a product price, production marginal cost. Analyse what the importance of differences in these values between two markets is.

Solutions

Ad 1

Solve the profit maximization problem determining the optimal supply and optimal levels of prices.

The profit function takes a form:

$$\begin{aligned}\pi(y_1(t), y_2(t)) &= r_1(y_1(t)) + r_2(y_2(t)) - c^{tot}(y_1(t), y_2(t))\\ &= p_1(y_1(t)) \cdot y_1(t) - p_2(y_2(t)) \cdot y_2(t) - (c(t)y(t) + d(t)).\end{aligned}$$

We need first to derive inverted functions $p_i(y_i(t))$ $(i = 1, 2)$ of the consumer demand:

$$\begin{aligned}y_i(t) &= -a_i(t)p_i(t) + b_i(t)\\ a_i(t)p_i(t) &= -y_i(t) + b_i(t)\\ p_i(t) &= -\frac{1}{a_i(t)}y_i(t) + \frac{b_i(t)}{a_i(t)}.\end{aligned}$$

The total supply of the monopoly consists of supplies of the product intended for two markets:

$$y(t) = y_1(t) + y_2(t).$$

Substituting the inverted functions of the consumer demand into the profit function and using the form of the production total cost function we get:

$$\pi(y_1(t), y_2(t)) = \left(-\frac{1}{a_1(t)}y_1(t) + \frac{b_1(t)}{a_1(t)}\right)y_1(t) + \left(-\frac{1}{a_2(t)}y_2(t) + \frac{b_2(t)}{a_2(t)}\right)y_2(t)$$
$$- c(t)(y_1(t) + y_2(t)) - d(t) = -\frac{1}{a_1(t)}(y_1(t))^2 + \left(\frac{b_1(t)}{a_1(t)} - c(t)\right)y_1(t)$$
$$- \frac{1}{a_2(t)}(y_2(t))^2 + \left(\frac{b_2(t)}{a_2(t)} - c(t)\right)y_2(t) - d(t).$$

The necessary condition for existence of a maximum of this function takes a form of two equations:

$$\frac{\partial\pi(y_1(t), y_2(t))}{\partial y_i(t)} = -\frac{2}{a_i(t)}y_i(t) + \frac{b_i(t)}{a_i(t)} - c(t) = 0 \quad i = 1, 2$$

and gives the optimal supply intended for each market:

$$\overline{y}_i(t) = \frac{b_i(t) - a_i(t)c(t)}{2} \quad i = 1, 2.$$

The sufficient condition for existence of a maximum of the profit function takes a form of two inequalities:

$$\frac{\partial^2\pi(y_1(t), y_2(t))}{\partial y_i(t)^2} = -\frac{2}{a_i(t)} < 0, \quad i = 1, 2$$

and is satisfied.

The optimal total supply of the monopoly consists of the optimal supplies of the product intended for two markets:

$$\overline{y}(t) = \overline{y}_1(t) + \overline{y}_2(t) = \frac{b_1(t) + b_1(t) - c(t)(a_1(t) + a_2(t))}{2}.$$

The optimal price set by the monopoly on each market takes a form:

$$\bar{p}_i(t) = p_i(\overline{y_i}(t)) = -\frac{1}{a_i(t)}\bar{y}(t) + \frac{b_i(t)}{a_i(t)}$$
$$= \frac{b_i(t) + a_i(t)c_i(t)}{2a_i(t)} = \frac{1}{2}\left(\frac{b_i(t)}{a_i(t)} + c(t)\right) \quad i = 1, 2.$$

Ad 2

Present trajectories[13] of the product optimal supplies intended for each of the markets and trajectories of the optimal prices of the product on each of the market (Figs. 5.12, 5.13 and 5.14).

---

[13] A MATLAB file to obtain these trajectories is called Exercise_5_15.m.

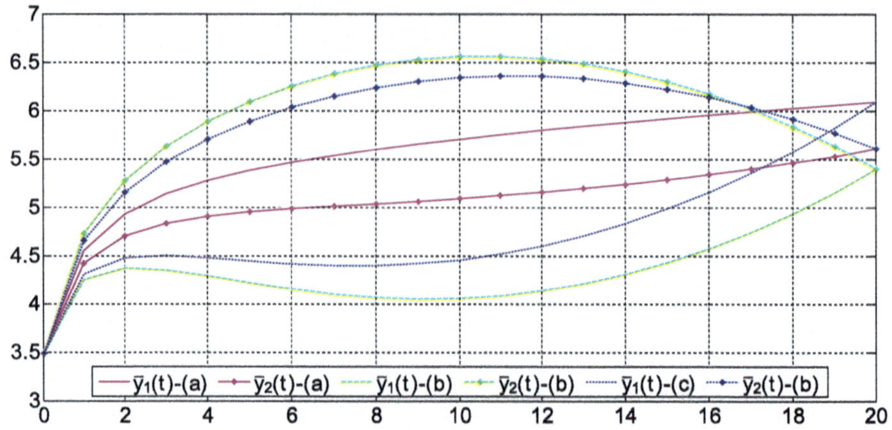

Fig. 5.12 Optimal supplies intended for the first and second markets (E5.15)

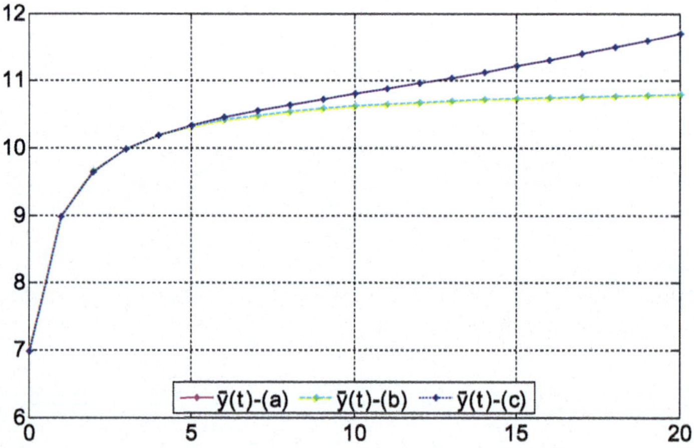

Fig. 5.13 Optimal total supply (E5.15)

Ad 3

Analyse how the optimal supplies and the optimal prices of the product supplied to both markets react to changes (*ceteris paribus*) in values of parameters describing the markets: market capacities, consumers' sensitivities to changes in a product price, production marginal cost. Analyse what the importance of differences in these values between two markets is.

Reactions of the optimal supply intended for i-th market ($i = 1, 2$), of the optimal total supply and of the optimal price on i-th market to a change in i-th market capacity are expressed as:

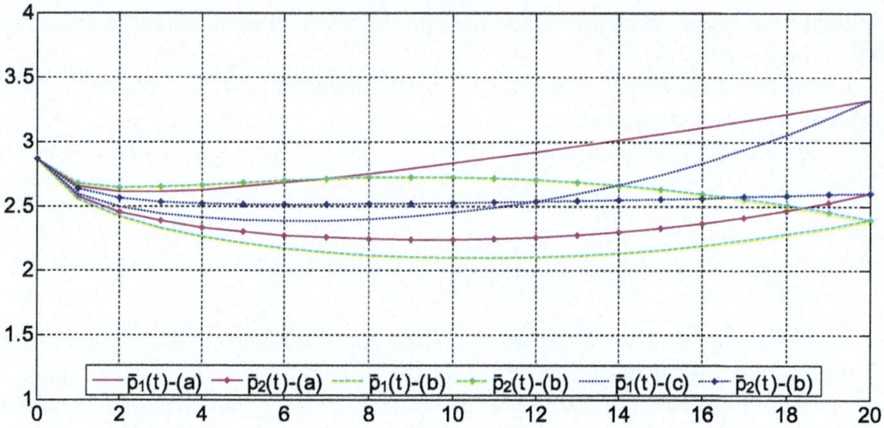

Fig. 5.14 Optimal prices on the first and second markets (E5.15)

$$\frac{\partial \overline{y}_i(t)}{\partial b_i(t)} = \frac{1}{2}\ \frac{\partial \overline{y}(t)}{\partial b_i(t)} = \frac{1}{2}, \qquad \frac{\partial \overline{p}_i(t)}{\partial b(t)} = \frac{1}{2a_i(t)} > 0 \quad i = 1, 2$$

and mean that when the capacity of i-the market increases $c.p.$ (*ceteris paribus*) by one physical unit, then the optimal supply intended for i-th market increases by 0.5 of the physical unit, the optimal total supply increases the same and the optimal price on i-th market increases.

Reactions of the optimal supply intended for i-th market ($i = 1, 2$), of the optimal total supply and of the optimal price on i-th market to a change in the sensitivity of i-th market consumers to changes in a price of the product on i-th market are expressed as:

$$\frac{\partial \overline{y}_i(t)}{\partial a_i(t)} = -\frac{1}{2}c(t) < 0, \qquad \frac{\partial \overline{y}(t)}{\partial a_i(t)} = -\frac{1}{2}c(t) < 0, \qquad \frac{\partial \overline{p}_i(t)}{\partial b(t)} = -\frac{b_i(t)}{2(a_i(t))^2} < 0, \qquad i = 1, 2$$

and mean that when the sensitivity of consumers on i-the market increases $c.p.$ (*ceteris paribus*), then the optimal supply intended for i-th market decreases, the optimal total supply decreases the same and the optimal price on i-th market decreases as well.

Reactions of the optimal supply intended for i-th market ($i = 1, 2$), of the optimal total supply and of the optimal price on i-th market to a change in the marginal cost of production are expressed as:

$$\frac{\partial \overline{y}_i(t)}{\partial c(t)} = -\frac{1}{2}a_i(t) < 0, \qquad \frac{\partial \overline{y}(t)}{\partial c(t)} = -\frac{1}{2}(a_1(t) + a_2(t)) < 0, \qquad \frac{\partial \overline{p}_i(t)}{\partial c(t)} = \frac{1}{2}, \qquad i = 1, 2$$

and mean that when the marginal cost of production increases $c.p.$ (*ceteris paribus*) by one money unit, then the optimal supply intended for i-th market decreases, the optimal total supply decreases while the optimal price on each market increases by 0.5 of the money unit.

Let us recall the form of the optimal supply intended for i-th market and of the optimal price on i-th market:

$$\overline{y}_i(t) = \frac{b_i(t) - a_i(t)c(t)}{2} \quad i = 1, 2$$
$$\overline{p}_i(t) = \frac{1}{2}\left(\frac{b_i(t)}{a_i(t)} + c(t)\right) \quad i = 1, 2.$$

From the forms of these values, it results that the bigger is the capacity of i-th market, the higher price can be set by the monopoly and the bigger supply is intended for this market. It results also that the bigger is the sensitivity of i-th market consumers to changes in a price of the product on i-th market, the lower price has to be set by the monopoly and the smaller supply is intended for this market. Finally, it results that the bigger is the production marginal cost, the higher price is set by the monopoly on each market and the smaller supply is intended for each market.

E5.16. Two producers having equal positions act on a market of some homogeneous product. The demand for this product evolves according to a demand function:

$$y^d(p) = -ap + b, \quad a, b > 0.$$

Production total costs for the first and for the second firm, respectively, are as follows:

$$c_1^{tot}(y_1) = c_1 y_1 + d_1, \quad c_1, d_1 > 0,$$
$$c_2^{tot}(y_2) = c_2 y_2 + d_2, \quad c_2, d_2 > 0.$$

The total output by both producers matches the demand for the product reported by consumers by a given price:

$$y_1 + y_2 = y^d(p).$$

1. Determine an equilibrium state in the Cournot duopoly model by the following assumptions:

   (a) $a = 2, \quad b = 20, \quad c_1 = 1, \quad c_2 = 1,$
   (b) $a = 2, \quad b = 20, \quad c_1 = 2, \quad c_2 = 1,$
   (c) $a = 2, \quad b = 200, \quad c_1 = 2, \quad c_2 = 1.$

2. Present a mechanism of reaching the equilibrium state when:

   (a) the first producer decides about the level of supply as first, assuming the competitor's supply equals 0,

(b) the second producer decides about the level of supply as first, assuming the competitor's supply equals 0.

State what the number of iterations in determining the levels of supply by each producer needed to reach the equilibrium state is.

3. Present trajectories of the optimal supplies by both producers.

Solutions

Ad 1

Determine an equilibrium state in the Cournot duopoly model.

From the description of the Cournot duopoly model,[14] one knows a form of reaction lines of producers:

$$\overline{y}_1 = \frac{b - ac_1}{2} - \frac{y_2}{2} \quad RL_1$$
$$\overline{y}_2 = \frac{b - ac_2}{2} - \frac{y_1}{2} \quad RL_2,$$

a form of optimal supplies by the producers:

$$\overline{\mathbf{y}}^{(C)} = \left(\overline{y}_1^{(C)}, \overline{y}_2^{(C)}\right) = \left(\frac{b - a(2c_1 - c_2)}{3}, \frac{b - a(2c_2 - c_1)}{3}\right)$$

and a form of optimal price of their product:

$$\overline{p}^{(C)} = \frac{b + a(c_1 + c_2)}{3a}$$

$$a = 2, \quad b = 20, \quad c_1 = 1, \quad c_2 = 1,$$

(a) $\overline{y}_1^{(C)} = \overline{y}_2^{(C)} = \dfrac{20 - 2(2 \cdot 1 - 1)}{3} = 6$

$$\overline{y}^{(C)} = \overline{y}_1^{(C)} + \overline{y}_2^{(C)} = 12 \quad \overline{p}^{(C)} = \frac{20 + 2(1 + 1)}{3 \cdot 2} = 4$$
$$a = 2, \quad b = 20, \quad c_1 = 2, \quad c_2 = 1,$$

(b) $\overline{y}_1^{(C)} = \dfrac{20 - 2(2 \cdot 2 - 1)}{3} \approx 4.67 \quad \overline{y}_2^{(C)} = \dfrac{20 - 2(2 \cdot 1 - 2)}{3} \approx 6.67$

$$\overline{y}^{(C)} = \overline{y}_1^{(C)} + \overline{y}_2^{(C)} \approx 11.33 \quad \overline{p}^{(C)} = \frac{20 + 2(2 + 1)}{3 \cdot 2} \approx 4.33$$

[14] Having the standard assumptions that the demand function and the functions of production total cost are linear.

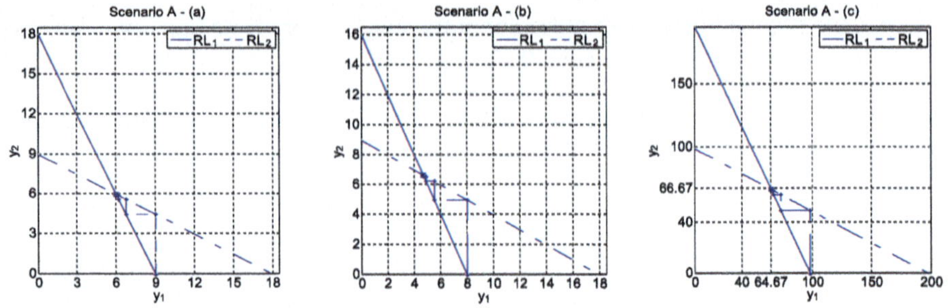

Fig. 5.15 Mechanism of reaching equilibrium state—first producer decides as first (E5.16)

$$a = 2, \quad b = 200, \quad c_1 = 2, \quad c_2 = 1$$

(c) $$\overline{y}_1^{(C)} = \frac{200 - 2(2 \cdot 2 - 1)}{3} \approx 64.67 \quad \overline{y}_2^{(C)} = \frac{200 - 2(2 \cdot 1 - 2)}{3} \approx 66.67$$

$$\overline{y}^{(C)} = \overline{y}_1^{(C)} + \overline{y}_2^{(C)} \approx 131.33 \quad \overline{p}^{(C)} = \frac{200 + 2(2 + 1)}{3 \cdot 2} \approx 34.33$$

Ad 2

Present a mechanism of reaching the equilibrium state.

State what the number of iterations in determining the levels of supply by each producer needed to reach the equilibrium state is.

(A) The first producer decides about the level of supply as first, assuming the competitor's supply equals 0 (Fig. 5.15).

  (a) The equilibrium supply is obtained by the first producer in 17-th iteration,[15] by the second producer in 18-th iteration. Thus, the equilibrium state is reached in 18-th iteration.
  (b) The equilibrium supply is obtained by the first producer in 17-th iteration, by the second producer in 18-th iteration. Thus, the equilibrium state is reached in 18-th iteration.
  (c) The equilibrium supply is obtained by the first producer in 21-st iteration, by the second producer in 20-th iteration. Thus, the equilibrium state is reached in 21-st iteration.

(B) The second producer decides about the level of supply as first, assuming the competitor's supply equals 0 (Fig. 5.16).

[15] In a MATLAB file called Exercise_5_16.m one can find commands to obtain the numbers of iteration in which the equilibrium supplies are reached:

t1_A = find(abs(y1-yC1) < 0.00009)and t2_A = find(abs(y2-yC2) < 0.00009).

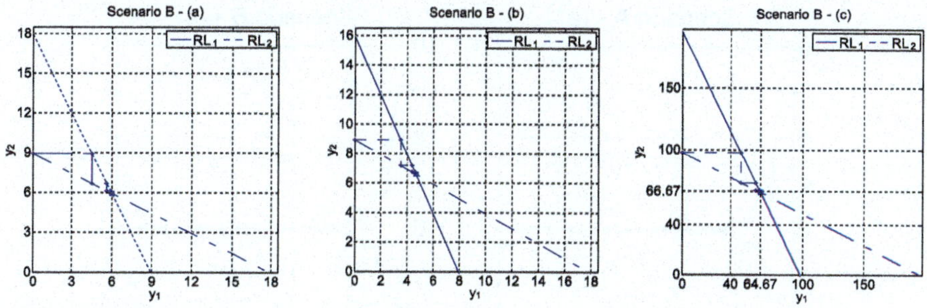

Fig. 5.16 Mechanism of reaching equilibrium state—second producer decides as first (E5.16)

(a) The equilibrium supply is obtained by the first producer in 18-th iteration,[16] by the second producer in 17-th iteration. Thus, the equilibrium state is reached in 18-th iteration.
(b) The equilibrium supply is obtained by the first producer in 16-th iteration, by the second producer in 17-th iteration. Thus, the equilibrium state is reached in 17-th iteration.
(c) The equilibrium supply is obtained by the first producer in 20-th iteration, by the second producer in 21-th iteration. Thus, the equilibrium state is reached in 21-st iteration.

Ad 3

Present trajectories of the optimal supplies by both producers (Figs. 5.17, 5.18 and 5.19).

E5.17. Two producers act on a market of some homogeneous product. The first of them has a position of the leader and the other a position of the follower. The demand for this product evolves according to a demand function:

$$y^d(p(t)) = -2p(t) + 20, \qquad a(t), b(t) > 0.$$

The total output by both producers matches the demand for the product reported by consumers by a given price:

$$y_1(t) + y_2(t) = y^d(p(t)).$$

Production total costs for the leader and for the follower, respectively, are as follows:

$$c_1^{tot}(y_1(t)) = c_1(t)y_1 + 1,$$

[16] In a MATLAB file called Exercise_5_16.m one can find commands to obtain the numbers of iteration in which the equilibrium supplies are reached:
T1_A = find(abs(Y1-yC1) < 0.00009)and T2_A = find(abs(Y2-yC2) < 0.00009).

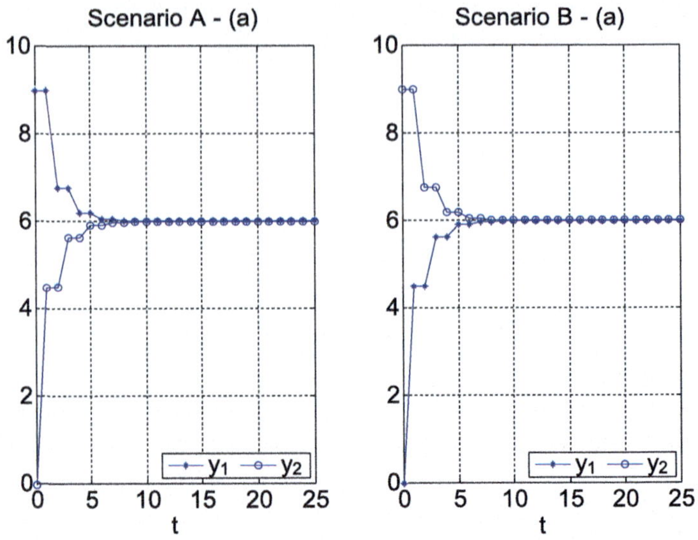

Fig. 5.17 Trajectories of optimal supplies by both producers—(a) (E5.16)

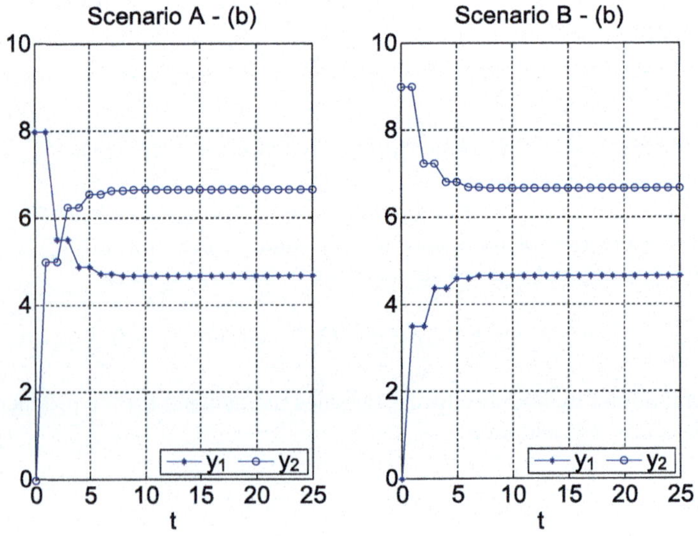

Fig. 5.18 Trajectories of optimal supplies by both producers—(b) (E5.16)

$$c_2^{tot}(y_2(t)) = 2.5y_2(t) + 1,$$

where

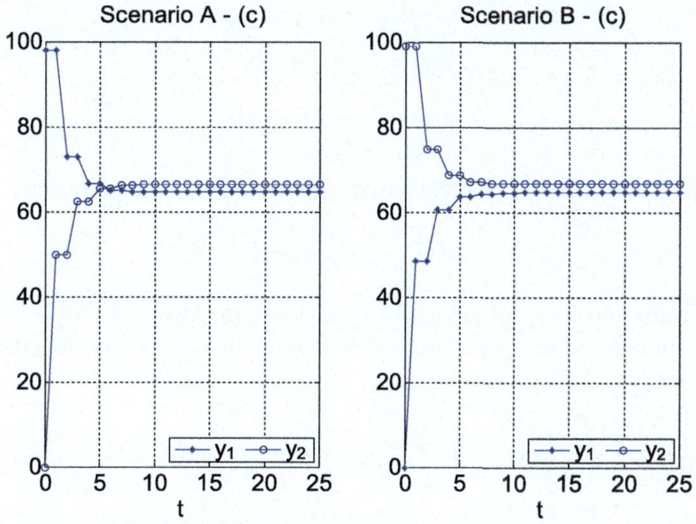

Fig. 5.19 Trajectories of optimal supplies by both producers—(c) (E5.16)

$$c_1(t) = -\frac{5}{16}t + 6\frac{1}{4}, \quad \forall t \in [0; 20].$$

1. Determine an equation describing a line of reaction of the follower and an equilibrium state in the Stackelberg duopoly model when the production marginal cost for the leader varies in time. Present a graph of the follower's reaction line and the equilibrium states depending on changes in the marginal cost for the leader.
2. At which moment are marginal costs for the leader and for the follower equal? What are then their shares in the market of a product?
3. Present trajectories of the optimal supplies by the leader and by the follower.

Solutions

Ad 1

Determine an equation describing a line of reaction of the follower and an equilibrium state in the Stackelberg duopoly model when the production marginal cost for the leader varies in time. Present a graph of the follower's reaction line and the equilibrium states depending on changes in the marginal cost for the leader.

The profit function of the follower takes a form:

$$\pi_2(y_2(t)) = r_2(y_2(t)) - c_2^{tot}(y_2(t)) = p(t) \cdot y_2(t) - c_2^{tot}(y_2(t)).$$

We need first to derive an inverted functions $p(y(t))$ of the consumer demand:

$$y(t) = -2p(t) + 20$$
$$2p(t) = -y(t) + 20$$
$$p(t) = -\frac{1}{2}y(t) + 10.$$

The total supply on the market consists of supplies by both producers:

$$y(t) = y_1(t) + y_2(t).$$

Substituting the inverted function of the consumer demand into the follower's profit function and using the form of the production total cost function for the follower, we get:

$$\begin{aligned}
\pi_2(y_2(t)) &= \left(-\frac{1}{2}y(t) + 10\right) \cdot y_2(t) - (2.5y_2(t) + 1) \\
&= \left[-\frac{1}{2}(y_1(t) + y_2(t)) + 10\right] \cdot y_2(t) - (2.5y_2(t) + 1) \\
&= (10 - 2.5)y_2(t) - \frac{1}{2}(y_2(t))^2 - \frac{1}{2}y_1(t)y_2(t) - 1 \\
&= 7.5y_2(t) - \frac{1}{2}(y_2(t))^2 - \frac{1}{2}y_1(t)y_2(t) - 1 = \pi_2(y_1(t), y_2(t)).
\end{aligned}$$

Since among variables $y_1(t)$, $y_2(t)$, the second producer can decide only about $y_2(t)$ the necessary condition for existence of a maximum of this function takes the form of one equation:

$$\frac{d\pi_2(y_1(t), y_2(t))}{dy_2(t)} = 7.5 - y_2(t) - \frac{1}{2}y_1(t) = 0$$

and gives the reaction line of the follower (Fig. 5.20):

$$\overline{y}_2(t) = 7.5 - \frac{1}{2}y_1(t).$$

The sufficient condition for existence of a maximum of the follower's profit function takes a form:

$$\frac{d^2\pi_2(y_1(t), y_2(t))}{dy_2(t)^2} = -1 < 0$$

and is satisfied.

The profit function of the leader takes a form:

$$\pi_1(y_1(t)) = r_1(y_1(t)) - c_1^{tot}(y_2(t)) = p(t) \cdot y_1(t) - c_1^{tot}(y_1(t)).$$

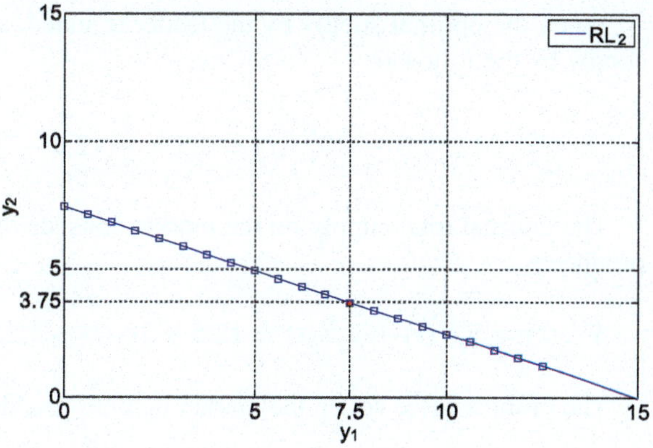

Fig. 5.20 Reaction line of follower and equilibrium states depending on production marginal costs (E5.17)

Substituting the inverted function of the consumer demand and the supply by the follower found above into the leader's profit function and using the form of the production total cost function for the leader, we get:

$$
\begin{aligned}
\pi_1(y_1(t)) &= \left[-\frac{1}{2}(y_1(t) + y_2(t)) + 10\right] \cdot y_1(t) - (c_1(t)y_1(t) + 1) \\
&= (10 - c_1(t))y_1(t) - \frac{1}{2}(y_1(t))^2 - \frac{1}{2}y_1(t)y_2(t) - 1 \\
&= (10 - c_1(t))y_1(t) - \frac{1}{2}(y_1(t))^2 - \frac{1}{2}y_1(t)\left(7.5 - \frac{1}{2}y_1(t)\right) - 1 \\
&= (6.25 - c_1(t))y_1(t) - \frac{1}{4}(y_1(t))^2 - 1
\end{aligned}
$$

The necessary condition for existence of a maximum of this function takes a form:

$$\frac{d\pi_1(y_1(t))}{dy_1(t)} = 6.25 - c_1(t) - \frac{1}{2}y_1(t) = 0$$

and gives the optimal supply by the leader:

$$\overline{y_1}^{(S)}(t) = 12.5 - 2c_1(t).$$

The sufficient condition for existence of a maximum of the leader's profit function takes a form:

$$\frac{d^2\pi_1(y_1(t))}{dy_1(t)^2} = -2c_1(t) < 0$$

and is satisfied whenever the marginal cost of production $c_1(t)$ is positive.

When the optimal supply by the leader is stated, one can determine the optimal supply by the follower:

$$\overline{y}_2^{(S)}(t) = 7.5 - \frac{1}{2}\overline{y}_1^{(S)}(t) = 7.5 - \frac{1}{2}(12.5 - 2c_1(t)) = 1.25 + c_1(t).$$

The optimal total supply on the market consists of the optimal supplies by both producers:

$$\overline{y}^{(S)}(t) = \overline{y}_1^{(S)}(t) + \overline{y}_2^{(S)}(t) = 12.5 - 2c_1(t) + 1.25 + c_1(t) = 13.75 - c_1(t).$$

The optimal price set on the market by both producers takes a form:

$$\overline{p}^{(S)}(t) = p^{(S)}\left(\overline{y}^{(S)}(t)\right) = -\frac{1}{2}\overline{y}^{(S)}(t) + 10 = -\frac{1}{2}(13.75 - c_1(t)) + 10 = 3.125 + c_1(t).$$

Ad 2

At which moment are marginal costs for the leader and for the follower equal? What are then their shares in the market of a product?

The production marginal costs have the same value for both producers at moment $t = 12$: $c_1(12) = c_2(12) = 2.5$. Then the equilibrium state is $\overline{\mathbf{y}}^{(S)}(12) = \left(\overline{y}_1^{(S)}(12), \overline{y}_1^{(S)}(12)\right) = (7.5, 3.75)$. Their shares in the market of the product are:

$$\overline{U}_1^{(S)}(12) = \frac{7.5}{7.5 + 3.75} \approx 0.67 \quad \text{for the leader}$$
$$\overline{U}_1^{(S)}(12) = \frac{3.55}{7.5 + 3.75} \approx 0.33 \quad \text{for the follower.}$$

Ad 3

Present trajectories of the optimal supplies by the leader and by the follower.

In Fig. 5.21, we can notice that at moment $t = 8$, both producers have the same optimal supplies. At this moment, the production marginal cost for the leader is:

$$c_1(8) = -\frac{5}{16} \cdot 8 + 6.25 = 3.75.$$

Then the optimal supplies are obtained as:

$$\overline{y}_1^{(S)}(8) = 12.5 - 2 \cdot 3.75 = 12.5 - 7.5 = 5$$
$$\overline{y}_1^{(S)}(8) = 1.25 + 3.75 = 5.$$

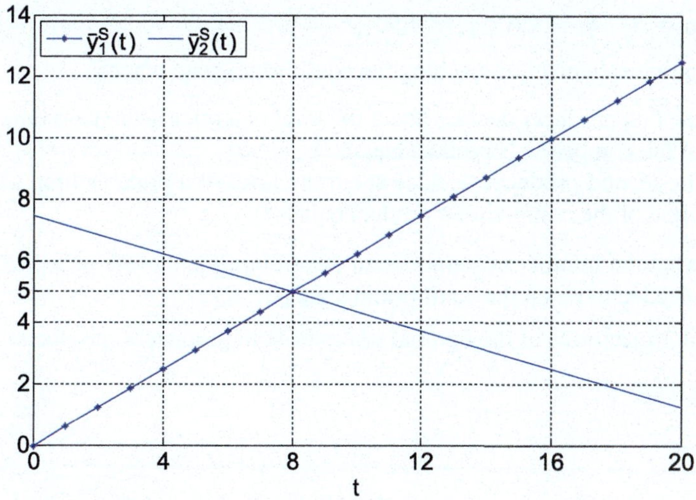

Fig. 5.21 Optimal supplies by leader and by follower (E5.17)

E5.18. Two producers having equal positions on a market offer two substitute products. The demand for these products evolves according to the following demand functions:

$$y_1^d(p_1, p_2) = -a_1 p_1 + \gamma_1 p_2 + b_1,$$
$$y_2^d(p_1, p_2) = -a_2 p_2 + \gamma_2 p_1 + b_2, \quad a_i, \gamma_i, b_i > 0, a_i > \gamma_i \quad i = 1, 2.$$

Production total costs for the first and for the second firm, respectively, are as follows:

$$c_1^{tot}(y_1) = c_1 y_1 + d_1, \quad c_1, d_1 > 0,$$
$$c_2^{tot}(y_2) = c_2 y_2 + d_2, \quad c_2, d_2 > 0.$$

An output level of each product matches the demand reported by consumers for this product by its given price:

$$y_i = y_i^d(p_1, p_2), \quad i = 1, 2.$$

1. Determine an equilibrium state in the Bertrand duopoly model by the following assumptions for $i = 1, 2$:

   (a) $a_i = 2, \quad b_i = 20, \quad \gamma_i = 1, \quad c_i = 1,$
   b) $a_i = 3, \quad b_i = 20, \quad \gamma_i = 1, \quad c_i = 1,$
   (c) $a_i = 2, \quad b_i = 21, \quad \gamma_i = 1, \quad c_i = 1,$
   (d) $a_i = 2, \quad b_i = 20, \quad \gamma_i = 1.9, \quad c_i = 1,$
   (e) $a_i = 2, \quad b_i = 20, \quad \gamma_i = 1, \quad c_i = 2,$

(f) $a_i = 3, \quad b_i = 21, \quad \gamma_i = 1.9, \quad c_i = 2.$

2. Present a mechanism of reaching the equilibrium state when:
   (a) the first producer decides about the level of a price as first, assuming a price of the competitor's product equals 0,
   (b) the second producer decides about the level of a price as first, assuming a price of the competitor's product equals 0.

State what the number of iterations in determining the levels of a price by each producer needed to reach the equilibrium state is.

3. Present trajectories of the optimal prices of both producers' products.

Solutions

Ad 1

Determine an equilibrium state in the Bertrand duopoly model.

From the description of the Bertrand duopoly model,[17] one knows a form of reaction lines of producers:

$$\overline{p}_1 = \frac{b_1 + a_1c_1}{2a_1} + \frac{\gamma_1}{2a_1}p_2 \qquad RL_1$$
$$p_2 = \frac{b_2 + a_2c_2}{2a_2} + \frac{\gamma_1}{2a_2}p_2 \qquad RL_2,$$

a form of optimal supplies by the producers:

$$\overline{p}_1^{(B)} = \frac{2a_2(b_1 + a_1c_1) + \gamma_1(b_2 + a_2c_2)}{4a_1a_2 - \gamma_1\gamma_2}$$
$$\overline{p}_2^{(B)} = \frac{2a_1(b_2 + a_2c_2) + \gamma_2(b_1 + a_1c_1)}{4a_1a_2 - \gamma_1\gamma_2}$$

and a form of optimal price of their product:

$$\overline{y}_1^{(B)} = \frac{a_1\left[2a_2(b_1 - a_1c_1) + \gamma_1(b_2 + a_2c_2 + \gamma_2c_1)\right]}{4a_1a_2 - \gamma_1\gamma_2}$$
$$\overline{y}_2^{(B)} = \frac{a_2\left[2a_1(b_2 - a_2c_2) + \gamma_2(b_1 + a_1c_1 + \gamma_1c_2)\right]}{4a_1a_2 - \gamma_1\gamma_2}.$$

(a) $a_i = 2, \quad b_i = 20, \quad \gamma_i = 1, \quad c_i = 1,$

$$\overline{p}_1^{(B)} = \overline{p}_2^{(B)} \approx 7.33 \qquad \overline{y}_1^{(B)} = \overline{y}_1^{(B)} \approx 12.67$$

[17] Having the standard assumptions that the demand function and the functions of production total cost are linear.

(b) $a_i = 3, \quad b_i = 20, \quad \gamma_i = 1, \quad c_i = 1,$

$$\overline{p}_1^{(B)} = \overline{p}_2^{(B)} = 4.6 \qquad \overline{y}_1^{(B)} = \overline{y}_1^{(B)} = 10.8$$

(c) $a_i = 2, \quad b_i = 21, \quad \gamma_i = 1, \quad c_i = 1,$

$$\overline{p}_1^{(B)} = \overline{p}_2^{(B)} \approx 7.67 \qquad \overline{y}_1^{(B)} = \overline{y}_1^{(B)} \approx 13.33$$

(d) $a_i = 2, \quad b_i = 20, \quad \gamma_i = 1.9, \quad c_i = 1,$

$$\overline{p}_1^{(B)} = \overline{p}_2^{(B)} \approx 10.48 \qquad \overline{y}_1^{(B)} = \overline{y}_1^{(B)} \approx 18.95$$

(e) $a_i = 2, \quad b_i = 20, \quad \gamma_i = 1, \quad c_i = 2,$

$$\overline{p}_1^{(B)} = \overline{p}_2^{(B)} = 8 \qquad \overline{y}_1^{(B)} = \overline{y}_1^{(B)} = 12$$

(f) $a_i = 3, \quad b_i = 21, \quad \gamma_i = 1.9, \quad c_i = 2$

$$\overline{p}_1^{(B)} = \overline{p}_2^{(B)} \approx 6.59 \qquad \overline{y}_1^{(B)} = \overline{y}_1^{(B)} \approx 13.75.$$

Ad 2

Present a mechanism of reaching the equilibrium state.[18]

State what the number of iterations in determining the levels of a price by each producer needed to reach the equilibrium state is.

(A) the first producer decides about the level of a price as first, assuming a price of the competitor's product equals 0 (Fig. 5.22; Table 5.10).
(B) the second producer decides about the level of a price as first, assuming a price of the competitor's product equals 0(Fig. 5.23; Table 5.11).

[18] We present the graphic results only for point (a). For the remaining points (b)–(f), the graphic results are similar.

Table 5.10 Number of iterations needed to reach the equilibrium supply—first producer decides as first[19]

	Number of iterations needed to reach the equilibrium supply		
	by the first producer	by the second producer	by both producers
(a)	9	10	10
(b)	7	8	8
(c)	9	10	10
(d)	17	16	17
(e)	9	10	10
(f)	11	10	11

Ad 3

Present trajectories of the optimal prices of both producers' products.[21] (Fig. 5.24)

Table 5.11 Number of iterations needed to reach the equilibrium supply—second producer decides as first[20]

	Number of iterations needed to reach the equilibrium supply		
	By the first producer	By the second producer	By both producers
(a)	10	9	10
(b)	8	7	8
(c)	10	9	10
(d)	16	17	17
(e)	10	9	10
(f)	10	11	11

[19] In a MATLAB file called Exercise_5_18.m one can find commands to obtain the numbers of iteration in which the equilibrium supplies are reached. t1_A = find(abs(p1-pB1) < 0.00009) and t2_A = find(abs(p2-pCB2) < 0.00009).

[20] In a MATLAB file called Exercise_5_18.m one can find commands to obtain the numbers of iteration in which the equilibrium supplies are reached. T1_A = find(abs(P1-pB1) < 0.00009) and T2_A = find(abs(P2-pCB2) < 0.00009).

[21] We present the trajectories only for point (a). For the remaining points (b)–(f) trajectories are similar.

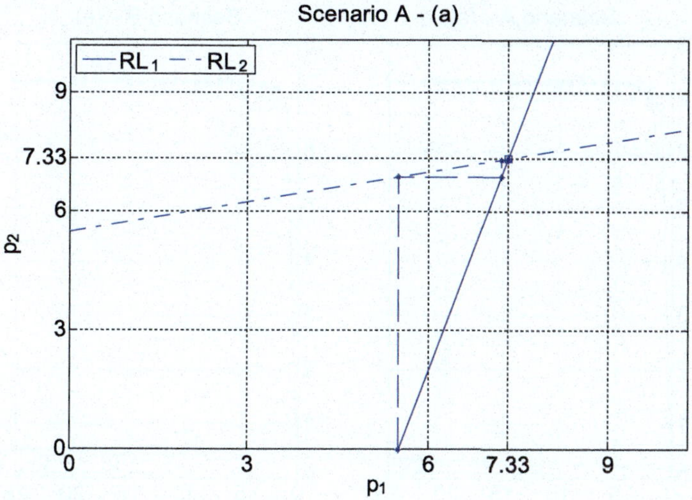

Fig. 5.22 Mechanism of reaching equilibrium state—first producer decides as first (E5.18)

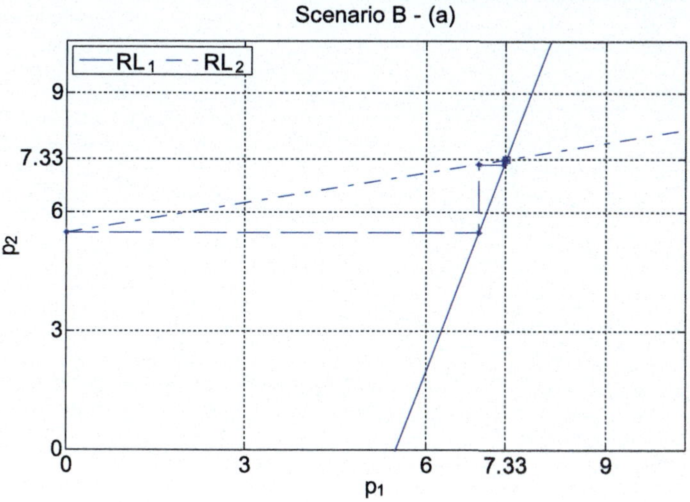

Fig. 5.23 Mechanism of reaching equilibrium state—second producer decides as first (E5.18)

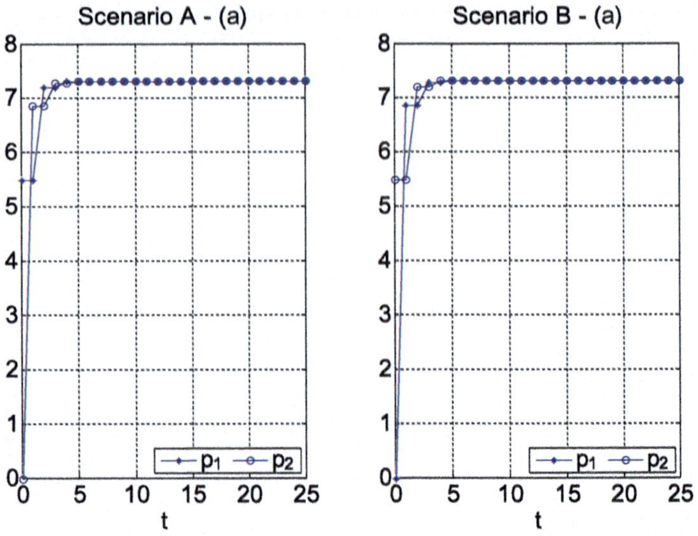

Fig. 5.24 Trajectories of optimal prices (E5.18)

Chapter 6
Rationality of Choices Made by Groups of Producers and Groups of Consumers

This Chapter presents 7 exercises that help in understanding the problem of describing behaviour of the community of consumers and producers. They concern two different types of static and dynamic two-commodity models: 1) with supply functions and functions of demand for a product that are defined exogenously, 2) with supply functions and functions of demand for a product that are defined endogenously—that is the Arrow-Debreu-McKenzie general equilibrium models. The dynamic models are considered in a discrete-time and in a continuous-time versions. In particular the focus of the exercises is to deal with a concept of the Walrasian general equilibrium and its existence, uniqueness and asymptotical global stability.

E6.1. There is a market of a homogeneous product with exogenously determined demand function: $y^d(p) = -ap^\alpha + b, \quad a, b > 0$ and supply function: $y^s(p) = cp^\alpha + d, \quad c, d > 0$.

1. For a product price, the demand and the supply levels determine intervals of values resulting from analytical forms of the demand and supply functions.
2. Draw graphs of both functions in space $\mathbb{R}^2_+$ (in one figure). Determine by what values of parameters $b, d > 0$ there exists the equilibrium price and indicate this price in the figure, when:

   (a) $\alpha \in (0; 1)$,
   (b) $\alpha = 1$,
   (c) $\alpha > 1$.

3. Determine the equilibrium price.
4. Determine elasticities of the equilibrium price with regard to parameters of the supply and the demand functions that determine this price and give their economic interpretation.

K. Sobczak and K. Malaga, *Workbook for Microeconomics*, Springer Texts in Business and Economics, https://doi.org/10.1007/978-3-031-41947-8_6

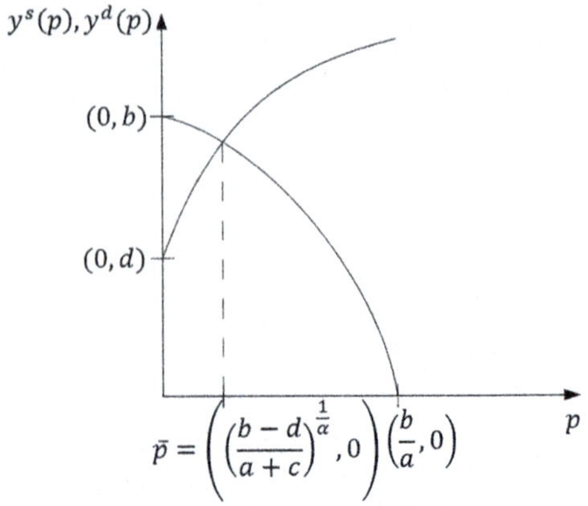

Fig. 6.1 Demand function and supply function, $\alpha \in (0; 1)$ (E.6.1a)

Solutions

Ad 1

$y^d(p) = -ap^\alpha + b, \quad a, b > 0 \quad$ and $\quad y^s(p) = cp^\alpha + d, \quad c, d > 0.$

If $\; p = 0 \;$ then $\; y^d(p) = b \;$ and $\; y^s(p) = d.$

If $\; y^d(p) = 0 \;$ then $\; -ap^\alpha + b = 0 \;$, so $\; p = \left(\frac{b}{a}\right)^{\frac{1}{\alpha}}.$

$$p \in \left[0; \left(\frac{b}{a}\right)^{\frac{1}{\alpha}}\right]$$
$$y^d(p) \in [0; b]$$
$$y^s(p) \in [d; +\infty).$$

Ad 2a (Fig. 6.1).

Ad 2b (Fig. 6.2).

Ad 2c (Fig. 6.3).

Ad 3a

$$\alpha \in (0; 1)$$

(1) $\exists_1 \overline{p} = \left(\frac{b-d}{a+c}\right)^{\frac{1}{\alpha}} > 0, \quad y^d(\overline{p}) = y^s(\overline{p}), \quad \forall b, d > 0, \quad b > d$

(2) $\exists_1 \overline{p} = 0, \quad y^d(\overline{p}) = y^s(\overline{p}), \quad \forall b, d > 0, \quad b = d$

3) $\neg \exists \overline{p} \geq 0, \quad y^d(\overline{p}) = y^s(\overline{p}), \quad \forall b, d > 0, \quad d > b.$

Ad 3b

$$\alpha = 1$$

Fig. 6.2 Demand function and supply function, $\alpha = 1$ (E.6.1b)

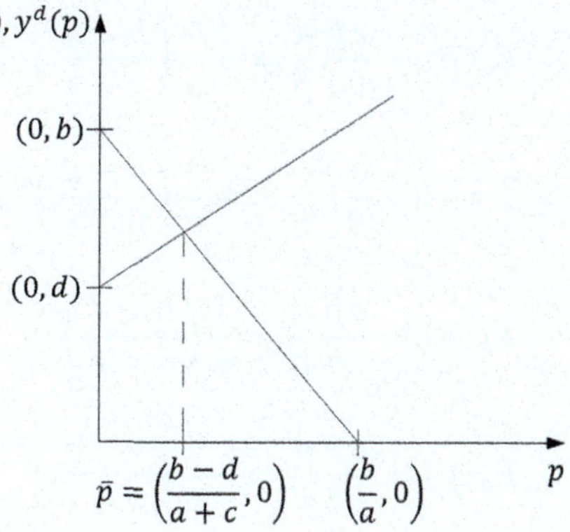

Fig. 6.3 Demand function and supply function, $\alpha > 1$ (E.6.1c)

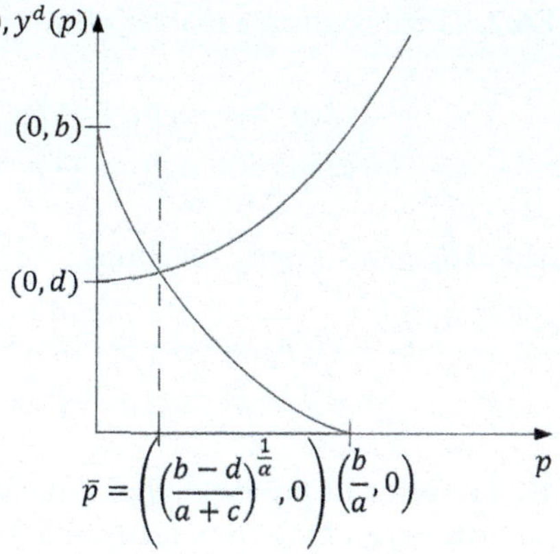

$$\begin{aligned}
&(1)\quad \exists_1 \overline{p} = \tfrac{b-d}{a+c} > 0, \quad y^d(\overline{p}) = y^s(\overline{p}), \quad \forall b, d > 0, \quad b > d\\
&(2)\quad \exists_1 \overline{p} = 0, \quad y^d(\overline{p}) = y^s(\overline{p}), \quad \forall b, d > 0, \quad b = d\\
&(3)\quad \neg\exists \overline{p} \geq 0, \quad y^d(\overline{p}) = y^s(\overline{p}), \quad \forall b, d > 0, \quad d > b.
\end{aligned}$$

Ad 3c

$$\alpha > 1$$

$$\begin{aligned}
&(1)\quad \exists_1 \overline{p} = \left(\tfrac{b-d}{a+c}\right)^{\frac{1}{\alpha}} > 0, \quad y^d(\overline{p}) = y^s(\overline{p}), \quad \forall b, d > 0, \quad b > d\\
&(2)\quad \exists_1 \overline{p} = 0, \quad y^d(\overline{p}) = y^s(\overline{p}), \quad \forall b, d > 0, \quad b = d\\
&(3)\quad \neg\exists \overline{p} \geq 0, \quad y^d(\overline{p}) = y^s(\overline{p}), \quad \forall b, d > 0, \quad d > b.
\end{aligned}$$

Ad 4

$$\exists_1 \overline{p} = \left(\frac{b-d}{a+c}\right)^{\frac{1}{\alpha}} > 0$$

$$E_a(\overline{p}) = \frac{\partial \overline{p}}{\partial a}\frac{a}{\overline{p}} = -\frac{1}{\alpha}\left(\frac{b-d}{a+c}\right)^{\frac{1}{\alpha}-1}\frac{(b-d)}{(a+c)^2}\frac{a}{\left(\frac{b-d}{a+c}\right)^{\frac{1}{\alpha}}} = -\frac{a}{\alpha(a+c)} < 0[\%]$$

$$E_c(\overline{p}) = \frac{\partial \overline{p}}{\partial c}\frac{c}{\overline{p}} = -\frac{1}{\alpha}\left(\frac{b-d}{a+c}\right)^{\frac{1}{\alpha}-1}\frac{(b-d)}{(a+c)^2}\frac{c}{\left(\frac{b-d}{a+c}\right)^{\frac{1}{\alpha}}} = -\frac{c}{\alpha(a+c)} < 0[\%]$$

$$E_b(\overline{p}) = \frac{\partial \overline{p}}{\partial b}\frac{b}{\overline{p}} = \frac{1}{\alpha}\left(\frac{b-d}{a+c}\right)^{\frac{1}{\alpha}-1}\frac{b}{(a+c)}\frac{1}{\left(\frac{b-d}{a+c}\right)^{\frac{1}{\alpha}}} = \frac{b}{\alpha(b-d)} > 0[\%]$$

$$E_d(\overline{p}) = \frac{\partial \overline{p}}{\partial d}\frac{d}{\overline{p}} = -\frac{1}{\alpha}\left(\frac{b-d}{a+c}\right)^{\frac{1}{\alpha}-1}\frac{d}{(a+c)}\frac{1}{\left(\frac{b-d}{a+c}\right)^{\frac{1}{\alpha}}} = -\frac{d}{\alpha(b-d)} < 0[\%].$$

E6.2. There is given a market of two products with exogenous demand functions:

$$y_1^d(\mathbf{p}) = -a_1 p_1 + \gamma_1 p_2 + b_1,$$
$$y_2^d(\mathbf{p}) = -a_2 p_2 + \gamma_2 p_1 + b_2, \quad a_i, b_i, \gamma_i > 0, \quad i = 1, 2$$

and exogenous supply functions:

$$y_1^s(\mathbf{p}) = c_1 p_1 + \delta_1 p_2 + d_1,$$
$$y_2^s(\mathbf{p}) = c_2 p_2 + \delta_2 p_1 + d_2, \quad c_i, d_i, \delta_i > 0, \quad i = 1, 2.$$

1. For price of products, the demand and the supply levels determine intervals of values resulting from analytical forms of the demand and supply functions.
2. Check if the two products are:
   (a) independent,
   (b) complementary,
   (c) substitute,

to each other.

3. Draw graphs of these functions in space $\mathbb{R}_+^3$ (in one figure). Determine by what values of parameters $b_i, d_i > 0$ $(i = 1, 2)$ there exists the equilibrium price vector and indicate this vector in the figure.
4. Determine the equilibrium price vector.
5. Determine elasticities of the equilibrium prices with regard to parameters of the supply and the demand functions that determine the prices and give economic interpretation of these elasticities.

Solutions

Ad 1- 2a Independents Products

$$y_1^d(p_1) = -a_1 p_1 + b_1, \quad y_2^d(p_2) = -a_2 p_2 + b_2, \quad a_i, b_i, \gamma_i > 0, \quad i = 1, 2$$

Fig. 6.4 Demand function and supply function, first product (E.6.2)

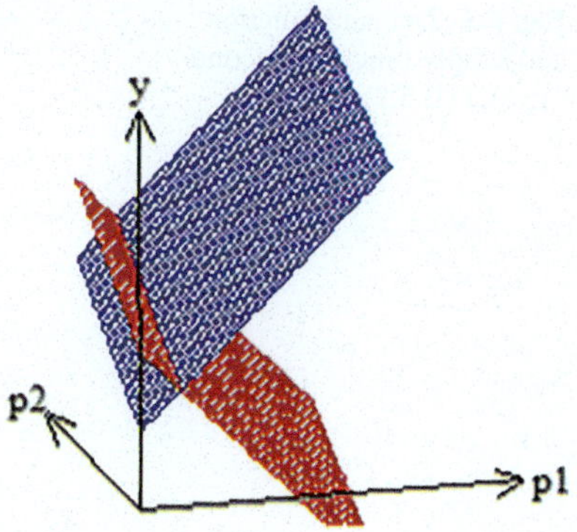

$$y_1^s(p_1) = c_1 p_1 + d_1, \quad y_2^s(p_2) = c_2 p_2 + d_2, \quad c_i, d_i, \delta_i > 0, \quad i = 1, 2$$
$$y_1^d(p_1) \in [0; b_1], \quad y_2^d(p_2) \in [0; b_2]$$
$$y_1^s(p_1) \in [d_1; +\infty), \quad y_2^s(p_2) \in [d_2; +\infty)$$
$$p_1 \in \left[0; \frac{b_1}{a_1}\right], \quad p_2 \in \left[0; \frac{b_2}{a_2}\right].$$

Ad 3

Since we are interested only in positive prices, the equilibrium price vector exists when $b_1 > d_1$ and $b_2 > d_2$. These two conditions have to be satisfied simultaneously.

We present figures for exemplary values of the demand functions and the supply functions:

$$y_1^d(\mathbf{p}) = -a_1 p_1 + \gamma_1 p_2 + b_1 = -p_1 + \frac{1}{2} p_2 + 2$$
$$y_1^s(\mathbf{p}) = c_1 p_1 + \delta_1 p_2 + d_1 = p_1 + \frac{1}{2} p_2 + 1$$

and $b_1 = 2 > 1 = d_1$

$$y_2^d(\mathbf{p}) = -a_2 p_2 + \gamma_2 p_1 + b_2 = -2p_2 + \frac{1}{2} p_1 + 2$$
$$y_2^s(\mathbf{p}) = c_2 p_2 + \delta_2 p_1 + d_2 = 2p_2 + \frac{1}{2} p_1 + 1$$

and $b_2 = 2 > 1 = d_2$ (Figs. 6.4 and 6.5).

There exists only one point belonging to all four planes. This point indicates the equilibrium price vector $\overline{\mathbf{p}} = (\overline{p}_1, \overline{p}_2) = \left(\frac{b_1 - d_1}{a_1 + c_1}, \frac{b_2 - d_2}{a_2 + c_2}\right) = \left(\frac{2-1}{1+1}, \frac{2-1}{2+2}\right) = \left(\frac{1}{2}, \frac{1}{4}\right)$ (Fig. 6.6).

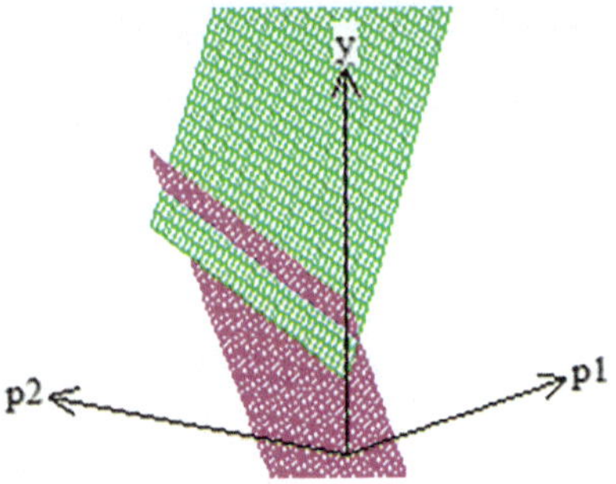

Fig. 6.5 Demand function and supply function, second product (E.6.2)

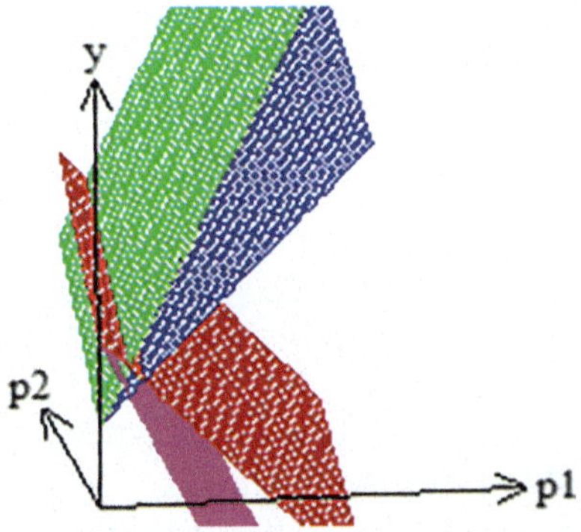

Fig. 6.6 Demand functions and supply functions, both products (E.6.2)

Ad 4

$$y_1^d(\overline{p}_1) = y_1^s(\overline{p}_1) \Rightarrow \overline{p}_1 = \frac{b_1 - d_1}{a_1 + c_1} \quad \text{if} \quad b_1 > d_1 \quad \text{then} \quad 0 < \overline{p}_1 < \frac{b_1}{a_1},$$
$$y_2^d(\overline{p}_2) = y_2^s(\overline{p}_2) \Rightarrow \overline{p}_2 = \frac{b_2 - d_2}{a_2 + c_2} \quad \text{if} \quad b_2 > d_2 \quad \text{then} \quad 0 < \overline{p}_2 < \frac{b_2}{a_2}.$$

Ad 5

$$E_x(\overline{p}_i) = \frac{d\overline{p}_i}{dx}\frac{x}{\overline{p}_i}, \quad i = 1, 2,$$
$$E_{a_1}(\overline{p}_1) = -\frac{a_1}{a_1 + c_1} < 0, \quad E_{a_2}(\overline{p}_2) = -\frac{a_2}{a_2 + c_2} < 0,$$
$$E_{b_1}(\overline{p}_1) = \frac{1}{a_1 + c_1} > 0, \quad E_{b_2}(\overline{p}_2) = \frac{1}{a_2 + c_2} > 0$$
$$E_{c_1}(\overline{p}_1) = -\frac{c_1}{a_1 + c_1} < 0, \quad E_{c_2}(\overline{p}_2) = -\frac{c_2}{a_2 + c_2} < 0,$$
$$E_{d_1}(\overline{p}_1) = -\frac{1}{a_1 + c_1} < 0, \quad E_{c_2}(\overline{p}_2) = -\frac{1}{a_2 + c_2} < 0.$$

E6.3. Present the model of a market of a single good from Exercise E6.1 as:

(a) a dynamic discrete-time model,
(b) a dynamic continuous-time model.

Check whether in these models, Walras's law is satisfied for an excess demand function. Selecting proper values for parameter $\sigma > 0$ in the dynamic discrete-time model determine a feasible price trajectory for 10 subsequent periods: $t = 1, 2, \ldots, 10$.

Solutions

If $y^d(p(t)) = -ap(t)^\alpha + b$, $a, b > 0$, and the supply function $y^s(p(t)) = cp(t)^\alpha + d$, then:

$$z(p(t)) = y^d(p(t)) - y^s(p(t))$$
$$= -ap(t)^\alpha + b - cp(t)^\alpha - d = -(a + c)p(t)^\alpha + b - d$$

Ad a

Dynamic discrete-time model

(1) $p(t + 1) = p(t) + \sigma(-(a + c)p(t)^\alpha + b - d)$
(2) $p(0) = p_0 > 0$
(3) $t = 1, 2, \ldots, 10.$

Ad b

Dynamic continuous-time model

(1) $\frac{dp(t)}{dt} = \sigma(-(a + c)p(t)^a + b - d)$
(2) $p(0) = p_0 > 0$
(3) $t \in [0; 10]$.

E6.4. Present the model of a market of two goods from Exercise E6.2 as:

(a) a dynamic discrete-time model,
(b) a dynamic continuous-time model.

Check whether in these models Walras's law is satisfied for a vector function of the excess demand. Selecting proper values for parameter $\sigma > 0$ in the dynamic discrete-time model, determine feasible price trajectories for 10 subsequent periods: $t = 1, 2, \ldots, 10$.

Solution

In exercise E6.2, the static model of a market of two goods is given. The demand for goods is described by functions:

$$y_1^d(\mathbf{p}) = -a_1 p_1 + \gamma_1 p_2 + b_1$$

$$y_2^d(\mathbf{p}) = -a_2 p_2 + \gamma_2 p_1 + b_2 \quad a_i, b_i, \gamma_i > 0 \quad i = 1, 2.$$

The supply of goods is described by functions:

$$y_1^d(\mathbf{p}) = c_1 p_1 + \delta_1 p_2 + d_1$$
$$y_2^d(\mathbf{p}) = c_2 p_2 + \delta_2 p_1 + d_2 \quad c_i, d_i, \delta_i > 0 \quad i = 1, 2.$$

Functions of excess demand for goods take the following forms:

$$z_1(\mathbf{p}) = y_1^d(\mathbf{p}) - y_1^s(\mathbf{p}) = -a_1 p_1 + \gamma_1 p_2 + b_1 - (c_1 p_1 + \delta_1 p_2 + d_1)$$
$$= -(a_1 + c_1) p_1 + (\gamma_1 - \delta_1) p_2 + b_1 - d_1$$
$$z_2(\mathbf{p}) = y_2^d(\mathbf{p}) - y_2^s(\mathbf{p}) = -(a_2 + c_2) p_2 + (\gamma_2 - \delta_2) p_1 + b_2 - d_2.$$

A price vector of the Walrasian equilibrium $\overline{\mathbf{p}}$ is a solution to the following system:

$$\begin{cases} z_1(\mathbf{p}) = 0 \\ z_2(\mathbf{p}) = 0 \end{cases}$$

that gives

$$\begin{cases} -(a_1 + c_1)p_1 + (\gamma_1 - \delta_1)p_2 + b_1 - d_1 = 0 \\ -(a_2 + c_2)p_2 + (\gamma_2 - \delta_2)p_1 + b_2 - d_2 = 0 \end{cases}$$

$$\overline{\mathbf{p}} = \left(\frac{(\gamma_1 - \delta_1)(b_2 - d_2) + (b_1 - d_1)(a_2 + c_2)}{(a_1 + c_1)(a_2 + c_2) - (\gamma_1 - \delta_1)(\gamma_2 - \delta_2)}, \frac{(\gamma_2 - \delta_2)(b_1 - d_1) + (b_2 - d_2)(a_1 + c_1)}{(a_1 + c_1)(a_2 + c_2) - (\gamma_1 - \delta_1)(\gamma_2 - \delta_2)} \right).$$

(a) The dynamic discrete-time model has a form:

$$p_i(t+1) = p_i(t) + \sigma z_i(\mathbf{p}(t)) \quad i = 1, 2, \quad t = 0, 1, 2 \ldots$$
$$p_i(0) = \text{const.} > 0 \quad i = 1, 2$$

(b) The dynamic continuous-time mode has a form:

$$\frac{dp_i(t)}{dt} = \sigma z_i(\mathbf{p}(t)) \quad i = 1, 2, \quad t \in (0; +\infty)$$
$$p_i(0) = \text{const.} > 0 \quad i = 1, 2.$$

Let us recall the Walras's law:

$$\forall \mathbf{p} > 0 \quad \langle \mathbf{p}, \mathbf{z}(\mathbf{p}) \rangle = p_1 z_1(\mathbf{p}) + p_2 z_2(\mathbf{p}) = 0.$$

From the form of the excess demand function, one can notice tat in general, the Walras's law is not satisfied in the models considered in this exercise. But the equation

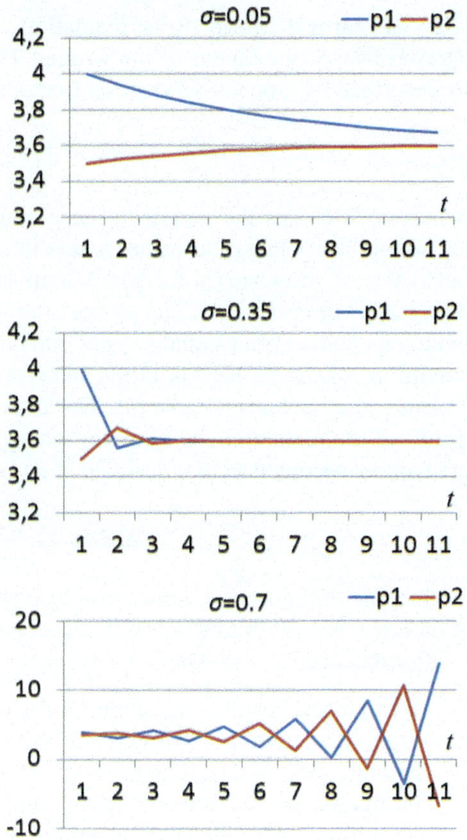

Fig. 6.7 Price trajectories in discrete-time model (E6.4)

of the Walras's law is satisfied for these models in a special case, when prices are the equilibrium prices:

$$\langle \overline{\mathbf{p}}, \mathbf{z}(\overline{\mathbf{p}}) \rangle = p_1 z_1(\overline{\mathbf{p}}) + p_2 z_2(\overline{\mathbf{p}}) = 0$$

since $z_1(\overline{\mathbf{p}}) = 0$ and $z_2(\overline{\mathbf{p}}) = 0$.

Let us now consider different values for parameter σ, to see by which values of this parameter we get feasible price trajectories. When $\sigma = 0.05$, the price trajectories are feasible but the equilibrium is not reached in time horizon $T = 10$. When $\sigma = 0.35$, the price trajectories are feasible and the equilibrium is reached in period $t = 5$. When $\sigma = 0.7$, the price trajectories are not feasible. The price trajectories[1] in all three cases are presented in Fig. 6.7.

E6.5. owner of a strawberry plantation hires one worker who has 24 units of time. The employee can allocate part of the time to work and part to rest. He/she owns

[1] The price trajectories are obtained in a file called Exercise 6.4.xlsx.

20% of shares in profits of the plantation. The only production factor in producing strawberries is the labour of the worker. The process of production of strawberries is described by a power production function of a form:

$$w_1 = f(n_2) = n_2^{0.5},$$

where w_1 denotes the output in the production process and n_2 denotes the input of labour. The plantation owner wants to maximize her/his profit from production and sales of strawberries for which their market price equals p_1 per unit (e.g. one kilogram, one crate, etc.). The source of production cost is hiring the labour force for which its market price equals p_2 per one hour. The plantation owner, as a consumer, wants to maximize her/his utility $u^1(x_{11})$ described as an increasing function of consumed strawberries' quantity. Her/his income consists of 80% of shares in the profit of the plantation. The worker wants to maximize her/his utility described as an increasing function of consumed strawberries' quantity and of leisure:

$$u^2(x_{21}, x_{22}) = x_{21}^{0.5} x_{22}^{0.3}.$$

Income of the worker consists of 20% of shares in the profit of the plantation and a money value of 24 time units allocated partly to work and partly to leisure.

For the static Arrow-Debreu-McKenzie model:

1. Write a space of the net output of the strawberries' plantation. Note: according to the description of the exercise the input n_1 of strawberries equals 0. While labour is not produced, hence $w_2 = 0$.
2. Formulate and solve the profit maximization problem for the plantation owner.
3. Formulate and solve the consumption utility maximization problems for the plantation owner and for the worker.
4. Write a form of an excess demand function.
5. Determine a system of general equilibrium conditions and a Walrasian equilibrium price vector.
6. Determine components of a Walrasian equilibrium allocation.

Solutions

Ad 1

Write a space of the net output of the strawberries' plantation. Note: according to the description of the exercise, the input n_1 of strawberries equals 0. While labour is not produced, hence $w_2 = 0$.

A vector of the net output of the strawberries' plantation is given as:

$$\begin{aligned}\mathbf{y}^1 &= (w_1 - n_1, w_2 - n_2) = (w_1 - 0, 0 - n_2) \\ &= (w_1, -n_2), \quad \text{where} \quad w_1 \le n_2^{0.5},\ n_2 \ge 0\end{aligned}$$

Hence, the space of the net output of the strawberries' plantation can be written in the following way:

$$Y^1 = \{\mathbf{y}^1 \in \mathbb{R}^2 : \mathbf{y}^1 = (w_1, -n_2),\ \text{where} w_1 \le n_2^{0.5}, n_2 \ge 0\}.$$

Ad 2

Formulate and solve the profit maximization problem for the plantation owner.

The profit maximization problem for the plantation owner takes a form:

$$\begin{aligned} &w_1 = f(n_2) = n_2^{0.5} \\ &\pi(n_2) = p_1 w_1 - p_2 n_2 = p_1 n_2^{0.5} - p_2 n_2 \\ &\pi(n_2) \to \max \quad n_2 \ge 0 \end{aligned}$$

The decision variable for the plantation owner is an input n_2 of labour. Hence, a necessary condition for existence of a maximum of the profit function takes the following form:

$$\frac{\mathrm{d}\pi(n_2)}{\mathrm{d}n_2} = 0.5 p_1 n_2^{-0.5} - p_2 = 0$$

and gives the optimal input of labour:

$$\overline{n}_2 = \left(\frac{p_1}{2p_2}\right)^2.$$

A sufficient condition for existence of a maximum of the profit function takes a form:

$$\frac{\mathrm{d}^2\pi(n_2)}{\mathrm{d}n_2^2} = -0.25 p_1 n_2^{-1.5} < 0$$

and is satisfied since $p_1 > 0$.

The maximum profit obtained in the plantation is:

$$\max \pi(n_2) = \pi(\overline{n}_2) = p_1 \overline{n}_2^{0.5} - p_2 \overline{n}_2 = p_1 \cdot \frac{p_1}{2p_2} - p_2 \left(\frac{p_1}{2p_2}\right)^2 = \frac{p_1^2}{4p_2} = \pi(\mathbf{p}).$$

The optimal supply of strawberries is:

$$\overline{w}_1 = \overline{n}_2^{0,5} = \frac{p_1}{2p_2}.$$

Now we can also write a function of supply of the plantation taking into account all products considered (strawberries and the labour):

$$\bar{\mathbf{y}}^1(\mathbf{p}) = [\bar{y}_{11}(\mathbf{p}), \bar{y}_{12}(\mathbf{p})] = \left[\frac{p_1}{2p_2}, -\left(\frac{p_1}{2p_2}\right)^2\right].$$

Let us emphasize that the supply of labour is written with the negative sign since in fact in this vector, it expresses the demand of the plantation owner for labour needed in the production of strawberries.

Ad 3

Formulate and solve the consumption utility maximization problems for the plantation owner and for the worker.

The consumption utility maximization problem for the plantation owner takes a form:

$\mathbf{a}^1 = (0, 0)$—initial endowment of the plantation owner.

$u^1(x_{11})$— the plantation owner's utility function depending only on consumption of strawberries

$$u^1(x_{11}) \to \max \quad x_{11} \geq 0 \quad p_1 x_{11} \leq I^1(\mathbf{p}) = 0.8\pi(\mathbf{p})$$

$u^1(x_{11})$ is an increasing function, hence $\frac{du^1(x_{11})}{dx_{11}} > 0$.

Because of the insatiability phenomenon reflected in the increasing utility function instead of the inequality above, one considers an equality which means that the plantation owner wants to spend all her/his income:

$$p_1 x_{11} = I^1(\mathbf{p}).$$

From this equation, we can find the demand of the plantation owner for strawberries:

$$\bar{\mathbf{x}}_{11}(\mathbf{p}) = \frac{I^1(\mathbf{p})}{p_1} = \frac{0.8\pi(\mathbf{p})}{p_1}.$$

Now, we can also write a function of demand of the plantation owner, being a consumer, taking into account all goods considered (strawberries and the leisure):

$$\bar{\mathbf{x}}^1(\mathbf{p}) = \left[\frac{0.8\pi(\mathbf{p})}{p_1}, 0\right].$$

Let us emphasize that the plantation owner's demand for leisure equals zero because her/his decision how much time he/she wants to spend working and how much resting is irrelevant for other agents in the economy, here only the worker. The plantation owner does not offer her/his hours of work to other employers; he/she is not employee in any company.

The consumption utility maximization problem for the worker takes a form:
$\mathbf{a}^2 = (0, 24)$— initial endowment of the worker

$$u^2(x_{21}, x_{22}) = x_{21}^{0.5} x_{22}^{0.3} \to \max \qquad x_{21}, x_{22} \geq 0$$
$$p_1 x_{21} + p_2 x_{22} \leq I^2(\mathbf{p}) = 0.2\pi(\mathbf{p}) + 24 p_2.$$

Again, because of the insatiability phenomenon reflected in the increasing utility function instead of the inequality above, one considers an equality which means that the worker wants to spend all her/his income. Hence, we have one equation of the system of two equations. The other equation results from the second Gossen's law. The system is:

$$\begin{cases} KSS_{12}^2 = \frac{0.5x_{21}^{-0,5} x_{22}^{0,3}}{0.3x_{21}^{0,5} x_{22}^{-0,7}} = \frac{5}{3} \cdot \frac{x_{22}}{x_{21}} = \frac{p_1}{p_2} & \Rightarrow x_{22} = \frac{3p_1}{5p_2} x_{21} \\ p_1 x_{21} + p_2 x_{22} = 0.2\pi(\mathbf{p}) + 24 p_2 \end{cases}$$

and is transformed to:

$$p_1 x_{21} + p_2 \frac{3p_1}{5p_2} x_{21} = 0.2\pi(\mathbf{p}) + 24 p_2$$
$$\frac{8}{5} p_1 x_{21} = 0.2\pi(\mathbf{p}) + 24 p_2$$

giving the demand reported by the worker:

$$\begin{cases} \overline{x}_{21}(\mathbf{p}) = \frac{5(0.2\pi(\mathbf{p})+24p_2)}{8p_1} = \frac{\pi(\mathbf{p})}{8p_1} + 15\frac{p_2}{p_1} \\ \overline{x}_{22}(\mathbf{p}) = \frac{3(0.2\pi(\mathbf{p})+24p_2)}{8p_2} = \frac{0.6\pi(\mathbf{p})}{8p_2} + 9 \quad \text{the demand for leisure.} \end{cases}$$

The time the worker wants to spend working in the plantation is the labour supply:

$$24 - \overline{x}_{22}(\mathbf{p}) = 24 - \frac{0.6\pi(\mathbf{p})}{8p_2} - 9 = 15 - \frac{0.6\pi(\mathbf{p})}{8p_2}.$$

Now, we can write a function of demand of the worker, taking into account all goods considered (strawberries and the leisure):

$$\overline{\mathbf{x}}^2(\mathbf{p}) = \left[\frac{\pi(\mathbf{p})}{8p_1} + 15\frac{p_2}{p_1}, \frac{0.6\pi(\mathbf{p})}{8p_2} + 9\right].$$

Ad 4

Write a form of an excess demand function.

A function of the excess demand is defined as:

$$\mathbf{F}(\mathbf{p}) = \bar{\mathbf{x}}(\mathbf{p}) - \bar{\mathbf{y}}(\mathbf{p}) - \hat{\mathbf{a}} = (F_1(\mathbf{p}), F_2(\mathbf{p}))$$

where the excess demand for strawberries is:

$$F_1(\mathbf{p}) = \bar{x}_{11}(\mathbf{p}) + \bar{x}_{21}(\mathbf{p}) - \bar{y}_{11}(\mathbf{p}) = \frac{0.8\pi(\mathbf{p})}{p_1} + \frac{\pi(\mathbf{p})}{8p_1} + 15\frac{p_2}{p_1} - \frac{p_1}{2p_2}$$

and the excess demand for leisure is:

$$\begin{aligned} F_2(\mathbf{p}) &= \bar{x}_{12}(\mathbf{p}) + \bar{x}_{22}(\mathbf{p}) - \bar{y}_{12}(\mathbf{p}) - a_{22} \\ &= 0 + \frac{0.6\pi(\mathbf{p})}{8p_2} + 9 - \left(-\left(\frac{p_1}{2p_2}\right)^2\right) - 24 \\ &= \left(\frac{p_1}{2p_2}\right)^2 - \left(15 - \frac{0.6\pi(\mathbf{p})}{8p_2}\right). \end{aligned}$$

The excess demand for leisure can be seen as well as the excess demand for labour, hence the difference between the demand for labour and the labour supply.

Ad 5

Determine a system of general equilibrium conditions and a Walrasian equilibrium price vector.

A system of general equilibrium conditions is derived from equalizing the excess demand function with **0**:

$$\begin{cases} \frac{0.8\pi(\mathbf{p})}{p_1} + \frac{\pi(\mathbf{p})}{8p_1} + 15\frac{p_2}{p_1} - \frac{p_1}{2p_2} = 0 \\ \left(\frac{p_1}{2p_2}\right)^2 - \left(15 - \frac{0.6\pi(\mathbf{p})}{8p_2}\right) = 0 \end{cases}$$

which can be also presented in a form showing the equalization of the demand and the supply, thus partial equilibrium on market of each product, hence the general equilibrium conditions:

$$\begin{cases} \frac{0.8\pi(\mathbf{p})}{p_1} + \frac{\pi(\mathbf{p})}{8p_1} + 15\frac{p_2}{p_1} = \frac{p_1}{2p_2} \\ \left(\frac{p_1}{2p_2}\right)^2 = 15 - \frac{0.6\pi(\mathbf{p})}{8p_2}. \end{cases}$$

From point 2, we know that the profit obtained in the plantation is:

$$\pi(\mathbf{p}) = \frac{p_1^2}{4p_2}.$$

Substituting this profit into each equation of the system, we get the same relationship prices of both products, that is p_1 of strawberries and p_2 of the labour:

$$\frac{43}{160}\frac{p_1^2}{p_2^2} = 15 \quad \Leftrightarrow \quad p_1^2 = \frac{2400}{43}p_2^2$$

which gives an equilibrium prices in a form of the following relationship:

$$\overline{p}_1 \approx 7.47 \cdot \overline{p}_2$$

This relationship shows a structure of the Walrasian equilibrium price vector:

$$\overline{\mathbf{p}}_\lambda \approx \lambda(7.47, 1), \quad \lambda > 0.$$

That is why one says that the Walrasian equilibrium price vector is defined with an accuracy of a structure. This means that any prices p_1, p_2 being in such a relationship satisfy the equilibrium conditions, thus guarantee the equilibrium on all markets considered.

Ad 6

Determine components of a Walrasian equilibrium allocation.

By the Walrasian general equilibrium prices, the demand of the plantation owner for strawberries and the leisure is:

$$\overline{\mathbf{x}}^1(\overline{\mathbf{p}}) = \left[\frac{0.8\pi(\overline{\mathbf{p}})}{p_1}, 0\right] = \left[\frac{0.8}{\overline{p}_1} \cdot \frac{\overline{p}_1^2}{4\overline{p}_2}, 0\right] = \left[\frac{0.8}{4} \cdot 7.47, 0\right] = [1.49, 0]$$

and the demand of the worker for strawberries and the leisure is:

$$\begin{aligned}
\overline{\mathbf{x}}^2(\overline{\mathbf{p}}) &= \left[\frac{\pi(\overline{\mathbf{p}})}{8p_1} + 15\frac{p_2}{p_1}, \frac{0.6\pi(\overline{\mathbf{p}})}{8p_2} + 9\right] \\
&= \left[\frac{1}{8p_1} \cdot \frac{\overline{p}_1^2}{4\overline{p}_2} + 15\frac{\overline{p}_2}{\overline{p}_1}, \frac{0.6}{8\overline{p}_2} \cdot \frac{\overline{p}_1^2}{4\overline{p}_2} + 9\right] \\
&= \left[\frac{1}{32} \cdot 7.47 + \frac{15}{7.47}, \frac{0.6}{32} \cdot 55.81 + 9\right] = [2.24, 10.05].
\end{aligned}$$

Thus, the time the worker wants to spend working, that is her/his labour supply is:

$$24 - 10.05 = 13.95.$$

The supply of the plantation by the Walrasian general equilibrium prices is:

$$\overline{\mathbf{y}}^1(\overline{\mathbf{p}}) = \left[\frac{\overline{p}_1}{2\overline{p}_2}, -\left(\frac{\overline{p}_1}{2\overline{p}_2}\right)^2\right] = \left[\frac{1}{2}\cdot 7.47, -\left(\frac{1}{2}\cdot 7.47\right)^2\right] = [3.73, -13.95].$$

E6.6. Consider a discrete-time version of the dynamic Arrow-Debreu-McKenzie model for the same data given as in Exercise E6.5. Initial prices are:

$$\mathbf{p}(0) = (10, 2).$$

Using formulas for the excess demand function and for a structure of the Walrasian equilibrium price vector derived in Exercise E6.5 for the static Arrow-Debreu-McKenzie model:

1. Determine trajectories of a price vector satisfying a system of equations of the dynamic discrete-time Arrow-Debreu-McKenzie model, taking a proportionality coefficient σ equal to 0.01, 0.05 and 0.1. Calculate price ratios $\frac{p_2(t)}{p_1(t)}$ and compare them with the equilibrium price ratio $\frac{\overline{p}_2}{\overline{p}_1}$.
2. State which of trajectories determined in point 1 are feasible.
3. State if and when (in which period) a structure of prices stabilizes around the equilibrium price structure and whether it reaches this structure in time horizon $T = 30$.
4. Present graphs of the price trajectories in the state space.
5. Present graphs of the price trajectories as functions of time.

Solutions

Ad 1

Determine trajectories[2] of a price vector satisfying a system of equations of the dynamic discrete-time Arrow-Debreu-McKenzie model, taking a proportionality coefficient σ equal to 0.01, 0.05 and 0.1. Calculate price ratios $\frac{\mathbf{p}_2(\mathbf{t})}{\mathbf{p}_1(\mathbf{t})}$ and compare them with the equilibrium price ratio $\frac{\overline{\mathbf{p}}_2}{\overline{\mathbf{p}}_1}$.

The dynamic discrete-time Arrow-Debreu-McKenzie model in case of two goods has a general form:

$$\begin{aligned} &p_i(t+1) = p_i(t) + \sigma F_i(\mathbf{p}(t)) \quad i = 1, 2, \quad t = 0, 1, 2\ldots \\ &p_i(0) = \text{const.} > 0 \quad i = 1, 2. \end{aligned}$$

On the basis of the results of exercise E6.5, we have the excess demand function given as:

[2] The trajectories are obtained in a file called Exercise 6.6.xlsx.

$$F_1(\mathbf{p}(t)) = \frac{0.8\pi(\mathbf{p}(t))}{p_1(t)} + \frac{\pi(\mathbf{p}(t))}{8p_1(t)} + 15\frac{p_2(t)}{p_1(t)} - \frac{p_1(t)}{2p_2(t)}$$

$$F_2(\mathbf{p}(t)) = \left(\frac{p_1(t)}{2p_2(t)}\right)^2 - \left(15 - \frac{0.6\pi(\mathbf{p}(t))}{8p_2(t)}\right).$$

Starting from the initial condition $\mathbf{p}(0) = (10, 2)$, one can find levels of prices of both goods in all subsequent periods.

Ad 2

State which of trajectories determined in point 1 are feasible.

It turns out that all trajectories are feasible. However, when $\sigma = 0.1$ the trajectories are oscillatory (Fig. 6.9).

Ad 3

State if and when (in which period) a structure of prices stabilizes around the equilibrium price structure and whether it reaches this structure in time horizon T = 30.

This can be stated on the basis of calculations provided in a file (Exercise 6.6.xlsx). From the static Arrow-Debreu-McKenzie model, we know that the Walrasian equilibrium price vector is $\overline{\mathbf{p}}_\lambda \approx \lambda(7.47, 1)$; thus, we can focus on $\frac{p_1(t)}{p_2(t)} \approx 7.47$ and when this equation is satisfied for the first time. It turns out that when $\sigma = 0.01$ the equilibrium state is reached in period $t = 51$, when $\sigma = 0.05$ it is reached very quickly because already in period $t = 7$, when $\sigma = 0.1$, it is reached very slowly because not earlier than in period $t = 822$. In this last case, the price trajectories are oscillatory but one can notice that the oscillations are smaller and smaller in time.

Ad 4

Present graphs of the price trajectories in the state space (Fig. 6.8).[3]

Ad 5

Present graphs of the price trajectories as functions of time (Fig. 6.9).[4]

E6.7. Consider a continuous-time version of the dynamic Arrow-Debreu-McKenzie model for the same data given as in Exercise E5.

1. Determine trajectories of a price vector satisfying a system of equations of the dynamic continuous-time Arrow-Debreu-McKenzie model taking a proportionality coefficient σ equal to $0.01, 0.05, 0.1$ and determine whether these trajectories are feasible.
2. Determine if and when (at what moment) a structure of prices stabilizes around the equilibrium price structure.

---

[3] The trajectories are obtained in an Excel file called Exercise 6.6.xlsx.

[4] The trajectories are obtained in an Excel file called Exercise 6.6.xlsx.

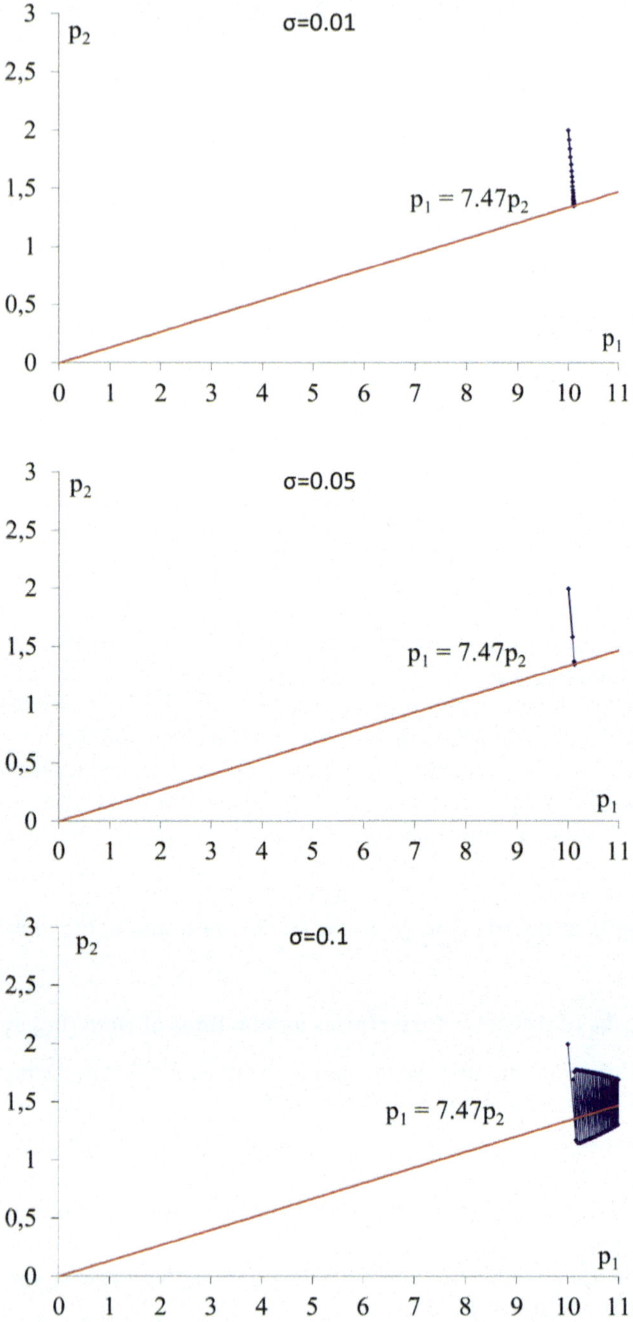

Fig. 6.8 Price trajectories in state space (E6.6)

Fig. 6.9 Price trajectories as functions of time (E6.6)

3. Present graphs of price trajectories as functions of time.

Solutions

Ad 1

Determine trajectories of a price vector satisfying a system of equations of the dynamic continuous-time Arrow-Debreu-McKenzie model taking a proportionality coefficient σ equal to 0.01, 0.05, 0.1 and determine whether these trajectories are feasible.

The dynamic continuous-time Arrow-Debreu-McKenzie model in case of two goods has a general form:

$$\frac{\mathrm{d}p_i(t)}{\mathrm{d}t} = \sigma z_i(\mathbf{p}(t)) \quad i = 1, 2, \quad t \in (0; +\infty)$$
$$p_i(0) = \text{const.} > 0 \quad i = 1, 2.$$

On the basis of the results of exercise E6.5, we have the excess demand function given as:

$$F_1(\mathbf{p}(t)) = \frac{0.8\pi(\mathbf{p}(t))}{p_1(t)} + \frac{\pi(\mathbf{p}(t))}{8p_1(t)} + 15\frac{p_2(t)}{p_1(t)} - \frac{p_1(t)}{2p_2(t)}$$

$$F_2(\mathbf{p}(t)) = \left(\frac{p_1(t)}{2p_2(t)}\right)^2 - \left(15 - \frac{0.6\pi(\mathbf{p}(t))}{8p_2(t)}\right).$$

To find levels of prices of goods in subsequent moments, one can approximate the original continuous-time model with a discrete-time model in the following way:

$$p_i(t + \Delta t) = p_i(t) + \sigma F_i(\mathbf{p}(t))\Delta t \quad i = 1, 2, \quad t \in [0; +\infty)$$
$$p_i(0) = \text{const.} > 0 \quad i = 1, 2,$$

where Δt means a time increment.

Having this discrete-time approximation of the continuous-time model and starting from the initial condition $\mathbf{p}(0) = (10, 2)$, one can find levels of prices of both goods in all subsequent moments.

To find feasible price trajectories, one can use various values for σ and for the time increment Δt. We use following sets of these parameters:

$$\sigma = 0.01, \quad \Delta t = 1$$
$$\sigma = 0.05, \quad \Delta t = 0.5$$
$$\sigma = 0.1, \quad \Delta t = 2.$$

It turns out that all trajectories are feasible.

Ad 2

Determine if and when (at what moment) a structure of prices stabilizes around the equilibrium price structure.

The structure of prices in a sense $\frac{p_1(t)}{p_2(t)}$ stabilizes around the equilibrium price structure, that is $\frac{\overline{p}_2}{\overline{p}_1}$ at following moments:

when $\sigma = 0.01$, $\Delta t = 1$ – in 51-th step, thus at moment $t = 51 \cdot 1 = 51$,
when $\sigma = 0.05$, $\Delta t = 0.5$ – in 17-th step, thus at moment $t = 17 \cdot 0.5 = 8.5$,
when $\sigma = 0.1$, $\Delta t = 2$ – in 22-nd step, thus at moment $t = 22 \cdot 2 = 44$.

Ad 3

Present graphs of price trajectories as functions of time (Fig. 6.10).[5]

[5] The trajectories are obtained in an Excel file called Exercise 6.7.xlsx.

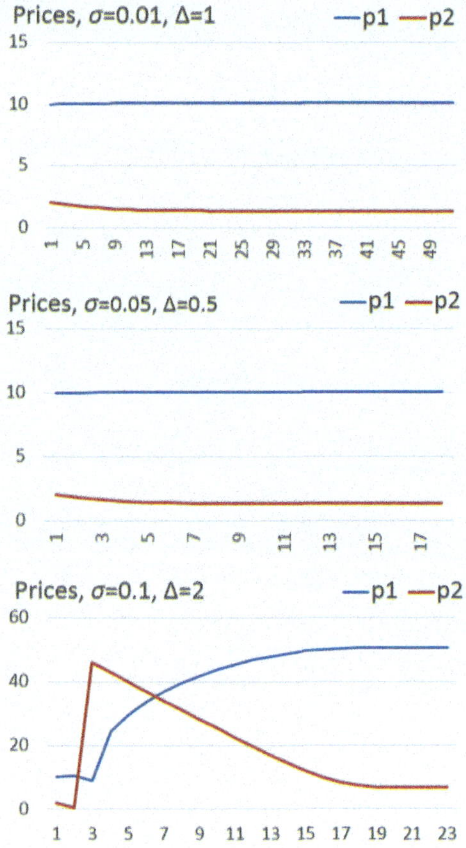

Fig. 6.10 Price trajectories as functions of time (E6.7)

References

Anholcer, M. (2015). *Mathematics and management examples and exercises.* MD 290. Wydawnictwo Uniwersytetu Ekonomiczego w Poznaniu.
Chiang, A. C., & Wainwright, K. (2005). *Fundamental methods of mathematical economics.* Mcgraw-Hill Education.
Jacques, I. (2006). *Mathematics for economics and business* (5th ed.). Prentice Hall.
Malaga, K., & Sobczak, K. (2021). *Advanced microeconomics, learning materials for Ph.D. students. MD 367*. PUEB Press.
Malaga, K., & Sobczak, K. (2022). *Microeconomics. Static and dynamic analysis.* Springer Nature.
O'Brien, R. J., & Garcia, G. G. (1971). *Mathematics for economists and social scientists.* Pitman Press.
Ostoja-Ostaszewski, A. (1996a). *Matematyka w ekonomii. Modele i metody* (Vol. 1). *Algebra elementarna.* PWN.
Ostoja-Ostaszewski, A. (1996b). *Matematyka w ekonomii. Modele i metody* (Vol. 2). *Elementarny rachunek różniczkowy.* PWN.
Sydsaeter, K., & Hammond, P. (2008). *Essential mathematics for economic analysis.* Prentice Hall.

K. Sobczak and K. Malaga, *Workbook for Microeconomics*, Springer Texts in Business and Economics, https://doi.org/10.1007/978-3-031-41947-8

GPSR Compliance

The European Union's (EU) General Product Safety Regulation (GPSR) is a set of rules that requires consumer products to be safe and our obligations to ensure this.

If you have any concerns about our products, you can contact us on ProductSafety@springernature.com

In case Publisher is established outside the EU, the EU authorized representative is:

Springer Nature Customer Service Center GmbH
Europaplatz 3
69115 Heidelberg, Germany

The manufacturer's authorised representative in the EU is Springer Nature Customer Service Centre GmbH, Europaplatz 3, 69115 Heidelberg, Germany. If you have any concerns regarding our products, please contact ProductSafety@springernature.com

Printed and bound by CPI Group (UK) Ltd, Croydon, CR0 4YY
01/10/2026
02225901-0001